alphabet
management

Other books by Nick Drake-Knight

FAST COACHING: The Complete Guide to New Code Continue & Begin®
Dandelion Digital, 2016
ISBN 978-1-905665-78-5

MEERKAT SELLING: Be the Best in Big Ticket Retail Selling
Dandelion Digital, 2008
ISBN 978-1-905665-70-9

BOOMERANG! Coach Your Team to Be the Best!
Dandelion Digital, 2007
ISBN 978-1-905665-51-8

200 insights to accelerate your
team management career

alphabet
management

The A-Z resource pack
for team managers

Nick Drake-Knight

Author of *Fast Coaching*

Dandelion Digital
13 Grayham Road
New Malden
Surrey
KT3 5HR

www.paperlionltd.com

First published in 2024 by Dandelion Digital,
an imprint of Paper Lion Ltd

Text © Nick Drake-Knight 2024
Illustrations © Rupert Besley 2024

ISBN paperback: 978-1-908706-52-2

The website links in this book were correct at the time
of publication, and the author and the publisher bear no
responsibility for the content of third-party websites.

Designed and set by seagulls.net
Cover design by Two Associates

Printed and bound in Great Britain by Lightning Source

Dedication

For Alf Knight, master joiner,
who taught me to measure twice, cut once.

Now I understand the pattern which connects.

reader reviews

"Like an extended dictionary for leaders, this book is a fantastic resource to simply open up and quickly dip in for what you need. Covering a huge amount of ground, I found myself skipping from one topic to the next, refreshing my knowledge on some, while learning new insights on others. The further reading suggestions are an extra gift from Nick. This is a resource every manager should have at their fingertips!"
– Caroline Carr, Head of Leadership and Talent Development, **AO.com**

"As a huge fan of 'Fast Coaching' I found Alphabet Management a mixture of Nick's pragmatic approach to people management, plus a treasure trove of insights and ideas. A 'must have' for any leader-manager, this book is guaranteed to be well thumbed."
– Steve Devonshire, EMEA Training Manager, **Bang & Olufsen**

"Readable, concise, and practical. Containing everything you would need to lead teams; the 200 tools and approaches allow you to think, and do..."
– Mike Notman, Managing Partner, **Bourton Group**

"Having known Nick for well over a decade, again a brilliant, no-nonsense, and practical guide to people management. It will stand new and experienced managers in good stead, to get the best from their people, and for their organisation."
– Tristan Dhalla, Senior Global Learning Manager, **BT**

"There's no silver bullet to delivering excellent customer service. Getting it right boils down to everything you do day-in, day-out. This is why taking proactive steps to change 'habits' is so critical to the ongoing success of a customer service department. This, alongside a comprehensive A-Z of insights, makes this a great book for any team manager to read."
– Megan Jones, Editor, **Call Centre Helper**

"Straightforward, accessible, yet a powerful and comprehensive roadmap which is a 'must read' for team leaders. Nick's new book captures his extensive experience and conveys key concepts for a successful approach to team management."
– Julia Pascu, Director, **Finger on the Pulse Research**

"It is great to see Goal Mapping being used more and more in team management and achievement by organisations at all levels. I am so very pleased that my long-term friend Nick Drake-Knight has included it in Alphabet Management. There is great value in having such an easy to access reference book for managers."
– Brian Mayne, Author of **Goal Mapping**

"Nick has complied a brilliant A – Z with many ideas to explore. A great read and a reminder on the key concepts to be a great manager."
– Graham Paine, Regional Operations Manager, UK & Ireland,
Helly Hansen and **Musto**

"Whether you're a new or experienced manager, there's a wealth of tips and guidance in here to help you be successful and develop your skills. Change is inevitable and the best managers adapt. This book gives you the skills to support your navigation to successful management."
– Charlotte Deprez, National Showroom Sales Manager,
MKM Building Supplies

"Nick's valuable experiences and insights provides a clear steer and mechanism of support for all managers, irrespective of sector, size of team, or focus of endeavour. It will be useful to those new to management or experienced in their field."
Nigel Hartley, CEO, **Mountbatten Hospice Group**

"By demystifying complex theory into simple and practical insights, Nick has created a guide for managers to develop their skills; an essential reference whether you are experienced or new to a management role, it will help make you a more confident and effective leader."
– Simon Parrott, Customer Experience Consultant, **MSX international**

"Nick has again produced an easy-to-read 'go to' manual for those dealing with the complex area of managing people. The A-Z format provides a fantastic resource to be read in its entirety and as a reference source when required. This book is ideal for those new to management and for existing managers."
– Katie Woods-Ruddick, Chief People Office, **px Group**

"Nick offers curated management wisdom, combining common sense and pragmatic advice with great storytelling."
– Wilf Walsh, Chair, **Racecourse Association**

"This book will build confidence and help any user excel on the 'know what you know'. It shares important approaches, techniques, and context to develop leaders and teams, in a bitesize format that doesn't require you to read end to end. A fantastic read for today's busy leaders!"
– Craig Mundy, Global PMTDR Programme Manager, **Shell**

"Keep this by your desk, it's an invaluable reference guide. It will help you manage situations, throughout your management career."
– Mike King, Commercial Manager, **Simply Asset Finance**

"It is a skill to take a complex idea and simplify it enough to implement. Nick has achieved this 200 times in this book. The new essential reference for managers and leaders – from someone who knows his onions."
– Steve O'Neill, Founder, **sondevelopment**

"Nick's ability to simplify the complex makes this a must-read book for any manager and / or leader. Whatever your experience this will open your mind to practical day to day improvements in your business."
– Mark Rogers, Director, **St James's Place**

contents

About the author. 1

Foreword by Dame Irene Lucas-Hays, DBE, DL. 3

Introduction 5

About team management – an overview. 7

Accountability 10

Act 12

Act As If. 13

Adaptive team management. 15

Adverbs, superfluous. 17

Agile team management. 18

Aims & objectives, clarity on 20

Air Cover sponsorship. 22

Analogue marking 23

Appraisals and performance reviews 24

Assertion and assertiveness 26

Assumptions 29

Authentic team management 31

Barriers to professional development 33

Behaviours and values, what is expected?. 34

Behaviour breeds behaviour 36

Behaviour change request. 38

Being comfortable, dangers of. 41

Beliefs, you can choose or change. 43

Brainstorming, esrever, and thought showers 45
But Monster®, The 47

Calmness 49
Can't to Can Belief Busting® 50
Celebrating successes – pot fillers 53
Certainty and Uncertainty, management of. 54
Change, or Evolution? 56
Chocolate Praise™ 64
CITO management. 65
Clean Language 67
Coaching 68
Coaching, Continue & Begin Fast Coaching® 71
Cognitive bias 74
Commitment mantra 75
Communication. 76
Continuous Professional Development [CPD] 78
CPD cascading. 79
Criticism and failure focus 81
Culture. 82
Customers, internal 84

Decision making, navy style. 86
Decision-making tools. 87
Delegating. 89
Deletion. 91
Desktop of the mind 92
Difficult people, managing 93
Distortion. 96
Diversity, Equity, Inclusion (DEI), or Equity, Diversity,
    Inclusion (EDI) 98

Emotional choice 103
Emotional Drivers™ 104

Emotional intelligence (EQ). 106
Empathy 108
Employee engagement. 109
English is Rubbish™ 113
Every Customer Wants® 115
Experiential learning. 117
Explicit standards 120

Failure, or feedback 122
Feel, felt, found 123
Fight, flight, play dead. 124
Floppy language 126
Focus. 127
Forcefields 128
Framing and reframing 130
Freedom questions 132
Friends, managing them at work 133
Future feeling. 135
Fuzzy language 136

Games people play 139
Generalisations 141
Get Even Better Ats (GEBAs) 142
Get inside their world. 143
Goal Mapping® by Brian Mayne 145
Good and less good 147

Habit. 149
Hallucinations of meaning 150
Halo and horns 152
Health and safety management 153
Hope and the Hope Factor 155
Horizon scanning 156
Huddles. 158

Human leadership 159

I know you don't know 163
I/Me ownership 164
Imagination. 166
Imposter syndrome 167
Induction, preboarding, onboarding, reboarding 169
Insights visits 174
Interest. 176
Irrational thinking. 177

JIT and float time 179
Job enrichment. 180
Johari, adapted for management. 181
Judgements and observations 183

Kanban 186
Key Performance Indicators 189
KPI/OKR overload 189
KIT meetings 190
KITAs 191
Knowledge. 193

Language to help 196
Language which hurts. 197
Language, written, redundancy and repetition. 199
Leadership and management. 201
Lean management. 203
Listening 206
Looking out of the window thinking 208

Management competencies 210
Management style 211
Maps of the territory 216

Matching and mirroring. 217

Measure twice, cut once 219

Meetings. 220

Mentoring 224

Meta thinking. 225

Metaphors 227

Milton Model 229

Modelling excellence. 230

Monkeys, management of. 232

Motivation. 234

NDK Performance Model®. 237

Networking (internal & external) 239

95% (ninety-five percentage) management. 241

Nominalisations, behaviour versus thing 242

Objectives, management by (MBOs and OKRs) 244

Obsession, compelling 246

Occam/Ockham's razor 248

Options and choices 249

Ownership 250

Past 252

Patterns which connect 253

Performance management 256

Persistence. 258

PESTLE. 259

Planning 261

Positivity 262

Pre-framing 263

Presentations. 264

Presentation behaviours. 267

Presentations Goal Map® 271

Presuppositions 273

Pride, encouragement of 274
Procrastination, Hammer it! 276

Quality and TQM 278
Quality Circles and Kaizen 280
Quality standards 282
Quality and 5S 284

Rapport 286
Rapport, advanced skills 287
Rarely, sometimes, always 290
Reading 291
Receive, and transmit 292
Remote working, remote management 294
Resilience 298
Resistor busting 299
Review and reflection 302
Root cause analysis 304

Scrums and sprints 306
Secondary and tertiary impact: The Law of Unintended
    Consequences 307
Secondary gain 309
Self-awareness 311
Self-talk, critical inner voice, empowering inner voice 317
Servant leadership 319
Significance 322
Sleep on it 324
Stoicism 325
Stress management, Mrs Erickson's mindfulness relaxation
    technique (5-4-3-2-1) 327
Stress management, self-trance 330
Stress management, patterns of healthy thinking 333
Structure of Well-Done-Ness® 336

Supervision sessions. 337
Surface structure, deep structure, specificity. 339

Team evolution 344
Teeth, show them (if necessary). 346
Tentative is no good. 347
Thank You. 350
Time is a budget item 352
Timeline empowerment 361
Time off. 363
Tissue paper prisons. 365
To be expected. 367
Training doesn't work 368

Unconscious mind, trusting the 371
Universal quantifiers. 373
Useful fiction 374

VAK(OG) representational systems 376
Value Stream Mapping 379
Visual management. 382
VUCA management. 384

What am I here for? What is my management purpose? 387
Why? Purpose and meaning. 391
Win-Win 393
Words, song, and dance 394
Work life balance 396
World's worst question 399
Worry. 402
Would you follow you? 404

X Factor management and leadership 409

Yes Sets, building confidence in others 411

Zzzzz – REM sleep 413

Reflections 417
And to follow 418
Acknowledgements 419
Case Study: On Growing Managers [and our Business] 421
Appendix 1
    Continue & Begin Fast Coaching®: its application in call centre
    operations 425
Appendix 2
    Greatest Band Ever Test – Answers 440
Bibliography 441

about the author

"Nick Drake Knight is a trainer, coach and consultant in people management. He is committed to equipping leaders to prioritise staff confidence and self-image, in the knowledge that that when people feel good about themselves then resourcefulness increases and innovation and productivity improve.

He is an authority on using therapeutic principles to introduce healthy employee growth strategies. Nick travels extensively helping global businesses develop their people strategies. Over the course of his colourful career, he has trained the business leaders of global and national brands and SMEs, in the UK, Europe, and extensively in the Former Soviet Union. He has worked across sectors from automotive and retail, to telecoms and financial services. He is an international conference speaker on employee growth. Nick's first taste of management development came in the leisure industry, following spells as a merchant seaman and police officer.

In the 1990s Nick lectured in management, and gained prestigious awards for his students through his innovative approach to learning. He developed the confidence-boosting method of (what became) Continue & Begin Fast Coaching® which had early successes during tutorials with student managers. The techniques are explained in his previous book, FAST

COACHING. Consulting work followed as Nick became an advisor and then board member of the UK's largest Business Link operator, focusing on management development. Throughout the 2000s, Nick was co-director of the UK's leading multi-media customer insights agency, consulting for a wide range of clients from the private and public sectors in the UK, Europe and the Middle East. He continues to equip managers to empower their staff by encapsulating the insights gained over his career into the resource-packed book that is ALPHABET MANAGEMENT.

Nick lives by the sea on the Isle of Wight on the southern coast of England. He is a retired amateur rugby player, incompetent mountain biker, proud dad, and devoted grandfather."

foreword

Dame Irene Lucas-Hays, DBE, DL

Team leaders and operational managers are at the heart of organisations. Business strategy is implemented at the front line, and its success depends on high quality team management skills.

Class-leading brands ensure supervisory staff have the underpinning knowledge and understanding to manage colleagues professionally. Investment in their learning and development is a vital element in building management competences.

At Hays Travel we have embraced and embedded *Continue & Begin Fast Coaching*® within our business. The training and content provided by Nick has been instrumental in developing the skills of our management team.

In *Alphabet Management* Nick has designed a highly effective tool for busy managers who require an easy-to-use resource to support their daily role.

This book re-ignites and refreshes good management practice, providing a "quick dip" facility, and a great signpost to encourage further academic reading to support on-going personal development.

Dame Irene Lucas-Hays, DBE, DL
Chair, Hays Travel

introduction

Organizations employ more frontline managers and team supervisors than any other form of management, yet few receive appropriate management and leadership training.

This book addresses the specific development needs of those team managers.

Here I offer over 35 years of my management development teachings in an easy access compendium, presented alphabetically. Formulas for developing managers are compiled in bite-sized chunks, with a mix of new knowledge and handy reminders. There are some refreshingly quirky approaches, and a selection of tried and trusted 'standard business school' notes. All are proven as performance enhancing, across diverse sectors.

The result is a non-threatening entry to pragmatic learning about the role. The alphabetical presentation makes it easy to dip in wherever you like and pick ideas relevant to your topic of interest.

Management of people is an inspiring and rewarding role. It is also time consuming, frustrating, and angst-inducing. In worst case scenarios the role can even impact on emotional and physical health. *Alphabet Management* provides a resource pack of insights pared down to practical methods, to help managers operate effectively and healthily.

This is more than a business book

Nestled within the management tips are techniques to help professionals cope healthily with today's workplace. There are patterns which connect, incorporating methods from therapeutic disciplines, applied to the world of business and specifically, to managing a team.

Each topic is introduced succinctly, in one or two pages. Occasionally the subject matter requires a longer passage to address constituent parts, for example in *Change* and in *Time is a budget item*. Every topic has Signposts to Further Reading, for readers to continue exploration into areas of specific interest.

There is a human element too, with stories from my varied management career, including 'aha' moments and whopper size errors of judgement, each presented with (I hope) humour and humility.

Who is the book for?

Likely beneficiaries are team leaders, and their managers, HRM and learning professionals, entrepreneurs, SME owner-managers, and of course, business school students and graduate entrants. Global brands use my learning materials to develop teams in healthy ways, and to revitalise tired organisational habits; and managers from all sectors will find new understandings.

Would you like to be 10% more effective in your management role? How about 20%? More? Whatever your ambitions for continuous improvement, this book will help.

NDK

Andros, 2024

A

About team management – an overview

"There is nothing so useless as doing efficiently that which should not be done at all." *– Peter Drucker*

As the industrial age matured from the late 19th into the early 20th centuries, management emerged as a discipline, and later as a recognised profession. Thinkers and writers of the time included,

- Frederick Winslow Taylor – *scientific management.*
- Max Weber – *bureaucratic management.*
- Henri Fayol – *administrative functions.*
- Mary Parker Follett ('the mother of modern management') – *humanistic and matrix management.*
- Elton Mayo and others (Hawthorne studies) – *environmental impact on employee behaviour.*

By the 1940s, 50s and 60s, researchers were questioning the validity of early classical theories, with increased recognition of 'human motivation' as a key variable. Humanist commentators included,

- Abraham Maslow – *hierarchy of needs.*
- Kurt Lewin – *unfreeze, change, refreeze.*
- Douglas McGregor – *theory X, theory Y.*
- David McClelland – *achievement, power, affiliation.*
- Frederick Herzberg – *hygiene factors, motivators.*

- Clayton Alderfer – *existence, relatedness, growth.*
- Victor Vroom – *expectancy theory.*

Peter Drucker proposed new models of management in his consulting work and writing. Drucker developed many of the standard management tools still in use today, over half a century after his ideas first emerged.

Management by Objectives

- *Management by Objectives* (*MBO*) were popularised by Drucker.
- An evolution of *MBO* became *Objectives and Key Results* (*OKRs*) developed by John Doerr (2018).
- *S.M.A.R.T.* objectives (*Specific, Measurable, Achievable-Agreed, Realistic, Time-bound*) first appeared in George Doran's article *"There's a S.M.A.R.T. way to write management's goals and objectives"* (1981).

Decentralisation and the delegation of tasks was a theme in Drucker's teachings. He suggested that ineffective managers tend to try and do everything themselves, to maintain control, or in belief only *they* can execute assignments correctly. Drucker was one of the first to recognise that there is an essential connection between delegation of responsibility and the empowering and growth of team members.

Drucker's forward thinking still finds relevance today. His ideas about *knowledge workers*, a revolutionary concept at the time, is now commonplace in professional organisations.

Mary Parker Follett may have been the *mother of modern management*; Peter Drucker is universally recognised as the *father of modern management.*

Contemporary management

Today's management thinking adopts a systems approach, considering a range of interests, including external factors (see **PESTLE**), and internal, intrinsic elements which are inter-related and co-dependent.

In well managed organisations managers and their team members are working towards common goals of the wider enterprise. Genuinely common goals, in my management consulting experience, are uncommon. Silo mindsets of personal agendas, and small group ambitions, generally trump organisational direction, unless carefully monitored by managers, with reminders to refocus where necessary.

Contingency management

Beyond theoretical management approaches are the realities of circumstance. *Contingency* management recognises the nature of real-world situations and the value of adopting a flexible approach to managing and leading a team. Variable conditions require agile thinking (see **Agile management**) and adaptive behaviours, to deal with the range of issues modern managers face.

This is the real challenge for today's managers; deciding on which skills, methods and thinking patterns are the best fit for each specific circumstance. There is no best *style* of management. This book offers management ideas, and options to consider.

Management resources

Managers implement plans and strategies through available resources. We can identify common categories of resource,

- Supply chain materials.
- Machinery and equipment.
- Working space.
- Time.
- Budget.
- Information and data.
- Social media and other communications channels.
- Personal expertise.
- Processes and logistics.
- *People: Teams and the individuals within a team.*

People management

People management is the theme of this book. Its purpose is to provide ideas to help in your managerial role. It's not a fully comprehensive code of practice, or a business school standard text. It is pragmatic. It offers practical tools I've found useful in getting the best out of the thousands of people I have worked alongside, during almost 40 years of business leadership, in operations, consulting, and management teaching.

Beyond my original thinking are examples of excellence drawn from wide-ranging contexts, including ideas outside the world of work. As you progress through the book, you'll become familiar with the concept of *patterns which connect* (see **Patterns which connect**), where methods of outstanding performance may be modelled, codified, sometimes reshaped a little, and then re-applied to achieve similarly impressive results in a team management environment.

- You may like to navigate the book by subject matter, searching alphabetically using the Contents list, or enjoy progressing alphabetically, page by page.
- Some topics are cross-referenced to other headings, (for example, see **What am I here for? What is my management purpose?**).
- Each chapter has signposts to further reading, helping broaden your underpinning knowledge and understanding.

I hope you find this book a valuable reference in your management career.

Further reading

Chartered Management Institute | www.managers.org.uk

Management and Organisational Behaviour | Pearson, 2023 (13th Edition) | Mullins, L., Rees, G.

Essential Drucker: The Best of Sixty Years of Peter Drucker's Essential Writings on Management | Harper Business, 2008 | Drucker, P.F.

Measure What Matters. OKRs – the Simple Idea That Drives 10x Growth | Penguin Random House, 2018 | Doerr, J.

There's a SMART Way to Write Management's Goals and Objectives | Journal of Management Review, 1981 | Doran, G.T. | https://www.scribd.com/document/458234239/There-s-a-S-M-A-R-T-way-to-write-management-s-goals-and-objectives-George-T-Doran-Management-Review-1981-pdf#

Good Managers Don't Grow On Trees | The Motivation Agency, August 2023 | Atria, A

Accountability

"If you light a lamp for somebody, it will also brighten your path."
– *Buddha Siddhartha Guatama Shakyamuni*

Here is an important distinction; there is a difference between *accountability* and *responsibility*.

As manager, you may delegate key elements of your job function to team members. Colleagues within your team become responsible for specific activities or duties. It's a sensible thing to do, freeing up your time and headspace to think about bigger things, about how to enhance your team's operational performance.

Team members may become *responsible* for a task. You remain *accountable*. You will be asked to report on performance – to give an *account*.

This means, even though someone else is doing the work, you are still liable for delivery. Astute managers learn the art of delegation, identifying duties to delegate to appropriate team members, and then train, coach, and mentor as they grow into becoming fully competent.

As team members develop their skills and competencies, and as they build confidence, you can expand the scope of some individuals' job role, helping them enrich their work experience and develop as professionals. This releases your energies for the important stuff of identifying opportunities for continuous improvement (see **Quest for Continuous Improvement – QCI**).

The RACI framework, used in project management, identifies colleague functions in a project. It's a useful format for managers to consider when thinking through project roles for team members,

- *Responsible* – the person, or people, who will be carrying out an activity.
- *Accountable* – the (one) person who has authority to make significant decisions and is required to report on performance.
- *Consulted* – the person, or people, who will be consulted with to aid decision making during the project activity.
- *Informed* – the person, or people, who will be updated as the project develops.

Think about your team management role. Which *responsibilities* could be delegated, and for which do you remain *accountable*?

Further reading

Accountability Vs. Responsibility: Is There a Difference? | Science of People, December 2022 | Brown, K | https://www.scienceofpeople.com/accountability-vs-responsibility/

What is a RACI matrix? | Project Management.com, October 2022 | Morris, L. | https://project-management.com/understanding-responsibility-assignment-matrix-raci-matrix/

Act

"A goal without a plan is just a wish."
– Antoine de Saint-Exupéry

Saint-Exupéry was right up to a point; but planning alone achieves nothing. Action is required.

"A plan without action is not a plan. It's a speech."
– T. Boone Pickens, American financier.

Boone was closer. Developing an idea and then deciding on a management plan is one thing. Taking action to implement the plan is the difference that makes the difference. Plenty of great change plans are not implemented and as a result the status quo remains.

Procrastination, dithering, not getting on with it – this is not the way to manage professionally. Action is required. Get up. Get moving. Energy. Zest. Passion. Get on with it!

Stoic philosopher Epictetus had similar views,

"And whenever you encounter anything that is difficult or pleasurable, or highly or lowly regarded, remember that the contest is now: you are at the Olympic games, you cannot wait any longer…"

To make change happen, action is required. For modest change, *modest* action may be adequate. For major change, *MASSIVE, sustained* action is required!

Here's the formula for getting things done at work, and outside of work too,

1. Decide.
2. Plan.
3. Act

No procrastination, no ponderous inaction, no tentative thinking, or timid behaviour (see **Procrastination, hammer it!**). Decide – Plan – Act.

Think about this little riddle,

Five little dickie birds, sitting on a tree.
Two decide to fly away.
How many are left?

Three?

No, five. Two decided to fly away, and they planned in detail; but didn't act.

Further reading

The Art of Taking Action: Lessons from Japanese Psychology | To Do Institute, 2014 | Krech, G.

Eat That Frog! Get More of The Important Things Done Today | Hodder, 2013 | Tracy, Brian

Act As If

"Act as though I am, and I will be." – Hans Vaihinger

A quick and effective way to develop managerial skills is to *Act As If.*

Hans Vaihinger, the German philosopher, had a term for beliefs we know are not true but still come in handy: he called them 'useful fictions' (see **Useful fiction**) in his book *The Philosophy of As If.* He suggested acting *as if* something were true may be beneficial for us in a range of circumstances.

The philosophy of *As If* is a handy tool for developing a team manager's skills. Ask yourself a series of empowering questions (see the table below). You may wish to seek out more knowledge before answering some of the questions, and that's fine. Part of continuous professional development is to research best practice.

Go and find out. Read, listen, observe, ask questions of managers who are already exhibiting these management attributes. Through modelling accomplished managers (see **Modelling**) you'll build a blueprint to work to, adapted to your own style. *Act As If* and you'll soon discover how quickly you are developing new skills.

Here are a few management behaviour questions to consider. You may wish to add to the question list; these are a starter pack to get you on the move, thinking about how to *Act As If* you are already a talented team manager (you may already be so!).

You can write notes in the spaces beneath each question. Be brave! You won't get told off, it's your book, and if it's not, write in pencil.

What do successful managers do?	How would I think?
What self-talk would I have?	How would I prepare each day, week, month, quarter, year?
What habits should I adopt, to Act As If I was a successful manager?	What management strategies would I employ?
What would I do to build credibility?	What model of leadership would I follow?
What types of words should I use?	How should I relate to team members?
What tonality would I use?	How would I prepare before a meeting?
How would I use my body?	How would I review my performance?
How would I dress?	How could I continually improve my skills?
Additional questions to consider?	

Explore your responses to these behavioural questions and build your blueprint. Maybe you could chat through your ideas with a mentor, or a colleague. Once you have built up a working model you can apply your learning and *Act As If* you are an (even more) gifted manager.

Act As If. It's only pretend, and it works.

Further reading

The Philosophy of As If: A System of the Theoretical, Practical and Religious Fictions of Mankind | English translation from CreateSpace Independent Publishing Platform, 2015 | Vaihinger, H., 1922

The As If Principle. The Radically New Approach to Changing Your Life | Simon & Schuster, 2014 | Wiseman, R.

Adaptive team management

"The species that survives is the one... able to adapt to, and to adjust best to, the changing environment in which it finds itself..."

– Charles Darwin*

Improvise, adapt, and overcome is a phrase associated with the US Marines. Charles Darwin identified this dynamism as a feature of successful evolution.

Team managers need to be flexible in thought and deed. Circumstances change, business context and environmental factors are constantly shifting, at times evolving gradually, at other times dramatically and at speed.

Think about the 2008 financial crash, and the 2020 coronavirus pandemic, or technological advancements and environmental concerns. These and other influences have radically reshaped the way we do business. The PESTLE framework (see **PESTLE**) is a reference point for thinking about continuing change; what are the political, economic, social, technological, legal, and environmental factors for managers to consider? What might be coming? A variant is PESTEC, where *culture* is a feature.

At operational level, team managers are discovering a new landscape of employees' expectation from work. Covid radically affected perspectives

---

* This is an apocryphal quote attributed to Darwin, not found anywhere in his book *On the Origin of Species*. We can consider it a *useful fiction* (see **Useful fiction**). Whether it is true or not, it is helpful to consider it so.

and priorities of the global workforce. Life choices began to impact on attraction and retention of staff. Managers are more aware of recruitment and retention challenges and the shifting expectations of employees about their experience at work, its shape, and where it fits with their wider life. Managers are learning to think more deeply about the emotional and pastoral elements of their colleagues, to empathise and reshape working patterns to suit the needs of the employee's whole life, not simply work priorities (see **Human leadership**).

In a changing world, adaptation is a necessary skill. Barriers emerge, new obstacles appear. Established practices may not work so well. Maybe it's time to review and update our thinking. If old habits are no longer working in this evolving landscape, try something different. Yes, it might feel uncomfortable thinking and acting in new ways. The alternative, though, is gradual deterioration in performance.

Adaptation is necessary to remain competitive and survive.

What were once proven protocols may no longer be so, no matter how hard people work at them. Like the wasp's attempts to escape from a closed window, repeating ineffective strategies result in the same unsuccessful outcomes.

Some years ago, at a train-the-trainer event for an international home improvement retailer, one of the new trainers, Michael, was using the wasp analogy to make a point about adapting to new behaviours. I remember his broad Glaswegian accent,

> "I said, yah stupid wasp, adapt! Use the <u>open</u> windae... I was talking tae him, aye... and I don't even speak 'wasp'..."

Michael's delivery was funny, and his point well made.

Today's perceptive managers are ready to *improvise and adapt;* to adjust to a more flexible work environment and the changing needs of an evolving workforce.

Note: *adaptability* and *agility* are not the same thing (see **Agile team management**).

- *Adaptability* is a *reactive* capacity, an aptitude for modifying management processes or behaviours to accommodate changed circumstances or evolved conditions. Adaptive managers evaluate and reflect on new factors, think through options, make plans, and devise a plan. Adaptation is considered and measured.

- *Agility* is a *proactive* management capability, a skill developed <u>in readiness</u> for the potentiality of change. Agility means being ready to deal with the unexpected, to be immediately flexible in approach, *light on the feet.* Agile managers are ready for the inevitability of short notice situational changes and take swift, decisive action where appropriate.

Further reading

The Adaptation Advantage | Wiley, 2020 |
McGowan, H., Shipley, C.

On the Origin of Species | Wordsworth Editions (1998) | Darwin, C.

Adverbs, superfluous

"I believe the road to hell is paved with adverbs."

– Stephen King

Class-leading managers are masters of written communication. Most people I work with have ambitions to develop their writing skill. For some, school wasn't the best experience and consequently their vocabulary, grammar, and sentence construction are limited. Elegant verbal communicators I work with have challenges when it comes to putting their thoughts into an email. That's ok, we work on it and over time learn patterns of success, and methods of construction, to make their 'written comms' professional and effective.

Typical of many managers is overuse of adjectives (descriptors of nouns, e.g., *red* appl*e*) and adverbs (descriptors of verbs, or modifiers of adjectives, e.g., *amazingly* helpful). It's easy to spot adverbs where they end in *-ly*, e.g., *extremely, incredibly, hugely.*

At work, adverbs of *magnitude* are problematic. These adverbs describe the size, scope, or scale of the thing being referenced. They are intended by managers to add emphasis and intensity to a statement. Except in team communications, they do not.

Managers think adding a *very,* an *ever so, really, amazingly, extremely, incredibly, fantastically, highly,* will be *enormously* beneficial in emphasising your point. It doesn't, it weakens it.

I remember as a young leisure industry manager, being guided by a senior manager, Bob, whom I admired,

> "Nick, the content of your reports is fine. The language though, is flowery. The adjectives and adverbs get in the way of your message. Simplicity, with politeness, will be more impactful."

Bob was right. I listened and adapted my report writing.

Think about your communications at work. Lose the adverb and stick to the facts. The power of a message is in its directness. Make your statements direct.

- This book will *really* (superfluous) help you manage.
- This book will help you manage.

Further reading

Highly delighted, bitterly disappointed, ridiculously cheap: adverbs for emphasis | Cambridge Dictionary Blog, 2014 | Walter. L. | https://dictionaryblog.cambridge.org/2014/10/22/highly-delighted-bitterly-disappointed-ridiculously-cheap-adverbs-for-emphasis/

The Use of Adjectives and Adverbs in Journalism | Media Helping Media (undated) | Eggington, B. | https://mediahelpingmedia.org/basics/the-use-of-adjectives-and-adverbs-in-journalism/

Agile team management

"Change is the only constant in life." – *Heraclitus*

The Covid-19 pandemic stimulated a flurry of innovation, creativity, and ingenuity. We searched for invention and originality, simply to survive. Employing organisations, and their team managers, discovered the value of agility and adaptation. We learned to perform in the most difficult of circumstances.

Let's look at a pattern which connects (see **Patterns which connect**) flexible, adaptive team management with software development disciplines. Looking outside our day-to-day working patterns highlights new ways of thinking about team management.

Agile is a methodology employed by software engineers to ensure project builds remain relevant to the changing needs of sponsors and end users. *Agile* allows continuous adaptation of a software design specification. Progress is monitored at regular intervals. The project is broken down into small sections and is worked on during *sprint* phases. Development is then reviewed at team meetings known as *scrums* (see **Scrums and sprints**).

Although project meetings take design engineers away from 'dev time', there is a valuable return on time investment. Why? Because of the sustained focus on project relevance, aligned to the requirements of customers, both external and internal (see **Customers, internal**). *Agile* assesses how environmental factors may be evolving. It ensures project outcomes remain valuable and fit for purpose.

An alternative approach in the software engineering world is known as *Waterfall*, where a project is mapped in advance and engineers work methodically through a list of design tasks, step by step, sequentially, until the build phase is complete. *Waterfall* works well when the project is clearly scoped in advance and there is low probability of customer requirements shifting, or environmental change during the development and commissioning phase.

Agile *team management* is a pattern which connects with software development. Professional team managers spend time, regularly, with internal or external customers and check on short notice requirements, which are sometimes unexpected. They consider the service that is being developed by the work team, and any iterations to incorporate. Keeping the work team updated on customer requirements is a vital part of maintaining team engagement and their commitment to service quality.

In a volatile world of rapid change (see **VUCA management**), forward-thinking managers recognise the dangers of complacency in delivering *same-old-same-old* to customers. Adapting to customers' needs, and new external factors, may mean new ways of working, and sometimes radical changes.

Covid-19 presented a challenging obstacle for team managers. Sadly, not all organisations were able to adapt, some struggled to make radical shifts in behaviours. We learned valuable lessons about readiness for change, and about preparing work teams to be alert, ready to adjust and modify working methods at a moment's notice. Those lessons can be applied in day-to-day operations, by creating a team culture of *expecting* change, embracing the uncertainty of how it will appear, and being ready to shapeshift in an *agile* fashion (see **To be expected**).

Agility then, is the mark of an effective modern-day team, encouraged and supported by leaders and managers.

Note: in team management *agility* and *adaptability* are not the same thing (see **Adaptive team management**).

Agility is a *proactive* management capability, a skill developed <u>in readiness</u> for potential change. Agility means being ready to deal with the unexpected, to be immediately flexible in approach, *light on the feet*. Agile managers are ready for the inevitability of short notice situational changes and take swift, decisive action where appropriate.

Adaptability is a *reactive* capacity, an aptitude for modifying management processes or behaviours to accommodate changed circumstances or evolved conditions. Adaptive managers evaluate and reflect on new factors, think through options, make plans, and devise a plan. Adaptation is considered and measured.

Further reading

Keith Ferrazzi on How the Pandemic Taught Organizations to Be "Crisis Agile" | Harvard Business Review, March 2022 | Ferrazzi, K. | https://hbr.org/2022/03/keith-ferrazzi-on-how-the-pandemic-taught-organizations-to-be-crisis-agile

The Rise of the Agile Leader: Can You Make the Shift? | Prominence Publishing, 2020 | Mollor, C.

Aims & objectives, clarity on

"In a world deluged by irrelevant information, clarity is power."

– Yuval Noah Harari

Task clarity is an imperative for employees. To do well, employees want to fully understand the expectations of their job role, how it is to be delivered, and what goals and standards have been identified as performance measures.

It's reasonable for employees to expect clarity on these fundamental questions,

- "What am I required to do?"
- "How well am I expected to do it?"
- "How can I measure my progress?"
- "What help can I expect if I am finding difficulty?"

Client organisations I support are often insufficiently specific on their expectations of employees. Even a cursory inspection reveals role definitions as fuzzy, ambiguous, and imprecise. This leads to difficulties for employees and their managers. Team managers have a role to play in resolving these uncertainties.

Managers use a range of instruments to be explicitly clear on expectations

- Job role description, or 'specification'.
- SMART objectives (see **Objectives, management by [MBOs and OKRs]**).
- Performance management remedial objectives (see **Performance management**).
- Policies and procedures, or Standard Operating Procedures (SOPs).
- Explicit standards (see **Explicit standards**).
- Appraisals (see **Appraisals and performance reviews**).
- Competency definitions .
- Induction (see **Induction, preboarding, onboarding, reboarding**).
- Coaching sessions (see **Coaching**).
- Informal 121s (see **KIT meetings** and **Supervision sessions**).
- Short term project goals.

Employees thrive when they understand what, specifically, is expected in their work role. How clearly defined are aims and objectives for your team members?

Management role clarity

The same principle applies to the managers of teams. Does job role clarity exist for you (see **What am I here for? What is my management purpose?**)?

Further reading

Goal Clarity, Task Significance, and Performance: Evidence from a Laboratory Experiment | Derrick M. Anderson, Justin M. Stritch, Arizona State University | Journal of Public Administration and Theory Advance Access, 2015

Radical Clarity for Business: How to Empower People for Better Results at Work | Clarity Press, 2020 | Jones, C.

Air Cover sponsorship

"As a middle manager, you are in effect a chief executive of an organization yourself… As a micro-CEO, you can improve your own and your group's performance and productivity, whether or not the rest of the company follows suit." – Andy Grove

A plea to the senior management team; please sponsor your managers with *Air Cover* at new initiative time. To function effectively, operational managers need the confidence of knowing senior players have their backs. Implementation can be a rocky road.

Direction and strategy happen at senior level.

Execution at operational level is a more pragmatic activity and challenging for front line managers. Delivery of change plans reveals uncertainties within a work group, and occasionally a reluctance to shift from established habits. Not everyone is as committed to the new approach as senior policy makers.

Air Cover sponsorship means championing an operational manager with vocal advocacy. It means accepting that glitches will happen during early experimentation and learning phases and being ready to remind observers of this. In fact, difficulties are to be expected (see **To be expected**).

Regular contact checking-in on progress and offering reassurance between senior leader and operational manager will be comforting. How is the manager getting on? Could the senior manager deploy further influence to oil the wheels of change?

When a manager believes their boss is actively promoting their work effort and rooting for them, it boosts their moral and enthusiasm. It means a lot to feel protected, particularly during controversial periods of change.

So, senior leaders, are you offering supportive *Air Cover* sponsorship to your operational managers?

Further reading

Sponsors Need to Stop Acting Like Mentors | Julia Taylor Kennedy, Pooja Jain-Link | Harvard Business Review, February 2019 | https://hbr.org/2019/02/ sponsors-need-to-stop-acting-like-mentors

How to Manage Managers | Society for Human Resource Management, July 2021 | Janzer, C. | https://www.shrm. org/resourcesandtools/hr-topics/people-managers/pages/managing-managers.aspx

Analogue marking

"I speak two languages, Body and English." – *Mae West*

When we communicate through words, tone, and bodily expression (see **Words, song & dance**) we can choose to emphasise specific messages through *analogue marking.*

Analogue marking is the reinforcement of an *element* of a message, or a suggestion, through tonal or physiological shift. This emphasis is designed to be noticed and registered by the unconscious mind of the message recipient, whilst being unseen or unheard by the conscious mind.

The effect of analogue marking is to *mark* in the mind of the receiver, a specific message or part of a message. The master of this subtle methodology was Milton Erickson, the celebrated hypnotherapist.

During a patient intervention Erickson would

- Turn his face to one side to say certain words or phrases, to briefly change the direction of voice.
- Raise or lower the volume, change cadence, or soften or harden his speaking at specific points.
- Move his finger, hand, arm, leg, head, facial expression, or other physiological distraction to emphasise a suggestion.

These, and other techniques, were used by Erickson to place emphasis on precise elements of his conversation.

Sophisticated communicators use analogue marking to fix important parts of messages and embed suggestions to an audience. Stand-up comedians are masters of the art, as are professional actors. You can learn to do it too. You can see extensive use of analogue marking in NDK videos on YouTube.

Further reading

Ericksonian Approaches: A Comprehensive Manual | Crown House Publishing, 1999 | Battino, R., South, T.

New Code Continue & Begin® – Analogue Marking | Continue and Begin Ltd, 2016 |

Drake-Knight, N. | https://ndk-group.com/news-updates/

YouTube Nick Drake-Knight channel | https://www.youtube.com/channel/UCbiVddbHqtlhXLGEE24iDOA

Appraisals and performance reviews

"Managers don't like giving appraisals, and employees don't like getting them. Perhaps they're not liked because both parties suspect what the evidence has proved for decades: Traditional performance appraisals don't work." *– W. Edwards Deming*

Your organisation may have an established format for performance reviews. Maybe there's a reflective section, referencing back to a previous appraisal meeting. Perhaps there's space to review old objectives and decide on new ambitions, presented in SMART or OKR format. The framework document may ask about a personal development plan and learning options (see **About team management – an overview** and **Objectives, management by [MBOs and OKRs]**).

A more radical question asked by people management revolutionaries is *why?* Why is it necessary to have an annual or half yearly date set aside for this process? A process which, on a given date, addresses a team member's historical performance, celebrates successes, addresses shortfalls, reviews previously set objectives and maps out new ones, and identifies a development plan for the employee. Why is this not a continuous discussion?

The key to performance momentum is regular and continuous joint monitoring, not an annual assessment.

Maybe your organisation has a combination of formal appraisal reviews and regular, self-evaluative coaching? If so, great. Make sure (documented) outputs from the coaching sessions are brought along and integrated into the appraisal discussion. Growth is continuous, not something scheduled at a single critical meeting once or twice a year.

The best appraisals are celebratory and developmental, and most importantly, take place inside the team member's world (see **Get inside their world** and **Maps of the territory**). Whatever the format, remember the performance review activity will be more significant to the appraisee than it is for you. You cancel, postpone, rush it, or give lip service, at your peril.

Good team managers create their own supportive review approach. Regular conversations with team members help managers feel informed, and employees feel appreciated. Work related discussions don't need to be formal. A relaxed chat over coffee is often useful to keep up to speed on how a team member is doing, how they're feeling, and any support the manager can help to make the employee's work life thrive (see **KIT meetings**).

There's a place during conversation to consider any barriers to a team member's effectiveness, or to explore streamlining processes, or ineffective systems. Coffee chats can cover coaching opportunities, mentoring, or additional training for a team member to build capability and bring value to the team. It doesn't need form filling.

These low-key contacts of keeping in touch and staying aware of a colleague's world are invaluable (see **Get inside their world**). The annual *Appraisal and Performance Review* is a contrived, artificial, activity which attempts to compensate for poor team managers not doing what good managers do.

Further reading

The Performance Management Revolution | Harvard Business Review, 2016 | Capelli, P., Tavis, A. | https://hbr.org/2016/10/the-performance-management-revolution

Why Appraisals Are Pointless for Most People | BBC Work, May 2019 | Woolston, C. | https://www.bbc.com/worklife/article/20190501-why-appraisals-are-pointless-for-most-people

Assertion and assertiveness

"The only healthy communication style is assertive communication."
– Jim Rohn

Despite millennia of evolution, humans are still fundamentally mammals, with mammalian drivers of behaviour. We seek *feelings* we would like, and work to remove or avoid *feelings* we don't want (see **Emotional Drivers™**).

This manifests itself in our styles of behaviour. As societal animals, we act in ways designed to move us towards, or away from, circumstances in which specific feelings may be stimulated. Our primitive approach to achieve our feeling-goals was limited to two broad behavioural strategies,

Aggression

Domination of others provided *wins*. Humans could achieve goals and ambitions by subjugating others, by conquest, to get the outcome they wanted, and the feeling(s) being sought. Over time, repeated bouts of aggression were necessary to maintain dominance and authority. The wins were dependant on continued superiority.

In today's workplace, physical aggression may thankfully be less common, although non-physical aggressive behaviour stimulates the same hormonal responses in recipients, as fear of physical injury.

Psychologically brutal aggression still exists in some forms of workplace intimidation, leveraging fear of job loss and associated security fears. Abraham Maslow's Hierarchy of Needs included security as a factor in emotional well-being, and workplace performance.

In work teams, aggression may come in more subtle, covert, forms. Manipulative aggression is a form of twisting circumstances and situations to suit the aggressor. It is still driven by an urge to get what I want. It pressurises and demands compliance, even if the aggressor's behaviour may seem 'reasonable' at face value.

The core purpose of aggression is to get what I want. It's a rubbish way of operating as a team leader. The limitations of aggression are as follows,

- Aggression creates personal movement, not inner motivation.
- People do things because they must (negative implications if they don't), not because they want to.
- Projects become management-owned, not team-owned. There is less buy in to the mission.
- Aggression stimulates remembered pain, and future resistance, often in the form of passive-aggressive responses, go-slows, minimal effort, doing enough to avoid more aggression. It's employees' ways of getting back at the aggressor, without overt confrontation. Passive aggression is common in workplace organisations. Maybe you've experienced this?
- Management aggression becomes normalised in the experience of team members, so the power of threat diminishes over time.
- Aggressors may get a win once, maybe twice. Over time subsequent wins become less likely.

Submission

Avoidance of conflict (see **Fight, flight, play dead**) as a short-term tactic, or longer-term strategy, is intended to minimise the likelihood of pain. In a society of pack leader hierarchies, humans could appease aggressors and lessen the chances of personal attack. The strategy of submission, or passivity, is *to let you have what you want, so you don't hurt me.*

Submission exists in workplace teams. Think about the people you work with and the dynamics of your team. Are there instances of submissive behaviours?

The long-term results of submissive behaviour are damaging for everyone, for team members, managers, and the employing organisation,

- Emotional damage to the submissive individual.
- Feelings of resentment towards the dominator(s).
- Stimulation of passive-aggressive responses to being *put upon.*
- Diminished innovation and free thinking.
- Poor team morale.
- Reduced performance levels.
- Staff turnover.
- Increased recruitment, onboarding, and retention costs.

- Despite this, in today's world of work these primitive approaches of aggression and submission are still at large.

So, what is assertion, or assertiveness?

Assertion begins with an internal mindset. Remember, you can choose your mindset. One excellent starting point is to consider Franklin Ernst's *OK Corral.*

I'm **not** ok You're ok	I'm ok You're ok
I'm **not** ok You're **not** ok	I'm ok You're **not** ok

When we enter dialogue with another person, or persons, we can choose how we feel about ourselves and our co-communicators. Look at the four quadrants above. The most likely approach to gain maximum benefit from an encounter is a mindset of mutual respect, the *I'm ok, You're ok* position.

Assertive behaviours help us communicate honestly and directly about *what is relevant.* Transparency of communication allows free flowing of ideas, without the need to be aggressive, submissive, or passive-aggressive. Assertion means communicating thoughts and feelings without fear, whilst respecting another's position.

It takes practice, and courage, to communicate directly and openly. At first, like most new skills, it may feel awkward and uncomfortable. With time you'll discover the benefits, and the feeling of freedom, which openness and direct communication brings.

Eric Berne offers informative reading for people managers (see **Behaviour change request** and **Win-Win**).

Further reading

Games People Play: The Psychology of Human Relationships | Penguin, 1968 | Berne, E.

Assertiveness Pocketbook | Management Pocketbooks, 2011 | Eggert, M.A.

The Ernst Ok Corral | Ernst, F.H. | www. ernstokcorral.com

Assumptions

"Rational discussion is useful only when
there is a significant base of shared assumptions."
– Noam Chomsky

We make assumptions in our daily life to survive. Assumption is a short-cut strategy to get on, to avoid clarification questioning and delay. Accuracy generally improves with experience in any field of endeavour, including people management. Assumptions are dangerous though. The cheesy *'it makes an ASS of U and ME'* mantra may be trite, but it is not far off the mark. Assumptions are experiential shortcuts. They are also a function of our prejudices (see **Cognitive bias**).

Here's a fun way to demonstrate assumptions. Read the following 112 words paragraph. Allow yourself a whole minute to ensure you fully understand the contents. The information is factually accurate. Visualise the story as it unfolds. When answering the questions, refer to the story if you need to. Tick the box marked either, *True, False* or *Information Not Given* for each statement.

Once you have answered each question, please do not make changes to previous answers, otherwise it's no fun!

Rob, Mart, and George drove up to the Greatest Band Ever gig. Mart put on one of their CDs. There were thousands of people at the NEC, and they got there late. Rob heard a door steward say, "No drinks in the hall" and he put down the beer. They could hear the music from outside. They stood up throughout the performance. George thought the drumming sounded cool and Mart was into the slap bass. Mart got a nosebleed and Rob found some tissue paper for his brother. George had promised to get his sister a T-shirt for her birthday. They travelled home together and told Rosie all about it.

Check these statements. Is each statement True, False or Information not given? You decide.

	Greatest Band Ever Test	True	False	Info not given
1	Rob, Mart, and George drove up to the gig in one car, together			
2	Mart played a Greatest Band Ever CD in the car			
3	The gig was at the NEC			
4	The Greatest Band Ever got there late			
5	The doorman told Rob "No drinks in the hall"			
6	The beer was in a can			
7	The drumming was cool and so was the slap bass			
8	Rob and Mart are brothers			
9	George bought a Greatest Band Ever T shirt for Rosie's birthday			
10	Rob, Mart, and George are brothers			

You can find answers to the *Greatest Band Ever Test* in Appendix 2.

Further reading

6 Assumptions You Shouldn't Make – and 1 You Always Should | Forbes, 2017 | Goman, C.K. | https://www.forbes.com/sites/carolkinseygoman/2017/01/15/6-assumptions-you-shouldnt-make-and-1-you-always-should/?sh=7e23a83676f0

Are You Guilty of Making Too Many Assumptions? | Psychology Today, September 2019 | Guttman, J. | https://www.psychologytoday.com/us/blog/sustainable-life-satisfaction/201909/are-you-guilty-of-making-too-many-assumptions

Authentic team management

"What you leave behind is not what is engraved in stone monuments, but what is woven into the lives of others." – *Pericles*

Authenticity in team management is a feature of successful operations. Authentic managers behave and communicate with transparency. They are honest, genuine, and open about what is required of the work group, offering clarity of expectation (see **Aims & objectives, clarity on**) and perspective on how the team's function fits with wider business goals.

Patterns connect here with *Human Leadership* (see **Patterns which connect** and **Human leadership**).

A starting point for considering your own team management authenticity is self-awareness. Authentic managers are conscious of their character traits and acknowledge these to themselves and team members. Where appropriate, managers share how they are developing their behaviour patterns and communication style, as part of their own commitment to continuous professional development (see **Continuous professional development [CPD]**).

Authentic team managers have common behavioural characteristics. They,

- Show humility and a personal willingness to grow in their management role.
- Offer insights into their own personalities, sharing themselves with colleagues.
- Recognise and publicly acknowledge their own mistakes and judgement errors.

- Empathise with others. They invest effort to understand each team member and what is important to them at work, and outside of work (see **Emotional drivers™**, **Emotional intelligence [EQ]** and **Empathy**).
- Encourage contribution of ideas from team members regarding quality and process improvement and listen without interruption.
- Adopt a balanced assessment and evaluation of employee suggestions.
- Are honest about what's relevant (see **Assertion and assertiveness**)
- Maintain a horizon focus, considering long-term concerns, offering reminders of goals and ambition, as well as maintaining focus on short-term delivery.
- Create a work environment of 'safe space' to raise concerns or worries (see **Johari, adapted for management**).
- Celebrate genuine successes.
- Address team or individual performance dips if necessary (see **Performance management**).
- Embrace integrity by behaving in ways which reflect the values of the work group, doing what they said they would do, aligned to group values, and building trust and respect from team members.

Think about the above authenticity characteristics. How do you currently shape up as an authentic team manager? What can you continue to do well? What might you like to begin to do differently?

Further reading

Authentic: How to be yourself and why it matters | Piatkus, 2016 | Joseph, S.

Dare to Lead: Brave Work. Tough Conversations. Whole Hearts | Vermilion, 2018 | Brown, B.

B

Barriers to professional development

"The barriers are not erected which can say to aspiring talents and industry, 'Thus far and no farther.'" *– Ludwig van Beethoven*

We can easily make a compelling list of barriers to professional development. Here are typical justifiers,

- There's no time in my life for studying, too much going on at home, too much pressure at work.
- I'm not the studying type, I wasn't successful at school.
- There aren't any promotion prospects, so what's the point?
- Even if I get development training I'm not thought of as management material.
- I'm not very confident, people wouldn't respect me in a more senior position.
- I know what I need to know already.
- It's all theory anyway; I'm a practical, hands-on manager.
- My finance / English / IT / presentation / skills are poor.

Do any of these seem familiar?

But wait...if we become negative in our thinking, barriers *will* seem insurmountable, and we convince ourselves study is too difficult a challenge 'at this time' (a great way to delay).

Many of the barriers are simply thoughts – the barriers don't exist; we think we do. We have built what are known as *constructs*, belief systems to live our lives by. We can choose to remove the barriers if we want to (see **Beliefs, you can choose or change, Beliefs, limited, Can't to Can Belief Busting,** and **Irrational thinking**).

Of course, sometimes the barriers are put in place as a means of generating a secondary gain (see **Secondary gain**), a benefit usually associated with avoidance of pain or discomfort; for example, not having to invest energy, or concentrated effort. Or maybe a more pleasurable activity might be threatened by having to make way for a learning commitment?

The danger of barrier beliefs is they become self-fulfilling prophecies. We get what we focus on with our repeated self-talk. (see **Focus** and **Self talk, inner dialogue**).

Almost all are barriers are surmountable if we think differently about how to overcome them.

What is your *current* thinking about professional development?

Further reading

Personalize Your Management Development | Harvard Business Review, 2003 | Shope Griffin, N. | https://hbr.org/2003/03/personalize-your-management-development

Continuing Professional Development: Ensuring you have the skills to face a challenge | Chartered Management Institute | https://www.managers.org.uk/education-and-learning/continuing-professional-development/

Behaviours and values, what is expected?

"There's no magic formula for great company culture.
The key is just to treat your staff how you would like to be treated."
– Richard Branson

Check out your organisational values and expectations of employee behaviours. They will be around somewhere, on a wall poster, in a staff handbook or on the website. Team managers have a role in encouraging team members' behaviours to reflect these expectations. Are values and expected behaviours in your team lived to? If so, great. Or is colleague engagement a bit patchy?

During preliminary discussions with project sponsors, I make a point of asking senior players what their organisational values and behaviours are.

Few of the senior teams can answer directly without checking the board-room walls for clues.

I had one experience (I did well not to laugh out loud) a few years ago, consulting for a European household name retailer with a network of over 400 stores. We were in the head office boardroom, two directors, a senior manager and me. As we discussed ambitions for a customer experience programme, I asked for an insight into the brand's values, and how we could blend these into the project work.

There were mutters and glances exchanged, and a stuttered start from one director referring to one, then two of the brand values. It was obvious these were not at the forefront of their minds. How on earth, I wondered, were customer-facing employees going to live the values of the brand if their leaders didn't know what the values were?

The reason I found it so difficult not to laugh was because the brand values were printed in a large funky design font, behind them, on the wall of the boardroom. I had spotted these (difficult not to) when I'd entered the room prior to our meeting. I knew at that point it would be a challenging project. It was.

World-class organisations work hard to ensure directors, team managers and front-line staff all live to the values and behaviours of the enterprise, and these are not words left on a wall (see **NDK Performance Model®**).

How is it going in your world?

Further reading

Make Your Values Mean Something | Harvard Business Review, 2002 | Lencioni, P. | https://hbr.org/2002/07/make-your-values-mean-something

Are workers really quitting over company values? | BBC Worklife, February 2022 | Christian, A. | https://www.bbc.com/worklife/article/20220223-are-workers-really-quitting-over-company-values

Behaviour breeds behaviour

"Just as ripples spread out when a single pebble is dropped into water, the actions of individuals can have far-reaching effects."

– Dalai Lama

It's a truism that *behaviour breeds behaviour*. How one person behaves impacts and creates response from others. It's a stimulus – response mechanism, a pattern common to home life and work.

Your role as a people manager demands qualities which stimulate enthusiasm and energy in team members. Your people will replicate (at least some of) your deeds and manners. Savvy team leaders exhibit positive traits as an example to follow. Culture starts at the top.

Performance Damaging Behaviours

Stay alert for performance limiting patterns, in yourself and in others. The illustrations here are a bit of fun and as with much said in jest, there is a degree truth in them. Do you recognise these traits?

- *PLOMs – Poor Little Old Me.* Self-pity and an urge for attention from others. Permanently hard done by, and in their own world, deserving of sympathy from everyone in their sphere of influence. Focused on self, not team effort.
- *R-BUTs – "Ah, but it won't work because…".* Stimulus-response negativity towards new proposals. Cynics.
- *CAVE dwellers – Continuously Against Virtually Everything.* Like R-Buts. Patterns of negativity as a default behaviour. Transfer negativity to others, affecting colleague morale and customer feeling.
- *BMWs – Bitchers, Moaners, and Whiners.* The full fat version of negativity, guaranteed to bring down team energy and positive impact.
- *ICBAs* (ick-bahs) *– I Can't Be Arsed.* Patterns of low motivation and commitment to team goals.
- *Energy Vampires and Mood Hoovers.* Suck energy and positivity from others.

- *MGs – Moaners & Groaners.* Often in pairs, one moans, the other groans. Misery loves company.
- *RSPs – Reluctant Service Providers.* Keep these characters away from external and internal customers.
- *JAJs –* It's *Just A Job.* Low employee engagement.
- *20:20s –* 20 years' experience, and their behaviour hasn't evolved since year one. In a changing world, year one behaviour has been replicated twenty times. Dinosaurs.

These characters are difficult to love, aren't they?

Performance Enhancing Behaviours

How about the up siders?

My favourites are the *Makers*, the people who make things happen. They have no time for the *Behaviour Breeds Behaviour* styles listed above. They drive teams on, filled with energy and optimism, inspiring colleagues, and stimulating like-mindedness. Just as elite sports athletes do, they believe in possibility and opportunity. They plan for success and invest sustained energy. They persist. And they do it with a smile!

You can be a *Maker*

Make it easy for team members to enjoy their work, by being bright and cheerful. Remember the power of smiling in your communications with employees (see **Words, Song and Dance**), include those colleagues working remotely, and help people feel respected and valued.

Of course, no-one is cheery all the time. We all struggle to put on a friendly face when we're not feeling too great. The best people managers work on their presenting style and 'turn on' their performance when needed. For some, it is a mental switch – a thought process or inner voice which initiates their *Act As If* behaviours (see **Act As If**).

Further reading

Boomerang! Coach Your Team to Be the Best | Dandelion Digital, 2007 | Drake-Knight, N.

https://www.audible.co.uk/pd/
Fast-Coaching-Audiobook/B07TTKD13T

Fast Coaching. The Complete Guide to New Code Continue & Begin® | Dandelion Digital, 2016 | Drake-Knight, N. | Audible

The Motivation Agency | https://
themotivationagency-online.com/course/
begin

Behaviour change request

"The secret of change is to focus all of your energy,
not on fighting the old, but on building the new." – *Socrates*

In my late twenties I came across an assertion technique for influencing the behaviour of others. It helped me feel better about myself, because I learned to take positive action and address situations which were bothering me.

The technique was developed by Sharon and Gordon Bower and is known as DESC. It revolutionised my approach to difficult communication issues, and I have shared the Bowers' ideas to family, friends, colleagues, students, and clients. It incorporates a form of 'I statement' where the communicator owns their feelings and shares them with a co-communicator.

The DESC model, or at least my version of it, is structured as follows:

- **Describe** the *behaviour* of the other person, in context, and be as specific as possible. Make sure the description is accurate and factual. A skewed account of circumstances will undermine your proposal.
- **Express** the *feelings* you experience when this behaviour occurs. Again, be specific in your description. It may be uncomfortable for your message recipient to hear. This is the powerful part because no-one can argue with how you *feel. What you feel, you feel,* it's an experience only you can verify.
- **Specify** the *change* to the other person's behaviour you would prefer. Be specific and practical.
- **Consequences** – explain how your proposed change will help, the *positive consequences* of this, and the benefits to both parties. By contrast, if the other person's behaviour continues, describe how it will impact negatively.

A version of this approach helped me, as a young manager in a corporate organisation.

It was 1989, I was a 29-year-old learning and development manager. One of my tasks was to write and deliver training events for leisure industry business units across the UK. Our company was fast-growing; it had a portfolio of hotels, restaurants, bars, nightclubs, casinos, leisure centres, landmark tourism attractions, bookmakers, and bingo halls. It was a lot of fun working in the company and I loved every minute. I was creating something, developing management good practices, and helping to build an organisational culture I believed in.

Clouds were on the horizon though. Interest rates were rising steeply, finance repayments became difficult for the business to service, and challenging trading conditions began to bite. The rapid growth became rapid downsizing. Each day it seemed another desk was empty at head office. I began to worry I might be next for redundancy. I was married with three, soon to be four, young children and a mortgage I could barely pay each month.

The HR Director (let's call him Rod) had previously made a point of meeting with me on Monday afternoons to bring me up to speed on what he could share from the Board meeting earlier in the day. I enjoyed his trust, as he shared headline news on business performance and the next stage in our growth ambitions. The Monday afternoon meetings had stopped some weeks ago. I was gripped by paranoia, *"What isn't he telling me?"*.

I remember spending an uncomfortable weekend thinking about how I could address this with Rod. I picked up my notepad and began to compile a DESC conversation framework. On the following Monday I waited until Rod returned from the Board meeting, walked down the corridor, and knocked on his door. I took my notebook with me.

"Come in! Hi Nick, how's it going?" I could feel my Adam's apple bob up and down as I swallowed nervously.

"Rod, can I share something with you?" Trembling voice.

"Of course, fire away…" And this is how it went…

Describe "Rod, I enjoyed the briefings you used to give me after Board meetings each Monday. It's not happened for the past few weeks and it's bothering me. Because you haven't been meeting with me… and with the redundancies going on…"

Express "I feel anxious, and it's affecting me at home as well as at work."

Specify "If you felt able to restart the Monday briefing with me… even if there are things you can't share, it would be helpful for me."

Consequences "If you could, I'd feel involved and less worried about what's happening in the company. I'd be able to get on with the great things we're doing in L&D. If you think you can't I'll understand… except I'll worry more and it's affecting my concentration. Could you offer the briefings again?"

There, I'd done it. Now for the response from Rod…

"Oh Nick, I'm so sorry, you're right, I haven't been meeting with you recently, I'm so sorry. I've got a lot on my plate at the moment, and it's a difficult time, as I'm sure you know…"

[Learning point for NDK, it wasn't all about me! Rod, the poor guy, had a whole company HRM strategy to manage in difficult conditions].

"Of course, yes, let's make sure we get back to briefings, every Monday afternoon, if I'm able to. I'll share with you what I can. I didn't realise what an impact it was having on you… I'm so sorry."

What a top bloke! I felt bad for not realising his map of the territory, the incredible amount of strain he must have been under and how he was coping. He was a nice man, and our Monday meetings were re-instated.

Then I asked him one lunchtime if he thought I should apply for an opportunity I'd seen in another organisation. *"Yes"* was his response, and I did. Within a month I had been appointed as Lecturer in Management at a further education college, teaching front line managers, team leaders, and middle managers. The leisure company went into administration not long afterwards.

DESC assertion had helped me during a difficult time. So, thank you, Sharon Anthony Bower, and Gordon H. Bower; your insightful thinking has helped so many people manage the process of discussing troubling communication topics with others. I recommend reading their book *Asserting Yourself.*

Further reading

Asserting Yourself – Update Edition: A Practical Guide for Positive Change | De Capo Press, 2004 | Bower, S.A., Bower, G. H.

Are 'I' Statements Better Than 'You' Statements? | Psychology Today, November 2012 | Johnson, J.A. | https://www.psychologytoday.com/ca/blog/cui-bono/201211/are-i-statements-better-you-statements

Study Reveals a Conversation Trick That Motivates People to Change Their Behavior | Forbes, January 2016 | Morin, A. | https://www.forbes.com/sites/amymorin/2016/01/22/study-reveals-a-conversation-trick-that-motivates-people-to-change-their-behavior/?sh=5657b4eb6ff0

Being comfortable, dangers of

"Don't be afraid to expand yourself, to step out of your comfort zone.
That's where the joy and the adventure lie." *– Herbie Hancock*

How employees become motivated at work has been a subject of study for generations. Research is well documented, with business school references including Herzberg, McClelland, Maslow, Vroom and Alderfer and others (see **Motivation**).

Shapiro and Doyle proposed a set of three internal drivers for professional *salespeople* which they suggested are common motivational factors. These included,

1. *Ego Driver* – being the best, the top performer.
2. *Reward Driver* – compensation received, bonus.
3. *Sales Task Clarity* – understanding precisely what is required to be successful.

These are valid observations in sales management. Except Shapiro and Doyle missed an internal driver, a motivator for some employees,

4. *Be Comfortable* – do just enough.

There is a group of employees in any organisation who are self-motivated to just *Be Comfortable*. Sales environments are well-known for this, employees who work just enough to reach the target line each month, but no more. Long service sales pros know the game and manage their energy investment and customer networks so next month gets off to a flying start. Known as *putting it in the fridge*, it means the sales order is held back and kept 'chilled' until the 1st of the following month. It's a fact, ask any experienced sales manager.

This is not only a phenomenon of the sales world. *Be Comfortable* is rife in many sectors. Team members who are doing enough to keep you off their backs are playing the *Be Comfortable* game. Experienced, long service team members are particularly prone to this condition (see **Games people play**).

Be Comfortablers feel there's something missing in their professional lives; there's a lack of spark, inner drive, or passion to achieve. *Be Comfortablers* often have outside interests providing the stimulus they don't experience at work.

Getting to know the team member's professional history, their career highlights, and disappointments, helps gain deeper insight into the person behind the performance. A feeling of lack of interest in them by 'management' is a common factor in low motivation. Most *Be Comfortablers* I've worked with respond well to authentic interest and empathy from their manager (see **Difficult people, managing, Empathy, Employee engagement** and **Human leadership**).

You may think,

"If they are delivering the goods, then who cares?"

If there is untapped potential and spare capacity not being fully utilised, there's a conversation to be had about what, specifically, has to happen to provide a stimulating challenge for the team member, when they clearly have more to offer (see **Freedom questions**).

When managers invest time to learn about a colleague's background, their past achievements, and their internal *movement away* and *movement towards* motivators (see **Emotional Drivers™**), there is potential for finding more meaning through work.

Abe Maslow suggested we all have an urge to 'self-actualise', meaning to fulfil our potential. If the work experience is shaped in a way which attracts the interest of a *Be Comfortabler*, there's hope for a re-energised approach towards achievement. This could include,

- Special responsibilities, or project management.
- Colleague training and coaching.

- New product or service development.
- Reshaped goals and ambitions.
- Revised reward and recognition system for outstanding performance.

The question is, are you willing to put up with *Be Comfortable* behaviour patterns? Or do you want to address the employee's mindset? If you do, think about exploring the employee's world. There may be an opportunity waiting to be uncovered.

Further reading

Make the Sales Task Clear | Harvard Business Review, November 1983 | Shapiro, B., Doyle, S. | https://hbr.org/1983/11/make-the-sales-task-clear

How to Motivate Your Problem People | Harvard Business Review, January 2023 | Nicholson, N. | https://hbr.org/2003/01/how-to-motivate-your-problem-people

Beliefs, you can choose or change

"If you don't change your beliefs, your life will be like this forever. Is that good news?" – *W. Somerset Maugham*

We have chosen our belief systems. As life goes on, we continue to add new beliefs, new 'certainties', to our collection. Our beliefs were influenced by significant others during our early development years. Some of those certainties may have changed as we've navigated through life. Do the cultural and political views of our parents, or carers, still mirror ours now? I grew up believing the daily newspaper in our house was *The Truth*. Maybe life experiences have caused us to question some of our early influences?

Questioning our belief systems is a healthy activity. Why? Because now, as adults, we can choose which beliefs are helpful for us. At some point *we decided* to have a specific belief, otherwise it wouldn't have become embedded in our mind. We can *undecide* these if we wish. Once this reality lands with managers I work with, eyes light up and new opportunities emerge.

Beliefs may be helpful, or self-limiting. Managers share their beliefs with me, sometimes consciously, at other times unconsciously through their words, tonality, and physiology (see **Words, song, and dance**).

Beliefs relate to self-perception, about abilities and areas of expertise, and limitations. In their book *Hypnotic Language*, John Burton and Bob Bodenheimer describe the impact a belief change has on performance,

> "Altering beliefs usually results in a change in behaviour because we behave in ways consistent with our beliefs."

I hear managers share impoverished beliefs about self,

> "I can't give formal presentations."

> "I'm not cut out for that role."

> "I hated school, I'm not one for learning."

> "I can't write reports."

> "I don't have enough time for 121s with my team members."

> "I'll never get to grips with the new software."

> "I'm not good with managing discipline."

> "I lose my words when I'm talking to bosses."

Whatever your beliefs are right now, on any subject, know *you can change them* to whatever new paradigm you would like to have. It may require an investment of energy, in learning, or in practising a new skill; it can be done though, and the starting point is a change in thought patterns. For many people, this simple awareness has a profoundly positive affect on their feelings about freedom of choice, options for living and how they wish to associate with others.

When a team member reveals a belief system inhibiting their performance at work, it may be appropriate, as a coaching activity, to explore their embedded thinking and tease out opportunities to grow. This is a potent skillset for managers to deploy.

A proven method for breakthrough, to loosen the grip of limiting beliefs, is the change tool *Can't to Can Belief Busting®* (see **Can't to Can Belief Busting®, Johari, adapted for management,** and **Case Study: On Growing Managers [and our Business]**).

Further reading

Boomerang! Coach Your Team to Be the Best | Dandelion Digital, 2007 | Drake-Knight, N.

Fast Coaching. The Complete Guide to New Code Continue & Begin® | Dandelion Digital, 2016 | Drake-Knight, N. | Audible https://www.audible.co.uk/pd/Fast-Coaching-Audiobook/B07TTKD13T

The Motivation Agency | https://themotivationagency-online.com/course/begin

Provocative Therapy | Meta Publications, 1974 | Farrelly, F., Brandsma, J.

Hypnotic Language: Its Structure and Use | Crown House Publishing, 2000 | Burton, J., Bodenhamer, B.

Brainstorming, esrever, and thought showers

"It is better to have enough ideas and some of them to be wrong, than to be always right by having no ideas at all." *– Edward de Bono*

Problem solving doesn't get more fun than this! Reverse brainstorming (in my experience) is more effective in stimulating creative thinking patterns than 'standard' brainstorming sessions. I've used this approach with global brands to work through customer experience issues. You may have a different topic; the approach will be the same.

Incidentally, it's appropriate in some environments to refer to brainstorming as *thought showers*. So, I guess we are referring here to *Reverse Thought Showers*. Anyway, this is how it works...

Assemble a team for the problem-solving activity. A group size of between eight and twelve contributors creates the right blend of energy and opportunity for all group members to participate. One facilitator can usually manage this, although it helps (and is more fun) if you appoint a 'scribe' to make rapid written notes on a flipchart. You'll need to tear off each completed flipchart sheet and stick them on the walls of your room.

Select the 'problem', in reverse mode. Write the problem in a prominent position, for example, *"How can we make our customers' experience as awful as possible when they visit our stores?"*

Starting the process will require energy on the facilitator's part. Most employees are conditioned to think they'll be expected to offer up positive proposals. You may need to encourage subversive, troublemaker thinking, with a few suggestions of your own, for example,

"Avoid eye contact at all costs."

"Scowl at the customer and keep your arms folded."

"Make sure the store is as messy and dirty as possible."

"If asked a question about a product, say 'Dunno.'"

It won't take long to get the group going. It's a treat for most employees to be naughty and misbehave. Emphasise there is to be no evaluation of suggestions, make it as nutty as each contributor likes.

Once you have plenty of flipcharts on the walls, covered in crazy ideas, you can begin the process of reversing the statements into positive, constructive ideas. So, we could take the above list of negative proposals about customer service and reverse them like this,

- ~~Avoid eye contact at all costs.~~ Make a point of looking at each new customer as they enter and acknowledge them.
- ~~Scowl at the customer and keep your arms folded~~. Smile at the customer, turn towards them, and have your arms by your side.
- ~~Make sure the store is as messy and dirty as possible.~~ Keep the store professionally presented, tidy, and clean in line with *Store Standards*.
- ~~If asked a question about a product, say 'Dunno.'~~ Use your product knowledge or make use of the instore product tablets to demonstrate

our range, their features, benefits, and the positive feelings customers can expect from using the product.

These solutions have been developed by the team, not you. The power of employee-created solutions is more impactful than yet another session of telling.

Enjoy *Reverse Brainstorming*, or *Reverse Thought Showers*, it's fun.

Further reading

Do It All Wrong! Using Reverse-Brainstorming to Generate Ideas, Improve Discussions, and Move Students to Action Sage Journals | Hagen, M., Bernard, A., Grube, E., 2016

Forget Traditional Brainstorming—Instead, Try This Technique to Spur New Levels of Team Creativity | Forbes, July 2021 | Brownlee, D. | https://www.forbes.com/sites/danabrownlee/2021/07/28/forget-traditional-brainstorming-instead-try-this-technique-to-spur-new-levels-of-team-creativity/?sh=2468ca174d13

But Monster®, The

The But Monster® is a conjunction, a word joining two sentences together. Used carelessly, it acts as a destructive rapport breaker. In therapeutic contexts the word 'but' is acknowledged as potentially damaging to counsellor-client progress.

Consider the following examples from a call centre environment,

"You were quite friendly with the customer…
but (Monster) you should've stayed on the call longer."

"Yes, when he called you did acknowledge him…
but (Monster) you should have used his name."

"Your performance dealing with the enquiry was good…
but (Monster) you need to up-sell more while you are processing the customer details."

Have you noticed the impact of the But Monster? It negates all before it and creates tension in the mind and body of the message recipient. *However* is just a posh way of saying *but*. It's a *But Monster* in disguise.

A healthy alternative to the *But Monster* is to, either,

- Substitute *but* with the word *and* in its place.
  or,
- Break the sentence in two. End the first observation statement, and start the request for change message in a second statement,

Using the phrase *even better* is a nice way to stay positive, and of course an upward tonality breathes energy into any dialogue. Also, in the above examples, lose the qualifying word *quite*: it minimises and is disempowering.

Let's try those sentences again, adapted:

"You were ~~quite~~ friendly with the customer… **and**… it would be great next time if you could spend more time on the call."

"Yes, when he called you did acknowledge him… **and**… next time you could use the caller's name to build rapport even more quickly."

"Your performance with the enquiry was good! … **full stop, deep breath, new sentence**… You know, you could make your performance even better by offering linked services while you record the customer's details."

The But Monster® bites! Please consider alternatives when communicating with your team (see **Language to help** and **Language which hurts**).

Further reading

Boomerang! Coach Your Team to Be the Best | Dandelion Digital, 2007 | Drake-Knight, N.

Audible https://www.audible.co.uk/pd/ Fast-Coaching-Audiobook/B07TTKD13T

Fast Coaching. The Complete Guide to New Code Continue & Begin® | Dandelion Digital, 2016 | Drake-Knight, N. |

The Motivation Agency | https:// themotivationagency-online.com/course/ begin

C

Calmness

Operational management can be frustrating, even maddening. A prime driver of frustration is people. People you work alongside, line managers, your direct reports, customers, suppliers, and other stakeholders.

In my management coaching work, we explore the parts of a manager's job they find most troublesome, and how they respond to those circumstances, and usually they are people related. Managers report how they occasionally react to provocation with knee jerk, stimulus-response behaviours. We reflect on these automatic patterns and investigate the reasons behind them. Most managers acknowledge the impact of their reflex communication may be *less helpful* (see **Good and less good**).

Managers are human and susceptible to the same emotional responses as everyone else. It's how we learn to control our natural reflexes that makes the difference. Talented managers are skilled (knowingly or unknowingly) at dissociation, that is, stepping back from a circumstance and considering *what is going on here?* They take the emotion out of thinking. They're empathetic towards emotional message givers without using emotive language themselves (see **Empathy**).

A dissociative approach gives a more independent perspective, more room to consider what is happening in the moment, and less likelihood of an immediate emotional response. It helps to take a pause, nod acknowledgment of what has happened or is happening, and think through decision making options and likely impact, both immediate and subsequent (see **Secondary and tertiary consequences**).

Where a team member is reporting a challenging circumstance, and seeking guidance, an experienced manager may make use of Ken Blanchard's *One Minute Manager* approach and ask, *"What do you think should be done about this?"*

In our coaching sessions we discuss personal strategies to address stress-inducing incidents, and how, even in the face of profound irritations, managers can stay calm. Remember the wise words of Epictetus (see **Stoicism**),

"It is not events which disturb men's minds, but their thinking about events."

A simple technique to prevent a knee-jerk reaction was Jefferson's suggestion; count to ten. Or one hundred.

Further reading

Little Book of Calm at Work | Penguin, 1999 | Wilson, P.

The One Minute Manager | Penguin Putman, 1997 | Blanchard, K.H.

Can't to Can Belief Busting®

"Whether you think you can or think you can't – you're right."
– Henry Ford

Managers and team members have limiting beliefs, everyone does. When those thinking restrictions get in the way of effective performance it is time to use *Can't to Can Belief Busting*®. You can learn to use *Can't to Can*® for yourself, for your team members, or outside of work. Typical limiting beliefs I hear are,

"I can't do presentations… I can't deal with difficult customers… I can't write reports… I can't speak at conference… I can't be assertive with my boss…"

Well, of course colleagues can do these things, even though they choose to belief they can't (see **Beliefs, you can choose or change**, and **Secondary gain.** Virginia Satir (1972), the family therapist said,

"We can learn something new anytime we believe we can."

We could ask, *"Why can't you do it?"*, except this results in a justification for the belief (see **World's worst question**). Much better is to use the *Can't to Can*® method. I get more correspondence from users thanking me for this technique than any other NDK creation. It is powerful.

Can't to Can® has a structure for breaking through limiting beliefs. It uses the framework on the next page.

The two *Freedom Questions* at the heart of *Can't to Can Belief Busting*® do the unlocking, *"What would happen if you could?"* releases thoughts of possibility (see **Freedom questions**).

Once released, *"What would have to happen to make that happen?"* asked repeatedly, and phrased differently each time, seeks out implementation planning and action.

So, the seven steps of the *Can't to Can* framework are,

1. *"What is your limiting belief? … the 'I can't…' topic?"*
2. *"What would happen if you could* (do that thing)*?"* … the feeling benefit identified… the emotional leverage for creating change.
3. *"What would have to happen to make that happen?"* … repeated questioning to isolate change strategies, implementation plans, and action.
4. Timescale.
5. Summary.
6. Emotional Drivers™ health check.
7. Commitment.

Can't to Can Belief Busting® is a technique included within *Continue & Begin Fast Coaching*® (see **Coaching, Continue & Begin Fast Coaching**®, **Emotional Drivers**™, and **Case Study: On Growing Managers [and our Business]**).

New Code Can't to Can Belief Busting

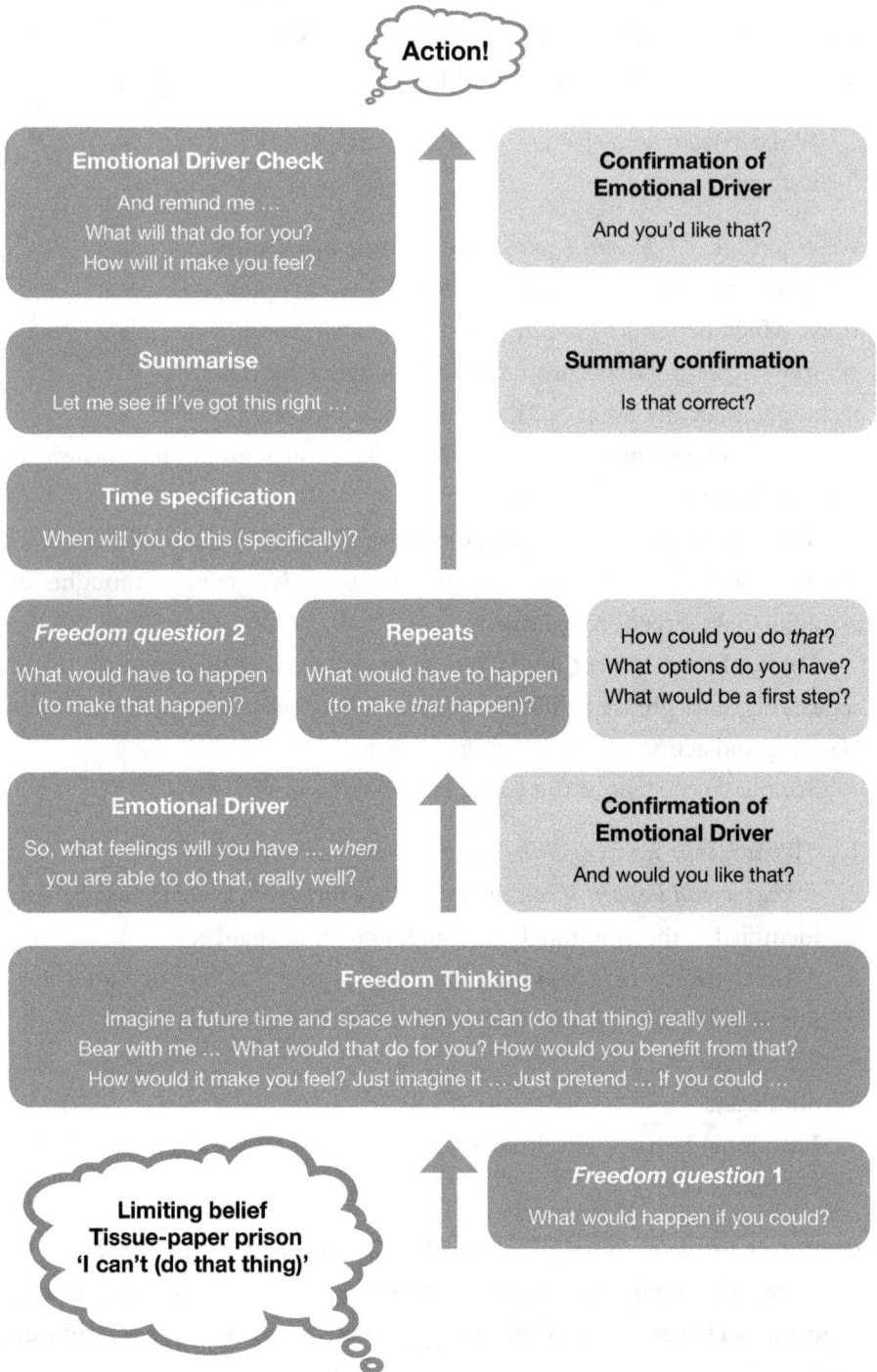

Action!

Emotional Driver Check

And remind me …
What will that do for you?
How will it make you feel?

**Confirmation of
Emotional Driver**

And you'd like that?

Summarise

Let me see if I've got this right …

Summary confirmation

Is that correct?

Time specification

When will you do this (specifically)?

Freedom question 2

What would have to happen
(to make that happen)?

Repeats

What would have to happen
(to make *that* happen)?

How could you do *that*?
What options do you have?
What would be a first step?

Emotional Driver

So, what feelings will you have … *when*
you are able to do that, really well?

**Confirmation of
Emotional Driver**

And would you like that?

Freedom Thinking

Imagine a future time and space when you can (do that thing) really well …
Bear with me … What would that do for you? How would you benefit from that?
How would it make you feel? Just imagine it … Just pretend … If you could …

**Limiting belief
Tissue-paper prison
'I can't (do that thing)'**

Freedom question 1

What would happen if you could?

Further reading

Peoplemaking | Science and Behavior Books, 1972 | Satir, V.

Boomerang! Coach Your Team to Be the Best | Dandelion Digital, 2007 | Drake-Knight, N.

Fast Coaching. The Complete Guide to New Code Continue & Begin® | Dandelion

Digital, 2016 | Drake-Knight, N. | Audible https://www.audible.co.uk/pd/Fast-Coaching-Audiobook/B07TTKD13T

The Motivation Agency | https://themotivationagency-online.com/course/begin

Celebrating successes – pot fillers

"The more you praise and celebrate your life,
the more there is to celebrate." *– Oprah Winfrey*

Virginia Satir, the family therapist, used an analogy of a pot on the kitchen stove and the level of 'soup' it contained, either high or low. She referred to our feelings of self-confidence at any given time as being *high pot* or *low pot,* meaning high or low levels of confidence.

"I am convinced that the crucial factor in what happens both inside people and between people is the picture of individual worth that each person carries around with him – his pot. Integrity, honesty, responsibility, compassion, love – all flow easily from the person whose pot is high." *– Virginia Satir (1972)*

Team members work most effectively when they feel confident, resourceful, and empowered. This is the underpinning principle behind *Continue & Begin Fast Coaching®* (see **Coaching, Continue & Begin Fast Coaching®**).

When self-image, self-worth and self-esteem are high, employees and managers perform at optimum levels, making the most of their abilities. By contrast, if employees feel short of resourcefulness, have impoverished self-perceptions of ability and worth then enthusiasm, innovation and productivity will suffer (see **Significance**).

Managers of people can act as *pot fillers*. One way we can do this is to help team members celebrate their achievements, affirm their skills and abilities, and build resourcefulness. *Pot drillers*, by contrast, criticise and find fault in team members' performances, dragging down confidence, sowing seeds of doubt and diminishing resourcefulness.

Be a *pot filler*, not a *pot driller*.

Further reading

Peoplemaking | Science and Behavior Books, 1972 | Satir, V.

Virginia Satir: the Patterns of Her Magic | Real People Press, 1991 | Andreas, S.

Certainty and Uncertainty, management of

"Without the element of uncertainty, the bringing off of even the greatest business triumph would be dull, routine, and eminently unsatisfying." *– J. Paul Getty*

The world of work is changing at an increasing rate of acceleration. That means the speed of change is getting faster. Certainty is in low supply; there is little to be certain about. How you accommodate uncertainty into work contexts will determine how effective you are in your management role.

Living comfortably with uncertainty is a step towards becoming less anxious at work, at home, and in relationships.

Successful strategies for embracing uncertainty involve forward thinking and planning on key areas of management interest; being prepared for the inevitability of new, maybe unexpected, scenarios.

Listed below are a few ideas on how uncertainty might be mitigated by a manager thinking ahead,

- Create resource and supply chain flexibility.
- People planning.
- Skills requirements assessments – for self and others.
- Regular updates to 'what if' scenarios.
- Contextual awareness updates (see **PESTLE**).
- Knowledge of competitor activities.
- Industry evolution.
- Market monitoring.
- Consumer behaviours.
- Risk assessments.
- Adopting an agile management mindset (see **Agile team management**).

Where are you in relation to the certainty factors in this table?

NDK Certainty Scale	Certain Uncertain									
Your management role stability	10 Certain	9	8	7	6	5	4	3	2	1 Uncertain
Future evolution of the management role	10 Certain	9	8	7	6	5	4	3	2	1 Uncertain
Future value of your personal skills	10 Certain	9	8	7	6	5	4	3	2	1 Uncertain
Employer stability	10 Certain	9	8	7	6	5	4	3	2	1 Uncertain
Industry / profession continuity	10 Certain	9	8	7	6	5	4	3	2	1 Uncertain
Workplace relationships	10 Certain	9	8	7	6	5	4	3	2	1 Uncertain
Future career progression	10 Certain	9	8	7	6	5	4	3	2	1 Uncertain
Health, physical/emotional	10 Certain	9	8	7	6	5	4	3	2	1 Uncertain
Future financial securities	10 Certain	9	8	7	6	5	4	3	2	1 Uncertain

How did you score?

- How can you become *even more* comfortable with uncertainty?
- Would it be helpful to talk to someone about how you feel?
- How can your team members become comfortable with uncertainty?
- The world of work is changing, and its changing fast. How do you feel about that reality?

Further reading

How to Lead When the World's Gone Crazy | Management Today, 2019 | Hazlehurst, J. | https://www.managementtoday.co.uk/lead-when-worlds-gone-crazy/long-reads/article/1523413

Dealing with Uncertainty | HelpGuide.org | Robinson, L., Smith, M. | https://www.helpguide.org/articles/anxiety/dealing-with-uncertainty.htm

Change, or Evolution?

"No man ever steps in the same river twice, for it's not the same river and he's not the same man." *– Heraclitus*

Change is here to stay; the Ancients knew this.

Years ago, management development programmes would include a separate module on *Change Management*. Today we are accustomed to a state of flux, aware of the inevitability of change within our organisations. We know more change is coming. It's a given. What then, is to be learnt about managing in an environment of perpetual progression?

Eckhart Tolle (2006) states in his book *A New Earth: Awakening to Your Life's Purpose*,

"Awareness is the greatest agent of change."

John Kotter (2012), respected Harvard professor, included awareness in his suggested process for leading change. Kotter proposed an 8-step approach,

1. Create urgency (through *awareness*).
2. Form a powerful coalition of like-minded advocates for change.
3. Create a vision for change.
4. Communicate the vision.
5. Remove obstacles.
6. Create short term wins.
7. Build on the change (more wins).
8. Anchor the changes in corporate culture. Front line managers are interested in team culture.

Change, how it is labelled

Think about the word *change*. For some it represents impending discomfort, uncertainty, maybe anxiety. It's an emotive word describing a difference between now and the future. There will be people within your team who find this unnerving.

I propose the word *evolve* as a more natural, graduating term. It suggests evolution, a wholesome process in which we participate as a natural part of life. That's what organisational change is, isn't it? A workplace team adapting, within a developing working environment, in an evolving industry sector or commercial context. That's life. *Evolution* continues, and we are attuned to the idea. *Change* by contrast suggests radical shift.

Think carefully about the name labels assigned to team progression. How it is framed in language will impact on colleagues.

Ask the people

Before setting out on a planned *evolution* initiative it makes sense to consider differing perspectives.

In Robert Townsend's classic business book *Up the Organisation* (also presented alphabetically) he suggested if you want to know the answer to anything in an organisation, seek advice from employees. Chances are they will also have a solution ready to offer. Seasoned business leaders ask their team members what they think. It is a sign of a strong manager when colleagues are asked for ideas. As Townsend and Bennis (2007) proposed,

"Ask the people – they know where the wheels are squeaking!"

Communicating transition

People like to understand the reasons behind new work practices. Hard facts are crucial, they want to understand the 'why' of revisions. Most folk like to live within their comfort zones, with regular, structured activities they can rely on. Only a few people thrive on constantly shifting circumstances – they are usually a minority. Employees embrace change when they understand *Why* things need to be different and are consulted on the *How*. Team member consultation gains engagement and ensures that local issues are considered (see **Why? Purpose and meaning**).

Some reasons for change are listed below. Which topics are relevant for you in your team?

Reasons for Change Requirement	Change Significant for You? Yes/No
Legal requirement	
Competitors catching up, or already ahead	
Consumer / market expectations	
Technology opportunities	
Increasing costs	
Reducing profitability	
Ageing workforce	
Staff turnover	
Growing business volume	
Reducing business volume	
Changes to product / service portfolio	
Supply chain / fulfilment channel impact	
Relocation opportunities	
Merger/takeover	
Other reasons?	

Organisational vs emotional

Changing systems and processes is relatively simple. It's a logical and procedural activity with a start date, process map and completion date. There's a *change plan*.

Emotional change doesn't work so simply. People can't be 'processed mapped' in the same way. The effects of change on people can last for months, even years, as workers, managers and stakeholders come to terms with new ways of operating. Some employees don't make the shift from old ways, they jump ship and leave.

Organisational (rational thinking) transition

In organisational change management, the period of transition is scheduled and usually described by a project plan. It is a logical, unemotive process activity. Plans, flow diagrams, revised structures, and Gantt charts, all offer a visual representation of the move from *current state* to *future state*.

```
┌─────────────────┐                    ┌─────────────────┐
│  Current State  │───────────────────▶│  Future State   │
└─────────────────┘                    └─────────────────┘
```

Human (emotional thinking) transition

The emotional impact of change for team members and managers is less easily mapped by project planning. Effect impact is indeterminable. People get nervous during times of change. Irrational and sometimes paranoid thoughts come to the surface.

Reassurance from you, the team manager, is important to minimize anxiety and help employees feel 'ok' about what is to come. Progress reports are important, too. The mantra to adopt is *Communicate, Communicate, Communicate,* even when there is little to report, it's good to let people know that. Just being updated helps reduce worry and anxiety.

```
┌─────────────────┐                    ┌─────────────────┐
│    Familiar     │                    │      New        │
│  experience     │───────────────────▶│  experience     │
│   is ending     │                    │  is beginning   │
└─────────────────┘                    └─────────────────┘
```

Emotionally intelligent managers are acutely aware of the likely *feeling* impact of change on team members, individually and collectively. It is important to think through how to mitigate discomfort for colleagues. Thinking ahead is a critical people management habit (see **Horizon Scanning**).

Change 'Models'

There are plenty of frameworks and acronyms for this subject matter.

Change 'models' include ideas about how change is perceived by a workforce, and about how it should be introduced and managed. Quite rightly, change management specialists focus on the human factor, about how people will feel before, during and after a new initiative.

Here are a few frameworks commonly used during organisational change planning. A recognised leader in change management thought is Jeff Hiatt, founder of Prosci, a consultancy specialising in change management.

ADKAR®

The Prosci *ADKAR®* model, or thinking process, considers five stages in managing a change project,

A	Awareness	• do people understand the need for change?
D	Desire	• is there a willingness, or hunger, to make change happen?
K	Knowledge	• is there sufficient knowledge within the team to make change happen?
A	Ability	• do team members have the ability to make changes happen, and stick?
R	Reinforcement	• what is needed to embed the change and make it habitual?

CLARC

Prosci suggests people managers have five roles to play during times of change:

1	Communicator	• sharing personal impact messages with direct reports about the change.
2	Liaison	• engaging with and supporting the project team.
3	Advocate	• demonstrating support for the change.
4	Resistance Manager	• identifying and mitigating resistance to the change.
5	Coach	• helping employees through the change process.

How do you rate, or have you rated, in these five influencing roles during times of change?

4 Ps of Change Management

The 4 Ps is a simple framework for managers to consider when initiating changes, at any order of significance within an organisation. It's a great self-check, before launching into action. Taking time to work through these steps will help your clarity of thinking,

1	**Project**	• the specific initiative or project that requires change. • implementing a new system? Restructuring a team?
2	**Purpose**	• what are the goals or intended outcomes of this project?
3	**Particulars**	• specific details related to the change effort. Who will be impacted? • what are the specific changes being implemented?
4	**People**	• how to engage and support employees during the transition?

There are a lot of 'P models' in management studies. This one relates to change management. Yet, even within this one topic, other 'P' versions exist. You may come across these variants of the 4Ps,

- People, Purpose, Process, Performance.
- Purpose, Picture, Plan, Part.
- Process, Prepare, People, Perform.

Choose what works for you and the people in your team.

Balogun & Hope-Hailey's Change Model

This is a useful reference to consider the nature of a change programme, in order of its radicalism. It's an ideal visual for discussing change factors with senior managers, and as a means of explaining to team members what is planned within the business. Adaptation? Evolution? Reconstruction? Revolution?!

1. Adaption
2. Evolution (a healthier, less daunting phrase than 'change')
3. Reconstruction
4. Revolution

		End Result	
		Transformation	Realignment
Nature of Change	Incremental	Evolution	Adaptation
	BIG BANG!	Revolution	Reconstruction

Whatever models, frameworks, or concepts are used within your organisation, *It makes sense, to make sure, it makes sense* for your team members. High level concepts are of little interest to the 75% + of colleagues who are 'doing-the-job'. It's important for organisational behaviour modelling to be meaningful for frontline team members and presented in language which is understood. Team managers often have a job to do in translating *management-speak* into pragmatic communication with team members.

For a fun and effective series of messages about change, *Who Moved My Cheese?* is a great little book, written in an easy to digest (no pun) format. It explains in a simple metaphor, how we can learn to adapt to evolution and environmental shifts.

Fatigue

Where organisations are in a constant state of flux, especially in large macro change programmes, constant shift becomes wearisome. Fatigue comes when the most recent restructuring, reorganising, and reprocessing is not bedded in, or is incomplete, before the next round of transformation is introduced. There are methods you can use to ease the tension of change fatigue; here are a few ideas,

- Re-state the original reason for the plan, and its benefits.
- Show how far you have come – what has been achieved so far?
- Show some light at the end of the tunnel – what is the next significant goal in the project plan?
- Have you identified what is working and what is not?
- Do you need help from your team to make it happen?
- Ask the team members the great question, *"What would have to happen... to get this programme revitalized?"*

Bus stop reviews

Take time out regularly and see how far you've come.

Every now and then *get off the bus.* There will be stages in a development scheme when it makes sense to take stock of where you are at. *Bus Stop* progress reviews are valuable in letting your people know how far they've come; how resilient they are and how new ways of working are already making a difference. This is a strong message validating the reasons for the change and preparing employees for what is still to come.

Have a think about your next planned change. When would be sensible staging points to schedule in *Bus Stop Reviews*?

Further reading

A New Earth: Awakening to Your Life's Purpose | Penguin, 2006 | Tolle, E.

Managing Change | Pearson, 2017 (7th edition) | Burnes, B.

Dealing with organisational change: Can emotional intelligence enhance organisational learning? | International Journal of Organisational Behaviour, 2004 | Jordan, P.J.

Exploring Strategic Change | Balogun, J., Hope Bailey, V., Gustafsson, S. | Pearson, 2015

Management and Organisational Behaviour | Pearson, 2016 (11th Edition) | Mullins, L.

Who Moved My Cheese: An Amazing Way to Deal with Change in Your Work and in Your Life | Vermilion, 1999 | Johnson, S.

Leading Change | Harvard Business Review Press, 2012 | Kotter, J.P.

Up the Organisation: How to Stop the Corporation from Stifling People and Strangling Profits | Jossey-Bass, 2007 | Townsend, R., Bennis, W. | Prosci ADKAR® model | https://www.prosci.com/

Chocolate Praise™

"He who praises everyone, praises no-one." *– Samuel Johnson*

'Nice' judgement phrases such as, *"You did really well there... well done... it was excellent"* are *Chocolate Praise*™ and of limited value. I refer to these language patterns *as Chocolate Praise* because, as when you eat a piece of chocolate, blood sugar levels go up and it feels good, but not for long, before it comes crashing down again.

"Well done" feels good; it's a temporary feeling.

We all like a pat on the back from time to time. It feels nice but it doesn't help us reflect and isolate what it was, specifically, that we did, which made our performance so impressive. *Chocolate Praise* doesn't help us understand the *Structure-of-Well-Done-Ness®*, the building blocks of excellence that make the performance so outstanding (see **Structure of Well-Done-Ness®**).

Effective team managers, and workplace coaches, help team members recognise for themselves those building blocks, the key things that happened, which made their performance worthy of celebration.

They do this by asking targeted questions related to the explicitly described standards for the team member's job role. Examples of these are presented in the *NDK Performance Model®* (see **NDK Performance Model®**).

When managers encourage colleagues to identify for themselves the things they've done well, in relation to a known set of standards, then self-awareness and sustainable learning prospers. By contrast, bland statements of congratulation achieve little, and even then, only for a moment.

Pay attention to the celebratory language you use with your team and listen out for your own *Chocolate Praise*™ (see **Judgement and observation**).

Further reading

Boomerang! Coach Your Team to Be the Best | Dandelion Digital, 2007 | Drake-Knight, N.

Audible https://www.audible.co.uk/pd/ Fast-Coaching-Audiobook/B07TTKD13T

Fast Coaching. The Complete Guide to New Code Continue & Begin® | Dandelion Digital, 2016 | Drake-Knight, N. |

The Motivation Agency | https:// themotivationagency-online.com/course/ begin

CITO management

> "We've had three big ideas at Amazon that we've stuck
> with for 18 years, and they're the reason we're successful:
> Put the customer first. Invent. And be patient." **– Jeff Bezos**

Some years back I worked with a large European retailer where we used an acronym for emphasising to store colleagues the importance of prioritising customer interaction over store tasks. We called it TOCI (*tocki*), meaning *Task Out, Customer In.*

Fast forward a decade and the same conversation was taking place with a global adventure sports apparel retailer. We considered TOCI. A bright spark in the project team suggested she liked the principle behind TOCI, except the emphasis was in the wrong order! We had been discussing the value of 'think customer first' and the nature of language, including its sequence (syntax) in how we prioritise.

The team member suggested we should reflect our thinking in the acronym and change TOCI to CITO (*see-toh*), emphasising *Customer In* as the first thought for retailing teams. The senior management team agreed, and we went on to roll out a customer experience training programme which included CITO as a core principle.

CITO doesn't mean *no task*; of course, tasks need to be completed. It means a first thought about customer requirements, the design specification they would like, and what would offer best value for them. These are fundamental considerations for any quality management approach (see **Quality and TQM**).

Now, transfer this idea to the internal marketplace of most organisations, where teams and departments are either suppliers or customers (or both) to other parts of the business. The commodity being supplied or received may be a physical item, for example in a manufacturing plant where value is added at each stage of the production process. Or perhaps the product is information, either as raw data, or adapted for further use; for example, work schedules, payroll information, marketing plans, sales reports, departmental KPIs, staffing rotas, and so on.

When team culture is centred on providing an outstanding service to internal customers, remarkable changes happen. The mindset of team members has more purpose, there is meaningful motive behind the daily grind, to supply *customers* with great service. Teams who provide first class customer experience to their internal market soon gain a reputation for professionalism, and the feedback loop becomes motivational. It may take a while for colleagues to feel fully engaged as part of a supply chain, that's to be expected. With perseverance and sustained emphasis on service quality, the mindset will come, and behaviours will follow.

Which customers do your team supply in the organisation's internal market?

Further reading

Build a Customer-First Culture | The Wall Street Journal, 2017 | Horn, H., Sloan, N., Benjamin, B. | https://deloitte.wsj.com/articles/build-a-customer-first-culture-1512968535?tesla=y&tesla=y

The Toyota Way: 14 Management Principles from the World's Greatest Manufacturer | McGraw-Hill, 2004 | Liker, J.

Clean language

"We always translate the other person's language into our own language." – *Milton. H. Erickson*

The idea of *clean language* originated in therapeutic work. David Grove and colleagues developed a method for verbally exploring an individual's language, metaphors, and ideas, in a way which does not contaminate the other person's thinking. There are dangers in paraphrasing someone's speech, using our own word versions of the other persons communication, because it pollutes the mental processing of our co-communicator. By sticking to *their* language patterns and key phrases, including colloquialisms, metaphors, and analogies, we can build rapport, gain understanding, and strengthen the communication process.

We can adapt this therapeutic approach to the world of work. Here is an extract from my book *Fast Coaching* (Dandelion Digital, 2016),

… if I use the same words as you, *particularly when you use idioms, analogies, or metaphors,* then we have a greater possibility of creating a rapid rapport based on mutual use of language.

The less we try to paraphrase or adapt the language used by other people into our own preferred language, and the more we use *their* chosen words and sentence construction, the more likely it is our fellow communicators will feel a sense of understanding and empathy from us.

This has proven to be a powerful rapport building technique. Where possible, key words from the speaker's language patterns are repeated back by the rapport builder. The skill is in identifying which words to repeat back and when, so that the other person experiences the process as a natural activity rather than a conscious, contrived, 'technique'.

You have the opportunity at any time during a conversation, to 'use the words the speaker uses' to confirm and demonstrate that you do understand what she is saying.

Clean language reassures our co-communicators that we are listening attentively (see **Listening**). Think about the application of clean language in managing your team members.

Note: the above application of Clean Language is my own (NDK) adaptation for team management purposes. It is a variant of the therapeutic approach, not intended as an accurate representation of Grove's model.

Further reading

Clean Language: Revealing Metaphors and Opening Minds | Crown House Publishing, 2008 | Sullivan, W., Rees, J.

What is Clean Language? | Clean Learning (Walker and Way Ltd) | https://cleanlearning.co.uk/about/faq/what-is-clean-language

Coaching

"Good character is not formed in a week or a month.
It is created little by little, day by day. Protracted and patient
effort is needed to develop good character." *– Heraclitus*

It still surprises me how few managers use a coaching style to develop colleagues.

Coaching is not about telling, training or refresher training, nor is it guidance, signposting, mentoring, counselling, or 'supporting'. Coaching is about helping people, through excellent questioning, to explore their own world and identify opportunities to make changes to their lives, professional or personal, should they wish to do so. Coachees are encouraged to find their own answers. A coach helps the coachee find their own solutions.

How do you think that went?

Most effective coaching methods ask the *coachee* to consider their topic of choice and identify their *current state* in relation to it. The coach asks the coachee to think about where they are at, whether this is acceptable to them, and if not, what would the coachee prefer? Once a preferred *future state* is identified and described in specific form, the coach can then ask the coachee through tailored questioning, to consider strategies to achieve their ambitions.

When a strategy has been identified, a skilled coach will encourage the coachee to think about implementation planning, resource requirements, and actions to make the strategy become a reality.

There are numerous coaching methods in use in business, many of which are excellent, and are usually a variation on this framework,

- Where are you?
- What do you want?
- What choices or options do you have?
- Which choice/option would you like to go for?
- What do you need to do to for that to happen?
- When are you starting?
- How will you review?

Common models

Typical coaching frameworks are,

- **ACHIEVE** – Assess situation, Creative brainstorming, Hone goals, Initiate options, Evaluate options, Valid action design, Encourage momentum.

- **GROW** – Goal, Reality, Options, Way forward.
- **OSCAR** – Outcome, Situation, Choices, Actions, Review.
- **STAR** – 6-pointed star comprising two triangles, one inverted. One represents the coachee's role (desire to change, commitments, values/ beliefs), the other the coach's role (engagement, awareness, action).
- **STEPPPA** – Subject, Target identification, Emotion, Perception, Plan, Pace, Action/amend.

Other coaching models exist with similar components and formats. There is a challenge with some of these approaches,

1. The time involved to work through each stage of the exploratory process. These methodologies are slow to work through. That's fine if sufficient time is available to explore topics in detail.
2. There is little, and in some methods zero, emphasis on strengthening the self-confidence of the coachee prior to embarking on personal 'change'.
3. Insufficient emphasis and leverage are placed on *future feeling*, the emotional pull of succeeding in new ways.
4. Commitment might be wishy washy, tentative, or not addressed at all. The absolute, total, complete dedication to make change happen is *the difference that makes the difference* in performance coaching. Fine ambitions unravel, like a loose thread, if commitment is uncertain.

The coaching models described above, and others, are useful frameworks for some professional contexts.

Further reading

Coaching for Performance: The Principles and Practice of Coaching and Leadership | Nicholas Brealey Publishing, 2017 (10th edition) | Whitmore, J.

Boomerang! Coach Your Team to Be the Best | Dandelion Digital, 2007 | Drake-Knight, N.

Fast Coaching. The Complete Guide to New Code Continue & Begin® | Dandelion Digital, 2016 | Drake-Knight, N. | Audible https://www.audible.co.uk/pd/ Fast-Coaching-Audiobook/B07TTKD13T

The Motivation Agency | https:// themotivationagency-online.com/course/ begin

Coaching, Continue & Begin Fast Coaching®

"I cannot teach anybody anything. I can only make them think."

– Socrates

When I designed *Continue & Begin®* there were ambitions in my mind,

- To create a coaching approach quick to use and easy to learn.
- To strengthen the self-confidence of coachees and help them feel resourceful enough to take on personal plans for change.
- To use emotional leverage, an influential positive future feeling, as impulse and stimulus for an individual's motivation to change.
- To lock in personal resolution to *do the thing they said they would do.*

Continue & Begin Fast Coaching® strengthens self-worth and busts through limiting belief patterns. By following a specific flow of questions, carefully crafted for their impact, a practitioner can achieve phenomenal coaching results. Coachees become empowered and confident, fully resourced and determined to take on ambitious change. Quickly.

Continue & Begin® helps a coachee celebrate recent successes, no matter how minor they may seem to be, and builds confidence. The approach reminds the coachee of their resourcefulness, resilience, and proven ability to succeed. Once the coachee's confidence has been strengthened and celebrated, then and only then, does the *Continue & Begin®* coach help the coachee explore what they would like to *Begin To* do differently, or maybe *even better.*

71

Here is an overview,

Continue & Begin® is based on self-assessment, guided by precise questions. There are 3 parts to Continue & Begin Fast Coaching®,

1. **Celebrate:** In the first of the three parts, or *chunks*, we help a coachee *Celebrate* what they're already doing well, in relation to the explicitly described standards, ambitions, or goals the coachee is already working towards. During the celebration stage the coachee is encouraged to identify what they are already doing, specifically, which is working well. We can help them feel good about successes.
2. **Change:** When people are feeling good and resourceful, when their self-esteem and self-image is strong, then we can ask about what, from now on, they might want to do differently and perhaps, *even better.* This is chunk 2, the *Change* part.
3. **Commit**: The final chunk of Continue & Begin® is vital. It turns ideas into actions. This is the *Commitment* phase. This is about helping people do what they say they are going to do.

Where thinking barriers exist *Can't to Can Belief Busting®*, a *Continue & Begin®* tool, helps a coachee break through their limiting beliefs to achieve personal change (see **Can't to Can Belief Busting®**).

Continue & Begin Fast Coaching® is used around the world by global brands and public sector agencies, in families, in sport and in therapeutic contexts (see **Case Study: On Growing Managers [and our Business]**).

You can read more about *Continue & Begin®* in *Fast Coaching, The Complete Guide to New Code Continue & Begin®* or listen to the audiobook version.

Coaching, narrow & deep, shallow & wide

When a manager coaches a colleague 121, the activity is known in *Continue & Begin®* circles as *narrow and deep*. This means the intervention is helping one person in a reasonable degree of depth. Although the impact for the coachee may be significant, the spread of benefit is limited to one individual.

When 121 coaching action plans are shared across a wider audience, for instance to colleague team members, this is referred to in *Continue &*

Begin-speak as *shallow and wide*. *Shallow* because some of the relevance of the coaching plan may not fit all team colleagues and *wide* because of the sharing with other beneficiaries.

Some organisations using *Continue & Begin®* adopt a three-strand approach to coaching,

1. *Narrow and deep*, for each person coached.
2. *Shallow and wide*, for the wider team.
3. *Shallow and wide*, where the entire team reflect on recent performance and commit to a collective effort in achieving a single specific goal or objective, over an assigned period.

Continue & Begin Fast Coaching® benefits for team managers

Adopting the *Continue & Begin®* approach helps managers,

1. Focus on explicitly described performance standards (see **Explicit standards**).
2. Remove relationship dynamics (manager vs team member) from performance evaluation.
3. Develop coaching language skills.
4. Enhance questioning technique.
5. Stimulate positivity during team communication.
6. Build team member confidence.
7. Create a culture of continuous improvement (see **Quality and TQM**).
8. Maintain focus on team performance goals.
9. Aid performance consistency.
10. Aid performance sustainability.

Further reading and listening

Boomerang! Coach Your Team to Be the Best | Dandelion Digital, 2007 | Drake-Knight, N.

Fast Coaching, The Complete Guide to New Code Continue & Begin® | Dandelion Digital, 2016 | Drake-Knight, N. | Audible https://www.audible.co.uk/pd/ Fast-Coaching-Audiobook/B07TTKD13T

The Motivation Agency | https:// themotivationagency-online.com/course/ begin

Appendix 1: Continue & Begin Fast Coaching®: its application in call centre operations. Q&A Podcast transcript with www.callcentrehelper.com

Cognitive bias

"We can at least try to understand our own motives, passions, and prejudices, so as to be conscious of what we are doing when we appeal to those of others. This is very difficult, because our own prejudice and emotional bias always seems to us so rational."

– T.S. Eliot

We are influenced by our perceptions of the world and what we chose to think about a given set of circumstances (see **Maps of the territory**). Once we are consciously aware of this, we become more sensitive to the nuances of our thoughts, emotions, and subsequent behaviours.

Cognitive bias is a short cut mechanism developed over millennia to speed up the process of thinking, particularly in relation to survival. We build patterns from experience and start to compile *if-then* scenarios. The more we've experienced a scenario X and the more the outcome has been Y, the more likely we are to expect a Y outcome the next time we come up against an X. This is an efficient method of processing information.

It may be efficient, but it is not always correct.

There are numerous forms of cognitive bias. For example, a common bias is to look for evidence which supports our existing hypotheses or established beliefs, known as *confirmation bias*. Hundreds of bias 'types' have been documented. Here are a few examples,

Confirmation bias – looking for evidence which confirms a pre-existing opinion.	**Negative bias –** tendency to give more attention to negative news than neutral or positive information.	**Bandwagon, or Social Proof, bias –** beliefs embedded due to promotion by a group of others.
Curse of knowledge bias – belief others already know the same information as you.	**Focalism bias –** tendency to rely on first piece of information gained about a topic.	**Bias blindspot –** belief others have bias, but you don't.
Declinism bias – tendency to consider past more favourably than future.	**Dunning-Kruger bias –** unskilled people overestimating own ability, highly skilled people underestimating own ability.	**Functional fixedness –** limits the use of a tool or object to its traditional use.

Normalcy bias – not preparing for negative events which have not happened before (failure to 'what if').	**Present bias** – giving greater weight to an option producing present benefit than one with later pay-off.	**Semmelweis effect** – reject new evidence or new knowledge because it contradicts established norms, beliefs, or societal patterns.

The healthy question for a manager to consider in relation to decision-making is,

"Is my judgement on this matter being influenced by my cognitive bias?"

Further reading

Thinking, Fast and Slow | Penguin, 2012 | Kahneman, D.

Cognitive Bias: How We Are Wired To Misjudge | Simple Psychology, July 2023 | Ruhl, C. | https://www.simplypsychology.org/cognitive-bias.html

Commitment mantra

"Commitment is doing the thing you said you would do,
long after the mood you said it in has left you." *– George Zalucki*

This is one of the briefest sections in this book. Not because it is low in significance, but the opposite; the message is short, powerful, and bang on in its importance to team managers.

Zalucki's exhortation has become a theme throughout my work supporting client organisations and the managers within them. It encapsulates the persistence, dedication, and single mindedness necessary to get things done.

How many times have we made commitments (remember those New Year resolutions?), and allowed the original pact with ourselves to dissolve?

Lose weight, get fit, give up chocolate, no more alcohol, stop smoking, read more, study and gain qualifications, make these changes to my management style...

What is your commitment? Oh, yeah? Really? What about when the mood has left you?

Further listening

The Mind and Emotions Set | www. georgezalucki.com | Zalucki, G.

Grit: Why passion and resilience are the secrets to success | Vermilion, 2017 | Duckworth, A.

Communication

> "The single biggest problem in communication is the illusion that it has taken place." *– George Bernard Shaw*

The one phrase I have been hearing for decades from senior leaders and directors is, *"Our managers need to improve their communication skills"*. Communication is a HUGE word, incorporating a diverse range of meanings. It is one of the biggest generalisations in the language of work and is rarely dissected into precise topics for management development purposes.

Effective communication, in all its forms, is a required competency for professional managers. So, what does it include? In my experience, senior leaders' calls for a manager to *improve communication,* once dissected, usually references a person's,

- Empathy.
- Emotional intelligence.
- Authoritative or conciliatory style.
- Tendency towards assertion, aggression, or passivity.
- One-way information or two-way information flow.
- Testing of understanding.
- Balancing listening with talking.
- Telephone manner.
- Language patterns and vocabulary.

- Tonality, cadence, volume, pitch, intensity, inflection, monotony.
- Non-verbal communication, one-to-one, or in group settings, including,
  - Posture
  - Major and minor motor movements
  - Eye movement
  - Facial expressions, animation
  - Personal grooming and dress
  - Spatial awareness
- Email construction, format, and style.
- Report writing.
- Clarity of meaning.
- Conciseness of message giving.
- Regular communication with colleagues.
- Sharing of information.
- Over-communicating.
- Presentation and influencing skills.
- Relationship building through networks.

So, the next time you hear someone talk about someone's 'communication' you can ask for precision, *"Which specific elements of communication are you referring to?"*

This book explores a (non-comprehensive) set of communication topics. You can find these listed alphabetically,

See **Adverbs, superfluous**

See **Analogue marking**

See **Assertion**

See **But Monster®, The**

See **Clean language**

See **Chocolate Praise™**

See **Deletion**

See **Distortion**

See **Emotional intelligence (EQ)**

See **Empathy**

See **English is Rubbish™**

See **Floppy language**

See **Freedom questions**

See **Fuzzy language**

See **Generalisations**

See **Get inside their world**

See **I know you don't know**

See **'I' ownership**

See **Judgements and observations**

See **Language to help**

See **Language which hurts**

See **Language, written, redundancy and repetition**

See **Listening**

See **Metaphors**

See **Matching and mirroring**

See **Nominalisations**

See **Pre-framing**

See **Presentations** and
Presentations behaviours

See **Presuppositions**

See **Rapport**

See **Rapport, advanced skills**

See **Receive and transmit**

See **Reframing**

See **Self talk, inner dialogue**

See **Specificity**

See **Surface structure, deep
structure**

See **Tentative is no good**

See **Thank you**

See **VAK(OG)**

See **Universal quantifiers**

See **Words, song, and dance**

See **World's worst question**

Continuous Professional Development [CPD]

"People in general, and knowledge workers in particular, grow
according to the demands they make on themselves. They grow
according to what they consider to be achievement and attainment.
If they demand little of themselves, they will remain stunted. If they
demand a good deal of themselves, they will grow to giant stature—
without any more effort than is expended by the non-achievers."

– Peter F. Drucker

Human beings are learning machines. We are hard-wired to receive and process information to help us thrive and stay safe. It's a survival system. It only works if we use it, and the more we use it, the more efficient it becomes in storing learning for later use.

We begin our lives naturally curious and have significant others to encourage us in our learning. At school we have a structured programme set out for us to follow and we (mostly) navigate through the learning journey designed for us. College and university, or apprenticeships, offer a guided route along a syllabus roadmap. Basic training in any industry sector provides instruction on how to carry out a job.

There comes a point where the emphasis on learning necessarily shifts from *reactive* to *proactive*. Effective managers realise the liability for learning and skills development rests with themselves; they are personally responsible for their own growth in knowledge and professional practice. This is the era of do-it-yourself professional development. It's no longer acceptable to wait to be offered an opportunity.

You are responsible for your continuing professional development (CPD). No-one else, *you*. It is *your* responsibility to be curious, *your* responsibility to read, to take the necessary trainings, to actively listen, to explore, to seek out mentors, coaches, and guides. *You*. No-one is going to do it for you. It will be your own internal obsession to learn and grow which makes the difference.

I emphasise this to managers in brands I support. Changing the mindset of managers and their directors is the starting point for assignments. Responsibility for learning rests with the individual. The degree to which each manager grasps the learning nettle and drives on with enthusiasm and sustained persistence, over years, is a fair marker for how successful they will become (see **Case Study: On Growing Managers [and our Business]**).

Grandma was right about the ten two letter words; *If it is to be, it is up to me.*

Further reading

6 Ways to Take Control of Your Career Development If Your Company Doesn't Care About It | Harvard Business Review, 2018 | Cast, C. | https://hbr.org/2018/01/6-ways-to-take-control-of-your-career-development-if-your-company-doesnt-care-about-it

The Making of a Manager: What to Do When Everyone Looks to You | Portfolio, 2019 | Zhuo, J.

Continuing Professional Development | Kogan Page 2007 | Megginson, D., Whitaker, V.

CPD cascading

"In a world of change, the learners shall inherit the earth, while the learned shall find themselves perfectly suited for a world that no longer exists." *– Eric Hoffer*

Management learning gets stuck at each organisational level. New supervisors learn programme content A, departmental managers learn content B, middle managers content C, and so on up the management hierarchy. Yet, much of the learning content in each programme is applicable at all strata within an enterprise.

Business leaders serious about cultural modelling (*'how we manage things round here'*) and managerial succession planning, will recognise the value of good solid management principles applied across an organisation.

The section **Coaching, Continue & Begin Fast Coaching®** in this book explores the benefits of sharing a coachee's action plan *shallow and wide* for the benefit of a wider team audience. Extend this principle to management CPD outputs and cascade managers' learning to junior managers and team leaders. Managers have a *response-ability* (the ability to respond) to grow their people, by sharing their own learning,

The impact of this approach is phenomenal. It,

- Embeds new learning in the mind of the original direct learner. We know cascading a topic helps embed and reaffirm recently gained knowledge.
- Stimulates senior managers to develop colleagues.
- Reminds senior managers to *do* as well as *know.*
- Presents role model behaviours for more junior managers.
- Fast tracks the growth of direct reports.
- Promotes new methods by sharing enthusiasm from the original learner to new 'cascaded' learners.
- Extends management capacity.
- Accelerates cultural change.

I know this approach is working in an organisation when I experience junior managers exhibiting behaviours and language patterns learnt and applied by more senior colleagues (see **Case Study: On Growing Managers [and our Business]**).

Further reading

Cascading Change | Boston Consulting Group, 2009 | Tollman, P., Bixner, R., Keenan, P., Powell, K. | https://www.bcg.com/publications/2009/change-management-engagement-culture-cascading-change

CIPD Knowledge Hub 2020 | https://www.cipd.org/en/knowledge/

Criticism and failure focus

"He has a right to criticise, who has a heart to help."
– Abraham Lincoln

We all benefit from guidance, advice, and an occasional steer in the right direction. Critical feedback delivered constructively and with genuine warmth is invaluable, especially when balanced with recognition of successful performance.

Unfortunately, criticism can build momentum and become an avalanche of negativity and 'tell'. Criticism, even well intentioned, may have a damaging effect on the individual criticised. It seems the harmful impact on motivation and wellbeing is more significant than we previously thought. Recent research suggests negative critical assessment limits personal growth.

In *The Neurochemistry of Positive Conversations*, Judith, and Richard Glaser (2014) explore the hormones produced in our bodies when stimulated by 'the chemistry of conversations'.

When we experience criticism or negativity, or feel fear or rejection, the hormone cortisol is produced in our bodies. Cortisol prepares us, in the face of conflict, as a survival auto-response. We become more sensitized to threat, and hyper-aware of any indications of potential harm. We become *stressed*. We may perceive more threat than really exists. Cortisol stays in our bodies for several hours, potentially up to 26, and the more we think about our fear, the longer cortisol stays active in our bodies. If repeated, or sustained, cortisol causes health issues. It's not a nice feeling to have.

By contrast, celebratory conversations, positive affirmations, and recognition for achievement, produce oxytocin, often known as the feel-good hormone. Here's the challenge though, oxytocin dissipates more rapidly than cortisol, so it's positive impact on body and mind is short-lived.

What does this research tell us?

- *Critical commentaries*, when considered by the recipient to be threatening or potentially harmful, stimulate a chemical reaction. The research warns us of the long-term impact of cortisol-inducing commentaries.
- *Positive empowering observations* help people feel good about themselves and consequently they become more resourceful, with more positive self-image, and feelings of self-worth and self-esteem. It requires repetition to sustain the feel-good (see **Chocolate Praise™**).

The damaging outputs from using criticism to leverage change underscores the importance of considering the psychological and emotional wellbeing of employees. Managers can do this through ego strengthening of colleagues and affirmation of their competences and skills. Team managers have a duty of care. The health, safety and welfare of colleagues includes consideration of how communication can cause great good, or great harm.

Further reading

The Neurochemistry of Positive Conversations | Harvard Business Review, 2014 | Glaser, J.E., Glaser, R.D. | https://hbr.org/2014/06/ the-neurochemistry-of-positive-conversations   *Words Can Change Your Brain: 12 Conversation Strategies to Build Trust, Resolve Conflict, and Increase Intimacy* | Avery, 2012 | Newberg, A., Waldman, M.

Culture

"Culture eats strategy for breakfast." *– Peter Drucker*

Cultures may be formal or informal. One client organisation I supported had no formal dress policy for managers within the business and yet, without exception, all management staff replicated the preferred dress of the CEO, long-sleeve blue 'Oxford' cotton shirt with buttoned down collar, no tie, beige chinos, brown belt, and brown deck shoes. Managers were fashion clones of the boss.

Culture starts at the top, initiated by the most senior of executives, and is adapted at each subsequent level. Pockets of sub-cultures exist throughout organisations, sometimes differing markedly from the headline approach sponsored by the senior leadership team. Local cultural habits and behaviours might include,

Language patterns we use.	How we pre-frame, frame, or reframe circumstances.
Where we park our car.	How we respond to fresh challenges or tasks.
What time we start and leave work.	How we support team members under pressure.
Where and when we take breaks.	How we moderate language and behaviour.
How we manage our physical environment.	How we respect diversity.
How we manage personal phone use.	How we relate to other teams.
How we comply with minor rules.	How we celebrate or critique a colleague's work.
How we dress.	The nature of colleague relationships during work and outside of work.
How or if we interrupt meetings.	Whether we work late, or out of hours, to complete a task.
How we answer internal phone calls.	What we share and expect others to share about home life.
How we compile and phrase emails.	How we perceive the team's role in contributing to organisational goals.

In addition to *organisational* level cultural habits, local cultures are shaped in *teams*.

Managers have a responsibility and opportunity to influence team behaviours. Being congruent with the behaviours you'd like to be replicated in your team is a good starting point. The way you communicate and present yourself, the manner with which you address challenges and difficulties, the responses you make to team and individual successes; these are all reference points for employees (see **Behaviours and values, what is expected?** and **Behaviour breeds behaviour**).

What culture are you shaping in your team?

Further reading

Winning! | Hodder & Stoughton, 2004 | Woodward, C., Potanin, F.

The Art of Winning. Ten lessons in Leadership, Purpose, and Potential | Penguin, 2023 | Carter, D

Customers, internal

"Respect yourself, and others will respect you." *– Confucius*

There is an internal market within your organisation, a marketplace where suppliers provide goods, services, and information to colleague customers – *internal customers*. World-class team managers get their internal service proposition right; it shows respect towards colleagues.

Think about your own team environment. Who are suppliers within your internal market, and who are customers? What products, services and information are sought and provided? How do you know if the service is excellent? What is the customer experience, or 'CX' like?

Customer	Product, service, or information sought	Supplier	Criteria of success?
e.g. Payroll team	Employee timesheets	Managers and team members	On time, accurate

A professional approach to *internal* service management encourages healthy habits in caring for *external* customers; it becomes a habitual way for employees to operate, an embedded mindset. The same principles of providing leading-edge experience apply.

Astute managers operate as service quality exemplars internally, demonstrating habits of *CX* excellence, for team members to model and replicate. It starts with a culture of helping colleagues. What product do they need? What service? What information? What service level agreements (SLAs)?

Internal customers, like external consumers, deserve to have products, services and information delivered to them, right first time, on time, every time (see **Quality and TQM**).

The Continue & Begin Ltd *Every Customer Wants®* training programme highlights the internal customer marketplace as much as it does external end user customer contexts. Get customer experience right at home and it will be second nature when helping 'real' customers.

Every Customer Wants® (see **Every Customer Wants®**) offers a structure for service providers. Customers have three requirements, universally relevant, irrespective of the service sector,

- *Understand Me* – get inside my world, discover what's important to me.
- *Add Value for Me* – help me by providing something of value to me, a product, or a service.
- *Make it Easy for Me* – keep this simple for me, minimise my effort, make it hassle free.

These requirements apply equally to internal and external markets. How can your team apply commercial principles to your internal customer-supplier chain?

Further reading

Continue and Begin Ltd | https://ndk-group.com/conference-presentations-8/

The Motivation Agency | https://www.themotivationagency-online.com/course/everycustomerwants

D

Decision making, navy style

"In any moment of decision, the best thing you can do is the right thing. The worst thing you can do is nothing."

– Theodore Roosevelt

I joined the merchant navy at sixteen to begin life's great adventure, as a navigating officer cadet, a *midshipman*, on deep sea cargo vessels. I was fortunate to sail on four ships to most continents around the world (didn't get to Antarctica) and numerous ports.

It was a learning curve, experiencing the beauty and power of nature, particularly the big seas and swells of the Pacific and ferocious North Atlantic storms, my most terrifying experience. Life aboard and ashore with twenty officers and crew was educational in many ways.

One of the tasks for midshipmen (and women, my future wife Claire was a navigating cadet; we met on the M.V. Andros in Hong Kong harbour) was to manage the ballast system of the vessel, on instruction from the Chief Officer. This was a serious role for a fresh-out-of-school teenager. Nevertheless, cadets were expected to decide how best to use the pumps and valves in the ship's engine room to manage ballasting operations, pumping sea water into enormous wing tanks, double-bottom tanks, forward and aft tanks, or to eject ballast, for reasons of buoyancy and trim.

A family friend, 'Uncle' Eric was an experienced Royal Navy chief petty officer of thirty years' service. As a senior non-commissioned warrant officer, he had seen and done most things in his nautical career. He was familiar with supporting young officers new to leadership and management. Eric gave me a valuable piece of advice before I went off to sea,

> "An officer always makes a decision; good or bad, as long as he makes one. Got it nipper?"

> "Yes Eric".

A people manager who dithers and flip-flops around, procrastinating, is not helpful. A considered approach to decision making may make sense, of course, but not an unnecessary delay. It creates uncertainty and nervousness in team members.

Eric was right. A good officer gets on and makes the decision.

Although… there *was* that time on the M.V. Scotspark in the Indian Ocean when I filled the starboard wing tanks and emptied the port wing tanks rather than… erm… the other way around. No-one noticed until the Old Man's (Captain's) teacup slid off his table… oops.

Further reading

I Think I'll Go to Sea | You Write On Publishing, 2010 | Jackson, B.

Thinking in Bets: Making Smarter Decisions When You Don't Have All the Facts | Portfolio Penguin, 2018 | Duke, A.

Decision-making tools

> "Don't ever make decisions based on fear.
> Make decisions based on hope and possibility.
> Make decisions based on what should happen,
> not what shouldn't."
> **– Michelle Obama**

Decision making is a core management function. Managers are expected to address issues, take control, and come up with workable solutions, to keep your team running at optimum performance. Three forms of decisions are,

1. *Intuitive* – Decisions made instantly; instinctive decisions made very quickly, 'in the moment'.

Shall we summarise?

2. *Experiential* – Decisions made referencing previous occasions in (apparently) similar circumstances, either replicating, or avoiding, the same course of action.

3. *Calculated* – Decisions made after careful consideration, with a structured approach to evidence, options, and conclusion.

Proven decision-making tools are available for people managers,

- **Weighted scoring selection analysis.** Decisions are made based on a selection of criteria, each weighted by importance. Options are scored against the criteria and a cumulative calculation made. The highest scoring option is selected, subject to sense checking tests.

- **Root cause analysis.** Uncovering the *cause-of-the-cause* of a problem (see **Root cause analysis**).

- **Kepner-Tregoe selection analysis.** A troubleshooting approach, incorporating three elements; (current) problem analysis, decision analysis, and (potential) problem analysis.

- **Decision trees.** Considers alternate courses of action at each stage of a decision-making activity. The tree branches off to different potential options for calculated consideration.

- **Devil's advocate testing.** Be hyper-critical of the decision you are *thinking* of making. Test if the criticisms can be countered with a sound argument.

- **Descartes Decision Grid.** Credited to French philosopher and scientist Rene Descartes, the grid consists of four quadrants of question, each designed to explore the consequences of a possible decision,

What will happen if this happens?	What will happen if this doesn't happen?
What won't happen if this happens?	What won't happen if this doesn't happen?

These are classic management tools to aid decision making. There is one more idea which trumps all the above. Over the years I've found the most productive and engaging method is to remember Robert Townsend's proposition for consultation (see **Change, ask the people**)

"Ask the people – they know where the wheels are squeaking!"

Adept operational managers ask team members what they think. It is a sign of a strong leader who feels confident enough to ask for ideas. In which decision-making topics could you engage your team members?

Further reading

Knowledge Bank: Decision Making | Chartered Management Institute | www.managers.org.uk

Up the Organisation: How to Stop the Corporation from Stifling People and Strangling Profits | Jossey-Bass, 2007 | Townsend, R., Bennis, W.

Descartes Square: A Popular Decision Making Technique | Westminster Business Consultants, April 2017

Kogan, M. | https://wbcuk.wordpress.com/2017/04/07/descartes-square-a-popular-decision-making-technique/

With thanks to Mike Notman at Bourton Group https://www.bourton.co.uk/ for insights on this management topic.

Delegating

"No person will make a great business who wants to do it all himself or get all the credit." *– Andrew Carnegie*

You can't do everything, and even if you did, you'd be a *busy fool.* Your role is to manage, to get things done, not necessarily *to do* the things needing to be done. I meet plenty of busy fool managers.

Parts of your job can be delegated to team members. Maybe not all of it, and certainly some. Apart from freeing up time for you to do what you're employed to do (delivering performance and thinking how to improve), delegation allows your team members to grow. You're still *accountable*, ultimately answerable, for the tasks delegated, with tasks completed by people you make *responsible* (see **Accountability**).

Which parts of your job could you delegate? There's a simple and effective method for answering this,

1. Make a list of the key areas of responsibility in your role. If you're lucky, your job description will be up to date and will accurately describe this. If it's not, think it through and make the list anyway.
2. Next, identify the subsidiary tasks within each of the key areas. Again, a good job description will include many of these. If you don't have a good JD, think through a typical month of your activities, this will help.
3. Highlight the tasks which could be delegated to team members. The temptation is to be conservative and say, *"No, they're not capable"*. Be creative! Temporarily abandon evaluation and be radical in your thinking.
4. Now, begin the thinking of *who-with-what?* Who within your team is a good fit for which task? Who has the potential? Whose career will benefit from developing this capability?
5. Team members may not *today* be able to deliver on tasks you have highlighted for delegation. With training, guidance, mentoring and coaching they may. You'll keep a close eye on them to begin with, won't you? Gradually you can release the reins, reduce your micro-management, and allow team members to deliver on their enriched role.
6. You'll want to be kept up date. You're not abdicating this responsibility, only loaning it out.

Remember, although you're still *accountable* for the delegated task, you help team members grow by allowing them to be *responsible*.

Not everyone wants to be promoted. Delegation of key parts of your management responsibilities offers *job enrichment* opportunities for your team members (see **Job enrichment**).

Further reading

Managers Must Delegate Effectively to Develop Employees | Society of Human Resource Management, 2012 | Lloyd, S. | https://www.shrm.org/ResourcesAndTools/hr-topics/organizational-and-employee-development/Pages/DelegateEffectively.aspx

5 Strategies to Empower Employees to Make Decisions | Harvard Business Review, March 2020 | Lancefield, D. | https://hbr.org/2023/03/5-strategies-to-empower-employees-to-make-decisions

Deletion

"The most interesting information comes from children,
for they tell all they know and then stop." *– Mark Twain*

Deletion is an omission of parts of an intended message. The speaker does not include important information in the transmission. Bandler and Grinder built on earlier linguistics work in their book *Structure of Magic Volume 1.* Here are examples of deletions in a workplace context,

"I need some help."

"It will be fine."

"I don't know what to do."

"The meeting went well."

"I messed up the presentation."

"Today was awful."

"I nailed it!"

"They know I don't like it."

"The project isn't going well."

Notice how these spoken statements are missing content; they are impoverished by the deletion of the full representation of meaning. Impoverished communication occurs in all forms of human interaction. When speakers and writers delete elements of their experience or meaning it limits the accuracy of the information transfer.

Deletion reduces clarity, raises ambiguity, and increases the chances of the listener, or reader, misinterpreting the intended message. Assumptions, attempted mind reading, and misunderstandings become more likely. Listen out for communication deletion within your organisation.

We can challenge these deletions with questions.

Deletion challenges,

"Which project isn't going well? In what way, specifically, is it not going well? What causes you to think it's not going well?"

"In what way did you mess up the presentation? Messed up how, specifically?"

"It's great you nailed it. How do you know you nailed it? What, exactly, did you do to nail it?"

Deletion challenging is a valuable skill for people managers.

Further reading

The Structure of Magic: A Book about Language and Therapy | Bandler, R., Grinder, J. | Science and Behavior Books, 1975

Meaning Deletion in Coaching Communication | Continue and Begin Ltd | Drake-Knight, N. | https://ndk-group. com/language-deletion-generalisation-in-coaching-communication/

Desktop of the mind

"I feel it's the conscious mind that messes things up. The conscious mind is constantly telling you this might happen or that might happen, even before it has happened. Your conscious mind tells you the next ball might be an out-swinger, but when it's coming at you realize it's an in-swinger... so literally, you've played two balls." *– Sachin Tendulkar*

Our conscious minds can cope with a finite amount of data at any given time. It's like your desktop, there's only so much space. Too many programmes open, and it runs slowly, and sometimes crashes.

The psychologist George Miller (1956) researched into short term memory and our ability to consciously absorb and reproduce ideas. Miller was interested in the transfer of information to storage in our long-term memory. He promoted what he called *The Magical Number Seven Plus or Minus Two*.

Miller suggested most of us can satisfactorily manage a finite amount of activity in our short-term memory, between five and nine pieces of information. He proposed numbers were easier to retain and recall than words, which themselves are easier to recall than ideas. Subsequently, Alan Baddeley (1994), and others, have suggested the typical limit for short term memory is even shorter, between three and five ideas.

Sports team players know this experientially. The pre-match coaching instructions, and especially the half time exhortations to play in a certain way, have impact inverse to the number of messages given. The more instructions given by coaches, the less they will be absorbed and acted upon. I'm talking here of the grass roots sport most of our population are involved in; maybe top-level professional athletes have a greater capacity for retaining and acting upon instructions, I don't know.

Proficient coaches and team leaders minimise team focus onto a handful of hot topics. There is only a finite amount of desktop space available. Keep priorities to a minimum.

Further reading

The Magical Number Seven, Plus or Minus Two | The Psychological Review, 1956 | Miller, G. | http://psychclassics.yorku.ca/Miller/

The Magical Number Seven: Still Magic After All These Years? | Psychological Review, 101, 1994 | Baddeley, A.D.

What are the different types of memory? | Medical News Today, November 2020 | Villines, Z. | https://www.medicalnewstoday.com/articles/types-of-memory

Difficult people, managing

"Patience is bitter, but its fruit is sweet." *– Aristotle*

Managing difficult people is a topic worthy of its own book.

Experienced managers are familiar with different character types and their behavioural oddities. For recently appointed supervisors it may come as a shock to discover some team members present themselves as *challenging*.

Which behaviour patterns might be difficult for team managers?

Eric Berne (1968) described influence and manipulation methods people adopt and suggested their intended outcomes in his work on transactional analysis. Seasoned managers will recognize some of these presenting styles (see **Games people play**).

John Edmonstone (2003) explored categories of behaviour in his *Energy Investment Model*. Edmonstone discovered groups of responses from participants during 'action learning sets', a collective approach used for organizational problem solving.

Edmonstone's four box model presents categorized patterns in relation to mental attitude, and the energy people are willing to invest in their chosen behaviours. These include,

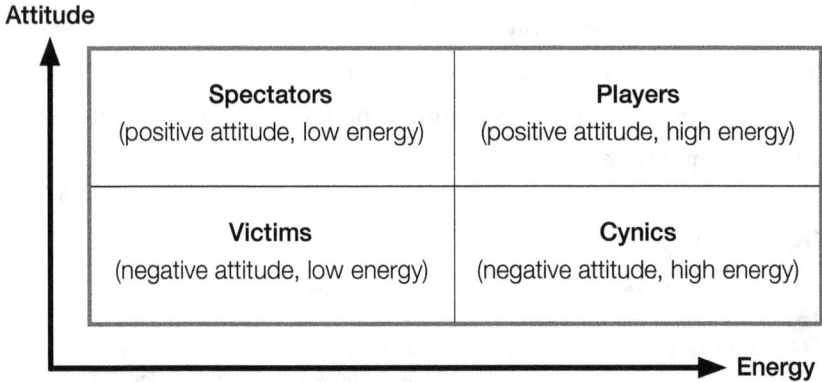

Attitude

Spectators (positive attitude, low energy)	Players (positive attitude, high energy)
Victims (negative attitude, low energy)	Cynics (negative attitude, high energy)

Energy

It's no surprise Edmonstone's model is often referenced when describing workplace team members. Each of these presenting styles require adaptive management thinking.

In this book I have introduced other awkward personalities; the *CAVE dwellers* – continuously against virtually everything, the *R-BUTs* – ah, but it won't work, the *PLOMs* – poor little old me, the *MGs* – moaners and groaners, and the *20/20s* – the one year of ancient experience, repeated without being changed or updated, for twenty years.

For additional tongue in cheek caricatures of challenging team members, see **Behaviour breeds behaviour.**

Employees motivated by a search for self-image may present as *Significance Seekers*. People want to feel worthy, and the nature of their worthiness isn't always aligned to business ambitions. Workplace behaviours coming from a need for personal importance come in varied forms and are awkward to manage (see **Significance**).

So, how can team managers handle challenging employee behaviour patterns, professionally? Is there a *pattern which connects*?

'Straightforward' underperformance is often easier to deal with than attitudinal presenting styles. Managers have tools to address performance standards (see **Explicit standards**, **NDK Performance Model**, and **Performance management**).

Less clear is how to approach the mental framing and behaviours of unhelpful team members.

A useful strategy, as with management of customer relationships, is to *understand*. Understanding a team member is the starting point. What is happening in their world (see **Get inside their world**)?

Everyone is carrying emotion. It may be well-hidden; it's always there though, and each team member, including the awkward character, is holding something. Enthusiasm and excitement would be great, of course. For some team members though, it might be anxiety, frustration, resentment from historical hurt, or other feelings about their life at work.

What is it? What *is* the feeling lurking behind the presenting style? What feeling(s) do they want to move away from or move towards (see **Emotional Drivers** and **Employee engagement**).

Is it even work related? Is there something outside work influencing attitudes and behaviours in their team role?

- Challenges at home?
- Childcare or carer responsibilities?
- Personal relationship difficulties?
- A capacity or capability issue?
- Learning needs?
- A health issue?
- Money worries?

All communication has a positive intent; people say and do things for an outcome purpose, even though they may be only *unconsciously* aware of their intent. Finding the underlying reason for troubling behaviours is the way to help team members feel more positive about life at work.

Understanding is the key.

Listening, asking sensitively phrased questions, and further attentive listening, is a useful place to begin your enquiry (see **Listening**).

Be patient though, not all employees will immediately open up and reveal their inner demons about work, their role in it, or your personal involvement in their professional life. It can take time, its own time, and may need a gradual approach. Trust comes eventually, not immediately.

Further reading

Games People Play: The Psychology of Human Relationships | Penguin, 1968 | Berne, E.

The Lost Art of Listening | Guildford Press, 2021 | Nichols, M.P., Straus, M.B.

You're Not Listening: What You're Missing and Why It Matters | Vintage, 2021 | Murphy, K.

Learning and development in action learning: the energy investment model | Industrial and Commercial Training Vol. 35, February 2003 | Edmonstone, J.

Action Learning in Health, Social and Community Care Principles, Practices and Resources | CRC Press, 2017 | Edmonstone, J.

Distortion

"To succeed, jump as quickly at opportunities as you do at conclusions." *– Benjamin Franklin*

Distortions include assumptions we make about people or circumstances, attempts at mind-reading, seeing things which don't exist, or choosing a selective meaning.

"She ignored me this morning, she doesn't like me."

"That customer is a dreamer; I can tell."

"The new software will mean job losses."

"I haven't heard from the customer. I think we've lost the sale."

"He didn't get the monthly report in on time; he doesn't care."

Notice here the speaker has made a leap in logic from the first part of their communication to the second. Statement A; therefore statement B. Yet the statements are not logically linked. The speaker is using imagination to form conclusions not backed by fact.

We can challenge these distortions with questions.

Distortion challenges,

"How does not getting the monthly report in on time mean he doesn't care?"

"When specifically, was the report submitted? What are the reasons given for the report being submitted late?"

"How does not hearing from the customer mean we've lost the sale? Have you contacted her since your meeting?"

"How can you tell the customer is a dreamer? Have you tested your assumption?"

As with deletion, *distortion challenging* is a valuable skill for a people manager. Distortions limit the accuracy of communication and understanding. Guessing what is meant by a speaker or writer leads to misinterpretation and logic errors. Assumption and attempted mind reading makes illogical conclusion more likely. Professional team managers challenge the distortions of colleagues.

Further reading

The Structure of Magic: A Book about Language and Therapy, Volume 1 | Bandler, R., Grinder, J. | Science and Behavior Bo oks, 1975

A Receiver's Role in Clear, Effective Communication Is an Important One: Protect Yourself Better Knowing What Goes Wrong in Conversations | ThoughtCo, July 2019 | Nordquist, R. | https://www.thoughtco.com/receiver-communication-1691899

Diversity, Equity, Inclusion (DEI), or Equity, Diversity, Inclusion (EDI)

"The sun shines on everyone." – *Gaius Petronius*

Today's world of work is populated by a diverse employee base, reflecting the communities and social make-up of our time. Team managers are required by law, and by sound ethical practice, to nurture an atmosphere of belonging and accessibility for all team members to thrive.

Legislation exists to protect against discrimination, including the workplace. In the UK, for example, it is against the law to discriminate against anyone because of 'protected characteristics' (www.gov.uk). These include,

- Age.
- Gender reassignment.
- Being married or in a civil partnership.
- Being pregnant or on maternity leave.
- Disability.
- Race including colour, nationality, ethnic or national origin.
- Religion or belief.
- Sex.
- Sexual orientation.

Laws are *push* factors – they demand compliance. In practice, legislation has limited ability to stimulate DEI cultures. *Pull* factors are more engaging, more inspiring, and more likely to result in sustained methods of working – they are driven by *movement towards* motivators (see **Emotional Drivers**). The *wants* (pull factors) are more influential than the *musts* (push factors).

So, what are the pull factors associated with a more diverse, equitable and inclusive working group?

Organisations are strengthened by multi-faceted teams. By contrast, insularity leads to repetitive thought patterns and stunted growth. Embracing new ways of thinking, introduced by team members with fresh perspectives, adds perspectives to business challenges. Innovation and problem-solving capabilities are enriched by original, perhaps previously unfamiliar reasoning.

Research suggests diverse teams are more effective at,

- Evaluation of data.
- Accuracy.
- Challenging and testing ideas within work groups.
- Managing financial performance measures.
- Creativity.

A diversity of background, culture, beliefs, and values, creates a rich talent pool from which ambitions can be addressed with a broader outlook.

From experience I know some managers and employees bemoan the requirement for DEI policies and expectations around workplace behaviours. Reservations seem most prominent in homogenous organisations and teams, where work group membership has patterns of 'sameness' with deep rooted thinking and embedded behaviours. In these environments change, even gradual evolution, is considered uncomfortable.

Managers may find terminology challenging, and fear 'getting it wrong' by using clumsy, awkward, or outdated language. Definitions, and the appropriateness of language labels do evolve, and it's difficult to keep up with society's changing expectations around how we communicate. Even name labels are tricky; is it DEI or EDI? Or JEDI – justice, equity, diversity, and inclusion? Or DEIB – diversity, equity, inclusion, and belonging? Equity or equality?

One model of definitions popular at the time of writing this book, is the shoe analogy,

- *Equality* is everyone getting a pair of shoes.
- *Diversity* is everyone getting a different type of shoe.
- *Equity* is everyone getting a pair of shoes that fit.
- *Acceptance* is understanding we all wear different types of shoes.
- *Belonging* is wearing the shoes you want without fear of judgement.

Whatever the definitions, managers have a responsibility to care for team members, to enable full access and engagement in workplace activities and opportunities. This is particularly important if barriers exist to an employee's involvement.

Management responsibility includes creating a climate and atmosphere of belonging and acceptance for all colleagues, with fairness and justice in mind, including employee exploration around personal mindsets. Helping colleagues become self-aware of their unknown bias (see **Cognitive bias**) and unintentional prejudice helps unfreeze ingrained beliefs. When colleagues grasp the benefits of embracing what may seem culturally (to them) unorthodox, new opportunities unfurl in the workplace.

So, what might be a managers' considerations for building a culture of equity, diversity, and inclusion? One instrument that I have used with managers asks for an honest self-assessment against potential prejudice. I use it myself, from time to time, as a check on my own unintended bias and latent discrimination. It's a self-scoring table, for personal use, so honesty is the key if it is to be of value.

"How do I feel about working with people who are different to me in terms of their…"

	Troubled				Not Sure			Relaxed		
Family background	10	9	8	7	6	5	4	3	2	1
Cultural values, beliefs, and behaviour	10	9	8	7	6	5	4	3	2	1
Language, dialect, or accent	10	9	8	7	6	5	4	3	2	1
Professional experience	10	9	8	7	6	5	4	3	2	1
Nationality	10	9	8	7	6	5	4	3	2	1
Regionality	10	9	8	7	6	5	4	3	2	1
Religion or spirituality	10	9	8	7	6	5	4	3	2	1
Sexual orientation	10	9	8	7	6	5	4	3	2	1
Birth sex	10	9	8	7	6	5	4	3	2	1
Gender identity or expression	10	9	8	7	6	5	4	3	2	1
Gender reassignment	10	9	8	7	6	5	4	3	2	1
Married or civil partner status	10	9	8	7	6	5	4	3	2	1

Pregnancy or maternity	Troubled				Not Sure				Relaxed	
	10	9	8	7	6	5	4	3	2	1
Physical ability or impairment	Troubled				Not Sure				Relaxed	
	10	9	8	7	6	5	4	3	2	1
Mental health ability or impairment	Troubled				Not Sure				Relaxed	
	10	9	8	7	6	5	4	3	2	1
Race	Troubled				Not Sure				Relaxed	
	10	9	8	7	6	5	4	3	2	1
Ethnicity	Troubled				Not Sure				Relaxed	
	10	9	8	7	6	5	4	3	2	1
Political views	Troubled				Not Sure				Relaxed	
	10	9	8	7	6	5	4	3	2	1
Academic achievement	Troubled				Not Sure				Relaxed	
	10	9	8	7	6	5	4	3	2	1
Age	Troubled				Not Sure				Relaxed	
	10	9	8	7	6	5	4	3	2	1

What was noticeable about your scoring today?

It may be worth revisiting this self-assessment scale, occasionally, for a health check on your DEI/EDI/DEIB personal bias.

Further reading

Why Diverse Teams Are Smarter | Harvard Business Review, November 2016 | Rock, D., Grant, H. | https://hbr.org/2016/11/why-diverse-teams-are-smarter

Sex vs Gender: What's The Difference And Why Does It Matter? | Simply Psychology, June 2023 | Simkus, J. | https://www.simplypsychology.org/sex-gender.html

Race and ethnicity, explained | National Geographic, February 2019 | Blakemore, E. | https://www.nationalgeographic.co.uk/history/2019/02/race-and-ethnicity-explained

47 Terms That Describe Sexual Attraction, Behavior, and Orientation | Healthline, February 2023 | Abrams, M. | https://www.healthline.com/health/different-types-of-sexuality

Building Inclusion: An Evidence-Based Model of Inclusive Leadership | Diversity Council Australia, 2015 | O'Leary, J., Russell, G. and Tilly, J. | https://www.dca.org.au/research/project/building-inclusion-evidence-based-model-inclusive-leadership

Equality vs Equity | American Journal of Law and Equality, 2021 | Minow, M. | https://direct.mit.edu/ajle/article/doi/10.1162/ajle_a_00019/107229/EQUALITY-VS-EQUITY

Positively Purple; Build an Inclusive World Where People with Disabilities Can Flourish | Kogan page, 2022 | Nash, K.

Equality | TUC Workplace Manual, November 2021 | https://www.tuc.org.uk/resource/equality

Equality, diversity, and inclusion (EDI) in the workplace | CIPD Factsheet | Chartered Institute of Personnel and Development, November 2022 | https://www.cipd.org/uk/knowledge/factsheets/diversity-factsheet/

Equality, equity, and inclusivity... What do they mean? | The Motivation Agency, April 2023 | Atria, A. | https://themotivationagency.co.uk/equality-and-inclusivity-is-changing-what-does-that-mean-for-organizations/

E

Emotional choice

"Thought and character are one, and as character can only manifest and discover itself through environment and circumstance, the outer conditions of a person's life will always be found to be harmoniously related to his inner state." *– James Allen*

We experience a range of internal feelings when managing a team,

Excitement, determination, optimism, apprehension, fun, annoyance, satisfaction, anger, humour, fear, thrill, frustration, and other emotions.

Emotional management is a healthy capability. Here's the good news,

You can choose your emotion!

There is a circularity, an emotional chain, which affects all of us. It is at the heart of how we live and operate at work and yet little is taught on this subject at school or in industry. Emotional chains have the following sequence,

Event/situation ⦙⦙⦙➡ **thought choice** ⦙⦙⦙➡ emotion selected ⦙⦙⦙➡ hormone release ⦙⦙⦙➡ behaviour and communication ⦙⦙⦙➡ consequence/situation ⦙⦙⦙➡ **thought choice** ⦙⦙⦙➡ emotion selected ⦙⦙⦙➡ hormone release… and round we go again.

Notice, the catalyst to each *consequence/situation* outcome is *thought choice*. How we choose to think about a set of circumstances will determine how the situation unfolds. Our thought choices lead to our emotions, the subsequent release of hormones, the behaviours, and communications we go on to exhibit, and the resultant outcome from this chain of input, all originate from our thinking about an event.

We can choose how we think about a situation. This life truism is woefully underplayed in education and the workplace. Marcus Aurelius understood this two thousand years ago.

> "Choose not to be harmed and you won't feel harmed. Don't feel harmed and you haven't been." *– Marcus Aurelius, Meditations, AD170*

Think about it; *she* made me angry; *it* made me sad. No, *she* didn't and no, *it* didn't; *you chose* to feel those emotions by the way you thought about and framed events.

The key to emotional management is the thinking choice made in each situation. Emotions, hormones, behaviours and communication, all flow from the starting point of that internal choice, how you choose to *think* (see **Framing, Reframing**).

Further reading

As a Man Thinketh | CreateSpace Independent Publishing Platform, 2006 | Allen, J.

Are Emotions a Choice? | MentalHealth. net May, 2013 | Matta, C. | https://www.mentalhelp.net/blogs/are-emotions-a-choice/

Emotional Drivers™

> "People's behaviour makes sense if you think about in terms of their goals, needs and motives." *– Thomas Mann*

All human behaviour has a positive intent. People do things for a reason. The reason is not always obvious to the outsider and sometimes not consciously recognised by the person exhibiting the behaviour.

Behaviour is driven by an underlying emotional need – an *Emotional Driver*™ – encouraging us to make a movement towards emotional or physical pleasure, or a movement away from existing or anticipated physical or psychological pain. Every employee's (and manager's) decision to act is based on one of two internal motivators, either,

Movement Away from Pain or Discomfort
~ including fear of potential future pain
or discomfort.

Movement towards Pleasure or Comfort
~ seeking feelings of relaxation, comfort,
or pleasure.

Movement Away? Movement Towards?
Which is driving behaviour? Sometimes it
will be both, but one driver will be the dominant, or initiating force. Consider every piece
of behaviour you are exhibiting now – every single movement or action is in
furtherance of one, or both, of these two *mammalian drivers!*

Is your team member driven by an urge to move away from discomfort?
Is that why she is behaving in that way? Or is she planning some pleasure?
Remember, employees commit to act for one, or both, of these reasons. We
can explore these inner levers during relaxed conversation with colleagues.
KIT meetings are a great time to chat through the driving forces making a
difference for them (see **KIT meetings** and **Get inside their world**).

Once a manager has insight into an employee's personal drivers it might
be possible to adapt work arrangements to provide a best fit motivational
stimulus.

What forces are driving the behaviour of your team members? What are
the *dominant* forces, *movement away* from discomfort, or *movement towards*
pleasure?

Further reading

Boomerang! Coach Your Team to Be the Best | Dandelion Digital, 2007 | Drake-Knight, N.

Fast Coaching. The Complete Guide to New Code Continue & Begin® | Dandelion Digital, 2016 | Drake-Knight, N. | Audible https://www.audible.co.uk/pd/Fast-Coaching-Audiobook/B07TTKD13T

The Motivation Agency | https://themotivationagency-online.com/course/begin

Meerkat Selling® | Dandelion Digital, 2008 | Drake-Knight, N.

The Motivation Agency | https://themotivationagency-online.com/course/meerkat

Emotional intelligence (EQ)

"All learning has an emotional base." *– Plato*

Understanding how our emotions function, and being able to manage them, are valuable skills.

The emotional part of the human brain aids our survival system, often referred to as *fight or flight* or *play dead* (see **Fight, flight, play dead**). When people's survival antennae are activated, strong responses emerge, such as fear, anger, or sadness. We are not always aware of how powerful our emotions are.

In contrast, the logical, rational part of our brain, which enables us to think clearly and make considered decisions, is not dominant. In an emergency, our emotional brain takes over and tells us to go with our *gut feel*. When we become upset or angry, happy, or euphoric, our logical thinking is compromised; we become more susceptible to stimulus-response behaviour.

Emotional intelligence, or EQ, is about being aware of our emotions, and heightening our logical and rational thinking, rather than being ruled by our feelings. Emotionally intelligent people are not immune from the influence of inner sensations. Being self-aware though, in tune with feelings, allows our logical brains to do more.

Therapists know the value of recognizing and naming a feeling being felt,

"I notice I am feeling competitive."

"I notice I am feeling anxious."

"I notice I am feeling excited."

"I notice I am feeling frustrated."

Recognition of our emotional state reduces subjectivity and achieves a degree of dissociation. It helps team managers act in a balanced, measured way. We can decide on the most productive actions, based on all the information available, rather than how we *feel*. It makes us easier people to work with and leads to better, clearer thinking at work.

Emotional intelligence is not purely about us. Having an awareness and sensory acuity towards the emotional wellbeing of others is part of EQ. An empathetic mindset is the mark of a mature team manager (see **Empathy**).

We can never fully associate and experience a team member's emotional state; what we can do is think through the most likely mental conditions of a colleague or colleagues, based on known factors, and test these with compassionate questioning (see the Milton Erickson and Carl Rogers quotes in **Get inside their world**).

Emotional intelligence is a pre-requisite for effective team management. Thinking through the likely impact of management decision making, and how it is communicated, is a trait of elegant professional managers (see **Secondary and tertiary consequences**).

I meet and work with managers, including senior executives, who have yet to master this competence. Too often communication from leaders is transactional and process focused, with attention centred on *the thing* requiring attention. Emotional impact on colleagues has been insufficiently considered or is not thought significant.

Military leadership expert John Adair encouraged officers and non-commissioned officers to think about balancing emphasis between task, the team, and individuals within the work group. This is a requirement of effective team management, not an optional luxury (see **Human leadership**).

How we communicate management instruction or commentary is the difference that makes the difference; *that is the difference*. Thinking through emotional conditions is an intelligent approach to team management. Being attuned, empathetically, to the impact of management communication is the mark of a sophisticated leader.

Further reading

Emotional Intelligence: Why It Can Matter More Than IQ | Bantam, 2005 | Goleman, D.P.

Em-Path Online | The Motivation Agency | https://themotivationagency-online.com/course/empath

With thanks to Ian Luxford and the team at The Motivation Agency www.themotivationagency.co.uk for insights on this management topic.

Empathy

"I call him religious who understands the suffering of others."
– Mahatma Gandhi

Empathy is the ability to understand the feelings of another. Empathy at work increases awareness of a colleague's inner world, how they think and feel, what is driving them, and the reasons behind this.

Empathy leads to stronger and more productive workplace relationships. Team managers who are empathic avoid making assumptions about another's world, nor do they project their own feelings or values onto others. Elegant team managers listen without judgement and seek to understand, rather than attempt to impose, or change a person's mind.

Empathy management is not about agreeing with others' feelings or offering advice to find solutions. It is about gaining an approximated understanding of what is happening for a colleague, in their experience of the world, and being able to see things as they see them, hear what they hear, feel as they feel, without changing your own views or position.

Empathetic communication is a desirable skill for working with team members and peers. Managing workloads, negotiating, dealing with conflict, supporting, and coaching, are more effective when conducted with an empathetic approach.

The Motivation Agency www.themotivationagency.co.uk state in their learning programme *Em-Path Online,*

> "Empathy is about being brave enough to sit and listen… connecting to their reality…".

What empathy is not

- Empathetic is not sympathetic. Sympathy offers commiseration and pity.
- Attempts at mind-reading are equally unhelpful. A common statement, with a damaging impact inverse to the speaker's positive intent, is,

> "I know what you mean. When X happened to me…".

No, no, no.

No-one *knows* another person's map of the territory. It is their map, drawn by them. Attempts to mind-read are almost always clumsy, superimposing a subjective perception based on guesswork (see **Maps of the territory**).

Listening

Empathy works through listening to gain as accurate an understanding as possible. Not *"I know how you feel"*, so much as *"I would like to know how you feel."* Empathy employs curiosity, rather than commentary, and certainly not *judgement* (see **Listening**).

Empathy offers connection and presence. It seeks, with permission, to get inside the world of the troubled or untroubled person, to join them, and gain an *approximation* of understanding.

Helping someone feel they have been listened to, with a genuine attempt to understand (doomed to be an approximation), is realistically about as much as empathy can achieve. Nonetheless, its impact is reassuring for team members. Team managers who employ empathetic behaviours are more likely to provide appreciated support to colleagues than those offering sympathy or benevolent advice.

Further reading

Practice Empathy as a Team | Harvard Business Review, February 2023 | Porath, C., Boissy, A. | https://hbr.org/2023/02/practice-empathy-as-a-team

The Empathy Effect: 7 Neuroscience Based Keys for Transforming The Way We Live, Love, Work, and Connect Across Differences. | Sounds True Inc, 2018 | Reiss, H., Neporent, L.

Em-Path Online | The Motivation Agency | https://themotivationagency-online.com/course/empath

With thanks to Ian Luxford and the team at The Motivation Agency www.themotivationagency.co.uk for insights on this management topic.

Employee engagement

"For a friend with an understanding heart is no less than a brother."

– Homer

There is no single definition of employee engagement. The term refers to the way people feel about their work, how committed they are to their employment organisation, and the extent to which they feel part of the *Why?* (see **Why? Purpose and meaning**).

Engaging for Success (MacLeod and Clarke, 2009) was a study of organisations demonstrating high employee engagement and performance. The report highlighted a relationship between how engaged people feel, and how well the enterprise performs.

The research identified that the common factors in high engagement/ high performance were Four Enablers,

1. **Strategic Narrative.** There is clarity about organizational direction and its people understand how to contribute to success.
2. **Engaging Managers.** Line managers listen, coach, and enable team members.
3. **Employee Voice.** People are encouraged to participate in planning and implementation; their experiences and ideas are actively sought and used.
4. **Integrity.** The enterprise does what it says it will do, it lives by its declared values, and is transparent about how it treats its people.

Managers can have an impact on the level of engagement within their teams, by:

- Making colleagues feel part of the *Why?* and demonstrating how to contribute to overall goals.
- Being engaging managers – listening, coaching, and enabling.
- Involving team members and giving them a voice.
- Leading by example.

How do you measure up against these team management activities? Are your team members fully engaged? If you are uncertain, *"What would have to happen to make that happen?"* (see **Freedom questions**).

Gallup Q12®

A respected method of measuring employee engagement is the Gallup Q12® survey. Q12® is a cross-industry yardstick against which an employer can calibrate engagement. Survey agencies around the world use Q12®, or a variant of it, as a source of engagement data. Gallup claims to have studied 2.7 million workers from 100,000+ employee teams, over 50 diverse industry groups.

The Q12® core question set from Gallup refers to *employee need*. It is structured as follows,

1. I know what is expected of me at work.
2. I have the materials and equipment I need to do my work right.
3. At work, I have the opportunity to do what I do best every day.
4. In the last seven days, I have received recognition or praise for doing good work.
5. My supervisor, or someone at work, seems to care about me as a person.
6. There is someone at work who encourages my development.
7. At work, my opinions seem to count.
8. The mission or purpose of my company makes me feel my job is important.
9. My associates or fellow employees are committed to doing quality work.
10. I have a best friend at work.
11. In the last six months, someone at work has talked to me about my progress.
12. This last year, I have had opportunities at work to learn and grow.

How would your team members respond to the Gallup Q12® employee engagement survey?

	Of the Q12® set, which three areas of investigation do you think might merit your attention?
1	
2	
3	

Variance to Q12®

Some agencies will adapt the Q12® question set to reflect areas of specific interest. A 'side hustle' question set will investigate topical areas of relevance during a particular period, perhaps related to recent reorganization, or a key issue of concern to the enterprise. Some brands will add to the Q12® to explore people engagement topics in more detail.

Here is an example question set of Q12® content, with added questions to suit the needs of a retail business. This is a ranking report, post survey, showing high scoring attributes within the respondent group, and areas of moderate or concerning performance. It is RAG rated, in this instance with >75% being green, 70% – 74.9% amber, <70% is considered red.

Rank	Attribute	Score
1	I know what is expected of me at work	86.6
2	I have a colleague I can talk to at work	83.7
3	I am aware of project scrums and sprints	81.2
4	I know how my work contributes to overall company objectives	75.6
5	If I had an issue, I would be comfortable in raising this with my manager	75.4
6	I am aware of bonuses and incentives available to me	75.3
7	At work I have the opportunity to do what I do best every day	74.7
8	I feel I can develop my career with the company in a technical or managerial role	73.6
9	My supervisor, or someone at work, seems to care about me as a person.	73.4
10	The mission or purpose of my company makes me feel my job is important.	71.4
11	This last year, I have had opportunities at work to learn and grow.	70.9
12	In the last seven days, I have received recognition or praise for doing good work.	69.3
13	This last year, I have had opportunities at work to learn and grow.	68.7
14	I have regular 121 coaching sessions with my line manager	66.4
15	I have regular keep-in-touch (KIT) meetings with my line manager	66.1
16	I have the materials and equipment I need to do my to do my job	65.0
17	My associates or fellow employees are committed to doing quality work.	64.8
18	I regularly contribute to team meetings	61.4
19	At work my opinions seem to count	61.3
20	This organization is a great place to work	60.9

What questions would you consider adding to the core Gallup Q12® employee engagement survey for your team?

Additional research possibilities

Most research agencies will offer survey tools to investigate other areas of employee interest. These might include,

- Voice of the employee 'VoE' – helps flag up early warning signals.
- Diversity & Inclusion – is everyone being treated fairly?
- Employee satisfaction – to investigate specific topics.

Employee engagement data collection offers valuable intelligence. Beware of overly frequent use though, there is a balance between gaining regular insights, and feelings of survey fatigue.

Further reading

Gallup's Employee Engagement Survey: Ask the Right Questions with the Q12® Survey | Gallup | https://www.gallup.com/workplace/356063/gallup-q12-employee-engagement-survey.aspx

Carrots and Sticks Don't Work: Build a Culture of Employee Engagement with the Principles of RESPECT | McGraw-Hill, 2010 | Marciano, P.L.

Engaging for Success | MacLeod, D., Clarke, N. | Department for Business, Innovation, and Skills, 2009

With thanks to Ian Luxford and the team at The Motivation Agency www.themotivationagency.co.uk for insights on this management topic.

English is Rubbish™

"There is no greater impediment to the advancement of knowledge than the ambiguity of words." *– Thomas Reid*

English is a dreadful language. So is German, French, Spanish, Italian, Portuguese, Mandarin, Arabic, Urdu, and others. All languages are inaccurate attempts at communicating because the words and sounds employed are approximations of meaning. Language is the menu to the food, the map to the territory. We do our best to communicate meaning, using the tools at our disposal – our native language.

Verbal communication washes over people like a wave of noise. Listeners can only get the broad idea of meaning from a communicator. A full representation of meaning is difficult to achieve and so messages in conversation or writing become generalised (see **Deletion**, **Distortion** and **Generalisation**).

Words are uncertain, non-specific, and ill-defined in meaning. Because our language system is so full of generalisation it is easy for transmitted communication to be misinterpreted by the recipient; that's to say, interpreted by the message receiver in a way the transmitter did not intend.

How many times have you heard, *"I didn't mean it like that!"*

Often the language heard by a recipient is so ambiguous we feel the need to ask questions to gain a more precise understanding of meaning. Even then, after asking a clarification question we will ask additional, probing, questions to gain what we believe to be an adequate amount of precision in our understanding. Phew! This language business is hard work!

If for example we were to ask a colleague about their weekend, they might say *"It was ok, didn't do much really"*. What does that mean, specifically? We have received a broad generalised message telling us very little about our colleague's experience. If we asked more specific questions, we may receive more precise information. It's always an approximation of experience and meaning.

Linguists know the difference between levels of communication transmission as *Surface Structure* and *Deep Structure*. Surface Structure provides a general overview message. Deep Structure is where richer, more detailed information exists (see **Surface structure, deep structure, specificity**).

Managers who understand ambiguity in communication recognise language containing imprecision and the dangers of leaving it untested. Artful managers use the words *specifically*, *precisely*, and *exactly* to encourage communicators to be more accurate in their description of meaning.

Further reading

Precision Questioning | Vervago, 2018 | https://www.vervago.com/skill-sharpeners/precision-questioning/

Boomerang! Coach Your Team to Be the Best | Dandelion Digital, 2007 | Drake-Knight, N.

Fast Coaching. The Complete Guide to New Code Continue & Begin® | Dandelion Digital, 2016 | Drake-Knight, N. | Audible https://www.audible.co.uk/pd/Fast-Coaching-Audiobook/B07TTKD13T

The Motivation Agency | https://themotivationagency-online.com/course/begin

Every Customer Wants®

"Life is largely a matter of expectation." – *Homer*

The internal marketplace in your organisation is a matrix of customer-supplier chains. How you and your colleagues manage these relationships will determine the quality of customer experience (see **Customers, internal**).

The *Every Customer Wants®* education programme, developed by Continue & Begin Ltd, offers guidance on how to raise customer experience to the highest levels. It offers to,

"Develop customer experience professionals' knowledge and skills, by learning to understand each customer's needs, and deliver added value through service quality, whilst minimising customer effort".

Research conducted across service sectors suggests three deliverables (wants) are important to *all* customers, including those in internal customer-supplier relationships.

1. **Understand Me** – get inside my world, discover what's important to me. Listen to my story, put yourself in my shoes, see things from my perspective. Understand what I want, and what I don't want.
2. **Add Value for Me** – help me by providing something of value to me, a product, or a service. Make a difference to my life, even if it's a small thing. Offer me help to make my life more comfortable.
3. **Make it Easy for Me** – keep this simple for me, minimise my effort, make it hassle free.

Every Customer Wants® explores these *wants* in more detail,

Understand Me
- *Every Customer Wants®* – Overview.
- Different Strokes
- Get Inside Your Customer's World
- First Impressions
- Words, Song & Dance
- Being Warm and Friendly
- Reflective Listening

- Help me!
- Customer Drivers™

Add Value for Me

- CITO Mindset
- Customer Segmentation
- Assumption Danger
- Moments of Truth
- Service Standards
- Linked Services or Products
- Becoming Your Customer's Friend
- Customer Service *Superhero*
- Internal Customers

Make it Easy for Me

- Customer Effort, Customer Ease
- First Contact Resolution
- Floppy Statements
- Framing & Reframing
- Handling Customer Concerns
- Behaviour Breeds Behaviour
- Finish on a High
- Reminder of *Every Customer Wants*® principles
- Make a Pledge

Think about the supply role your team plays within your organisation. What can you and your team members do to help internal customers feel,

"Thank you. You understand me."
To achieve this, we could...
"Thank you. You are adding value for me."
To achieve this, we could...
"Thank you. You are making it easy for me."
To achieve this, we could...

Note: *Every Customer Wants®* and *Understand Me, Add Value for Me, Make it Easy for Me®* are registered trademarks of Nick Drake-Knight.

Further reading

Stop Trying to Delight Your Customers | Harvard Business Review, August 2010 | Dixon, M., Freeman, K., Toman, N. | https://hbr.org/2010/07/stop-trying-to-delight-your-customers

Continue and Begin Ltd | https://ndk-group.com/conference-presentations-8/

The Motivation Agency | https://www.themotivationagency-online.com/course/everycustomerwants

Experiential learning

"What I hear I forget, what I see I remember, what I do I understand."
– Xunzi, 340 BC – 245 BC

Be wary of conceptual knowledge not proven by pragmatic application. There are enough *Scarf Draggers* out there (intellectuals, academic theorists) with limited experience of real-world implementation.

The same principle applies to you and your team members. Knowledge alone is unlikely to result in high skills delivery. There is a difference between knowledge and skills. Learning through knowledge application is known as *experiential learning*. It is by far the most effective strategy for embedding workplace practices.

Lombardo and Eichinger (1996) suggested a ratio for the effectiveness of learning avenues,

- 70% from experiential activity, where the experience is challenging.
- 20% from working with others, and feedback gained.
- 10% from formal learning, training, and course work.

Whilst the formula above has been criticised for the efficacy of its research, and the suspiciously rounded numbers, there's no doubt personal experience has profound impact on learning and ability.

Remember,

Knowing what to do, is not the same as doing what you know.

It is important to get out of intellectualism and *do*. Don't allow yourself or your colleagues to be the *Scarf Dragger* who says, *"I've read that book"*, or *"I went on that course."* Conceptual knowledge is valuable only if it results in new behaviour.

Some employees are artful at knowing, but not doing, because it suits them to do so.

I remember designing a spidergram for sales managers of a prestigious German automotive manufacturer, which addressed this point. We had been reflecting on the number of sales executives who, when challenged, apparently knew what to do, but didn't do what they knew.

I created the spidergram to illustrate visually how sales executives could plot themselves through self-assessment against six components,

1. Product portfolio knowledge.
2. Process knowledge (internal).
3. Knowledge of competitors in the marketplace.
4. Knowledge about customers, experiential expertise in customer communications.
5. Experience in the sector, or within sales and customer experience.
6. Personal belief in the brand and proposition.

Here's the spidergram illustrated with one scenario, that of an experienced sales executive, who *knows what to do* about organisational processes, but doesn't *do what he knows*. It's a common reality in many organisations where the employee *does it their way*.

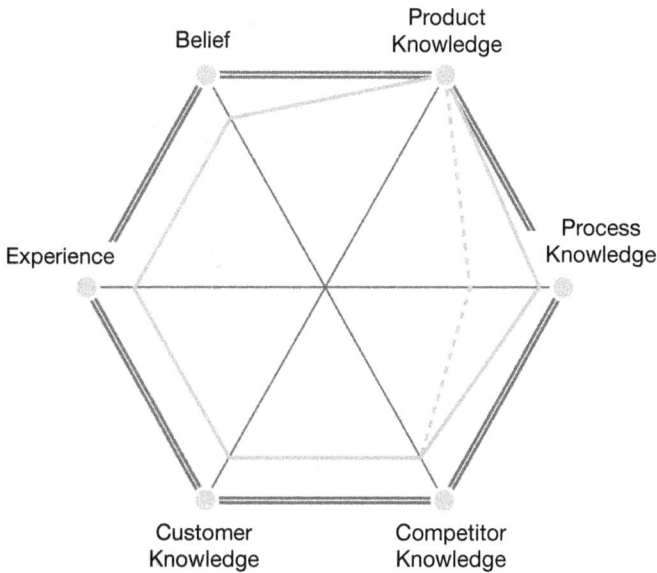

In this example, the sales executive is clearly experienced and competent, with self-assessed high scores.

Part of the development activity we were designing allowed sales managers to conduct their own perspective assessment of the sales executive, using the same spidergram model. Lay one alongside the other and inevitably differences are apparent. These becomes a focus for conversation.

Notice in the example above, the sales executive has scored highly on Process Knowledge. The dotted line represents the scoring of the sales manager who doesn't see the sales executive delivering behaviours which match self-perception knowledge. A gap exists. Why? Because the sales executive doesn't think it necessary to comply with explicitly described process. And so, that becomes a more significant conversation.

This is the essence of true understanding; being able to, and being willing to, *do* the thing you *know*. Do you and your team members know what to do, and how to do it? And do they *do* what they know?

Further reading

8 Reasons Why Experiential Learning Is the Future of Learning | eLearning Industry | Jayaraman, R. | https://elearningindustry.com/8-reasons-experiential-learning-future-learning

The Career Architect Development Planner | Korn Ferry, 1996 | Lombardo, M., Eichinger, R.

Sales Confidence | Continue and Begin Ltd | www.continueandbegin.com

Explicit standards

"Have you set high standards in the past that make it clear
what level of performance you demand?" *– Tom Peters*

If team members don't understand *exactly* what is required of them, how
can they be expected to deliver? Managers can achieve this by designing and
implementing explicit standards of performance, supported by appropriate
training and coaching.

Explicit standards could, for example, relate to,

- Presentation and maintenance of the workplace environment.
- Following internal processes or protocols.
- Expectations of employees' knowledge of product and process.
- Required communication behaviours.
- Compliance with, and 'living to', organisational values.

These can be set out in clear terms and transferred to employees through
training and promoted through visual management. Once standards have
been trained out into the workforce, and colleagues know what is expected
of them, on-the-job coaching will maintain delivery standards (see **NDK
Performance Model®**, **Performance management**, **Visual management**,
Coaching, Continue & Begin Fast Coaching® and **Case Study: On
Growing Managers [and our Business]**).

Clearly defined, unambiguous, and explicitly described standards become
the reference points for employee performances. Reference to standards
helps managers achieve consistent delivery across a team, and for quality to
be sustained. These might be referred to during keep-in-touch meetings,
coaching sessions, and at appraisal time (see **KIT meetings**, and **Appraisals
and performance reviews**).

Do you have clear, unambiguous, and explicitly described standards of
performance for your team to work to?

Further reading

Boomerang! Coach Your Team to Be the Best | Dandelion Digital, 2007 | Drake-Knight, N.

Fast Coaching. The Complete Guide to New Code Continue & Begin® | Dandelion Digital, 2016 | Drake-Knight, N. | Audible https://www.audible.co.uk/pd/ Fast-Coaching-Audiobook/B07TTKD13T

The Motivation Agency | https:// themotivationagency-online.com/course/ begin

F

Failure, or feedback?

"Failure is merely feedback that there is something blocking the path
of the emergence and expansion of the greatest version of yourself."
– Mother Teresa

Once we recognise any result informs and educates us, we begin to see
management as a learning experience. Think of your actions and decisions
which *did not* produce the outcome you wanted – these were all learning experiences and developments in your professional growth. You could
choose to think of these instances as 'failures' if you like; a disempowering
judgement (see **Framing and reframing**).

A more damaging mistake would be to transpose these experiences into
self-labelling, as *"I am a failure"* (see **Nominalisations**). It's your efforts
and strategy which created the outcome, not you the person.

Much more beneficial to you, and healthier, is to identify these events
as 'learns' and take your new knowledge onto the next phase of your
management career. There are plenty of high-profile stories illustrating how
astonishing achievements were preceded by repeated calamitous results.

Most of us have experience in how to foul up an opportunity. We are
fallible human beings who, from time to time, make unhelpful choices. It
is how we think about our results which determines our future. The NLP
(Neuro Linguistic Programming) community is good on reframing unwel-
comed outcomes,

There is no failure, only feedback.

For managers, this simple reframe encourages us to get up from knock downs, adapt our behaviours, and build new capabilities.

Here's a tip I know works well. Make a shortlist of experienced managers known to you, and whom you admire. Ask each of them for a brief mentoring session, maybe 30 minutes or so. Ask them for examples of their management decisions or activities which didn't go to plan, or circumstances and events where they learned a valuable, even harsh, lesson about managing.

I'm confident you'll gather insights and useful tips, and reassurance from your interviewees that even the most accomplished performers have had wobbly moments, and have learned from their successes and mistakes, just as you do.

Further reading

Unlimited Power | Simon & Schuster, 1986 | Robbins, A.

5 Ways to Reframe Failure | Success, November 2014 | Lombardo, E. | https://www.success.com/5-ways-to-reframe-failure/

Feel, felt, found

"If you think adventure is dangerous, try routine, it is lethal."

– Paulo Coelho

Feel, felt, found is used in sales environments to help a prospective customer rethink a concern they have about purchasing a product or service. The sales consultant understands the customer is feeling concerned. *"I empathise with how you feel, someone else felt the same, (but*) what they found was . . ."*

Feel-felt-found (FFF)'s influence is based on what psychologist Robert Cialdini refers to as *social proof.* The marketing industry has used social proof for decades as leverage to encourage undecided potential customers towards a proposition.

---

* Purposeful use of the *But Monster*®. In this scenario, we want to break the pattern of thinking of a co-communicator (see **But Monster®**).

FFF works on the principle of,

- I understand you.
- Someone else has knowledge you do not have.
- They had a positive experience.
- By implication, so will you.

Here is an example from face-to-face retail clothing,

> "I can understand your concern about the lining because it seems so lightweight. One of our regular customers had the same concern when she bought hers. She popped in last week and said it had kept her cosy in a nasty blizzard."

That's the application of *feel-felt-found (FFF)* in a sales context. How else can it be used? FFF is a universal communication tool to encourage participation.

Feel, felt, found is a great way for helping team members be adventurous, take on new ways of working, or stretch to new capabilities. Maybe they are unsure about a new software system? A change to their role? Workplace changes? Starting a course of study? A new team member joining?

How could you use *feel-felt-found* in your team management role?

Further reading

Meerkat Selling | Dandelion Digital, 2008 | Drake-Knight

Influence: The Psychology of Persuasion | HarperBus, 2021 | Cialdini, R. B.

The Motivation Agency | https://themotivationagency-online.com/course/meerkat

Fight, flight, play dead

> "I cannot do confrontation. You know that fight of flight thing? I'm flight. I just don't want the argument." *– Jennifer Saunders*

Robert Anton Wilson (1983) suggested humans are simply *domesticated primates.* He had a point. Anatomically and mentally, our evolution, which has programmed us to survive the threats of a primitive era, has yet to catch up with the world of work. Threats to our survival are different today,

- Performance criticism.
- Restrictions on advancement, or career opportunities.
- Loss of earnings.
- Potential redundancy.
- Removal of management 'love'.
- Being fired.

All these threats have a linkage back to survival in the form of security and physiological needs. What happens if I lose money? Lose my job? My mortgage or rent payments? My children?

We still respond to perceived danger in the same way as we did in prehistory. Threats to our wellbeing at work may be less obviously physical in nature today, and yet our bodies still react in readiness for one of three survival strategies,

1. Fight
2. Flight
3. Play dead. If I don't move, I might not be seen by the aggressor,
   I may stay safe.

The way our bodies instinctively prepare is to adopt a well-proven set of physiological changes,

- We increase blood pressure and our heart rate, it pumps rapidly. We will need to move blood around our body soon, ready for the *fight* or *flight*. *Playing dead* might not work and we will have to resort to one of the other survival strategies.
- We breathe shallow and fast, to load up on oxygenated blood, ready for action.
- We tense our muscles. We will need strength for *fight* or *flight*.
- We sweat. We are going to get hot and will need optimum body temperature.
- Our hairs stand up. If we are hairy, it will make us look bigger and a more challenging adversary. It will allow air to move around and keep us cool during the *fight* or *flight*.
- We dilate our eyes. We need as much light in as we can. We need to see our adversary.

Dramatic? Yes. And despite our modern sophistications, this is *still* what happens when we are faced with what we perceive as danger.

So, what is the connection between evolutionary responses to danger and today's people management?

When you criticise team members in a way which is perceived as threatening, their inner responses are mammalian. It causes physiological responses. The criticised employee becomes defensive, their urge is to *fight* (argue, obstruct, or be passive aggressive), to *fly* (exit discussion, or resign) or to *play dead* (not participate or contribute).

It is important we manage with care. We can cause harm to our people through clumsy communication (see **Criticism and failure focus** and **Get inside their world**).

Further reading

Prometheus Rising | New Falcon Publications, 1983 | Wilson, R.A.

Fight or Flight (The Adrenal Response) | Practical Psychology, March 2023 | https://practicalpie.com/fight-or-flight/

Floppy language

> "Believe in yourself! Have faith in your abilities! Without a humble but reasonable confidence in your own powers you cannot be successful or happy." *– Norman Vincent Peale*

Floppy language is communication content which undermine the strength of our proposition,

"I'm sorry to say…"

"I'm afraid I have to tell you…"

"I realise this might not be what you wanted to hear…"

"It's a bit expensive, but…"

"I'm sorry if this isn't quite what you expected…"

"It's the best we could do really…"

"I know it's not great, but…"

"We didn't have much time to prepare this…"

"I know I'm not very good at this…"

I was a police officer in Bristol, England during the 1980s. I remember being chastised at training school by the instructor when, during role play, I said,

"I'm afraid, I'm going to have to arrest you".

A booming voice shouted,

"Afraid? Afraid?! What are you afraid of Constable? Why are you apologising?"

I had been using floppy language. Floppy language undermines your credibility and your negotiating strength. Listen out for it in your patterns of speech, in your written work, and in the communications of your team members.

Note: floppy language is different to tentative language, which presents with hesitance and timidity (see **Tentative language**).

Further reading

Meerkat Selling | Dandelion Digital, 2008 | Drake-Knight, N.

The Motivation Agency | https://themotivationagency-online.com/course/meerkat

Floppy Language | Changingminds.org

Starker, D. | http://changingminds.org/techniques/language/modifying_meaning/floppy_language.htm

Focus

"Always remember, your focus determines your reality." *– George Lucas*

We get what we focus on. Motorcyclists and cyclists know this. When there is a wet and slippery drain cover in the middle of a corner, the worst possible strategy is to think (internal dialogue),

"I must not ride over that slippery drain cover."

Guess what happens? You're right, the biker rides straight over it. This is because our brains don't process negativity well. So, *do not think* about the colour of your... home front door... yes, the colour of your home front door... *do not think about it.*

You had to think about it to *not think* about it, right?

Much better if the rider had used a different self-talk message,

"It's a corner, so ride on the tarmac road surface."

We get what we focus on. Visualisation, goal orientation, and future orientation in time, all work well because we provide our brains with a clearly defined positive focus (see **Goal Mapping**® by Brian Mayne, **Future feeling, as motivational leverage**).

Alfred Adler's emphasis on goal-directed thinking highlighted how focus helps or hinders. The self-statements *"I am going to succeed"* or *"I am going to fail"* are equally influential and lead us towards our stated aim (succeed/failure). We find what we are looking for.

Wise people managers focus team members' attention on working towards positive outcomes, rather than avoiding negative results.

Further reading

What you focus on is what becomes powerful – why your thoughts and feelings matter | Hey SIGMUND, 2016 | Young, K. | https://www.heysigmund.com/why-what-you-focus-on-is-what-becomes-powerful-why-your-thoughts-and-feelings-matter/

Why You Get What You Focus On | Self Help for Life | Thomas, P. | https://selfhelpforlife.com/why-you-get-what-you-focus-on/

Understanding Life. An Introduction to the Psychology of Alfred Adler. | Adler, A., Brett, C. | One World Publication, 2009

Forcefields

"Change has its enemies." *– Robert Kennedy*

Force field analysis, created by the social psychologist Kurt Lewin, is an excellent management tool for creating shifts in team performance. Lewin's framework, adapted for commercial contexts, shows the *forces* at work in an organisation, or subsidiary team. A forcefield will include factors supporting or encouraging change, known as *driving forces,*

Example Driving Forces

- New business plans and strategies.
- New products and services.
- Automation.
- Focus on continuous improvement.
- HRM policies focused on personal growth and development of employees.

Other factors may be preventing change, known as *resisting forces*,

Example Resisting Forces

- Outdated processes, or non-value adding activities.
- Poor working environment.
- Silo mentality of team members.
- Limited management experience.
- Negative mindsets.

Here is an example of a forcefield for a manager planning business unit performance improvement,

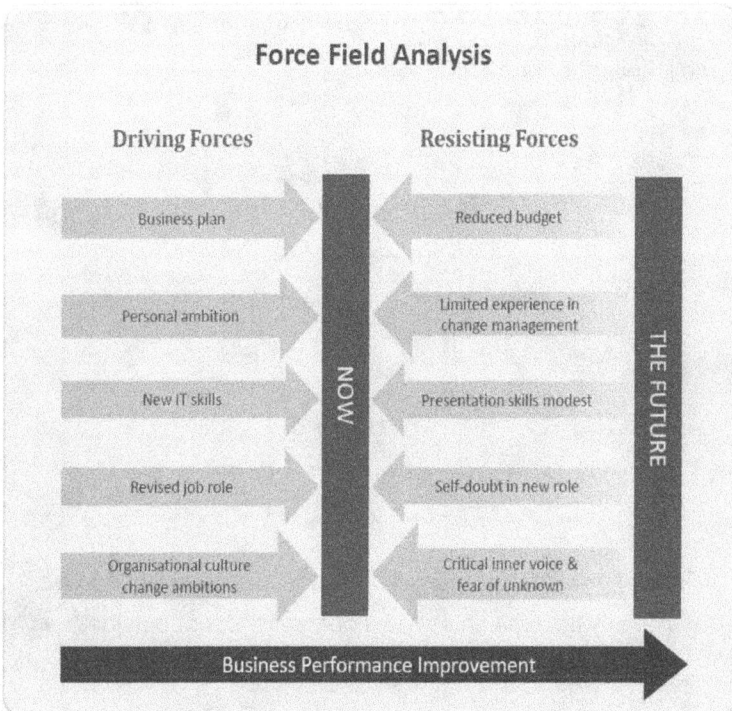

Force Field Analysis

Driving Forces | Resisting Forces

Business plan | Reduced budget
Personal ambition | Limited experience in change management
New IT skills | Presentation skills modest
Revised job role | Self-doubt in new role
Organisational culture change ambitions | Critical inner voice & fear of unknown

NOW | THE FUTURE

Business Performance Improvement

Imagine you are a recently appointed team manager, and this is your personal forcefield, carefully prepared. You would like to move from *Now state* to a developed level of performance, *Future state*.

Having a force field populated with drivers and resistors is helpful. It provides a *position statement*, which is informative, but on its own it changes nothing. To improve team performance, we need to ramp up the driving forces, or lessen the influence of the resisting forces.

What are the forces at work in your team's performance? Think about your management ambitions and draw a forcefield. Add in the Drivers and Resistors.

So, how to use the forcefield? How can we move from *Now state* to *Future state*?

- Should we increase the Driving Forces? No.
- Should we reduce the Resisting Forces? Yes (see **Resistor busting**).

Further reading

Field theory in social science | Harper, 1951 | Lewin, K.

Lewin's Force Field Analysis (Change Management) | Change Management

Insight, November 2019 | Tahir, U. | https://changemanagementinsight. com/lewins-force-field-analysis-change- management/

Framing and Reframing

"Today I escaped from anxiety. Or no, I discarded it because it was within me, in my own perceptions, not outside."

– Marcus Aurelius, Meditations

The thinking frame we put around circumstances has massive effect on how we feel and act (see **Emotional choice**).

The way a manager 'frames' events is important. If a messenger's glass is half empty, be sure the audience will feel the same way. If the glass is half full, you stand a chance of influencing your audience positively. Positive framing plays an important role in shaping team culture.

Aaron Beck (1979), the psychiatrist, developed what he called cognitive restructuring. It proved valuable for patients experiencing depressive episodes. He encouraged people to shift their mindsets from negative, disempowering thinking habits to more positive patterns of thought about the same set of circumstances. The more generalised, non-clinical, version of cognitive restructuring became known as *cognitive reframing*, or simply, *reframing*.

- **Framing**, influences an audience with a positive perspective on a situation.
- **Reframing**, influences team members through a positive perspective on negative thoughts and comments.

Here are some workplace situations you can use to practice reframing skills,

Circumstance, Thought, Comment	Frame or Reframe
"Oh no! We've made a terrible mistake and the customer is annoyed."	"Ok, we have a chance here to add some real value to the customer by showing how much we care about our mistake. We can also review our systems and processes to make mistakes less likely in future."
"The new Document Management System will be difficult to grasp."	"Once it's up and running the new Document Management System will save lots of time and free us up for fun activities!"
A unit manager reports in long-term sick	"Ok, this gives me a chance to up-skill another team member – it will be great for increasing team flexibility and giving someone an opportunity."

The more you practice framing and reframing, the more adept you'll become in its use. Make it habit-ual and many of life's frustrations will be minimised. I've been reframing situations for so long now its second nature to seek out positivity from events which initially may appear challenging. Remember the guidance from Epictetus,

> "It is not events which disturb men's minds, but how they think about events."

Here's a live example; I've just spent three days rewriting parts of this book. Earlier this week I carried out a health check on content and style and found over a dozen sections I was unhappy with; they clearly required re-work. Pretty daunting, eh? A major investment in time would be needed to make the necessary changes.

I'm not suggesting I wasn't initially frustrated, of course I was. It took only a few moments though to reframe the situation and celebrate the opportunity to make the manuscript *even better*. I decided, I planned, and I acted (see **Act**). Three days later I am feeling content knowing the changes have improved the text.

Start developing your framing and reframing skills and you'll be surprised how it positively affects your feelings about work, your colleagues' perceptions and morale, and productivity.

Further reading

Cognitive Therapy and the Emotional Disorders | Penguin, 1979 | Beck, A.T.

How Cognitive Reframing Works | Very Well Mind, May 2023 | Morin, A. | https://www.verywellmind.com/reframing-defined-2610419

Freedom questions

> "Sometimes I've believed as many as six impossible things before breakfast." *– Lewis Carroll*

Freedom questions ask about opportunity. They open up fresh thinking about what might be possible in a situation. *Freedom questions* have the magical ability to unlock imagination and release a person's hidden ambitions.

Linguists refer to these types of questions as *modal operators of possibility*. *Freedom questions* seems a more useable name. They are a useful management tool for breaking through restrictive thinking patterns (see **Can't to Can Belief Busting®**).

There are two *freedom questions:*

1. "What would happen if...?"
2. "What would have to happen...?" ("... to make that happen?")

For example:

- "What would happen if you took part in the software training day?"
- "What would happen if you <u>did</u> apply for the promotion?"
- "What would happen if you could make a great presentation?"
- "What would have to happen, for you to be comfortable with it?"

Freedom Questions give you a launch pad to explore possibilities further.

- "Ok, let's see if we can make it happen for you, shall we?"
- "Alright then, let's get this into your development plan."
- "Ok, we can come up with some options for that."

How could you employ freedom questions in your team management role? What would happen if this proved useful for you?

Further reading

Boomerang! Coach Your Team to Be the Best | Dandelion Digital, 2007 | Drake-Knight, N.

Audible https://www.audible.co.uk/pd/ Fast-Coaching-Audiobook/B07TTKD13T

Fast Coaching. The Complete Guide to New Code Continue & Begin® | Dandelion Digital, 2016 | Drake-Knight, N. |

The Motivation Agency | https:// themotivationagency-online.com/course/ begin

Friends, managing them at work

"I speak to everyone in the same way, whether he is the garbage man
or the president of the university." *– Albert Einstein*

Team leaders promoted from within may subsequently manage former peers, some of whom are good friends. It can feel awkward, I know because it happened to me as a young manager.

What are the issues at play here? The team leader may feel uncomfortable because there's now a requirement to be the 'boss' with friends, maybe even family? Employees might feel uncertain about how to communicate with a friend in a position of authority, someone who used to be *one of the guys*. The dynamic is different now.

Well, yes, it is. It doesn't mean friendships have to suffer though. It's helpful to have an open conversation about how the team leader and the friend, or friends, feel about the new arrangement. In the spirit of Johari (see **Johari, adapted for management**) being honest about hidden feelings is a healthy conversation to have. After all, you're friends.

I found, in one circumstance, having a conversation specifically about how my friend and I planned to relate to each other at work was healthy for our friendship and super productive professionally. We agreed on a few principles:

- We agreed our work relationship and our personal friendship were different dynamics.
- Our relationship would be founded on professional respect for each other. There would be no *"He won't mind if I do that thing, he's my chum"*.
- No *"Do this for me because we are mates"* or *"Let me get away with it because we are pals"*.
- We decided we would use our workplace standards as the reference point for discussions around performance. I don't think either of us expected benefits when we first sat down to discuss *How are we going to work together?* We did though, it felt healthy for us to have an independent marker to refer to. It became less about 'us' and more about 'the standard' (see **Explicit standards**).
- We would wear our business *masks* when in work, adopting our workplace alter egos, focussing on professional matters. We called it our *Work Heads*. We allowed ourselves downtime during lunchbreaks.
- Neither of us would allow our friendship to influence our workplace behaviour towards each other, or colleagues.
- Don't expect the manager to share confidential information.
- Don't expect the team member to reveal confidences from other team members.
- Once work was finished for the day, or week, we would resume our friendship style of communicating. Work stayed at work.

Having a set of when-at-work rules create clarity, and communication within a friendship at work will benefit. It means being respectful to each other.

It doesn't mean taking it easy as a team leader though. Far from it, professionalism demands performance be managed without fear or favour. If the team member friend is not delivering to work standards it's a professional matter, not a friendship issue. If they are not coming in at 9am, and think its ok because 'we are mates', it's an abuse of friendship.

Have a dedicated one-to-one conversation with your friend, or friends, and explore the rules you're going to respect. It may feel a bit weird, and it's worth the investment.

Further reading

The Business of Friendship: Making the Most of Our Relationships Where We Spend Most of Our Time | HarperCollins Leadership; Illustrated edition, 2020 | Nelson, S.

5 Things You Must Do When You Get Promoted Over A Friend | HuffPost, February 2022 | Torres, M. | https://www.huffingtonpost.co.uk/entry/friend-job-promotion-tips_l_5cbdf2bee4b0f7a84a732e0b

Future feeling

"When there's a goal, you feel able to overcome any problems as there's future success waiting for you". *– Alfred Adler*

Alfred Adler (1956), the psychologist, identified humans are 'teleological'; that is, we operate most effectively when oriented towards a goal, an objective or a specific ambition or outcome.

We are evolutionary, we move towards helpful change. When a future ambition forms in our mind as an imagined visual image (or video), an auditory representation (hearing sounds, voices, music), or a kinaesthetic experience (internal, or external feeling), an imagined smell, or an imagined taste, then the goal ambition becomes real for us. Our minds are masters of imagination (see **Imagination**).

When we ask a team member to think about *future feeling* and what, specifically, an achievement will stimulate for them, i.e., a *movement towards pleasure* feeling, or a *movement away from pain* feeling, we can influence the team member to act.

Future feeling is a powerful way to help people transport themselves to a future time and place when they are successfully performing new ambitions. Helping people access their imagination of future performance helps make achievement a teleological inevitability.

We can help people access *future feeling* simply, by including a carefully crafted question,

> "So, when you are doing this well/professionally/skilfully,
> how will you feel?"

Positive responses to this loaded question provide a manager with a platform for next steps (see **Can't to Can belief Busting** and **Freedom questions**), for example,

> "So, what would have to happen, to make that happen?"

The same principle applies to managers. How will you feel when you are successfully using the techniques offered in this book? What will be the positive feelings for you? So, what would have to happen, to make that happen?

Further reading

The Individual Psychology of Alfred Adler | Basic Books, 1956 | Adler, A.

How Thinking About the Future Makes Life More Meaningful | Mindful.org, May 2019 | Allen, S. | https://www.mindful.org/how-thinking-about-the-future-makes-life-more-meaningful/

Fuzzy language

> "It is in middles that extremes clash,
> where ambiguity restlessly rules." – *John Updike*

Fuzzy language is non-specific and imprecise. It has similarities to *generalisations* (see **Generalisations**); it has ambiguity. Fuzzy language is broader in its non-specificity as it includes other types of language, for example, *adverbs of frequency,* such as *sometimes, most of the time, occasionally.* These are imprecise terms, open to interpretation.

The danger of *fuzzy language* is the variation in understanding people have of the same word patterns. It highlights why precision and accuracy of language in teamwork is so important.

Clarification of meaning is critical to effective teamwork (see **English is Rubbish™**). Talented managers work hard to gain specificity in communication. They ask standard questions to gain accuracy,

- "What do you mean specifically?"
- "In what way?"
- "How precisely?"
- "When/where exactly?"
- "Who/which person specifically?"

Consider the table of words below and award a percentage score for a task undertaken by a team member, which you think each word represents. As an example, this task could be *product presentation in a retail store.*

For example, if you think *Not bad* means about halfway towards a required quality standard, award it a score of 50%, where 100% is an exact representation of expected standard. Other members of your team may think *Not bad* means 30%. Explore how you have differed perceptions of the same word or phrase. It's a great way to illustrate *fuzzy language.*

Product Presentation

Not bad	Pretty good	Excellent	It's OK
About right	Really good	Fine	Not quite up to standard
Reasonable	Not great	Almost there	Perfect

If you are familiar with retailing, you may be thinking *"Hang on, what are the quality standards for product presentation in this store?"* (see **Explicit standards**). If so, you are on the right track towards finding a reference point for performance measurement.

In this retail scenario, store standards are likely to form the basis for assessment. Communication becomes less fuzzy when performance is measured against clearly defined expectations of work, for example,

> "Point of Sale (POS) materials are to be displayed in line with latest Standards Operating Procedures (SOPs)."

Precise assessment then becomes possible, measured against explicitly described standards of performance. Managers and team members can identify which specific element(s) within the SOPs for POS materials have been complied with, and which, specifically, have not. Fuzzy language is minimised.

Using precise language is a skill for managers to develop, and one to encourage within a working group.

Further reading

Slippery terms: do you and I mean the same thing? | Vervago, 2020 | https://www. vervago.com/slippery-terms-do-you-and-i-mean-the-same-thing/

Definition and Examples of Vagueness in Language | Thought.Co, September 2018 | Nordquist, R. | https://www.thoughtco. com/vagueness-language-1692483

G

Games people play

Behaviours emerge in teamwork and organisational management which are roles, or *Games*, adopted to achieve personal benefit. Each role has a purpose, sometimes consciously employed, sometimes unconscious. Eric Berne (1968), the originator of *Transactional Analysis*, highlighted the nature of common games.

Here are typical Games played by employees (and managers?) working in a team,

1. *Stay quiet in meetings.* I don't want to contribute. I feel vulnerable in a group. Quietness minimises risk.
2. *Avoidance of task.* I'm not that kind of person. I'm not cut out for it. I feel threatened.
3. *Joker.* If I mess about and be funny, I can gain popularity. It gives me protection.
4. *Late night emails.* Look how hard I'm working.
5. *Social media posts.* See, I'm successful and happy! Aren't you envious of me?
6. *Dinosaur.* I've been operating like this for decades. I'm not going to change now, so don't ask. I feel uncomfortable operating in new ways. It makes me feel uncertain.

7. *Just Enough.* I'll do the minimum, and no more, to stay out of trouble (see **Being comfortable, dangers of**).

8. *Persecutor.* I am better than you. You are inferior. It makes me feel good.

9. *Rescuer.* I know more than you. You need me. I feel superior.

10. *Victim, or PLOM (poor little old me).* I am inadequate, you are better than me. Please have pity and be kind to me.

11. *Blemish.* You're fine except for a minor blemish – hair style, clothes, ability to achieve a task, communication style, chink in your armour… which spoils everything.

12. *Wooden Leg.* Surely you can't expect much from me when I have such a handicap – homelife, education, background…

13. *Inexperience.* I've never done it, so you can't ask me to step so far outside my comfort zone. Ask someone else.

14. *Sick.* You'll have to take into account I am feeling so ill.

15. *Best Interest.* I think you're gullible enough to believe my proposal is for your benefit.

16. *Now I've got you!* I've caught you making a mistake and now you're going to suffer.

17. *Deflector.* There are all these reasons why I haven't been able to deliver. There's always a reason.

18. *Avoider.* I hated school so you can't expect me to go on a training course.

Can you think of 2 more to make it 20?

Effective team managers recognise people's Games and challenge them appropriately. Exploring the motivation behind an employee's Game is helpful in uncovering the root cause (see **Root cause analysis**) of unhelpful behaviour patterns. There is always a reason, either conscious or unconscious, stimulated by an urge for feeling, or a wish to avoid feeling (see **Emotional Drivers™**).

A note of caution; beware your own Games!

Further reading

Games People Play: The Psychology of Human Relationships | Penguin, 1968 | Berne, E.

What Do You Say After You Say Hello: Gain control of your conversations and relationships | Corgi, 2018 | Berne, E.

Generalisations

> "To generalize is to be an idiot. To particularize is the alone distinction of merit. General knowledges are those knowledges that idiots possess." – *William Blake*

Generalisations are collective patterns of speech or written communication. They are non-specific sweeping comments minimising detail. Generalisations are an over-simplification of ideas. They include the set of universal quantifier patterns (see **Universal quantifiers**) *never, always, no-one, nobody, nothing, everything, all, none, totally, completely,* and others.

Here are examples of generalisation common in management and business, with the final example followed by a useful *generalisation challenge* question. Notice how speakers have chosen broad propositions, avoiding detail,

"We all love away days."

"Employees prefer it the old way."

"None of the managers know what they are talking about."

"Customers don't like change."

"Everyone knows what this about."

"Younger people don't want to get involved."

"It's too much – too little – too late – too (anything)."

"Every time it's mentioned you always get completely negative about everything."

"Software has a bad name around here."

Generalisation challenge question,

"Which software, specifically? A bad name with who, specifically? In what way?"

As with deletion and distortion, *generalisation challenging* is a practical skill for people managers.

Further reading

The Structure of Magic: A Book about Language and Therapy, Volume 1 | Bandler, R., Grinder, J. | Science and Behavior Books, 1975

Risks and Benefits of Generalizations | Life Well and Flourish | Van Slyke, C. | https://www.livewellandflourish.com/blog/risks-and-benefits-of-generalizations/

Get Even Better Ats (GEBAs)

"You cannot change your destination overnight, but you can change your direction overnight. If you want to reach your goals and fulfil your potential, become intentional about your personal growth. It will change your life." *– Jim Rohn*

In preparation for the first session of a 121 coaching intervention, I ask managers to think about what they would like to get *even* better at. We refer to these development areas as *GEBAs (jee-bahs)*. Typical GEBAs might be,

- GEBA 1 – giving formal presentations.
- GEBA 2 – managing conflict.
- GEBA 3 – communicating directly with senior managers.

GEBA topics are best kept to a small number, ideally three or less. Working on a long list of personal development ambitions is likely to be counterproductive; the conscious mind has limited capacity (see **Desktop of the mind**).

Once a set of GEBAs is clearly identified, we use coaching methods to help the coachee progress. GEBAs are great because the name label itself (*Get Even Better At*) suggests at least some degree of existing competency. This is compatible with the Continue and Begin Ltd philosophy of growing capability from a starting platform of positivity,

"I'm ok at (the skill); I'd like to be even better at it".

What are the GEBAs you would like to work on?

Further reading

Management and Executive Coaching | https://continueandbegin.com

The Business Skills Handbook | Kogan Page, 2009 | Horn, R.

Get inside their world

"They're not going to come into my world.
I'll have to go into their world." *– Milton Erickson*

Understanding, guiding, and supporting team members is best conducted inside the world of the employee, then cross referenced to the business imperatives of the organisation. Connecting with a colleague is dependent on building a relationship (see **Rapport** and **Rapport, advanced skills**).

Milton Erickson (1976), the hypnotherapist, was a master of building relationships, and could achieve intimate levels of connection with clients within minutes. His strategy was to *go into their world*.

Carl Rogers (1980), the psychologist, had a similar outlook about understanding and connection,

> "It means entering into the private perceptual world of the other and becoming thoroughly at home in it… It means temporarily living in the other's life."

Whilst exploring talented *connectors*, there is one character I recommend readers investigate: Frank Farrelly (1974), creator of *Provocative Therapy*. I had the privilege of attending one of Frank's two-day workshops and was fortunate to sit alongside him at lunch one day. We talked about his work and our shared passion for motorcycling. He was 75 at the time and still riding, much to the concern of his wife, so he told me.

Frank's innovative style of helping clients included a devil's advocate approach. He would get inside their world, gain an empathetic understanding (see **Empathy**), and feign agreement with their impoverished view of the world, pretending to share their views. After a while the client would realise Frank was teasing with provocation wrapped up in humour and heaps of warmth. He made people laugh as he gently taunted them. Clients giggled at his silliness and fought back against his teasing criticism, defending themselves, and breaking free of their restrictive thinking patterns.

Over lunch I shared how, during practice sessions, I was struggling to make his provocative therapy method work, I was clearly not getting inside the world of fellow delegates, acting as clients. I had been working hard to follow Frank's process and couldn't understand why I was missing the mark. I will always remember his reply,

> "Ah, you forgot… a twinkle in your eye… a smile around your lips… and an open heart".

After lunch, I took his advice, adopted Frank's non-verbal communication patterns, and achieved magical results. Remarkable.

Frank died in 2013. He left behind a legacy of how to connect with people. As he said about his mentor Carl Rogers, so I say about Frank, *"It was a blessing to know him."* What a wonderful man.

To be an effective manager of people it helps to make *connecting* a habit. Perceptive managers make efforts to understand their colleagues. Get inside their world.

Further reading

A Way of Being | Houghton Mifflin, 1980 | Rogers, C.

Provocative Therapy | Meta Publications, 1974 | Farrelly, F., Brandsma, J.

Hypnotic Realities: The Induction od Clinical Hypnosis and Forms of Indirect Suggestion | Irvington, 1976 | Erickson, M.H., Rossi, E.l., Rossi, S.I.

Goal Mapping® by Brian Mayne

"Goal Mapping® – an amazingly simple, yet extremely powerful way of setting and achieving and goals." – Brian Mayne

My good friend Brian Mayne is the creator of *Goal Mapping®*, an innovative approach to planning, implementing, and achieving a defined goal.

Most personal goals are driven by a desire to move away from pain or to move towards pleasure (see **Emotional Drivers™**). By committing goals to paper, a direct message is sent to our unconscious mind. The written text of goals works well for our left brain, the hemisphere of logical and analytical processing. However, it is difficult to recall the written word. Our brains are much better at recalling information stored visually in pictures and images.

Goal Mapping® requires left brain writing and right brain pictures which we can mentally photograph and use as reference and reminder. You can read, and hear, about Goal Mapping® at Brian's website www.goal mapping.com

At the top of the Goal Map® is the leverage to make the goal happen. The *Why?* question explores the underpinning personal driver to achieve the goal. It helps stimulate and sustain personal action.

As with root cause analysis (see **Root cause analysis** and **Why? Purpose and meaning**), repeated interrogation using the *Why?* question uncovers a core reason to act. These *feeling* drivers are the true motivators to achieve a goal ambition.

In this automotive sector example, an aftersales adviser's compelling obsession is to sell thirty (30) service plans in the three months period of July, August, and September (Q3 in the business' financial year). The adviser has drawn images as well as written words.

Notice how the main goal, to sell 30 service plans in Q3, is supported by a sub-goal, a steppingstone to his main ambition, in this case to sell 10 service plans in July. Actions required to help achieve the sub-goal and main goal are described sequentially, from bottom upwards, on the left side of the tree trunk. The person or people (including himself) who can help the aftersales adviser with each of the actions, is described to the right of the tree trunk. In both cases, time scoping, humour, and visual stimulus in the form of illustrations, are used to make the ideas memorable. The quality of drawing is irrelevant, although making the drawings as silly as possible seems to aid impact for some goalmappers.

Motivation to act is created by emotional leverage uncovered by repeatedly asking himself *"Why is this important to me?"* – in this case, personal pride in achieving his ambition. In the drawing, the goalmapper's ears are *puffed up with pride!*

Brian's Goal Mapping® approach has been proven over many years and continues to stimulate ambitious planning and goal achievements for people worldwide.

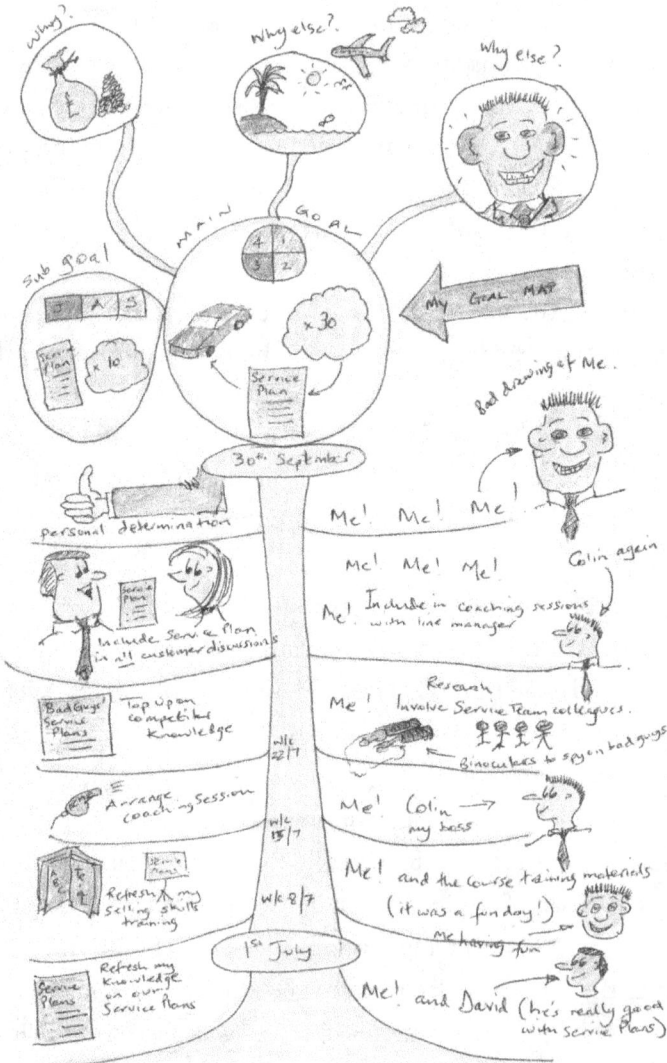

Further reading

Goal Mapping® | Watkins Publishing, 2020 | Mayne, B.

Self Mapping | Watkins Publishing, 2009 | Mayne, B

Life Mapping | Vermilion, 2003 | Mayne, B., Mayne, S.

Good and less good

"For what you see and what you hear depends a great deal on where you are standing. It also depends on what sort of person you are."

– C.S. Lewis

In the 1990s I worked as a consultant in the Former Soviet Union (FSU), in Poland, Slovakia and the former East Germany. I helped managers of former communist state enterprises understand the new free market economy. In the early days, I operated through an intermediary, Mariusz, a young graduate of Poznan University. Mariusz was full of energy and optimism. He embraced the new capitalism with relish and boundless enthusiasm.

Our first assignment was in Kalisz, west of Lodz (pronounced *wudge*). We were to run a business seminar the following day for senior managers from the local area, or Voivodeship. We were at Mariusz's dacha on a piece of land outside the town, drinking vodka and eating Polish sausage. We chatted about the adventure ahead.

"Mariusz, how many of the managers tomorrow can speak English?"

"Some of them..." Mariusz said, "Hmmm...their English is good. And some of them... hmmm... their English is... hmmm... less good."

The next day I met the managers. I could converse with those whose English was good. The managers with less good English? Well, my Polish was better than their English. Taka prawda! Mariusz habitually used this language pattern, *X good* and *Y less good.* It was a repeating pattern in his communication. For Mariusz, things were positive or less positive, helpful, or less helpful, good value or less good value. There was no *bad* for Mariusz; only *less good.* I was impressed by his positive framing and reframing (see **Framing and reframing**).

- Good and less good
- Productive and less productive
- Skilled and less skilled
- Informative and less informative
- Helpful and less helpful

You can make your own versions to suit your environment. How you think, how you talk and how you behave, whether with positivity, with stoicism (see **Stoicism**), or with negativity; these factors will determine your performance.

Good and *less good*. How could you apply this positivity framing in *your* role as a team manager?

Further reading

The Power of Positive Thinking | Touchstone; Reprint Edition, 2003 | Peale, N.V.

Awaken The Giant Within: How to Take Immediate Control of Your Mental, Emotional, Physical and Financial Life | Simon & Schuster, 2001 | Robbins, A.

H

Habit

"We are what we repeatedly do, therefore excellence
is not an act, but a habit." – *Aristotle*

High achievers sustain outstanding performances through habit; their
actions and behaviours become *habit-ual*. Habits are established or changed
through our active choice. We can select our belief systems and change our
habits to support them (see **Beliefs, you can choose or change**).

Hypnotherapists talk about engrams, grooves in the mind, created by
consistent behaviours and thinking patterns, like repeated walking along a
grassy area. Eventually a path is formed. Repeating your patterns over time
results in embedded, repetitive behaviours – habits. You can change them if
you wish.

The first step to changing a habit is to identify it as so. What are the
things you do, say, or think, which have evolved into habit?

- How you drive or use public transport.
- How you greet colleagues.
- How you answer the phone.
- The language patterns you use.
- How you dress and groom.
- What and how you eat at work.
- How you think (internal dialogue) as you prepare for a meeting.
- What you do in your non-work time.

- How you care for your body.
- How you care for your mind.

There was a time in the past where, in each of the above contexts, you selected what you thought was the most appropriate behaviour. Your choice will have been stimulated, directly or indirectly, by an *Emotional Driver*™ encouraging you to move towards comfort, or to move away from potential pain (see **Emotional Drivers**™).

After a while, your behaviour choice became an automatic stimulus-response pattern and, hey presto, a habit was formed.

Think about your habits in your role as a manager. Which are still supporting you and your team to perform at the optimum level? Which could do with a review? Which are certainly not helping? Which could do with being reset to a new empowering habit?

Remember, you can choose or change your habits.

Further reading

The Power of Habit. Why we do what we do and how to change | Random House, 2013 | Duhigg, C.

Atomic Habits | Random House Business, 2018 | Clear, J.

Hallucinations of meaning

"There are things known and there are things unknown, and in between are the doors of perception." *– Aldous Huxley*

When we communicate with another person, we hallucinate our meaning and theirs.

Consider this management situation; you are delegating to a colleague the requirements for an offsite team awayday. You have a set of ambitions for the type of venue, how you think the event meeting room should be laid out, the size and shape of room, lighting, the tables and chairs, your expectations for refreshments throughout the day and the calibre of customer experience from the venue.

You have a hallucination in your mind, vivid and lucid, of what you expect and require from a provider. You explain your thinking to a team colleague to whom you'll delegate the awayday project. Do you think your colleague has the same hallucination as you? No, they have not; they have their own perceptions of what you mean, through which they then create their own hallucinated version.

Manager hallucination   Team member hallucination

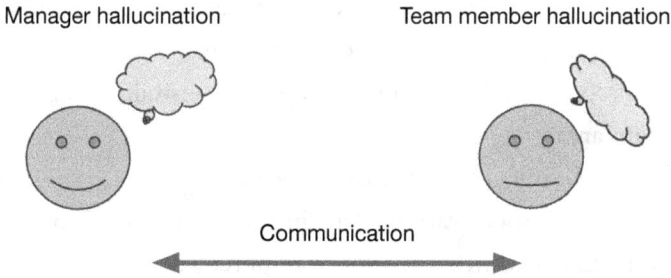

Communication

This is why misunderstandings take place, why team member delivery doesn't match your expectations.

The flipside is true as well. When a colleague is explaining a scenario to you, it's necessary for you to form your own imagined hallucination from their descriptions. Hallucinations are individualistic and unlikely to be mirrored by a co-communicator.

Shrewd managers are alert to the dangers of differing hallucinations. Precision language and questioning aids effective management (see **English is Rubbish™, Deletion, Distortion,** and **Generalisation**).

Further reading

Meerkat Selling | Dandelion Digital, 2008 | Drake-Knight, N.

The Motivation Agency | https://themotivationagency-online.com/course/meerkat

Understanding Other People: The Five Secrets to Human Behavior | ATA Press, 2009 | Flaxington, B.D.

Halo and horns

"We don't know where our first impressions come from or precisely
what they mean, so we don't always appreciate their fragility."
– Malcolm Gladwell

Managing selection and recruitment is a high risk, high benefit activity.
Getting recruitment right, or *less right*, has implications for team dynamics
and subsequent performance.

A professional hiring procedure will help. Protocols differ from one
organisation to another. Most human resource professionals will propose at
least some of the following preliminary actions:

- Conduct job role evaluation, agree post requirement, and outline scope.
- Create a job description (specification) to include job title, role
  purpose, reporting lines, main areas of responsibility, key tasks within
  each main area.
- Build a set of competences for the job role.
- Create a person specification, detailing likely attributes of a successful
  applicant, described in categories of required, desirable and if useful to
  do so, contra-indicators.
- Shortlist candidates from applications, or from agency recommendation.
- Conduct online skills assessments or job simulation exercises.
- Validate skills and check credentials.
- Invite for initial interview online, telephone, or in person.
- Conduct assessment at activity centre; or invite for a next stage interview.
- At some point recruitment decision makers will come face-to-face with
  candidates. It is at this stage where the *halo-and-horns effect* is most common.

We are programmed as mammals to make rapid assessments about survival.
We evaluate people we meet for the first time as potential threats or allies;
it is part of our unconscious wiring. We use our lifetime of experience to
assess the applicant's verbal and nonverbal clues. We calculate, very quickly,
whether the candidate in front of us is a threat and not right for our *tribe*,
(has *horns*, could cause damage) or a potential ally (has a *halo*, will help our
tribe, could make us stronger).

I participate in numerous assessment centres, helping clients recruit key players. I've lost count of the times senior and middle managers ignore the good preliminary work of establishing role competencies and a detailed person specification. They default to mammalian *halo-and-horns* perceptions and call it *instinct*, or *gut feel* – when it is evidently cognitive bias (see **Cognitive bias**).

It makes sense to use your management experience to aid candidate questioning, of course. My guidance to you is, be mindful of cognitive bias and the *halo-and-horns* effect.

Further reading

Blink: The Power of Thinking Without Thinking | Penguin, 2006 | Gladwell, M.

How To Stop the Halo and Horns Effect in Hiring and Reduce Unconscious Bias | Vervoe, May 2022 | Ross, L. | https://vervoe.com/halo-and-horns-effect-in-hiring/

Health and safety management

"When anyone asks me how I can best describe my experiences of nearly forty years at sea I merely say uneventful. Of course, there have been Winter gales and storms and fog and the like, but in all my experience I have never been in an accident of any sort worth speaking about." *– Captain E.J. Smith, RMS Titanic*

For several years I was a trades union tutor, training union representatives from a range of industry sectors. Health and safety at work is still an area of interest for me.

Protecting the safety, health and welfare of team members is a fundamental role for professional managers. In the UK the *Health and Safety at Work Act 1974 (HASAWA)* is the relevant legislation in force. Other countries have similar laws to protect employees. The HASAWA is a piece of *criminal* legislation. Breaches of this law can lead to prosecution of organisations and individuals, including managers.

In the UK, at least, subsidiary regulations and statutory instruments relate to specific elements of safe working practices, all of which fall under the HASAWA umbrella law, for example,

- The Management of Health and Safety at Work Regulations 1999
- The Workplace (Health, Safety and Welfare) Regulations 1992
- The Health and Safety (Display Screen Equipment) Regulations 1992
- The Personal Protective Equipment at Work Regulations 1992
- The Manual Handling Operations Regulations 1992
- The Provision and Use of Work Equipment Regulations 1998
- The Reporting of Injuries, Diseases and Dangerous Occurrences Regulations 1995

Each organisation employing five or more staff are required to provide a policy statement setting out senior management's commitment to health and safety, with an organisational plan for its management, and the arrangements put in place for ensuring the implementation of the policy and plan.

Team managers have a responsibility, as part of the policy, organisation, and arrangements, to care for the wellbeing of their team members whilst at work. HASAWA Section 2 states,

"It shall be the duty of every employer to ensure, so far as is reasonably practicable, the health, safety and welfare at work of all his employees."

To achieve this, employers need to:

- Provide and maintain safe plant and equipment.
- Ensure safe use, handling storage and transportation of any articles substances and materials used during work.
- Ensure the health and safety of their employees, by providing adequate information, instruction, training, and supervision as required.

- Provide and maintain a safe working environment, using safe systems of work, and
- Provide adequate welfare facilities such as toilets, first aid facilities and changing rooms, along with safe maintained access and egress.

Employers have a duty of care to their employees. They are accountable for health, safety, and welfare. Operational managers, in all sectors and industries, have a cascaded responsibility to comply with these requirements. Conducting a risk assessment of each employee's role is a fundamental management function.

It is LAW.

What are you doing to ensure your team members are safe, remain healthy, and have their welfare cared for whilst working in your team? If you are not sure, seek guidance.

Further reading

Managing for health and safety (HSG65) | Health and Safety Executive, 2013 | https://www.hse.gov.uk/pubns/books/HSG65.htm

Health & Safety – Reps Guide | TUC Workplace Manual, April 2021 | Trades Union Congress | https://www.tuc.org.uk/resource/health-and-safety-reps-guide

Hope and the Hope Factor

"The leader has to be practical and a realist, yet must talk the language of the visionary and the idealist." *– Eric Hoffer*

Motivation is driven by hope. Hope focuses on the future, of what is to come, of positive outcomes, of the good feelings we will experience when we achieve our goals (see **Emotional Drivers™**).

Hope runs half a step behind Maslow's hierarchy of needs; we hope to gain physiological comfort, we hope for security, we hope for warm relationships, we hope to further develop our self-esteem and sense of feel good, and we hope for personal growth to become the best version of ourselves. We hope for these ambitions to be satisfied. Hope is a powerful impetus for action.

Eric Hoffer (1951) knew about hope. In his insightful book *The True Believer* he outlined how hope has been the driving force behind some of humankind's most radical periods in history, and behind the emergence of leaders promising better times in the future.

Inspirational managers understand the importance of mapping out a compelling future for team members, a future of growth, of improvement, and achievement. Maybe a future of better conditions.

Business plans map out an organisational development plan. But what does this mean for team members? What is the Hope Factor for each employee?

What are the hope drivers in your team?

Further reading

The True Believer, Thoughts on the Nature of Mass Movements | Harper Brothers, 1951 | Hoffer, E.

Having Hope: Motivator, Comfort, or a Curse? | Mind Tools, April 2022 | Conradie, Y. | https://www.mindtools.com/blog/ having-hope-motivator-comfort-curse-mttalk/

The Theory of Human Motivation | Maslow, A., and Hudson, T.W. | Historical Recordings, 2020

Horizon scanning

"It is always wise to look ahead, but difficult to look further than you can see." *– Winston Churchill*

Future scoping, anticipating, opportunity spotting and risk analysis; these considerations are the mark of an insightful manager. Horizon scanning is not just for senior managers, in today's fast changing world of work front line managers need to stay ahead of the game at operational level. What works today may not work tomorrow.

The Institute of Risk Management (www.theirm.org) comments,

"If organisations manage their operations on the basis that previous success will ensure the future success of their business or operation, they are building-in failure through an inability to adapt to the changing environment. The world today is increasingly subjected to disruptive change. Present and future conditions are changing increasingly quickly due to interconnected activities and events, and decision making has become more complex as a result".

Horizon scanning is a useful activity in any sector. In my experience of growing managers and leaders, the ability to anticipate evolution is what identifies an individual as exceptional. These characters are prime candidates for fast-track career development.

At team management level horizon scanning could be an internal activity, considering the likely developments and changes within your organisation. In wider terms, contextual analysis using the PESTLE framework – political, economic, social, technological, legal, environmental – helps think through how the future may be influenced by external factors (see **PESTLE** and **Looking out the window thinking**).

In *scenario planning* games, managers (ideally with engagement from team members) construct multiple possible futures events, creating circumstances to consider and plan for. These may include plans for emergencies of danger or threat. They may equally consider preparedness for opportunity.

Contingency plans for imaginary futures may never be used. However, it is a truism of recent history to know externally driven sudden change is always a possibility.

Professional managers think about 'what ifs' and have a series of game plans ready to draw upon if needed. They think ahead, scan the horizon; and consider what *could* happen during the next quarter, this year, next year, or further ahead?

How could you incorporate horizon scanning into your management thinking?

Further reading

Horizon Scanning: A Practitioner's Guide | Institute of Risk Management, 2018 | https://www.theirm.org/news/horizon-scanning-a-practitioners-guide-revealed-at-irm-leaders/

See Sooner, Act Faster: How Vigilant Leaders Thrive in an Era of Digital Turbulence | The MIT Press, 2019 | Day, G.S., Schoemaker, P.J.H.

Huddles

"Talent wins games, but teamwork and intelligence
win championships." – *Michael Jordan*

A huddle is a short team meeting, usually of 10 minutes or less, conducted stood up. Standing up combined with brevity sends a strong message of the huddle being in preparation for impending action.

Huddles are usually convened at the beginning of each working day, facilitated by a huddle leader. A set time for each huddle encourages prompt attendance from the full team. Some organisations like to rotate the leadership role, so all team members feel engaged in the process. A huddle primes the work team for the day ahead with messages about topical items including performance measures, quality metrics and process changes. In a 24-hour service or manufacturing facility the huddle may act as a useful handover platform from shift to shift.

Huddles are particularly effective in maintaining momentum during project management roll out (see **Scrums and sprints**).

Good huddles incorporate visual management (see **Visual management and Kanban**) in the form of visual boards to illustrate relevant information and record comments from team members. This way, both audible and visual senses are involved in information processing and retention. Digital boards provide even greater flexibility and allow remote workers to be involved in distance huddles. Smart boards, handheld or wall mounted, allow for digital presentation of information and easy access to historical data on specific projects. Boards can also be used for alerts and notifications throughout the working day.

Some enterprises require huddle members to contribute a concern or a celebration from the previous workday. Celebrations help the team feel good, whereas problems or quality issues are noted on the visual board and addressed as a management activity *after* the huddle.

Effective huddles are quick, targeted and end with a thank you from the huddle leader and a call to action for the day. *"Ok, let's get to work!"*

Further reading

The Toyota Way: 14 Management Principles from the World's Greatest Manufacturer | McGraw-Hill, 2004 | Liker, J.

6 Team Huddle Ideas for the Workplace (With Tips) | Indeed | Editorial team, March 2023 | https://www.indeed.com/career-advice/career-development/team-huddle-

Can Huddles Really Help? | NHS England Blog, March 2019 | Shanmugalingam, S. | https://www.england.nhs.uk/blog/can-huddles-really-help/

Human leadership

"Friends show their love in times of trouble, not happiness." *– Euripides*

'Human' leadership recognises the interest of the person being led.

For team managers, human leadership means adopting an employee centred approach, considering the wellbeing of the collective team, and individuals within it. There are patterns here with the work of John Adair and his *Action Centred Leadership*, more commonly known as the 3 Circles leadership model (see **Management style**). Adair (2007) proposed effective leadership should balance task achievement ambitions with an equal focus on team harmony, and individual performance and welfare.

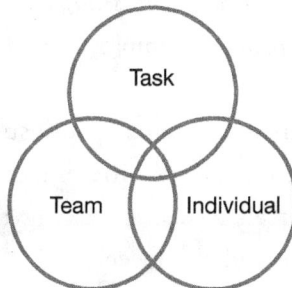

Today, team managers are still expected to maintain a balance between these three components of leadership. In many organisations, emphasis is shifting towards focus on people as the secret to operational success. Culture has been evolving rapidly in the workplace, with employees now less likely to thrive in a command-and-control environment, than in previous times.

For example, the demographic group known as *Generation Z, Gen Z,* or *Zoomers,* (born between 1997 and 2012) appear to have values and belief systems at odds with previously established working practices. Ethical issues, environmental concerns, and a new perspective on the purpose of work, have all been raised by a Gen Z workforce unafraid to express their expectations of an employer.

In addition, the impact of Covid-19 has created a new dynamic of workers reconsidering the importance of work within their lives. Lockdown, more time with family, and the health realities of the pandemic, caused some to reflect on humanistic factors. It seems, where there was previously an acceptance by employees of being *always-on* for work, this is now subsiding, with new priorities emerging beyond the world of employment.

For many, previously imposed requirements to work from home has morphed into a *work fusion* of hybrid working, with a mix of online remote work and communication, and a partial physical presence in the workplace. Lines between work and home have become blurred. For some this works, for others there is push back.

Arguments exist across sectors as to which working model is most effective; but most effective for whom? The organisation? The customer, internal or external? The team manager? Or the employee?

Increasingly, workers seek an employment experience in which they feel respected, cared for, and listened to. They want empathy and understanding from their employer. They expect work to be adaptive, to fit with their home lives, reflecting their values about *what's important.* There's a demand for integrity and authenticity from their employers and managers; a requirement for genuineness and 'no bull'.

No surprise then, human resource specialists, globally, are responding to labour markets demanding a different approach to employment. Organisational leaders, at all levels, are facing the reality of a changed dynamic between employer and employee.

Research conducted by Gartner in 2022 included consultation with HR managers, and a separate project exploring employee perspectives. Findings from the research highlighted expectations and requirements from today's workforce. Gartner suggest three components of Human Leadership,

1. Authentic (see Authentic team management)

- Being genuine, bringing your true self to the role of manager.
- Being honest about what is relevant.
- Being transparent and open, so far as commercial confidentiality allows.
- Sharing thoughts, feelings, and vulnerabilities with colleagues.

2. Empathetic (see Empathy and Emotional Intelligence [EQ])

- Being genuinely concerned about the wellbeing of team members, in good times and difficulty.
- Being caring and considerate, showing emotional intelligence.
- Recognising employees' concerns beyond the workplace, in family, social and domestic matters.
- Understanding and respecting the values and belief systems of each colleague.

3. Adaptive (see Adaptive team management)

- Reshaping working practices to suit the professional and personal needs of team members.
- Being flexible in management style relative to individual preferences.
- Accommodate work location, times, and schedules, to best fit the uniqueness of each employee.
- Be ready to modify workflow design as each team members' circumstances evolve.

How authentic are you in your leadership style? How empathetic? How adaptive?

Think about you and your team. Celebrate your human leadership successes. If gaps exist in your human leadership behaviours, what would you like to do differently, or even better?

Further reading

How to Grow Leaders: The seven key principles of effective leadership development. | Kogan page, 2007 | Adair, J.

The 3 Qualities You Need To Be A Really Effective Leader | Gartner, October | Turner, J. | https://www.gartner.com/en/articles/the-3-qualities-you-need-to-be-a-really-effective-leader

Gartner HR Research Identifies Human Leadership as the Next Evolution of Leadership | Gartner Newsroom, June 2022 |

https://www.gartner.com/en/newsroom/press-releases/06-23-22-gartner-hr-research-identifies-human-leadership-as-the-next-evolution-of-leadership

Human Leadership: What It Looks Like, And Why We Need It In The 21st Century | Forbes, November 2018 | Pir, S. | https://www.forbes.com/sites/sesilpir/2018/11/28/human-leadership-what-it-looks-like-and-why-we-need-it-in-the-21st-century/?sh=f990f2a29143

I

I Know You Don't Know

*"Although men are accused of not knowing their own weakness,
yet perhaps few know their own strength. It is in men as in soils,
where sometimes there is a vein of gold which the owner knows not of."*
– Johnathan Swift

Helping colleagues escape from their limiting belief patterns is occasionally thwarted by the blocking tactic *"Erm, I dunno"*.

When a colleague gets stuck in a negative mind set and is low on resourcefulness, it feels easier for them to rebuff questioning with a simple forward defensive (a cricketing term) to fend off further questioning. Responding to questions about possibility with *"dunno"* is less irksome than thinking through strategies for personal change, and all those challenges associated with self-development.

Fortunately, there is a language pattern available to unlock *dunno* thinking,

> "I know you don't know… and if you *did* know… what do you think
> you could do?",

or,

> "I know you don't know… and if you *did* know… what do you think
> the answer might be?",

The response, many times in my experience, will be something along the lines of,

"Well, I suppose I could think about…",

and away we go!

You may need to ask the question a couple of times before it unlocks potential; expect another *"dunno"*, maybe two, before progress gets underway.

"I know you don't know…" is a language pattern to use whenever you hear *"dunno"* from someone stuck in a limiting belief pattern of *"I can't"* (see **Can't to Can Belief Busting®**).

Further reading

Boomerang! Coach Your Team to Be the Best | Dandelion Digital, 2007 | Drake-Knight, N.

Audible https://www.audible.co.uk/pd/ Fast-Coaching-Audiobook/B07TTKD13T

Fast Coaching. The Complete Guide to New Code Continue & Begin® | Dandelion Digital, 2016 | Drake-Knight, N. |

The Motivation Agency | https:// themotivationagency-online.com/course/ begin

I/Me ownership

"I do my thing and you do your thing.
I am not in this world to live up to your expectations
And you are not in this world to live up to mine.
You are you and I am I,
And if by chance we find each other, it's beautiful.
If not, it cannot be helped."

– Fritz Perls

Listen out for the *you* language pattern; the speakers who comment on some aspect of *self* by using the avoidance pronoun *you* during conversation. For example,

"What works for you, is to…"

"So, then what you think is…"

"The thing is... what you do is..."

"What happens is, you feel kind of frustrated..."

In the examples above the speaker is promoting a personally developed idea whilst dodging reference to ownership of it. It is an avoidance tactic to deflect responsibility.

I notice this pattern of communication when coaching managers and executives. There is a reluctance in some managers to own their thoughts and feelings. Managers avoid taking personal *I/me* responsibility. I bring this to their awareness. The surprise, and sometimes shock, of realising their avoidance of *I/me* responsibility is an eye-opener for many.

I encourage managers to grasp personal responsibility with enthusiasm.

"So, when you say, 'you', do you mean 'I'?"

"Erm, well, yes, I suppose I do."

When a person talks in the first person using *I/me* patterns, ownership becomes more obvious and controllable. It accelerates self-awareness. Gestalt therapy, developed by Fritz Perls (1969), suggests only when a person has awareness of their own thinking, feeling, and behaviours can they be ready to embark on personal change.

A manager is responsible for owning thoughts, feelings, emotions, and behaviours. Language use is a mirror, reflecting the degree to which the manager is transparent about ownership. Self-awareness is the starting point for good management learning programmes.

Further reading

In and Out the Garbage Pail | Real People Press, 1969 | Perls, F.S.

4 Reasons to Take Ownership of Your Feelings | Psychology Today, July 2021 | Firestone, L. | https://www.psychologytoday.com/us/blog/compassion-matters/202107/4-reasons-take-ownership-your-feelings

Imagination

"Imagination is more important than knowledge.
Knowledge is limited. Imagination encircles the world."

– Albert Einstein (apocryphal)

A therapist tutor once advised me,

"Nick, so long as we have our imaginations, we can really disturb
ourselves, or make ourselves feel good. Which would you prefer?"

A good point.

We use our imaginations throughout our day, often in the form of
daydreams. Imagination is a powerful mindtool. We can even *choose* what
we daydream about! We can make our daydreams seem real and choose the
path they take.

Hypnotherapists understand how to steer a patient through a daydream,
although the details of the 'story' remain within the mind of the dreamer.

You may wish to think about… sitting comfortably in in a beautiful
garden or pasture… the spring sunshine warm on your face, on your
arms, your hands, and on your legs… you can rest for a while…
enjoy the calmness… the warmth… the rejuvenating rays of the sun.
You can allow relaxation and comfort to flow through your body.
A refreshing drink is close by. You can breathe and exhale… at ease.
Maybe even close your eyes for a moment…

How we use our imagination is the key to achievement and satisfaction.
What if we used our imagination as a mains feed for our compelling goals?

We know from Alfred Adler (1956), humans work well towards defined goals; we are *teleological* in nature (see **Focus** and **Future feeling**).

We can allow our imagination to think about the management activities needed to achieve our professional ambitions.

Perhaps it's an imagined presentation to annual conference? Maybe a well-managed meeting? Or will you imagine a professionally facilitated performance review? Or a difficult conversation with a team member – being well prepared, conducted calmly, and with structure?

We can imagine a positive and compelling future scenario. We can visualise, clearly, a future reality, hear the good sounds, notice our internal feelings, physical touch, even the good things we can smell or taste. And we can intensify those senses by doubling them, by increasing volume, brightening the picture, turning up the colours, until we experience the imagined future as a virtual reality.

Once we have a strong experience imagined, we begin the process of taking the steps to reach our future ambition – taking massive, persistent action towards our healthy and compelling obsession.

What would you like to imagine?

Further reading

Hypnotic Language: Its Structure and Use | Crown House Publishing, 2009 | Burton, J., Bodenhamer, B.

Hypnotic Realities: The Induction od Clinical Hypnosis and Forms of Indirect Suggestion |

Irvington, 1976 | Erickson, M.H., Rossi, E.l., Rossi, S.I.

The Individual Psychology of Alfred Adler | Basic Books, 1956 | Adler, A.

Imposter syndrome

"If I have the belief that I can do it, I shall surely acquire the capacity to do it, even if I may not have it at the beginning." *– Mahatma Ghandi*

Imposter syndrome is common. Newly appointed managers I work with during 121 coaching sessions report feelings of anxiety on their ability to deliver, about their limited experience, about managing people who until recently were teammates; and worries about imaginary scenarios. *"Am I worthy?"* becomes a repeating, circular, thought process.

It's not only front-line managers who experience this phenomenon. Senior executives are prone to feelings of doubt about personal capability. I regularly meet with senior managers, even CEOs who share their feelings of anxiety about worthiness for the role they've found themselves in. Big bosses are just people.

In some cases, management appointments are made because of prowess in a technical skill or behaviour. It can be tough though; technical and managerial skills are different disciplines. New team leaders learn quickly about the differences between doing and managing. It is inevitable feelings of uncertainty and self-doubt emerge. I help managers acknowledge these feelings are *"To be expected"*.

The challenge is to overcome disempowering thinking, including the critical inner voice, and gradually build up confidence in how best to manage resources, including of course, people.

In my career, I can think of numerous managerial appointments, either as an internal appointee or joining a new organisation, where I felt these feelings of self-doubt. On occasions I felt guilt from my own mental construct of having 'blagged' the interview and recruitment process. I worried I had hoodwinked the selection panel to believe I was capable, when internally I had significant doubts. You know what though? On each occasion resourcefulness, adaptability, and a resilience to setbacks, helped build a degree of competence I had at times thought unlikely.

There were mistakes aplenty of course (to be expected!) and major learning points, about consultation, about decision making, and most of all about judgement. I learned by trial and numerous errors, by modelling experienced and successful managers, through formal management training, through mentoring, from reading. And most valuable of all, I listened to my team members, during open conversations where I made myself vulnerable to criticism.

You're going to feel uncertain sometimes, its normal. To be expected. And you'll hear your own self-criticism when you make mistakes, small, medium, or large. The reality is you're a fallible human being, and errors will be made. You can thank your critical inner voice for its well-intended commentary on your foul up, laugh at yourself and then listen to a healthier internal dialogue,

"Hmmm, I messed up. What have I learned from this I can use in the future?"

Management competence builds over time. You won't be a perfect manager immediately, nor will you ever be. I still screw up regularly (I've learned to laugh), all managers do. It's how you respond to the screw ups which defines your ability to grow and mature as a team manager.

Temporary imposter feelings are fine if combined with a healthy frame of thinking (see **Framing and reframing**). Feeling uncertain about a new role or responsibility is entirely normal. It's great because it means you're about to have a growth experience. Stretch means learning.

Further reading

Vogue editor Edward Enninful: 'Impostor syndrome is what drives me.' | The Observer, 4th September 2022 | Wiseman, E. | https://www. theguardian.com/fashion/2022/sep/04/ vogue-editor-edward-enninful-impostor-syndrome-is-what-drives-me

How To Identify Imposter Syndrome and Deal With It In The Workplace | Forbes, April 2023 | Pham, E. | https://www.forbes.com/ sites/forbesbusinesscouncil/2023/04/03/ how-to-identify-imposter-syndrome-and-deal-with-it-in-the-workplace/?sh=4012b1 e24264

Cricket legend Ebony Rainford-Brent: "Anyone can suffer from imposter syndrome – it's part of who we are". | The Independent, July 2023 | Carnegie, M. | https://www.independent.co.uk/ life-style/galaxy-the-ripple-effect/ imposter-syndrome-anxiety-mental-health-work-wellness-b2369161.html

Induction, preboarding, onboarding, reboarding

"What is there more kindly than the feeling between host and guest?"

– Aeschylus

The early weeks of a new role are critical for any team member. Joiners are in a heightened state of awareness, often ambitious and enthusiastic, mixed perhaps with uncertainty and anxiety. Reassurance and a smooth immersion into the organization, and the role, makes transition a positive experience for new starters. Team managers have a prime role to play.

Feelings of *contribution* are important for a recruit, driven by an urge to make a positive impact, and being recognized as adding value. When the integration phase goes well, a new employee becomes productive and contributes rapidly.

When early days go *less well*, a new starter's experience may affect personal wellbeing, with potential for an early departure. High turnover of staff during the first few months of engagement is common across sectors.

Supervisors and first line managers have responsibilities for successful induction and onboarding. There has been investment of resources in the recruitment process, and a collective *hope* for the new colleague to add value in contribution to the team. It would be odd, wouldn't it, if the team manager wasn't closely involved in making the new appointment a success?

Pre-boarding, induction and *onboarding* are terms used to describe activities during the early stages of a colleague's employment.

Preboarding

There's a prequel to induction and onboarding, known as *preboarding*. This is the period between job offer and first day in role, when a manager can help or hinder the integration experience for new starters. If we acknowledge the volatility of early employment and the potential for early exit, it makes sense to do everything practicable, to help the appointee feel good about their career choice, before start date.

Maintaining positive momentum and reassurance during the pre-start period helps minimise risks of a recruit getting cold feet or looking elsewhere, or to consider other offers. Remember, the employee-to-be is in a heightened state of awareness, already in the market for change, and therefore vulnerable to alternative career options. *Ghosting* is a term now used to describe a new hire who simply doesn't show up on their start date.

Team managers can secure the commitment of new starters. Communication immediately after appointment, and through the intervening period to first day, is a time for regular, positive contact. Sharing news about the team, its recent successes, current assignments, and forthcoming ambitions, all helps an appointee feel part of the work group.

Forwarding pre-employment documentation for completion, or relevant policy documents to digest, will help maintain focus. These are rather dull engagement activities. Far more enthusing is to invite the new colleague to join group sessions or social events, in advance of their start date, to get a feel for the team, and for the team to get to know their new co-worker.

Induction

The term *induction* usually refers to process familiarization, often the administrative elements of an employee's introduction, involving data capture and mandatory training. Typical topics covered by induction programmes include,

- Statutory employment legislation documents.
- Organisation charts.
- 'Welcome aboard' documents.
- The *Why?* purpose explained, understood, and committed to (see **Why? Purpose and meaning**).
- Values and behaviours review.
- Health and safety matters.
- Culture, explicitly described.
- Site tour, introductions to immediate colleagues and network contacts.
- Jargon buster reference source, explanations of abbreviations and acronyms.
- Holidays procedures.
- Time off in lieu management.
- Absenteeism and sickness administration.
- Employment and HRM policies and protocols.
- Payroll information.
- HR advisory services.
- Benefits packages and how to access them.
- Employee assistance support.
- Mentoring schemes.
- Uniforms or branded clothing.
- Social networks.
- Buddy colleague(s).

And then onto the job itself,

- Job role.
- Main job purpose.

- Main areas of responsibilities.
- Key tasks.
- Quality management.
- Reporting lines, formal and informal.
- Regular workflows, schedules, and timetables.
- Productivity ambitions.
- Guidance on how the new starter can answer the question, *"How can I self-assess whether I'm doing a good job, or missing the mark?"* (see **Explicit standards**).

Onboarding

Onboarding has a broader scope, beyond induction. It includes helping new starters learn about the wider team, organizational ambitions, and why the contribution of the new starter will be so crucial.

Onboarding involves,

- Selection.
- Offer.
- Agreement and appointment.
- Preboarding.
- Induction administration.
- Job role familiarization.
- Early days care.
- Achieving early successes.
- Building loyalty to the brand and the activities of the team.
- Networking across the wider organization (if relevant).
- Cultural familiarization.
- Team manager check-ins and informal keep-in-touch meetings, preferably with no set agenda, allowing free flow conversation about topics important to the new colleague (see **KIT meetings**).
- Identification of any *hygiene factors* causing difficulty for the employee (see **Motivation**).

Team manager considerations

A proven tactic for building new starters' confidence, during early days, is to ask for their objective assessment of what is working well in the team, and where opportunities exist. Objectivity from recruits lasts for a few months, at best, and then dissipates. The fresh perspective of a new colleague is an asset. Don't lose it, ask,

"Which parts of what we do, do you think is silly?"

"Where are the blockages?"

"What is slowing us down?"

"What is impacting on our quality?"

"Where do opportunities exist?"

"What should we change?"

Even short-lived objectivity offers an opportunity for mini evaluations of what is working well, and what could be working better (see **Value Stream Mapping**).

Seek out early 'win' opportunities for the new hire. Where possible, provide chances for them to prove they are adding value. Early successes minimize the likelihood of *imposter syndrome*, a psychological feature common for employees promoted into challenging roles (see **Imposter Syndrome**).

Reboarding

On occasions colleagues leave, and subsequently return. Internally there's parental leave, long term secondments, extended breaks, and unpaid leave. When former employees return to a work team, tuned-in managers consider how to make re-entry as smooth as possible.

Circumstances change. Technologies, processes, and business emphasis all evolve over time. Colleagues do too. An extended period away may have created shifts in the employee's abilities, their values, or their ambitions. What is important to them, and to the business may have moved on.

Preboarding, induction, onboarding, and *reboarding* are team-shaping tasks for operational managers to master.

Further reading

Glassdoor for Employers | *3 Quick Wins for Establishing a Culture of Employee Engagement* | Glassdoor, May 2021 | https://www.glassdoor.co.uk/employers/blog/3-quick-wins-for-establishing-a-culture-of-employee-engagement/

Society for Human Resource Management | *Human Capital Benchmarking Reports* | www.shrm.org

CIPD | *Induction: A look at the induction process, and the purpose of induction for employer and employee.* | December 2022 |

https://www.cipd.co.uk/knowledge/fundamentals/people/recruitment/induction-factsheet

HRM Online | *A guide to reboarding an employee* | June 2021 | https://www.hrmonline.com.au/change-management/a-guide-to-reboarding-an-employee/

With thanks to Ian Luxford and the team at The Motivation Agency www.themotivationagency.co.uk for insights on this management topic.

Insights visits

"Break the pattern which connects the items of learning, and you necessarily destroy all quality." – *Gregory Bateson*

In my work with managers, at all levels of accountability, I emphasise the value of learning from patterns which connect from outside the team and organisation. Knowledge gleaned from pattern is a rich source of learning for CPD (see **Accountability**, **Patterns which connect** and **Continuous professional development [CPD]**).

For decades I've taken managers on *insights* days, visiting non-competitor organisations who offer patterns of interest for their own industry and organisation.

Time and again managers come away from site visits enthused by their experiences, keen to adapt new learning into their own operations. Somehow, reviewing another firm's work practices seems to create an enjoyable objectivity, and fresh energy, unshackled from day-to-day responsibilities. Or maybe it's just innate curiosity.

I find the best way to manage insights visits is to design a set of patterns to explore. It could be an operations focus, or manufacturing and production, or perhaps HRM practices, marketing strategies, sales processes, continuous improvement management, or systems development. Whatever the topics of interest, with the right host organisation and good up-front planning, insight sessions have a positive impact on visiting managers.

Visitors get to benchmark and compare, and become inspired and educated, on possible improvement strategies for their own businesses.

Agencies specialise in arranging commercial insights visits, though it is perfectly feasible to arrange your own. I've done it for years. You already have a network of potential hosts in your organisation's customer-supplier chains. That's a handy starting point. Don't be concerned too much about the 'relevance' of the host organisation; often a divergent sector is ideal in helping objectivity and interest. You and fellow managers will soon pick up on patterns which connect and innovative ideas to transfer into your own field. I encourage managers to think laterally, creatively, about how a method of work might be reshaped and used to good effect in their own roles.

Most hosts are only too pleased to share their successful strategies, it boosts their own sense of feel-good and pride about their operational practices. Wherever possible I promote a two-way dialogue between hosts and visitors. Some of my clients already have best practice systems their hosts would be keen to learn.

I'm no longer surprised at the positive impact insights visits have on managers who look beyond their own organisation, or industry sector, and discover gems of knowledge to incorporate into their management world.

A useful follow up activity is to ask insights visitors to prepare a brief report of findings, on how external excellence could be imported and integrated, with a simple cost-benefit analysis.

How soon will you arrange insights visits for you and your colleagues?

Further reading

Steps to an Ecology of Mind | University of Chicago Press, 1972 | Bateson, G.

Onsight Insights | https://onsiteinsights.org/

Lean Competency System | https://www.leancompetency.org/lean-company-visits-uk/

Interest

"Seek first to understand, then be understood." *– Stephen Covey*

The fastest, simplest, and most effective way to build trust and relationship is to *listen*. It will help you build relationships. Be *interested*, before *interesting*.

Showing interest encourages openness and transparency. It accelerates relationship building. Too many managers select the *transmit* button first and *receive* sometime afterwards; that's if they receive at all.

There is much to gain from listening to team members, to get inside their world (see **Get inside their world**). When we absorb messages from others, we build patterns of understanding, helping us gain insights.

- What is pressing on their minds currently?
- What anxieties are they revealing?
- What hopes and ambitions are important to them?
- What values and beliefs are they expressing?
- What information are they sharing, of which you were previously unaware?
- What have they *not* told you during this conversation?
- How are they processing information, through sight, sound, feeling, smell, or taste (see **VAK[OG] representational systems**)?
- What language patterns can you loop back into conversation in the form of clean language, to deepen rapport (see **Clean language**)?
- What questions can you ask, to highlight your listening mode, and gain deeper insights?
- From your learning, how can you offer support or add value?

People enjoy others showing interest. We all know charming characters who are attentive, and express sincere empathy, without being overly invasive. Their warmth and friendliness feel nice, and we like them. Consequently, their relationships blossom quickly and with genuine warmth.

Be interested. It will pay back dividends.

Further reading

7 Habits of Highly Effective People | Free Press, 1989 | Covey, S.R.

How to win Friends and Influence People in the Digital Age | Simon & Schuster, 2011 | Carnegie, D.

Showing Interest in Others Can Change Your Life! | Exploring Your Mind, November 2020 | https://exploringyourmind.com/ showing-interest-in-others-can-change-your-life/

Three Ways Great Leaders Show They Care About Their Team | Forbes.com, July 2018 | Henley, D. | https://www.forbes.com/sites/dedehenley/2018/07/20/three-ways-great-leaders-show-they-care-about-their-team/?sh=e7badd846e5c

Irrational thinking

"There are three musts that hold us back. I must do well. You must treat me well. And the world must be easy." *– Albert Ellis.*

I meet managers in my coaching work who fill their professional lives with irrational thoughts, placing unnecessary pressure on themselves. Here are a few common features,

Catastrophising

Making the worst possible future scenario a lucid reality in their imagination. Albert Ellis, the psychologist, referred to this tendency as *awfulizing*.

Paranoia

People (senior managers, peers, team members, customers, suppliers, others) are out to get me! This is brought to the surface during times of stress.

Past means future

Painful or disempowering historical events are brought into present thinking and overlay on top of a manager's *today* world. Burton and Bodenhamer (2000) refer to this as *looking at the present through the past*,

> "Doing this is sort of like using a mirror to look at the present, all you see is what's behind you and then mistake it for what is before you... so history repeats repeats (sic) itself."

Should-ing and Must-ing

I hear managers use what the NLP (neuro linguistic programming) community refer to as *modal operators of necessity*. MONs are language structures which demand compliance, such as *must, should, have to, got to, ought to*. These patterns induce stress and anxiety. When I hear managers use these patterns in relation to self, I suspect irrational thinking may be at work, e.g., *I must/must not, I should/should not, I have to/ought not to,* etc.

The key to escaping these disempowering thought processes is to actively listen to your inner dialogue and question the belief systems which stimulate them.

Challenging a belief system is a healthy strategy for reducing irrational thought. By changing the belief new resourceful choices may become apparent (see **Beliefs, you can choose or change**). Ellis provides a useful model to challenge irrational beliefs in his therapeutic model *Rational Emotive Behaviour Therapy*, or *REBT*.

Further reading

The Practice of Rational Emotive Behavior Therapy | Free Association Books, 1999 | Ellis, A., Dryden, W.

Rational Emotive Behavior Therapy: It Works for Me – It Can Work for You | Prometheus, 2010 | Ellis, A.

J

JIT and float time

"It takes great effort to follow the rules of a pull system ...
thus a half-hearted introduction of a pull system brings a
hundred harms and not a single gain." – *Taiichi Ohno*

Just In Time originated in Japan as a materials supply efficiency technique. With the right controls in place, *JIT* is an effective means of aligning materials supply chains with manufacturing schedules. Raw materials and components arrive *Just In Time* to be used in the manufacturing process. They are *pulled* from the supply chain at the right moment, as required. JIT therefore minimises inventory costs and associated cash flow requirements. JIT management is also used in the service sector.

Partnerships and mutual understanding, all along the supply chain, are critical to making JIT work. Inventory costs are reduced whilst ensuring production downtime is minimised and preferably eliminated.

High performing managers apply JIT principles to make the most of every workplace minute. They maximise diary efficiency and minimise downtime. Some will strive to optimise the *utilisation rate* of their personal time. Some will pull materials, components and often *information, Just In Time* for their needs. Others will apply *net time* principles and work on multiple tasks in parallel, where one activity has delay within its process, for example, making calls while waiting for a train, or listening to a CPD podcast while driving.

My guidance is to be careful with your own *Just In Time* approach to management; it doesn't always translate well to personal diary management.

JIT diary practitioners who are occasionally JTL (*Just Too Late*) cause stress for themselves and infect others with their angst. I had one sales colleague who insisted on leaving for client meetings at the absolute last minute (no point in wasting valuable selling time!) assuming all travel connections would run smoothly, without delays. You can guess what happened. It causes an unnecessary, self-inflicted anxiety.

Project managers refer to *float time*, a small cushion of time to allow for overruns. You can build float time into your daily plans as a contingency plan, or maybe use it for reflective thinking?

Further reading

The Toyota Way: 14 Management Principles from the World's Greatest Manufacturer | McGraw-Hill, 2004 | Liker, J.

JIT Implementation Manual – The Complete Guide to Just-In-Time Manufacturing | Taylor and Francis, 2009 | Hirano, H

Job enrichment

> "If you want people to do a good job, give them a good job to do — an enriched job." *– Frederick Herzberg*

Career advancement in organisations is associated with promotion, a step *up* the ladder, commonly thought of as a vertical progression *up* the organisation. But what if the structure is flat and management opportunities are limited?

In many organisations I have supported, a career development policy of job enrichment has radically shifted employees' and managers' perception of 'promotion'. Role growth becomes centred around psychological stimulation, exploring areas of special interest, and self-perceptions of adding value.

There is a difference between job *enrichment* and job *enlargement* or *horizontal loading*. Enrichment means more interest and intellectual challenge; enlargement means more work.

Projects management can be an engaging route to job enrichment, with responsibility for significant and meaningful ventures, encouraging employees to become the *czar* of a specialist field. Employees who feel recognised for their valuable contributions to strategic goals are more likely to be committed to the team effort and loyalty to the organisation. They will feel significant. Significance is a major motivator (see **Significance**).

From a practical perspective it makes sense too, for you, the manager. You can delegate parts of your role to suitable team members, offering learning and growth opportunities, whilst freeing you up to concentrate on developmental issues (see **What am I here for? What is my management purpose?**).

As a motivational approach and an aid to employee engagement (see **Employee engagement**), project responsibilities act as a fabulous spark to a sense of significance for employees, or to re-ignite the passions of a team member treading water. When colleagues are given opportunity to share their project progress with others, you'll see and hear enthusiasm and pride in their significance.

How do you, or could you, enrich the roles of your team members?

Further reading

One More Time: How Do You Motivate Employees? | Harvard Business Review Press 2008 | Herzberg, F. | https://hbr. org/2003/01/one-more-time-how-do-you-motivate-employees

What are the advantages and disadvantages of job enrichment? | Indeed | Editorial team, March 2023 | https://uk.indeed. com/career-advice/career-development/ advantages-and-disadvantages-of-job-enrichment

Johari, adapted for management

"Whenever two people meet, there are really six people present. There is each man as he sees himself, each man as the other person sees him, and each man as he really is." – *William James*

Psychologists Joseph Luft and Harry Ingham (Jo Hari) developed the Johari Window as a self-discovery tool to help people evaluate how they communicate with self and others. It is used in personal development circles, in counselling, and therapy contexts. It's an effective framework for self-evaluation.

Luft and Ingham proposed the value of increasing the *Open* area (or *Arena*) of the quadrant, to facilitate honest and transparent communication. I agree wholeheartedly with this.

Over the years I have adapted the original Johari quadrant to support management development activities. I use my version of the model to emphasise the importance of establishing a psychologically and emotionally safe culture within a workplace.

NDK adaptation of Johari

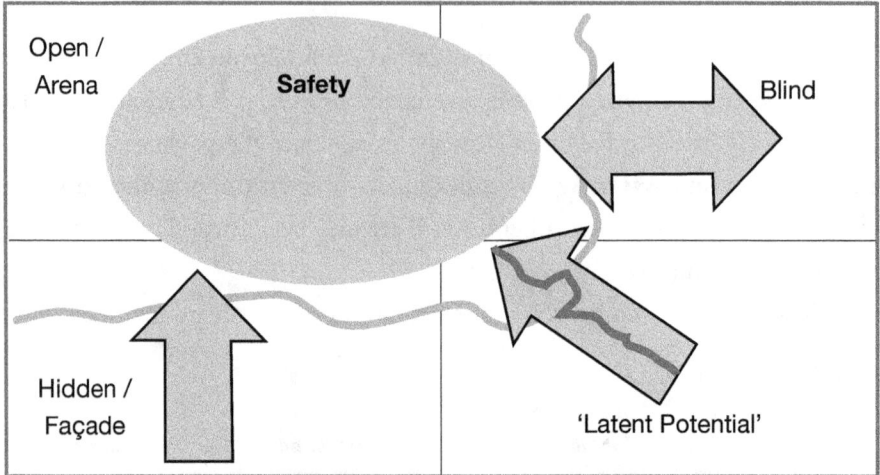

Qualifiers and adaptations which I apply in using Johari are,

1. Only when an employee (manager or team member) feels it *safe to do so*, will they be willing to share *hidden*, or *façade*, thoughts, feelings, and beliefs.
2. Only when an employee feels it *safe to do so*, will they be willing to actively seek commentary on their *blind* (or *blind spot*) behaviours.
3. For client work I change the original Johari Window lower right quadrant from *Unknown* to *Latent Potential*. Only when an employee feels it *safe to do so*, will they be willing to take on opportunities to explore new adventures in their work role, aware of stumbles along the way as inevitable.
4. I ask the managers I coach to consider,
    -   Do you feel there is a sufficiently safe culture for you to make your *Hidden, Blind,* and *Latent Potential* quadrants more *Open*?
    -   How do you think your team members feel about culture and safety, and their willingness to expand their *Open* quadrant?
    -   Is there work for you in making your culture more fertile for *Open* communication?

I find outputs from Johari Window (NDK adapted) coaching sessions quickly reveal the true culture at play within an organisation.

What would your response be to the questions above?

What would your team members report?

Further reading

The Johari window, a graphic model of interpersonal awareness | University of California, Los Angeles, 1955 | Luft, J., Ingham, H.

Management and Executive Coaching | Continue and Begin Ltd, 2016 | Drake-Knight, N. | https://continueandbegin.com/

Judgements and observations

"To be even minded is the greatest virtue." *– Heraclitus*

When a manager comments on a colleague's performance, the style of language used has significance.

Observational commentary, based on the facts of what has been seen or heard, is most likely to be accepted by an employee as accurate. Commentary driven by *judgement* (not a factual statement) is less likely to be accepted as fair; it invites defensiveness and conflict.

For example,

"When the customer asked about special offers, you weren't very helpful. You weren't interested in making a sale."

Here we have a judgement (*you weren't very helpful*) and an attempted mind-read (*you weren't interested*). Both invite defensive responses (see **Distortion**).

Compare the above judgement with this observation,

"When the customer asked about special offers, I noticed you didn't mention our '3 for 2' deal."

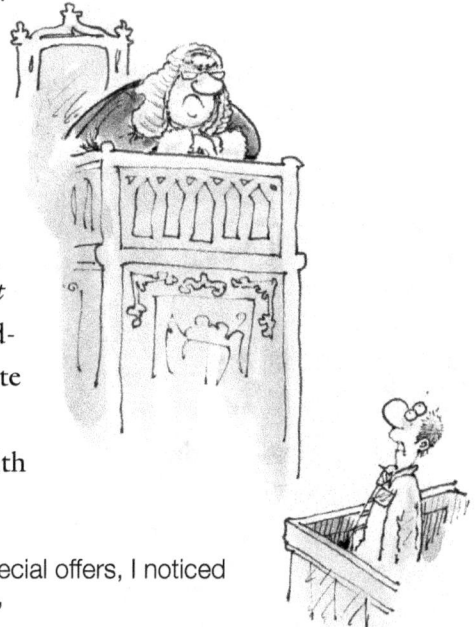

This is a factual statement leading to further discussion. *Observations* start the process of helping team members grow. *Judgements* hinder development.

Here are more examples. What do you think? *Judgement* or *observation?*

- "I was watching you with that customer – you didn't pay attention to her."
  J or O?

- "I heard you talking to that customer about three-bedroom semis. You weren't very friendly."
  J or O?

- "When you were laying out the table, you stayed focused on the task whilst you spoke to the customer. You didn't look up to gain eye contact."
  J or O?

- "When the customer asked you about accessories, you smiled at her, put down your paperwork and walked with her to the display."
  J or O?

- "You wrote that report really well."
  J or O?

- "You asked lots of questions to find out what the customer really needed, and then you took the customer to the display, showing her key features she'd said were important to her. You checked she was happy with the product and asked a trial close question."
  J or O?

- "You did a good job with that student."
  J or O?

Think about the language you use when commenting on a colleague's behaviours at work. Do you use observational, or judgemental, statements (see **Rarely, Sometimes, Always, Chocolate Praise™, Structure of Well-Done-Ness®** and **Coaching, Continue & Begin Fast Coaching®**)?

Further reading

Boomerang! Coach Your Team to Be the Best | Dandelion Digital, 2007 | Drake-Knight, N.

Fast Coaching. The Complete Guide to New Code Continue & Begin® | Dandelion Digital, 2016 | Drake-Knight, N. | Audible https://www.audible.co.uk/pd/ Fast-Coaching-Audiobook/B07TTKD13T

The Motivation Agency | https:// themotivationagency-online.com/course/ begin

K

Kanban

Kanban is a management method drawn from lean and quality principles (see **Lean management, Quality and TQM, Quality Circles and Kaizen, Quality Standards**, and **Quality and 5S**). It is a helpful visual management tool (see **Visual management**) for teams to use in organising and controlling workflow.

Effective team managers employ Kanban in the form of Kanban *boards* and Kanban *cards*.

Kanban boards are simple visual representations of work components in a flow pipeline and the tasks required of the team over a given period. The starting point of a Kanban project board is sometimes called the *Commitment Point*, with the end goal referred to as the *Delivery Point*.

Project tasks are identified as being at varying stages of evolution. Name labels for each stage vary from user to user, although common segment names are,

- *Pipeline* task loading.
- *Today* activities.
- *Underway*.
- *Obstacle* identified.
- Complete.

Some Kanban boards include an additional phase of *Review*.

A simple white board offers a great Kanban visual representation of pipeline workload. Electronic visual boards are excellent too, though beware of Kanban boards being lost in a computer filing system, even where file sharing is standard practice. The point of Kanban boards is to be highly visible, for immediate reference, not filed and hidden away from view.

Components of Kanban activity are often written on cards, either magnetic dry wipe cards on a white board, on simple sticky notes, or (if necessary) on a spreadsheet, although we're back to hidden information again with the tech approach. Some organisations will have the tech to display a Kanban board and its component cards on electronic boards.

Here's a simple Kanban board (see next page) for a marketing team managing an upcoming company conference. Notice how the Kanban cards move across the board as they progress towards completion. In this example Today (blue), Underway (orange), Obstacle (red) and Completed (green) are colour coded. Pipeline tasks greyed out have not been started yet. Cards are moved along the Kanban board as they progress each stage.

For Kanban boards where a team of people are allocated specific tasks, it's best to colour code or highlight specific cards to each team member, to identify who is working on which element of the project. Front end planning is a good time to do this and adapted as the project progresses at *scrum* time after each *sprint* (see **Scrums and sprints**).

Cards can be flagged with detailed information if it helps flow, and this may include time factors.

Project management professionals and software development teams are adept at developing sophisticated Kanban cards, often including detailed information. For most 'non-tech' team managers, a basic board (e.g., taped columns on wall space) with simple cards (sticky notes) is sufficient for a visual management space to review progress on deliverables.

How could you use Kanban boards and cards in your team?

Further reading

One Team on All Levels: Stories from Toyota Members | CRC Press, 2012 | Turner, T.

What is Kanban? | Atlassian | Agile Coach, 2019 | https://www.youtube.com/watch?v=iVaFVa7HYj4&t=15s

Annual Conference					
Pipeline [Commitment point]	Today	Underway	Obstacle	Completed [Delivery point]	Review
Allocate project team				1 Dec	
Agree budget with sponsor				2 Dec	
Agree conference date with Stakeholders				8 Dec	
Agree geographic location		Complete 13 Jan latest	EU delegates		
Visit potential venues, create shortlist		Complete 13 Jan latest			
Agree venue with stakeholders		Meet 20 Jan			
Arrange room layout, audio, lighting, timings		Site meet 21 Jan			
Arrange refreshments			Dietary needs?		
Arrange keynote speaker	Sponsor preference?				
Agree format and outline content with stakeholders		Request out to HODs			
Shortlist and invite supplier sponsors		Planning meeting 13 Jan			
Arrange delegate invitations					
Secure message content for delegate pack		12 Dec to HODs			
Design branding spec for delegate pack	Agency call				
Arrange print agency timeline	Timeline from agency				
Delegate materials, pens, lanyards, sponsor involvement					
Arrange parking			300 delegates		
Post-event delegate experience survey					

Key Performance Indicators

"If you can't measure it, you can't manage it." – *Peter Drucker*

Monitoring performance is a crucial activity for managers. Your role is to achieve a set of ambitions mapped out in your organisation's business plan.

How will you know your team is progressing?

Key performance indicators (KPIs) help the measurement process. You may have KPIs imposed on you, or they may be 'negotiated'. Mutually agreed KPIs are most likely to be addressed with enthusiasm. I remember one colleague manager complaining to a director, *"These are not my numbers, they're yours!"*. You may be more fortunate and have a degree of self-determination in designing performance indicators for your team.

What we can be sure of is: *what gets measured, gets done.*

John Doerr (2018) refers to *OKRs*, meaning *Objectives* and *Key Results* He suggested organisations should clearly define a set of objectives with calibrated results which may be performance monitored. Doerr dissects OKRs into the *What; the objectives*, and the *How; the key results* (see **Objectives, management by [MBOs and OKRs]**).

A limiting factor in KPIs is the historical nature of the data reported. KPIs look backwards, not forwards. By contrast, OKRs are dynamic, reporting on performance to date, with an eye to the future, aligned to a business Objective. The best OKRs engage team members in their development, rather than being designed and dictated by managers. OKRs relevant for local teams, aligned with wider business objectives, contribute to overall business performance.

KPI/OKR overload

The challenge in many organisations I work with is the tsunami of objectives and KPI/OKRs thrown at managers to deliver on, and measure against. There are usually too many.

If you are a senior manager reading this book, consider the primary delivery role of your team managers and isolate a small set of KPIs for each team manager, aligned to an Objective. This will focus the manager's mind on what is important, the core business outcomes required.

Managers, like everyone, can consciously focus on a limited set of ideas, so restrict KPI/OKRs to primary measures (see **Desktop of the mind, What am I here for?** and **Case Study: On Growing Managers [and our Business]**).

Further reading

Measure What Matters. OKRs – the Simple Idea That Drives 10x Growth | Penguin Random House, 2018 | Doerr, J.

OKRs: the ultimate guide to objectives and key results | Atlassian, undated. | Sparks, R. | https://www.atlassian.com/agile/agile-at-scale/okr

KIT meetings

"Know how to listen and you will profit even from those who talk badly." *– Plutarch*

Keep In Touch meetings support your team members when conducted regularly, perhaps monthly, or quarterly. There is something special about one-to-one time with a line manager which centres on the employee's welfare. Relaxed and informal, often with no specific agenda, KIT meetings provide space for free-flowing conversation about the work environment and the employees' world (see **Get inside their world**).

The best KIT meetings I have experienced are informal discussions, preferably in a nearby coffee shop, away from the workplace. Conversation is two-way, reflecting on 'what's going on' in the organisation and how the team member is feeling about work. Elegant team managers make the experience comfortable and relaxing.

KIT meetings are different to performance reviews or formal appraisal meetings. Nor are they *supervision* sessions (see **Supervision sessions**), common in the health and social care sector, where employees are encouraged to share or offload challenging experiences from their professional roles. KIT meetings are less intense than this, and more about – as the name suggests – staying in touch with the welfare of an individual team member and their world. Sometimes life outside work will be discussed, although this should be carefully managed; KITs are not an excuse to delve into an employee's private affairs.

KITs involve dedicated one-to-one facetime. Maybe you manage a remote team and face-to-face is through a digital meeting platform? Maybe you are keeping in touch during an employee's maternity leave or staying connected during sickness absence? You might feel the diary time involved is burdensome, particularly if you have a large team. Rest assured, the return on investment will be worth your energy.

Relaxed one-to-one time with you, over a coffee away from work, even conducted remotely, means more to your team members than it does for you.

Further reading

Make the Most of Your One-on-One Meetings | Harvard Business Review, November 2022 | Rogelberg, S.G. | https://hbr.org/2022/11/make-the-most-of-your-one-on-one-meetings

One-to-one meetings: a complete guide | Breathe, May 2023 | Sands, L | https://www.breathehr.com/en-gb/blog/topic/employee-engagement/one-to-one-meetings-a-complete-guide

KITAs

"Does he want to do a good job because he wants to do a good job? That's motivation. Does he want to do a good job because he gets a bonus, he wants a house, a car, a Jaguar? That's movement."

– Fred Herzberg

Fred Herzberg coined the phrase *KITA*, meaning *Kick in the Arse*, in relation to employee motivation at work. He argued team members could be encouraged to *move*, through the offer of reward – a positive KITA, or via a threat of impending pain – a negative KITA. An employee is likely to *move* in response to either of these stimuli.

Herzberg proposed *movement* is different to *motivation*, is temporary in its effect and requires repeated KITAs to stimulate further movement.

In my book *Fast Coaching* (2016) I include a transcript from a *Continue & Begin Fast Coaching*® train-the-trainer event, which illustrates this point,

> "So, my car is outside my house right now and I'm going to tell you it's filthy… and I mean really dirty … and it needs a proper clean, a proper valet, inside and out. What I would like you to do is… and it should only take you two or three hours … is to come round to my house and clean my car for me… would you?
>
> I live on the Isle of Wight in England by the way… yes, yes, I know it's a bit of a trek for you…. I realise there's a bit of travelling time for you… well, ok, yes… rather a lot of travelling time, yes. Anyway… if you would do that for me, that would be very kind. Would you like to do that please? Or… You'd prefer not? Oh.
>
> What about if I was to offer you some form of reward… I mean a serious reward. If I was to say in the back of my car there are tens of thousands of pounds, and you can have it all if you come and give my car a clean for a couple of hours… maybe you'd feel a little differently. You would? Oh, that's lovely, thank you. And yes, tomorrow would be fine.
>
> You see, I can get you to do it. Do you want to do it? No. But I can get you to **move.** Movement is different to motivation.
>
> What if I want you to move again? If I want you to clean my car again in the future? What have I got to do? I've got to give you some more reward… some more cash… or maybe some fear… some nasty threat… or some punishment.
>
> Do you want to do it? No… but will you do it? Yes.
>
> Movement is different to motivation. Motivation is when it comes from inside… when people are passionate about things… when they want to do it because… they want to do it. That's motivation."

Motivation is an internal driver, stimulated by self, and catalysed by the environment in which the employee works. Herzberg suggested meaningful, valuable work (see **Job enrichment**) offers employees opportunities to feel good about achievement and the recognition associated with successful performance. Motivation, in contrast to movement, is therefore self-driven and requires minimal external 'prodding' by managers.

In *Continue & Begin*® we emphasise the value of encouraging self-evaluation of performance against explicitly described standards of delivery (see **Coaching, Continue & Begin Fast Coaching**®, and **NDK Performance Model**®).

When team members are engaged in stimulating, meaningful work which adds obvious business benefit, and where employees are encouraged to self-assess their personal contributions to a set of explicitly described standards, the need for KITAs is eliminated. Employees become *self-motivated*, not externally *moved*.

Further reading

One More Time: How Do You Motivate Employees? | Harvard Business Review Press 2008 | Herzberg, F. | https://hbr.org/2003/01/one-more-time-how-do-you-motivate-employees

Motivation through a Kick in the Ass | Call Centre Helper, May 2009 | Drake-Knight, N | https://www.callcentrehelper.com/motivation-through-a-kick-in-the-ass-3448.htm

Boomerang! Coach Your Team to Be the Best | Dandelion Digital, 2007 | Drake-Knight, N.

Fast Coaching. The Complete Guide to New Code Continue & Begin® | Dandelion Digital, 2016 | Drake-Knight, N. | Audible https://www.audible.co.uk/pd/Fast-Coaching-Audiobook/B07TTKD13T

The Motivation Agency | https://themotivationagency-online.com/course/begin

Knowledge

"Human behaviour flows from three main sources; desire, emotion, and knowledge." *– Plato*

Knowledge is one of the five categories of *Explicit Standards* described in the *NDK Performance Model*® and presented in *Fast Coaching* (see **NDK Performance Model**®).

Knowledge growth with regular updating is fundamental to professional management, it's part of your commitment to continuous development. That's what professional managers do; they seek out opportunities for personal improvement. I wasn't always onboard with that proposition. As a young award-winning lecturer in management studies, I was confident I was fully informed on what I needed to know to continue to offer a great service to my customers – the management students I taught on qualification programmes, and their employers, the organisations paying their course fees.

I was offered the chance to enrol in an advanced management qualification. I was reluctant to sign up, partly (largely?) because of pride and ego. It meant in the next semester I would be studying alongside co-learners who were currently my students. What's more, I didn't have an appetite for another two years of intensive study, I was too busy with a large family, and life outside work. Further, the prospect of being taught by colleague lecturers, some of whom I had little professional respect for, did not appeal. There was considerable organisational pressure on me to enrol. I eventually did so with negligible enthusiasm. The course required attendance at lectures, one day and one evening every week, plus home study.

Thank goodness I did! I soon realised how little I knew about subject matters I thought I was well versed in. I wasn't. I knew what I knew and didn't know what I didn't know. Early in the course, I began to relish the new learning. I was sponge-like, absorbing new knowledge I had been unaware of. I abandoned my pomposity and resistance and fully immersed into studying.

I had been in denial about my lack of knowledge in key areas; in human resource management law, in financial accounting, in IT management, and in other areas. As a bonus I gained insights from fellow students, some of whom had been leading businesses in senior roles. I learnt so much from them.

One fellow student, Bob, was an experienced managing director of a construction company, in his mid-fifties. He became a valued source of learning and a good friend. Later, we became business associates as we worked together on economic development consulting projects in the Former Soviet Union.

Twenty years my senior, Bob's more informed perspectives always kept me on my toes when I thought I had an answer to a specific management question. I remember discussing financial dynamics with business owners in newly commercialised markets of Silesia in Poland and quoting the much-used proposition, *"Turnover is vanity, profit is sanity."* Bob was on hand to steer me in the right direction with an additional (and vital) third component, *"And always remember, cash is king!"*

I was hooked on learning. I read copiously and built up a library of knowledge I could refer to. Reading became a habit. *Leaders are readers.*

Up-to-date management knowledge is vital to business success. For example,

- *Legislation.* Is your knowledge current on legal matters relevant to your business?
- *Best Practice.* What are the latest trends in your sector?
- *Technological developments.* Are you at the cutting edge, or working with old technology?
- *Consumer behaviours.* Do you stay in touch with your customers, external and internal?
- *Market trends.* What is happening in your market? Are you sufficiently agile to adapt? How is the market behaving (see **Agile team management** and **Adaptive team management**)?
- *Networking.* What are you doing to keep up to speed with industry habits?
- *People management.* What is happening in human resource development? What are the emerging trends likely to affect your team (see **Human leadership**)?

How committed are you to continuous learning, to proactively seek out new knowledge and its potential added value for your team?

Further reading

The New Knowledge Management: Mining the collective intelligence | Deloitte Insights, January 2021 | Behme, F., Becker, S. | https://www2.deloitte.com/us/en/insights/focus/technology-and-the-future-of-work/organizational-knowledge-management.html

11 Ways To Stay Up On The Latest Industry Developments | Forbes.com Coaches Council | https://www.forbes.com/sites/forbescoachescouncil/2021/02/18/11-ways-to-stay-up-on-the-latest-industry-developments/?sh=e3f0d7b70fbc

L

Language to help

"Kind words can be short and easy to speak,
but their echoes are truly endless." *– Mother Teresa*

The words managers use, and their phrases and language patterns, have impact on team members.

I remember returning to a large leisure complex I had managed a year previously and chatting to former colleagues. We were discussing management styles and what had worked and hadn't worked for them when I was General Manager. I clearly recall Jeanette, the reception supervisor saying,

"When you were manager here, you said 'thank you' often, Nick.
It made a difference for us."

I had had no conscious memory of having thanked people 'often'; it may have been an unconscious habit. Mind you, Jeanette also told me my occasional non-verbal scowling was a major downer for colleagues, so I was far from the finished article in motivational team communications.

What this episode highlighted to me was the unknowing impressions managers have on team morale and individual experiences. I can still recall, vividly, the conversation with Jeanette, more than 30 years later.

Managers can have a profoundly positive affect on team members through careful use of language. Thanking people, recognising achievements, and encouraging self-celebration of successes are empowering approaches, growing resourcefulness and confidence in the hearts and minds of employees.

Be careful with *"Well done"* though. Praise only adds value when it recognises the specifics of successful behaviour (see **Chocolate Praise™** and **Structure of Well-Done-Ness®**).

Managers can help employees feel good about personal performance by recognising their specific patterns of behaviour contributing to success. You can do this through *noticing* and referencing to standard operating procedures (SOPSs), and by asking questions of the team member to stimulate self-assessment of their performance, and to stretch for even higher standards,

- *"Which parts of* (the SOPs) *did you succeed at?"*
- *"Tell me about how you did that so well?"*
- *"What specifically did you do, that made it so successful?"*
- *"How did you manage to do it, exactly?"*
- *"What did you like about the way you did it?"*
- *"What were you pleased with, specifically?"*
- *"What could you do to make the performance even better next time?"*

These patterns promote self-awareness and encourage professional development. They help employees feel responsible for their own successes and stimulate further personal growth. This is the basis of *Continue & Begin Fast Coaching®*.

Further reading

Boomerang! Coach Your Team to Be the Best | Dandelion Digital, 2007 | Drake-Knight, N.

Audible https://www.audible.co.uk/pd/ Fast-Coaching-Audiobook/B07TTKD13T

Fast Coaching. The Complete Guide to New Code Continue & Begin® | Dandelion Digital, 2016 | Drake-Knight, N. |

The Motivation Agency | https:// themotivationagency-online.com/course/ begin

Language which hurts

"A modest man, who has much to be modest about."

– Winston Churchill, on Clement Attlee

Words have the power to build up or to tear down. Some language patterns, whether used intentionally or unintentionally, have potential to cause harm,

damaging wellbeing, and personal effectiveness. Demanding obedience, and
being critical, are two such patterns,

Obedience

- *"You should…"*
- *"You must…"*
- *"You ought to…"*
- *"You have to…"*
- *"You've got to…"*
- *"You need to…"*

These are patterns demanding of an individual. The manager is placing a
compliance requirement on the team member. There may be repercussions
if the employee does not do what is demanded.

Should-ers, Must-ers and *Needers* bark insistent orders, compelling obedience. Such phrases may drive temporary compliance, but they do not create
enthusiasm or inner motivation. Employee responses may be submissive,
conforming reluctantly or with resistance, or through passive aggression (see
KITAs and the *Should-ers* story in **Metaphors**).

Criticism

- *"How many times have I told you this?"*
  Maybe help me in a different way then?
- *"I don't mean to criticise…"*
  But Monster® coming (see **But Monster®**).
- *"You could have done much better…"*
  Thanks for the encouragement.
- *"With the greatest of respect…"*
  You have none for me?
- *"If I were you…"*
  Well, you're not, so pipe down.

These language patterns are bombastic and overbearing, borderline bully-
ing. They hurt and run counter to a climate of confidence and enthusiasm.
They are, therefore, counterproductive.

Further reading

Podcast – Contact Centre Coaching: How to Sustain Learning and Make it Fun! | Call Centre Helper, October 2019 | https://www.callcentrehelper.com/podcast-contact-centre-coaching-148064.htm

Call Centre Etiquette: 15 Things You Should Never Say to a Customer | Call Centre Helper, February 2018 | https://www.callcentrehelper.com/11-things-a-call-centre-agent-should-never-say-but-many-do-68516.htm

Boomerang! Coach Your Team to Be the Best | Dandelion Digital, 2007 | Drake-Knight, N.

Fast Coaching. The Complete Guide to New Code Continue & Begin® | Dandelion Digital, 2016 | Drake-Knight, N. | Audible https://www.audible.co.uk/pd/Fast-Coaching-Audiobook/B07TTKD13T

The Motivation Agency | https://themotivationagency-online.com/course/begin

Language, written, redundancy, and repetition

"If language is not correct, then what is said is not what is meant.
If what is said is not what is meant, then what ought to be done,
remains undone." *– Confucius*

A common request I hear from senior managers is to help develop the written communication skills of supervisors and first line managers, even middle managers. During introductory 121 management coaching sessions participants often highlight development of their written work as a professional ambition, a *Get Even Better At* (see **Get Even Better Ats [GEBAs]**).

Managers explain how their career has evolved through professional or technical skills, time served, and experience gained within their industry sector. Most have modest academic or professional backgrounds; many have few if any formal qualifications. For some, the world of formal learning has been problematic. I hear disempowering experiences of school and feelings of discomfort when thinking about learning. Managers who express enthusiasm for reading, whether for professional or recreational purposes, are a minority.

Vocabulary building and eloquence are typical GEBA outputs from a first 121 coaching session. We focus on these ambitions with development plans suited to each coachee. Managers work on vocabulary content and the structure of their written communications. Most concerns are around the quality of email compilation.

Redundancy

A common work-on is to reduce word redundancy in emails and reports. Patterns of redundancy include habit words offering negligible value, for example,

- Adverbs (see **Adverbs, superfluous**)
- Common redundancies

  ...that...

  ...actually...

  ...basically...

  ...just...

  ...slightly...quite... really... very... (and other qualifiers)

  ...in order to...

  ...to be able to do...

  ...so that...

  ...it may be possible to...

  ...to be honest...

  ...it would seem...

  ...sometimes... occasionally... often... and other time ordinal descriptors, (see **Fuzzy language**).

  ...personally speaking... in my view... and other perspective and opinion phrases.

  ...she turned round and said... (did she really turn round?)

  ...swearing

And other padding words and phrases.

I suggest editing tools to search for phrases of redundancy in draft communications, particularly if this is a habit (see **Habit**). Most software programmes have a tool to help, and there's a range of online apps available, *Grammarly, Write, Quillbot* and others. Beware UK/US spelling variations.

Repetition

Managers I work with are aware of their tendency to overuse or repeat the same word within a sentence or paragraph.

This may be habit, or evidence of limited vocabulary. Rushed email compilation is a common cause, with insufficient time being taken to check on message quality. Once the flawed message has gone, it's too late.

Total Quality Management (see **Quality and TQM**) requires professionals to deliver materials or information, including emails, *right, first time, on time, every time.* Outbound written communication deserves a commitment to quality; to be *fit for purpose.* It means proofreading outbound written or electronic message before *Send.*

I encourage managers to adopt the carpenter's mantra of *measure twice, cut once.* When sending an email or other written communication, take time to review the draft message twice. Consciously seeking evidence of repetition in a draft is a professional approach.

Pressing *Send* without a quality inspection seems reckless, doesn't it?

Further reading

Top Email Etiquette Examples for Professional Communication | Indeed | Editorial team, July 2022 | https://www.indeed.com/career-advice/career-development/email-etiquette-examples

3 Useful Ways to Eliminate Redundancy from Written Reports | Vista Projects | Editorial team, September 2016 | https://www.vistaprojects.com/eliminate-redundancy-written-reports/

Leadership and management

> "Management is about persuading people to do things they do not want to do, while leadership is about inspiring people to do things they never thought they could." *– Steve Jobs*

Scarf draggers (academics) have been debating the distinctions between management and leadership for a long time. What is the difference? Why one rather than the other? The lines are blurred.

- **Leadership is the starting point.** Where are we going? What is our goal? In which direction will we travel? What strategy should we employ to get there? How can we inspire our people to take up the challenge?
- **Management follows.** How will I make it happen, specifically? What resources do I have? How can I make best use of them? What organisation do I need to make this happen? How can I measure and monitor our performance against target?

Leadership is more than a front-end activity. Effective managers use leadership principles as a theme throughout their work. We know managers have a set of resources available (see **About management – an overview**),

- Supply chain
- Machinery
- Space
- Time
- Finance
- Information
- *People*. The team and individuals within it.

It is the people resource to which this book refers, and to which leadership principles apply.

The classic management texts of Tannenbaum and Schmidt (leadership continuum), Adair (action centred leadership) and Hersey and Blanchard (situational leadership), all recognised the importance of team leadership as a common, continuous thread running through effective management.

Personal style seems important too. Jim Collins (2001) describes how great businesses are led by personally humble but professionally driven leaders. Patterns exist here with principles from Human Leadership, in authenticity, empathy and adaptability (see **Human leadership**).

Rugby

For over thirty years I captained rugby teams at amateur level. Our playing standards were by no means great, but I learned a thing or two about captaincy, leading hundreds of players during a lengthy on-field career. I learned early on, my team of players performed best when given a collective goal to achieve (to win), a direction (broad game plan), the strategy we will employ (specific game tactics), and a belief and trust in each player to do his job out on the field.

Each player was different, of course. Gary, a combative prop forward, responded well to a ferocious changing room challenge to bring out the beast inside him. Ian, an enormous man, performed wonderfully after a gentle chat, my arm around his huge shoulders, reminding him how talented he was and how much I admired him.

Rugby requires physical and mental courage. I instilled in my players a belief of winning being achievable, though only if they were willing to perform at their best, to be confident in their skills, and be brave in the face of confrontation. I made sure I was on the frontline during the game, in the thick of it, leading by example. It was a modest playing standard with *low skill* and *high will*.

Fortunately, at work, it is not necessary to be big and tough, but a willingness to get involved and lead from the front is.

Leadership sets out a goal. It inspires people to achieve remarkable feats. Management is the allocation and organisation of resources. It needs the support of leadership to drive performance.

Here is my own quote on the subject,

"Management without leadership is administration."

– Nick Drake-Knight

Further reading

Management Vs. Leadership: Five Ways They Are Different | Forbes, 2016 | Ryan, L. | https://www.forbes.com/sites/lizryan/2016/03/27/management-vs-leadership-five-ways-they-are-different/?sh=5c9d9f8c69ee

What's the difference between leadership and management? | The Guardian, July 2013 | Ratcliffe, R. | https://www.theguardian.com/careers/difference-between-leadership-management

Good To Great: Why Some Companies Make the Leap... and Others Don't | Random House, 2001 | Collins, J.

How to Choose a Leadership Pattern | Tannenbaum, R., and Schmidt, W.H. | Harvard Business Review Press (Reprint), 2009

Situational Leadership | Blanchard, K. | www.blanchard.com (accessed 07.07.24)

Lean management

"A bad system will beat a good person every time."

– W. Edwards Deming

Lean is fundamental equipment in any manager's toolkit.

The idea of Lean is to maximize customer value while minimizing waste. A popular misconception is Lean being suited only for manufacturing. Businesses in all industries and services, including healthcare and governments, are using Lean principles in what they think and do. Lean philosophies are effective in office environments as much as in production or operational contexts.

Lean, Transformation, or *Lean Transformation* characterizes an organisation moving from an old way of thinking to Lean thinking. To be fully effective, and embedded culturally, it requires a transformation in how an organisation operates. This takes long-term perspective and perseverance.

Lean principles originated in manufacturing industries, most notably in Toyota's approach to quality management (see **JIT and float time**, and **Quality and TQM**). The Toyota Production System achieved improvements in productivity, time efficiency and costs and became the benchmark approach for manufacturing industries.

Lean is a discipline comprising three propositions,

1. Deliver value (value = as perceived by your customer).
2. Eliminate waste (waste = anything which does not add value to your customer).
3. Continuously improve.

Service sector businesses and publicly funded organisations have adopted Lean because of its focus on customers' (including internal) perceptions of value.

Lean principles are built around customer needs and include five components,

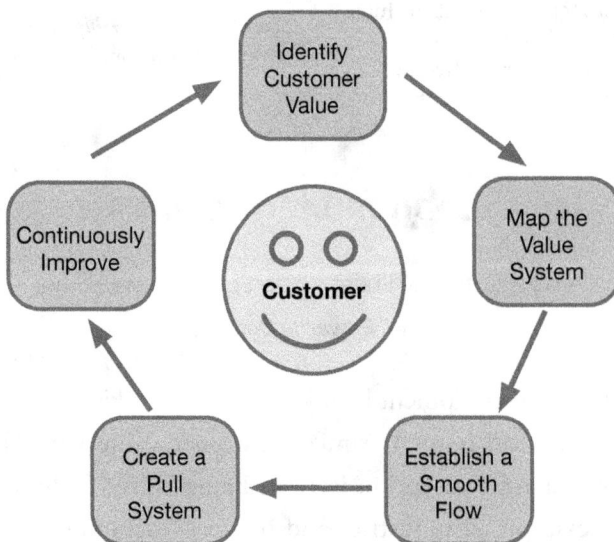

1. *Identify value.* What does the customer want? What is the customer willing to pay for?

2. *Value map.* Record the workflow of activities currently involved in producing value for customers. Which activities in the workflow do not add value and are therefore 'waste'.

3. *Establish continuous workflow.* Construct the activities of work teams to provide smooth delivery flow with minimal delays, blockages, or stop-starts in production time.

4. *Construct 'pull' systems.* Work is only undertaken if there is demand from internal or external customers. This minimises wasted activity and the overstocking of materials or finished product and associated costs.

5. *Continuously improve.* Technologies develop, customer requirements and expectations change, competition accelerates, and costs and profitability shift. To provide customer value, and remain competitive, it is necessary to focus on continuous improvement (see **Quality and TQM**).

Team managers can employ Lean principles and disciplines in day-to-day operations to improve efficiencies and provide even better value to internal and external customers.

How could you employ Lean in your management role?

Further reading

The Toyota Way: 14 Management Principles from the World's Greatest Manufacturer | McGraw-Hill, 2004 | Liker, J.

Applying Lean in an Office Environment | Bourton Group | Editorial team, September 2022 | https://www.bourton.co.uk/applying-lean-in-an-office-environment/

Lean Competency System | Lean Competency Services Ltd | Cardiff University | https://www.leancompetency.org/lean-company-visits-uk/

Listening

Nobody ever listens to a word I say –

"Most people do not listen with the intent to understand;
they listen with the intent to reply. They're either speaking or
preparing to speak. They're filtering everything through their own
paradigms, reading their autobiography into other people's lives".

– Stephen R. Covey

You can hone your listening skills. You might nod, smile empathetically, raise your eyebrows at appropriate times, lean forwards, cross your legs *towards* the speaker, or use continuity sounds such as, *ok... right... oh... really? ... wow...uh huh...* Using pauses as a continuity tool is also effective; simply nod and stay quiet. The speaker may have more to say.

Gentle questioning may help. Rudyard Kipling's poem, *The Elephant's Child*, provides a framework,

I keep six honest serving-men
(They taught me all I knew);
Their names are What and Why and When
And How and Where and Who.

A powerful approach to effective listening is to provide space and time, after questioning, for the speaker's communication to flow. Be patient, avoid interrupting, and allow the speaker to gradually reveal their thoughts and feelings (see **Get inside their world**).

The best listening manager I was privileged to work with was Brian. He was senior manager in a UK government business support agency. I was a team manager reporting to him. Brian was a master of listening. When approached for advice he could be relied upon to listen carefully, before making comment. His strategy was to be patient, to avoid the temptation to jump in early with advice. He allowed silence. Pauses encouraged his co-communicators to continue speaking.

Brian knew, instinctively, the limitations of surface structure language and the treasures which lie beneath (see **Surface structure, deep structure**).

NDK. "Brian, have you got a minute? I could do with a chat."

BB. "Sure, come in, take a seat."

NDK. "I've got something on my mind. It's troubling me..."

BB. "Ok..."

NDK. "(This thing) has happened and I'm uncertain how to deal with it."

BB. "Ok..." (gentle nodding, long pause)

NDK. "Its... well, I'm thinking about options..."

BB. "Right..." (gentle nodding, long pause)

NDK. "I've thought about (Options 1, 2, 3) and it seems to me we could (Option 3)"

BB. "Sure. You could do that... (pause, nodding). That is an option for you..." (long pause).

NDK. "Well, what I could do is..."

And without even knowing, with minimal words, Brian was coaching me through my decision-making process. As in so many coaching scenarios, the answer was right in front of me. I needed to get out of my own way by sharing the thinking process with a gifted listener. Brian was a wonderful people manager.

How are you at listening, patiently?

Further reading

You're Not Listening: What You're Missing and Why It Matters | Vintage, 2021 | Murphy, K.

How to Practice Active Listening: 16 Examples & Techniques | PositivePsychology.com, April 2023 | O'Bryan, A. |

https://positivepsychology.com/active-listening-techniques/

Just So Stories: Original Illustrated Edition | Kipling, J.R. | Independently Published, 2022

Looking out the window thinking

"The chief enemy of creativity is good sense." *– Pablo Picasso*

It was 1988. I was twenty-eight years old and had been unexpectedly promoted from deputy to general manager of a major leisure complex; three swimming pools, two restaurants, two bars, a golf course, squash, badminton and gymnasium facilities and a vintage car museum! In the summer months we employed around 120 staff and hosted tens of thousands of customers, including locals and visiting holidaymakers. At the time it was a big step up in my management career.

The managing director of the parent company was Steve, a gruff, chain-smoking senior executive, direct in his communication and uncompromising in his expectations about business performance.

Steve came to visit the site early in my tenure as general manager. I had a wonderful oak panelled office with two desks and a window view of the car park. I felt an imposter (see **Imposter syndrome**). Steve sat at one desk and lit a cigarette.

"I'm going to come and see you once a month, Nick, on Friday afternoons. And I expect to find you with your feet up on the desk, phone off the hook, looking out the window. Ok?"

"Erm, yes, Steve… (nervous half laughter)"

"I mean it. You have a job to do here promoting the importance of this site to the local community. I want you to think… to be creative and innovative… I want your energy focused on planning. I want you to look out of the window and contemplate. No phone interruptions:

tell your staff to leave you alone on Friday afternoons. Thinking Nick. It's what I expect you to do. Got it?"

"Yes Steve."

And so, I began to learn the importance of dedicated thinking time; developmental, growth focused thinking time. It has proven an invaluable strategy and I recommend it to every operational manager as a diarised item in your work schedule. Thinking time is an *important* task. It may not be *urgent*, but it is *important* and therefore merits an investment of your management time. Diarise it.

We digest and learn most effectively when in a relaxed state. I remember hearing Stephen Gilligan, therapist, coach, and author, saying,

> "Most people's hard thinking uses the same muscles as dealing with constipation."

When muscle tension softens, then learning begins. Hypnotherapists know this. Later in my management career I was to learn the benefits of relaxed focus and how to trust my unconscious mind in finding answers to work conundrums (see **Unconscious mind, trusting the**).

Turn your phone to silent, put your feet up, relax. Look out of the window at a distance point... focus on it... and allow your mind to wander (wonder)... in bigger terms. You may be surprised... and delighted... how quickly ideas and solutions come... into your conscious mind.

Further reading

The Creative Thinking Handbook: Your Step-by-Step Guide to Problem Solving in Business | Kogan Page, 2019 | Griffiths, C.

Generative Coaching Volume 1: The Journey of Creative and Sustainable Change | International Assoc. for Generative Change, 2021 | Dilts, R.B., Gilligan, S., Meza, A.

M

Management competencies

"I have no idols. I admire work, dedication, and competence."
– Ayrton Senna

Team managers deliver business objectives using a range of skills, or competences. A job description presents headline responsibilities for their management role, and a decent person specification may have helped in their selection and recruitment as the preferred candidate. What is commonly missing for managers I support is reference to a set of explicitly described management competences – the specific skills they are expected to exhibit.

A competency framework provides managers with guidelines for their role. Few newly appointed managers are fully competent across all areas; there is usually room for growth. A framework provides a measurement tool against which capability is assessed. It provides the basis for building a professional development plan for a manager.

Zenger & Folkman's *16 Differentiating Competencies* (2009) suggested some competencies as applicable at all levels of management. The sixteen competencies are presented within five categories,

1. Character – integrity.
2. Personal capability – technical expertise, problem solver, innovator, self-developer.
3. Focus on results – drives for results, stretch goals, initiator.
4. Interpersonal skills – communicates, inspires, relates, develops others, collaborates.

5. Leading change – strategic view, champions change, connects to outside world.

Zenger and Folkman's work offers a starting point for developing management competencies bespoke to a management team. For most brands I chunk down content to a more memorable (see **Desktop of the mind**) set of three *competency clusters* as follows:

1. Inspires and motivates others.
2. Communicates powerfully and prolifically.
3. Drives for results.

Each cluster has a subsidiary set of individual competencies, designed to the specific needs of the organisation. It's a canny move to engage a diagonal cross section of employees and managers to identify competencies best fitted to their brand (see **Change, ask the people**). The completed framework is used during management selection and development planning.

What are the management competencies you work to? Would they benefit from a review?

Further reading

The Extraordinary Leader: Turning Good Managers Into Great Leaders | McGraw-Hill, 2009 | Zenger, J., Folkman, J.

How to Be Exceptional: Drive Leadership Success by Magnifying Your Strengths | McGraw Hill, 2012 | Zenger, J., Folkman, J., Sherwin, R.H., Steel, B.

CMI Professional Standard | Chartered Management Institute | https://www.managers.org.uk/education-and-learning/professional-standards/professional-standard/

Management style

> "Pull the string and it will follow wherever you wish.
> Push it, and it will go nowhere at all." *– Dwight D. Eisenhower*

How would you define your management style? Which is the most effective approach? What options are available?

Newly appointed managers, including those promoted from within, have choices about how to establish themselves in the early days of their tenure.

Inexperienced managers seem prone to extremities of style. As one senior manager, David, expressed to me,

> "Newly elevated managers, from within a team, seem to go one of two ways; either they're too pally with their old mates, or they go old-school management – show them I'm the boss... I'm in control... I have to be tough."

It doesn't have to be either of these polarities.

Consultants have been proposing management styles since the days of Frederick Winslow Taylor and his *scientific management* approach in 1880s American steel works.

Considering *style,* we find writers and thinkers have blurred lines between management and leadership. John Adair promoted *Action Centred Leadership*, suggesting a balanced approach to task achievement, team harmony, and individual performance and welfare. These are factors relevant to both the management of people as a flexible resource, and to leadership style.

Douglas McGregor (1960) described his theory of X and Y style management, suggesting managers have two distinct perceptions of employees,

- In *Theory X*, a manager believes employees have little ambition, low motivation and are lazy. They work solely for income.
- In *Theory Y*, a manager believes employees, given opportunity, will enjoy their job role, will strive to be the best they can, and will take full responsibility for their work.

McGregor proposed benefits and drawbacks of both thinking models.

Robert Blake and Jane Mouton (1964) identified a balance between concern for task achievement and concern for the people carrying out the task, a variation of the Adair approach. They presented a grid to demonstrate options for managers, proposing optimum performance comes from a McGregor 'Y' pattern of thinking.

	Low			Concern for Production						High
High	1.9									9.9
			Accomodating				Team Performance			
Concern for People					Middle of the Road					
			Indifference					Authorative		
Low	1.1									9.1

Paul Hersey and Ken Blanchard (1969) suggested a variation of style to suit the levels of competence and enthusiasm of the employee,

- Telling/directing style.
- Selling/coaching.
- Participating/supporting.
- Delegating.

Referring to research by Hay McBer, Daniel Goleman (2000) recommended a flexible approach, incorporating different communication methods, subject to circumstance, and the emotional intelligence of the leader-manager. Six leadership styles were highlighted,

- Coercive (demanding compliance).
- Authoritative (directing towards a goal).
- Affiliative (creating emotional connection).
- Democratic (consensus seeking).
- Pacesetting (encouraging excellence).
- Coaching (develop team members).

Traditional business school curricula will present the above and many other models of management or leadership styles (Mintzberg, Bass, Burns and more) as part of a syllabus.

There is one management/leadership model (blurred lines again between these two roles) which, in my experience, stands out as the most value adding when considering *style*. Each time I introduce the Tannenbaum and Schmidt Leadership Continuum (2009) to managers, they quickly 'get it' and think of how it relates to their management and leadership role. Here is the model,

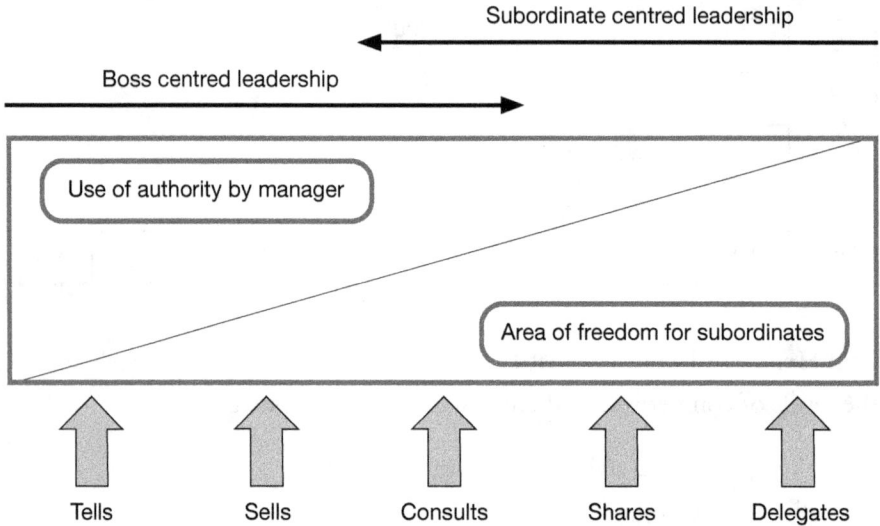

- **Telling:** At the extreme left of the continuum is complete control and directing authority of the manager-leader, *"Do this, then I'll tell you what else to do."*
- **Selling:** *"This is why my instruction is so great."*
- **Consults:** *"What do you think? Oh, ok thank you. Well, we're going to do what I think anyway."*
- **Shares:** *"Ok, let's talk and then have a vote."*
- **Delegates**: *"Over to you, you have the authority to do what you think is best."*

I have met managers who operate even further to the right of the continuum,

- **Abdication:** *"I don't care what you do or what happens."*

As with many of the style options described here, the key is *choice*. Managers can adopt a different style for different circumstances; they can move across the scale and back.

When team managers think of the Leadership Continuum, they recall the simple visual representation above and consider a small, easy to remember, number of ordered options, left to right, and back again (see **Desktop of the mind**). Tannenbaum and Schmidt's continuum helps managers think and adapt their communication style to suit circumstances and the team members involved.

Support or Control?

There's another fundamental consideration for team managers, regarding style. This applies to all levels of management and is worth a self-reflection from time to time. The matter concerns the balance between 'support' for your team members and 'control' of their activities and behaviours. A continuum provides a useful visual representation,

Manager Style – Controlling or Supporting?

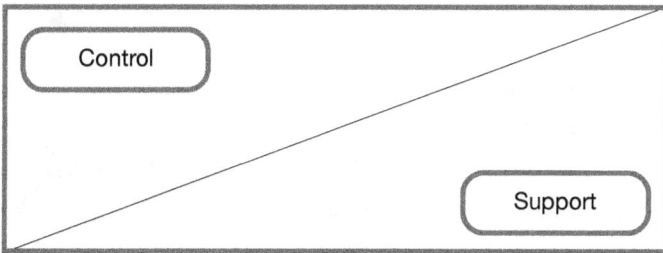

For team managers, there is an inevitable concern for management of performance and a temptation to *control* employees' work practices.

Think about the psychological impact of this on people; being *controlled*. Feelings of being monitored, measured, and under the microscope. The feelings of being untrustworthy to manage their own working activities to a suitable standard.

Compare this with feelings of being *supported* by a line manager. Feeling engaged, encouraged, resourced, trained, coached, and celebrated. Feeling trusted to get on with their job role, empowered to manage their own quality of performance, for which they have been employed.

The impact difference is phenomenal.

Of course, there are times, just as in the Tannenbaum and Schmidt model, where more direct involvement by managers makes good sense; with recent starters, or at times of particular difficulty, such as new working practices, new customer relationships, or when quality or safety concerns emerge.

Perhaps, in your working environment, there are good reasons for a balance between support and control?

Which management and leadership style(s) will you adopt?

Further reading

Leadership that gets results | Harvard Business Review, 2000 | Goleman, D.P. | https://hbr.org/2000/03/leadership-that-gets-results

The Human Side of Enterprise (annotated) | McGraw – Hill, 2006 | McGregor, D.

Leadership Styles: How To Discover And Leverage Yours | Leadership IQ press, 2019 | Murphy, M.

How to Choose a Leadership Pattern | Harvard Business Review Press, 2009 | Tannenbaum, R., Schmidt, W.H.

The Managerial Grid: The Key to Leadership Excellence | Houston: Gulf Publishing Co., 1964 | Blake, R.; Mouton, J.

Situational Leader | Prentice Hall & IBD, 1986 | Hersey, P.

Maps of the territory

"The map is not the territory." – *Alfred Korzybski*

Korzybski was interested in the limitations of language in describing experience. The mathematician Eric Temple Bell (1933) described the map idea more clearly as, *the map is not the thing mapped*. Other variations are, *the word is not the thing*, or the philosophical writer Alan Watts' version, *the menu is not the meal*.

We perceive circumstances in our own unique way. How we think about our environment at any one time determines how we understand our position and significance within it. The territory remains the same; it is our perception of the territory we choose to shape. We create our own versions of reality.

We may consider *maps of the territory* as a way of illustrating how language chosen to convey a circumstance, meaning, or feeling, will inevitably be inaccurate, at best an approximation of experience. How we describe our map to others brings challenges of communication.

This is relevant to you in your management role: there is variety in the 'map drawing' of different people describing the same territory. We all have different maps of the same circumstance. At work, and outside of work, we communicate with colleagues, friends and family members who all believe, with conviction, their map is the most accurate representation of each piece of territory. It is personal and bespoke to them. This is a valuable insight for managers (see **Receive and transmit**).

There is no one map, no single reality. It depends on your perception and choice of thinking. This is a critical awareness. Sagacious managers understand team members will have differing perspectives on the world. Recognising this truism and getting to know employees' different maps is the starting point for fruitful team communications.

Your map is not the *only* map.

Further reading

Science and Sanity: An Introduction to Non-Aristotelian Systems and General Semantics (1933) | Forest Hills; Institute of General Semantics, 1995 | Korzybski, A.

Numerology | Williams & Wilkins, 1933 | Bell, E.T.

Steps to an Ecology of Mind | University of Chicago Press, 1972 | Bateson, G.

Matching and mirroring

"Friends hold a mirror up to each other; through that mirror
they can see each other in ways that would not otherwise
be accessible to them..." – *Aristotle*

Learning to match and mirror will enhance your relationships with team members.

Therapists use verbal and non-verbal techniques to accelerate and deepen rapport with clients. One method is matching and mirroring. We like people like us, and we especially like people who *behave* like us. This is an under-pinning principle of rapport (see **Rapport**, and **Rapport, advanced skills**).

We know from *clean language*, using common patterns of speech as a co-communicator builds a bond between people, *"She speaks the same language as me"*. This applies with physiological, non-verbal, language too. By using similar major or minor body movements we create unconscious recognition of us being 'the same', stimulating trust. Our unconscious minds are busy waving friendship to each other at a frequency not consciously recognised (see **Clean language**).

The nuances of physiology may be subtle. Eye movements, facial expressions, the way we lean our head, hand gestures, shoulder positions, back posture, breathing patterns, are indicators of internal communication. Our bodies are never silent; they are always saying something about us and how we are thinking and feeling.

Behavioural matching is the display of non-verbal communication exhibited by another person. For example, she massages her right ear lobe with her right forefinger and thumb, you massage your right earlobe with right forefinger and thumb; this is matching. Sit opposite and massage your left ear with your left hand, this is mirroring.

Inexact matching and mirroring activities are effective and least likely to be identified as mimicry. For example, rather than massaging the right earlobe, a massage of the right side of the face is more subtle, yet still achieves unconscious recognition of similarity.

Battino and South (1999) comment on this,

> "You do not have to match all movements and postures. It is only necessary to match the general way the other person is sitting in a chair or to tilt your head to the right a bit if they are a head-tilter, or to nod your head a bit if they are a nodder, or move one of your feet if they are a foot tapper or wriggler."

It is best not to respond immediately to changes in your co-communicator's physiology. A lag of a few seconds or more before adapting your own body positioning or motor movements is elegant.

The unconscious is far more accomplished than the conscious mind (see **Unconscious mind, trusting the**). It knows rapport when it sees it, hears it, or feels it. There is no need to feel ill at ease about matching and mirroring. You and your co-communicator will know, intuitively, something rather pleasant is happening.

To strengthen your management communications with team members, stick to simple major and minor motor movements. Operate elegantly, use lag time, and be inexact.

You'll know you have deepened rapport through matching or mirroring when you change body position, and you notice your co-communicator has replicated your move.

Further reading

Use Mirroring to Connect with Others | Wall Street Journal, 2016 | Shellenbarger, S. | https://www.wsj.com/articles/use-mirroring-to-connect-with-others-1474394329

Ericksonian Approaches: A Comprehensive Manual | Crown House Publishing, 1999 | Battino, R., South, T.

Measure twice, cut once

"Alwaies measure manie, before you cut anie." *– John (Giovanni) Florio*

My stepfather Alf Knight was a talented craftsman, a master joiner and cabinet maker. His skills were admired in his community. Precision and accuracy contributed to his success and his mantra of *measure twice, cut once* became a family motto.

Years later, as I began my studies into personal development, I learned about *patterns which connect* (see **Patterns which connect**) from the anthropologist and polymath Gregory Bateson (1972). Alf's *measure twice, cut once* philosophy served me well in my management career, bar a few instances where I rushed into decision making and paid a price, and my poor professionalism caused harm.

Management thinking is an art worth practising. Mature managers know when to make an instant decision, and when a more considered approach is appropriate. Thinking through available choices, especially those related to people factors, requires contemplation (see **Decision making tools**).

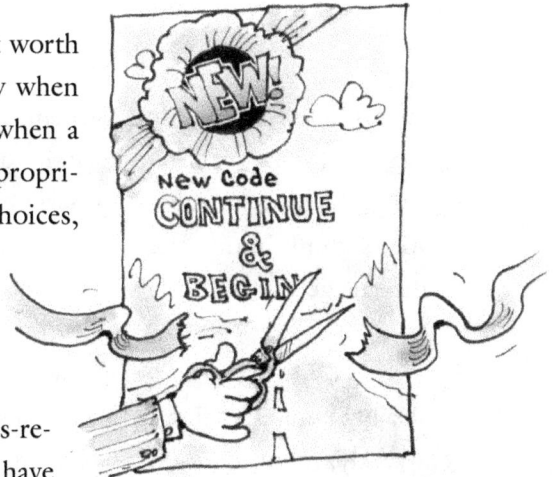

I made *horrific* management choices through knee jerk, stimulus-response decisions. Outcomes would have been more productive, and in some cases less damaging, if I had listened to my own propaganda and spent time engaged in *looking out of the window thinking* (see **Looking out of the window thinking**).

Where I got it right, my best thinking had come from daydreaming, followed up with evaluation of dreamy ideas and considered thought about strategies and tactics. Assessment of likely impact helped me check and double check the appropriateness of decisions (see **Secondary and tertiary consequences**).

Measure twice, cut once.

I have Alf's sturdy woodwork bench in my garage and I 'talk' to him regularly when I need advice on a maintenance or DIY project, or when I can' t find the right tool. He always comes up with the goods.

Further reading

Steps to an Ecology of Mind | University of Chicago Press, 1972 | Bateson, G.

Mind and Nature, A Necessary Unity | Hampton Press, 2002 | Bateson, G.

Measure Twice, Cut Once! | Psychology Today | Dwyer, D.J. | https://

www.psychologytoday.com/us/blog/got-a-minute/201202/measure-twice-cut-once

Measure Twice, Cut Once: Lessons from a Master Carpenter | Little, Brown, and Company, 1996 | Abram, M.

Meetings

"Everything we hear is an opinion, not a fact. Everything we see is a perspective, not the truth." *– Marcus Aurelius*

Managers have meetings, lots of them. How you make best use of the activity is crucial. Time is a budget item, and the more people involved in a meeting, the more time is being burnt (see **Time is a budget item**).

Let's think about the types of meetings in which team managers might engage.

Meeting Types

- Daily huddle standing up *get-going* sessions (see **Huddles**).
- Weekly/monthly workflow planning.

- Project preparation.
- Project status updates.
- Information gathering.
- Information sharing.
- Strategy and tactics planning.
- Decision making (see **Decision making, navy style** and **Decision-making tools**).
- Problem solving.
- Creative – innovation group sessions (see **Brainstorming, esrever, and thought showers**).
- Team relationship building.
- Project scrums (see **Scrums and sprints**).
- Bus Stop reviews (see **Change**).
- Functional topics; HR, IT, finance, production or manufacturing, marketing, sales, customer experience, logistics, and fulfilment.
- 121 meetings, KIT meetings, appraisal, and performance reviews (see **KIT meetings** and **Appraisals and performance reviews**).
- Performance management meetings (see **Performance management**).

… and multiple variants of the these.

How a meeting is managed influences its effectiveness. Despite the evolution of digital platforms as a standard medium for business meetings, the *way* in which meetings are facilitated remains crucial to their success.

Digital meeting management tools are available in abundance, and updating constantly, with new products on the market to aid scheduling and contribution during discussions. Technology may help of course, and yet the meeting still needs coordination and chairing.

Professional organisation and chairing of meetings require forward planning and consideration, no matter how frequently a regular meeting occurs, or how modest the topics under discussion.

Here are some ideas for managers to consider, in advance of arranging a workplace meeting,

20 Meeting Disciplines

1. Is the meeting necessary? Could information be transferred between parties electronically without locking in participants' face time, whether in person or digital?
2. If there is a genuine benefit to be gained from holding a meeting, *for whom* is the benefit?
3. What is the purpose of the meeting? What outputs are intended?
4. How will you know if the meeting has been successful?
5. What category of meeting will it be? *See types of meeting above.*
6. What *Terms of Reference* could be drawn up to explain the purpose of the meeting to participants?
7. Are all these people really required to attend? If so, how will you engage all participants to gain value from them? How will you balance attendees' contributions, to avoid overbearing meetings members dominating discussion, and encourage *wallflowers* to engage?
8. What is the agenda for the meeting?
9. Think ahead. What are the likely positions of participants, for each agenda item?
10. What allocation of time is appropriate for each item? Who will be timekeeper?
11. What will be the duration of the meeting, from start to end?
12. What preparatory work would be helpful for attendees to undertake?
13. What is the best date and time to schedule the meeting?
14. Who will chair or co-ordinate the discussion?
15. How will participants be able to contribute?
16. What pre-meeting discussions, between specific individuals, might be helpful?
17. Who is taking notes of discussion and actions?
18. How will actions be noted, allocated, time managed, and reviewed?
19. Who will circulate meeting notes and actions?
20. Is follow up required, or superfluous?

Meetings Contribution Culture

Is it safe for team members to express opinions during meetings in your organisation? That is; do participants *feel* safe to contribute? Meetings intended to gather the thoughts of colleagues will only succeed if team members feel comfortable in offering opinions.

I can smell the culture at play in a client business within minutes of attending an internal meeting. Leadership styles and organisational climate is revealed in a meeting environment. Tannenbaum and Schmidt's leadership continuum maps out a sliding scale of style, from an authoritarian *Telling* approach, through *Selling, Consulting, Sharing,* to a *Delegating* approach (see **Management style**). It's easy to spot.

Where there seems a cautionary approach to participation from attendees, there is a reason behind it. I'm a curious individual, and it's interesting for me to uncover the dynamics of meetings culture and the atmosphere within parts of a business.

I can quickly sniff out feelings of anxiety, even fear, about contributing to meeting discussions. This is common in larger group settings where a senior manager is co-ordinating a session, with limited time available for all participants to contribute. These meetings become downloading platforms. On occasions I've experienced targeting of underperforming attendees, even tellings-off, in a public forum. Participants learn to *keep mum*, and avoid offering potentially contentious thoughts, or ask questions (certainly *challenging* questions) which may place them in the meeting leader's spotlight.

It sounds sinister, doesn't it? That's because in some organisations I've witnessed, it *is* sinister.

In **Johari, adapted for management** I've explained how a large *Open* area helps create healthy interactive space within a work group. Open areas grow when the space in which to communicate is considered safe. When colleagues feel at ease in sharing thoughts, suggestions, and beliefs in meetings, they make themselves vulnerable. Freedom and encouragement to be open, without defensive counter comment from senior players, is an indicator of *Servant Leadership* (see **Servant leadership**).

I pose questions for team managers, and more senior managers and directors, about safety in the Open area,

- Do your direct reports feel safe in their transparency with you?
- With their peers?
- With more senior managers?

- How do you know that?
- How does safety manifest itself in meetings?

It is one thing to promote a safe Open area, and the benefits of freedom of expression during meetings; it is another altogether to live to those values, to be congruent in what you say you want (safe space for contributors), and how you behave. If there's a gap, communication in meetings is at best hamstrung, at worst doomed to tight lipped attendees.

- What *Meeting Types* do you facilitate, or attend?
- Which of the *20 Meetings Disciplines* do you adhere to? Which are worth considering?
- What is the *Meetings Contribution Culture* under your leadership?

Further reading

How to Lead Better Remote Meetings | Gartner, May 2020 | Mesaglio, M. | https://www.gartner.com/smarterwithgartner/how-to-lead-better-remote-meetings

How to Run a More Effective Meeting | New York Times Business, 2023 | Bryant, A. | https://www.nytimes.com/guides/business/how-to-run-an-effective-meeting

Dear Manager, You're Holding Too Many Meetings | Harvard Business Review, March 2022 | Laker, B., Pereira, V., Malik, A., Soga, L. | https://hbr.org/2022/03/dear-manager-youre-holding-too-many-meetings

Mentoring

"If I have seen further, it is by standing on the shoulders of giants."

– Isaac Newton

Professional team managers continually improve their skills. Team management presents different challenges every day. Sometimes an independent, third-party perspective brings objectivity and a judicious steer in a new direction. A mentor can help with this. Mentors are valuable sources of wisdom because they have already been there, seen it and done it, and will identify options for your management progression.

Mentoring is not coaching (see **Coaching**).

A mentor experienced and talented in a specific competence offers a fast-track for your CPD, transferring knowledge direct to you. Mentoring may involve a degree of teaching, or suggesting, by the mentor to you, the 'mentee'. A mentoring relationship may be a short-term arrangement focussing on a specific management function or could evolve into long-term support (see **Continuous Professional Development [CPD]**).

The right person to mentor you is usually *not* someone influential in your professional role, maybe not even in your organisation. A best fit mentor may be outside your everyday working life.

Most management challenges are common across employment environments. For example, introducing change, presenting to directors, negotiating with suppliers or customers, dealing with a difficult colleague, managing personal stress; these are typical management functions in any context. An external mentor can bring fresh thinking and a different perspective.

Support from an external mentor avoids relationship baggage in communicating with a line manager or other internal influencer. External mentors guide without agenda.

Do you have a management mentor? Would you benefit from mentoring? What would have to happen for you to find mentoring support?

Further reading

Mentoring Matters: Three Essential Elements of Success | Forbes, 2019 | Abbajay, M. | https://www.forbes.com/sites/maryabbajay/2019/01/20/mentoring-matters-three-essential-element-of-success/?sh=65fb64eb45a9

Mentoring Manual, The: Your Step-by-step Guide to Being a Better Mentor | Pearson Business, 2021 | Starr, J.

Meta thinking

"The world is full of magical things patiently waiting for our wits to grow sharper." *– Bertrand Russell*

Meta refers to higher levels of logical thought; it means *about itself*. For example, *Metathinking* is thinking about thinking, *metadata* means data about data, *metalanguage* is language used to describe languages.

We can use the pattern of *meta* to consider logical levels of thinking about most things, including team management.

Thinking at a higher logical level helps managers step away from immediate concerns, to think in bigger terms. Rather than thinking about *how* a tactical operation is being delivered, consider *whether* this specific tactic is the right approach to fit with a higher-level strategy, e.g., customer experience policy, process efficiency, human leadership commitments?

- Is the five second pick up rule for in-bound telephone calls the right consideration, or should we be asking if in-bound calls to this team is the best use of resource?
- Can the production bottlenecks be unblocked, or is an outsourced kit supply an option, delivered Just In Time (see **JIT and float time**)?
- Are customer queries transferred from call centre to the sales team working smoothly, or should we be considering a one-stop-contact facility with first time resolution?
- Are team members arriving for work on time, or should we be thinking about the best working pattern for workplace operations?

Meta thinking operates at a level above the current discussion. It is a continuous improvement philosophy. How could you employ meta thinking to resolve your management challenges?

Further reading

Everything You Can Do, You Can Do Meta

A psychological key to smarter life navigation that you've never heard of | Psychology Today, 2020 | Sherman, J.E.

Metathinking: The Art and Practice of Transformational Thinking | Springer, 2020 | Shannon, N, Frischherz, B.

Metathinking.org | https://metathinking.org/

Metaphors

Once upon a time there was a young prince who believed in all things
but three. He did not believe in Princesses, he did not believe in
islands, he did not believe in God. His father, the king, told him that
such things did not exist. As there were no princesses or islands in his
father's domains, and no sign of God, the prince believed his father.

– The Magus, Fowles, J.

Metaphor stories offer hidden meaning. Like parables, fables and folk tales, metaphors provide a story within a story, a hidden, or not so hidden, meaning which offers guidance to listeners or readers. Stories provide an indirect channel for imparting advice.

Therapists use metaphorical stories to highlight options and choices for patients. Sometimes the metaphor is obvious to the listener, sometimes less so. Stories may be brief or more detailed, allowing a listener to fully immerse and associate within the story teller's tale.

People remember stories. I use stories in conference, group, and individual work to embed messages and leave memorable references for listeners to reflect upon. The stories may be true, or they may be useful fictions (see **Useful fictions**) or might be a combination of truth and imagination. It doesn't matter, so long as the story interests the listener and offers a useful and memorable insight.

Here is a brief communications story, about demanding language styles, and its impact on relationships,

I have a rugby ex-teammate I enjoy a beer with, Jeff. We meet up now
and again for an evening of nostalgia… reminiscing about *Glory Days*

(they weren't) and *When We Were Kings* (we weren't) … harmless evenings of delusion. I'd knock on his door and say,

"I have beer tokens in my pocket Jeffrey! Would you like to come and spend them with me?"

Jeff would grab his coat and off we'd be off in a flash!

Then he got married and things changed. Well, when I used to call round for him… you know… to come out to play… his new wife Charlotte was there… and she was fine about us going out for a beer. She was friendly, and while I was waiting for the old rascal to find his wallet, she would ask about what I had been doing at work… and I might say…

"A busy one this week Charlotte, enjoyable though! Met up with a client in Edinburgh… a day trip to Frankfurt on Wednesday… and some business in London today… good fun!"

And then it would start…

"What you need to do Nick… is less travelling. You should spend less time at work at your age… you ought to be slowing down… you need to think about your health… you should go part time… that's what you need to do…"

Now, I go straight to the pub and meet Jeff there.

Metaphors are influential in team management. Stories referring to your own experiences, or the experiences of someone you know, or of someone known by someone you know (known as 'stacked reality' stories), offer a useful format for your metaphorical tale. True stories work well because you know them experientially and have deep understanding of their impact.

What metaphors of influence could you use in your team manager role?

Further reading

Therapeutic Metaphors: Helping Others Through the Looking Glass | Independently published, 2017 | Gordon, D.

How 8 Organizational Metaphors Impact Leadership | NOBL Academy | Editorial team, August 2019 | https://academy.nobl.io/gareth-morgan-organizational-metaphors/

Images of Organization | SAGE Publications, 2006 | Morgan, G.

Milton Model

"And sometimes the answers… seem to be one thing…
and turn out to be another." – Milton Erickson

An artful technique for helping team members find their own solutions is to use the Milton Model.

Milton Erickson, the hypnotherapist, used vague statements to allow his patients space, to find their own meaning and answers to whatever matter was troubling them. Carefully crafted open statements challenge a person's unconscious mind to search for their own answers; to fill in the gaps. There is no imposition or recommendation of what to do.

Pauses are used extensively in Milton Model statements to allow the subject thinking time and solution finding (see **I know you don't know**).

You can use the Milton Model in your management role to help team members find solutions to their workplace problems. Managers don't have to have all the answers. Employees have options and choices. The solution to their difficulty may be hidden, or temporarily mislaid in their mind. I continue to use Milton Model statements as an integral part of management coaching sessions, positioning solution-finding firmly in the hands of the coachee.

Here are some Milton Model style statements to stimulate a team member's thinking,

"You already know… there are certain opportunities for you… in your current job role… and you might be beginning to think about them…"

"There are always options… and you can consider your options…"

"You might be curious… about which option… offers the best outcome for you…"

"Your mind may wonder (wander)… which of your personal resources… will be most useful in resolving this…"

"There may be another opportunity… to consider… in more detail…"

"Because you already know the answer… it's there in your mind… somewhere…"

"Sometimes we forget to remember... how to deal with things... and that's ok... we are all fallible human beings... we can remember again..."

"You can sleep on it... and find the answer... later... you can do that... whenever you like..."

Erickson was skilled at influencing patients to take positive, helpful action. He encouraged people to enjoy life and have fun.

Think about how you could use vagueness in Milton Model statements to help your team members find their own solutions to problems.

Further reading

Ericksonian Approaches, A Comprehensive Manual | Crown House Publishing, 1999 | Battino, R., South, T.L.

Hypnotic Realities: The Induction od Clinical Hypnosis and Forms of Indirect Suggestion |

Irvington, 1976 | Erickson, M.H., Rossi, E.l., Rossi, S.I.

Patterns of the Hypnotic Techniques of Milton H. Erickson, M.D. Volume 1. | Meta Publications, 1975 | Bandler, R., Grinder, J.

Modelling excellence

"Success leaves clues." – *Tony Robbins*

You may know, or have known, managers who seem totally in control, exuding confidence, and competence. There seems a magic about them. There is no magic though, only structure. Talented managers may *consciously* think and act, and yet some parts of their 'magic' will be delivered through unconscious competence.

My friend Johnny was a fabulous rugby prop forward. Few opponents got the better of him. When he retired from playing, I asked him if he would coach youngsters at our club. *"I don't know what I do, it comes naturally."* There was a magic about his skill, yes. There was also a structure, of which he was unconsciously competent.

Studies of talented therapists and changemakers in the 1970s revealed practitioners were often unaware of which elements of their interventions were stimulating change. Frank Pucelik (2010) said 95% of a successful practitioner's performance was 'smoke'. What interested him was identifying the 5% making the difference.

Modelling is a method of unravelling the magic of a star performer, to reveal structure and process. Richard Bandler, John Grinder, and Frank Pucelik were instrumental in designing a methodology for modelling excellence. Bandler and Grinder's two volumes, *The Structure of Magic (Volumes 1 and 2)* describe their modelling work in detail.

Modelling excellence is a great tool for team managers. It involves asking good questions of a star performer to undercover their 'strategy', Pucelik's 5%. An example modelling question, in a customer facing environment, could be,

"How do you prepare, when approaching a prospective customer?"

A star performer's answer might be,

"As I approach, I say to myself, 'This customer has come here for a reason, she's interested in buying our product/service' It's my job to help her place an order."

This would be part of, and not all, of the star performer's strategy. What else do they think or do in this circumstance? You may be able to observe and listen to them in action. Effective modellers ask questions to uncover a star performer's internal thinking, their structure or process, and personal values.

Other questions might include,

- "How do you prepare yourself each day?"
- "What self-talk do you engage in?"
- "What personal 'rules' do you have?"
- "What language patterns do you use?"
- "How do you hold your posture?"
- "How do you breathe?"
- "How do you dress? "
- "What process do you follow?"
- "What work habits do you have?"
- "What haven't I asked you, and you would like to answer?"

Remember, most star players are unconsciously competent about their excellence. Like Johnny, they may not know how they do things, so it helps to remind them of a time when they were exhibiting their skills at their very best and get them to replay their experience as a video in their mind – to imagine they are doing that thing, *now*. Tony Robbins (1986) refers to this as putting *the cook in the kitchen*.

As the model recalls the experience, you can ask well-timed precision questions about what they were thinking and how they were operating. You will uncover at least some of their structure of excellence. In modelling, this is known as *eliciting the strategy* (see **Structure of Well-Done-ness®**).

You will need time with your star performer away from their workstation. And you will almost certainly need to explain what you are doing!

Modelling is an underutilised management tool. If excellence exists, model it.

Further reading

Whispering in the Wind | J & C Enterprises, 2001 | Bostic St. Clair, C., Grinder, J.

Frank Pucelik – His view on NLP's beginnings | NLP Academy, 2010 | Johnson, L. | https://www.nlpacademy.co.uk/articles/view/frank_pucelik_-_his_view_on_nlps_beginnings/

Unlimited Power | Simon & Schuster, 1986 | Robbins, A

The Structure of Magic: A Book about Language and Therapy, Volume 1 | Science and Behavior Books, 1975 | Bandler, R., Grinder, J.

The Structure of Magic 2, A Book About Communication and Change | Science and Behavior Books, 1976 | Grinder, J., Bandler, R.

Monkeys, management of

"I always delegate. If someone is very good at something, whatever it is, he will be in charge." – *Johan Cruyff*

When, as a young manager, I read the Harvard Business Review article, *Who's Got the Monkey?* I realised I was not alone in my (then) management style. It seemed I was busier than ever, with so many issues to deal with, many of them passed by team members for my decision and action.

Who's Got the Monkey? tells the story of a manager who takes on the problems of his team, promising to think about each issue and subsequently let the team member know his thoughts. The title refers to an analogy of feeding and caring for a monkey, where initially the monkey sits on the shoulder of a team member and, after consulting with the line manager, the monkey passes to the manager's shoulder for care and attention. In effect the subordinate has 'delegated up' the issue to the manager.

With a team of employees to manage, it is not long before the manager has a troop of monkeys to care for, all of which started out belonging to team members. The article encapsulates precisely what was going on in my management life. I was a busy fool and becoming less effective with each new monkey I was asked to care for.

Many newly promoted team managers think this ok, that they are managing well, *supporting* their team. This misperception of management, taking on the problems of individual team members, limits effectiveness, clogs up productivity and stunts the self-development of employees.

Competent managers make best use of the skills and attributes of team members. They delegate appropriately and regularly (see **Delegating**). They encourage employees to care for their own monkeys, and where appropriate, to take on additional or more challenging monkeys as part of professional development (see **Job enrichment**).

Wised-up team managers encourage a culture of personal responsibility in team members (see **Quality and TQM**). If consultation with the manager is necessary, the employee is expected to bring a considered set of options, including their proposed action.

Further reading

The One Minute Manager | Penguin Putman, 1997 | Blanchard, K.H.

Management Time: Who's Got the Monkey? | Harvard Business Review, December 1999 | Oncken, W., Wass. D.L. | https://hbr.org/1999/11/management-time-whos-got-the-monkey

Motivation

"Correction does much, but encouragement does more."
– Johann Wolfgang von Goethe

Much has been researched and written about motivation at work. It continues to be a topic
of discussion in employment across all
sectors. The question of how team
members can be *motivated* is perennial.

It remains a challenging subject
because it is not possible to *motivate*,
in the same way as it is not possible to excite,
inspire, annoy, frighten, instil happiness, anxiety, or other human emotions.
There is no authority within one person to select the feelings of another.
Although people may be influenced by others, or by circumstance, they
choose their own emotion, stimulated by thinking.

Managers can fashion an environment where employees understand
team purpose and opportunities and are given the resources to make a difference. Colleagues can choose to feel good about their contribution at work
(see **Pride, encouragement of**). Motivation comes from within. It needs a
fertile environment in which to flourish.

Command-and-control has short term influence and requires regular
reinforcement. Industrial psychologist Fred Herzberg (1987) dismissed
short term leverage as KITAs, the *kick in the arse* approach to stimulating
activity in employees. Herzberg suggested KITAs create *movement* rather
than *motivation* (see **KITAs**).

Herzberg proposed true motivational factors as,

- meaningful valuable work
- a sense of satisfaction from achievement
- recognition for achievement
- personal advancement and growth (in whatever form).

By contrast, Herzberg referred to many organisational considerations as
hygiene factors. He suggested elements were purely *potential dissatisfiers*, in

that no matter how good they are, employees are unlikely to jump out of bed in the morning, buoyed with ambition and personal drive because of the (for example) new software system, the reconditioned heating system, or the revised expenses claim form.

I use an analogy of hospital care to illustrate this idea. Imagine attending a hospital for treatment and the environment is spotlessly clean. No matter how hygienic the environment, your medical condition is unlikely to improve due to cleanliness alone.

Consider the opposite; imagine the hospital is rife with bacteria, Legionnaire's disease is in the water and air conditioning system, and the flesh-eating bug MRSA is rampant. Chances are some patients are likely to become more ill than when they first entered the hospital.

There's a similar pattern (see **Patterns which connect**) in workplace environments. Its improbable any of the factors listed below would inspire passion and drive, no matter how slick, or high quality, they may be. As *hygiene factors (potential dissatisfiers)* though, if less than adequate, they are likely to cause irritation and demotivation in team members.

- workplace temperature, heating, or air conditioning systems.
- software platforms.
- admin systems and process requirements.
- décor.
- workspace layout.
- seating and furniture.
- parking.
- toilet access.
- meal and rest breaks.
- kitchen and refreshments facilities.
- cleanliness.
- smell.

Fellow humanist-psychology writers McClelland, Maslow, Vroom and Alderfer offered their own motivation-at-work theories, not dissimilar to Fred Herzberg's ideas.

Celebration and ego strengthening are key to personal drive. When people feel good about themselves, when they feel resourceful and capable, then confidence grows, and personal drive is unleashed. Employees feel capable and willing to take on new challenges and ambitions, the self-actualisation Maslow suggested as the pinnacle of personal need. I explain more about internal motivation and the importance of confidence in my book *Fast Coaching* (see **Coaching, Continue & Begin Fast Coaching®**).

Today social media platforms are awash with *motivational* strategies, promoting philosophies and behaviours to optimise the workplace experience. Which doctrine team managers follow will be a function of their professional experience, personal beliefs, and biases (see **Beliefs, you can choose or change** and **Cognitive bias**).

What is certain, is the individualistic nature of internal motivation.

Effective managers understand the uniqueness of each team member's inner drive. Human Leadership principles (see **Human leadership**) shape workplace experiences to the distinct needs of employees. Empathy for each colleague, and adaptability to suit their work-life needs, is becoming an employee engagement factor in the post-Covid world of work.

But how? The key to unlocking inner drive within team members is for managers to understand the people they work with. This is why keep in touch meetings, and supervision sessions are so valuable (see **KIT meetings, Supervision sessions**, and **Get inside their world**).

Inspiring managers create a fertile environment to stimulate team members' feelings of personal achievement. How fertile is the motivational environment for your team? And how well do you know your colleagues and the nature of their inner drive (see **Emotional Drivers™**)?

Further reading

The Science of Improving Motivation at Work | PositivePsychology.com 2020 | Souders, B. | https://positivepsychology.com/improving-motivation-at-work/

One More Time: How Do You Motivate Employees? | Harvard Business Review Press, 2008 | Herzberg, F.

20 Most Popular Theories of Motivation in Psychology | Souders, B. | https://positivepsychology.com/motivation-theories-psychology/ (accessed 07.07.24)

N

NDK Performance Model®

"Excellent firms don't believe in excellence – only in constant improvement and constant change." – *Tom Peters*

There is a pattern which connects world-class organisations. They work to a common model of excellence emphasising continuous improvement. I designed the NDK Performance Model® as a way of illustrating the pattern (see **Patterns which connect**).

There are four levels of the NDK Performance Model,

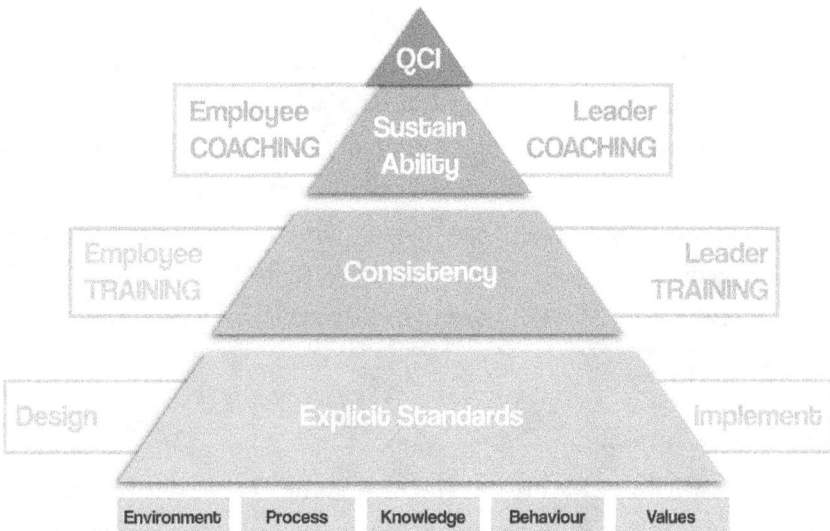

Level 1. Explicit standards

Class leaders have an explicit set of performance standards spelling out exactly what is required of employees. Team members need to know what is expected, if they are to work to a given standard. Explicitly described standards create transparency of job role. There are five categories of explicit standards described in the NDK Performance Model; there may be other considerations in your organisation.

1. *Environment* – the required standards of workplace order and presentation.
2. *Process* – the procedures and protocols employees are required to follow.
3. *Knowledge* – the knowledge required to effectively conduct a job role.
4. *Behaviour* – expected forms of behaviour at work.
5. *Values* – the ethics and principles an organisation aspires to uphold.

Designing a set of explicit standards, followed by their introduction and promotion is helpful, it provides a path for employees and managers to follow. On their own though, standards are not enough. I know plenty of organisations with an impressive set of explicitly described standards, which are not delivered.

Level 2. Consistency

Class-leading organisations strive for consistency of excellence across territories and functional teams. The same high standards are delivered in each operational area. Effective training can help achieve this, especially when competency based. Consistency is of limited value, however, if it is temporary. Top performing operators know performance excellence must be delivered day-in-day out, long after training initiatives have been launched. In some organisations, training has a short half-life. It's like throwing wet mud against the wall. Most of the mud slides off immediately, and the rest shortly after.

Level 3. Sustainability

Training, especially soft skills training, is a complete waste of energy and resource (and worst of all, *hope*) unless new behaviours are *sustained*. Key to sustainability is the development of a coaching capability for team managers to keep employees' plates spinning long after a training event has passed. Sustainability through local coaching keeps the momentum up and the training alive.

Level 4. QCI – Quest for Continuous Improvement (see Quality and TQM)

What is excellent today will not be good enough tomorrow. The best brands have a compelling obsession for never ending improvement, creating better quality products and services, delivered quicker, cheaper, and providing more value-added than today's version. QCI is a constant focus for best-in-class operators (see **Case Study: On Growing Managers [and our Business]**).

Think about your organisation and the team you manage. Which performance standards have been designed and made explicit to work to? How consistently are they delivered, by everyone, everywhere, in all circumstances? How are standards of delivery sustained? How is momentum maintained, day after day, week after week, month after month? Is QCI an embedded *habit-ual* mind-set?

Further viewing

NDK Performance Model® | https://www. youtube.com/watch?v=n4sPW5N7w9E | Drake-Knight, N., 2016

Fast Coaching. The Complete Guide to New Code Continue & Begin® | Dandelion Digital, 2016 | Drake-Knight, N. |

Audible https://www.audible.co.uk/pd/ Fast-Coaching-Audiobook/B07TTKD13T

The Motivation Agency | https:// themotivationagency-online.com/course/ begin

Networking (internal & external)

"If you want to go fast, go alone. If you want to go far, go with others."
– African proverb

A regular request I hear from directors and senior managers, is to encourage their operational managers to network, to build relationships, alliances, and improve co-operative lines of communication across the organisation. This is *internal* networking.

Plenty of departmental teams operate within self-limiting silos, inward looking, and competitive with other work groups rather than co-operative. Clever managers go out of their way to strengthen bonds and trust between internal teams.

Making regular contact with key individuals and teams, understanding the world they operate in, and learning how to help them, is a prudent management skill. Smile, be friendly, use people's names, be interested, and ask about them. These things go a long way (see **Interest, Human Leadership** and **Get inside their world**).

External networking might include suppliers, customer contacts, industry groups, professional bodies, even competitors. Social media platforms, particularly professional networks, offer ready-made opportunities. Networking outside the bubble of your organisation provides differing perspectives, and fresh thinking.

Building connections beyond your business will bring a return in investment, particularly in terms of personal learning. In my experience, external networking is often a long game, building associations and friendly relations which may go on for years without tangible business or career opportunity. Returns do come though. Many of my most rewarding consulting projects have come from long established contacts, people who recall an earlier positive experience.

I remember a politically minded senior manager, Colin, whose mantra for building relationships was *"Go and see them. Have a nice cup of tea."* He was right, at least in stimulating initial rapport (see **Rapport**).

Networking creates learning. It builds relationships. It will pay you back, in different ways and maybe not today.

Further reading

How to Win Friends and Influence People | Vermilion, 2006 | Carnegie, D.

The Complete Guide to Business Networking [+8 Key Tips You Should Leverage] |

Hubspot, February 2023 | Storm, A. | https://blog.hubspot.com/sales/what-is-business-networking

95% (ninety-five percent) management

"Good business leaders create a vision, articulate the vision, passionately own the vision, and relentlessly drive it to completion."

– Jack Welch

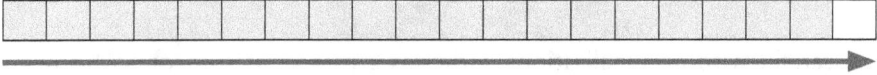

Some years ago, my board director colleagues, and I identified a recurring company phenomenon. A repeating behaviour pattern seemed to dog the business we were growing. We liked to think we were innovative and developmental in our thinking. We bounced off each other, stimulating great ideas and making commitments (see **Commitment mantra**) to implement our latest game-changer plan, which would, without any doubt, move us to the next stage in our business development.

Energy, resource, and hope was invested in each exciting new initiative. Excitement levels were high and all we had to do was design and implement the new idea. Time and again, we reached 'nearly done' stage and then lost momentum. Our brave new idea did not make it to operational implementation. We were almost there, on the cusp of application, except for the final pieces not being in place. Resisting forces were at large. Momentum slowed and we lost interest; we were by then on to the next *Big Idea*.

After a while, we recognised the pattern. We labelled it *95% Management*. It seemed to be the final stages of dedicated activity which we were failing to drive home. The pattern went on for years before we finally made a policy decision, no more 95% projects. It became an incantation for the business.

Never again would we allow ourselves to get excited, invest so heavily, and then abandon the project for something more topical.

Jack Welch of General Electric (GE) was right, *"...relentlessly drive it to completion."*

Further reading

Winning | Harper Collins, 2005 | Welch, J. with Welch, S.

The ultimate project completion checklist | Filestage, March 2023 | Skusa, M. | https://filestage.io/blog/project-completion/

Nominalisations, behaviour versus thing

"I am not a thing – an actor, a writer – I am a person who does things
– I write, I act – and I never know what I am going to do next. I think
you can be imprisoned if you think of yourself as a noun."

– Stephen Fry

Be careful with nominalisations, either as a user or as someone who hears them in use.

Nominalisations are language patterns where a verb is changed to a noun; a behaviour pattern is translated erroneously into a name label. For example,

"You are a failure, because you made a huge mistake".

Consider other similar phrases:

"You are stupid."

"I am a failure."

"She is an angry person."

"He is an idiot."

"That customer is a pain."

(In families) "You're a naughty boy/girl."

Notice how the phrases above create a *noun*, a *thing*. This is a clue to the irrationality of the thinking and the language being used by the speaker.

People are not *Stupids* or *Failures* – there are no such things. People may have 'failed' to complete a specific task or acted in a 'stupid' way. Someone is not an *Angry Person* although they may have acted in an angry manner.

When we use nominalisations to describe someone, including ourselves, we create a 'thing' which does not exist. Even though it does not exist we attempt to create it in the form of a nominalisation. This is irrational thinking.

Why the concern? Well, because nominalisations label people as being stuck in a behaviour pattern. Nominalisations cut out choice and opportunity, immediately. I can change my behaviour, whereas it is difficult to change me as a 'thing'.

Think about your language use. Are you prone to nominalising?

Further reading

The Structure of Magic: A Book about Language and Therapy, Volume 1 | R. Bandler, J. Grinder | Science and Behavior Books, 1975

10 Good Reasons Not To Label People (Or Yourself) | A Conscious Rethink | Editorial team, June 2023 | https://www.aconsciousrethink.com/13771/stop-labeling-people/

O

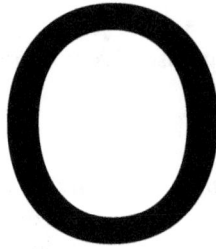

Objectives, management by (MBOs and OKRs)

"Management by objective works – if you know the objectives. Ninety percent of the time you don't." – Peter Drucker

As far back as Drucker, management thinkers were considering how best to set out ambitions and monitor delivery. *Management by Objectives* (MBO) was promoted as a formal administrative method in Drucker's book *The Practice of Management.* MBO is sometimes known as MBR, Management by Results. Not much has changed in the factors senior managers wish to address,

- What is our ambition?
- What, specifically, do we want to achieve?
- How can we break down our ambitions into digestible chunks?
- Who is best placed to deliver them?
- How can we monitor performance against ambition?

MBO begins with the identification of a set of objectives for a defined period, for example, annually. Subsidiary objectives are then determined for divisions of the organisation and contribute to overall results.

As MBO is cascaded through an enterprise it reaches individual employees who are charged with responsibility to deliver on work objectives specific to their job role. MBO is most effective for employees when team manager and member are both involved in drawing up mutually agreed work targets. Imposed objectives are less likely to provide inner motivation (see **KITAs** and **Motivation**).

Andy Grove of Intel expanded on MBO with what he called OKRs, Objectives and Key Results. He proposed an objective as a direction of travel, *"That's where we want to go!"*. He made Key Results the means of measuring performance as milestones in the journey towards the Objective. Critically, the Key Result must be measurable. As Grove said,

> "Milestones are only useful if you can see you've passed, or you've not passed. You don't 'maybe' pass milestones. You either do or you don't."

John Doerr picked up OKRs and introduced it during the early days of Google, with dramatic impact. Doerr's book *Measure What Matters* illustrates OKRs in detail.

- Objective is the *What*.
- Key Results are the *How*.

Below is an example of an OKR relating to sales performance. Notice how the OKR is presented as a live report, describing performance so far, and development required against plan. This is different to KPIs which do not address the goal or ambition ('Objective') and offer purely historical data.

OKRs are dynamic, they highlight *progress towards* as well as *distance travelled*.

Notice also, how the OKR is published to a select audience of stakeholders, in this case, the entire work group. Making OKRs public creates stimulus to team and stakeholder engagement.

Objective: Increase Branch Sales

Owner: Nick DK   Visibility: All colleagues

WHAT. Objective	Increase Branch Sales
HOW. Key Result 1. Target achievement: monthly	Increase LFL sales +3%
HOW. Key Result 2. Target achievement: year end	Increase ATV from £84 to £88
HOW. Key Result 3. Target achievement: year end	Increase GP% margin from 48% to 52%

WHAT. Objective: Increase Branch Sales		
Average of Key Results progress = 45%	➡	Progress 45%

Key Result 1 progress Increase LFL sales +3%, monthly				
0%	+2% ➡		+3%	Progress 66%

Key Result 2 progress Increase ATV from £84 to £88.00, year end			
£84.00 £85.60 ➡		£88.00	Progress 40%

Key Result 3 progress Increase GP% margin from 42% to 52%, year end			
42% 45% ➡		52%	Progress 30%

How do you, or could you, use MBO/MBR/OKR principles in managing your team?

Further reading

Measure What Matters; OKRs – The Simple Idea That Drives 10x Growth | Penguin Random House, 2018 | Doerr, J.

10 Great Retail Store Operations OKR Examples | Profit.co | https://www.profit.co/blog/okr-examples/10-great-retail-store-operations-okr-examples/

What is an OKR? Andy Grove, OKR inventor, explains. | https://www.youtube.com/watch?v=1ht_1VAF6ik (accessed 07.07.24)

John Doerr. OKRs. Objectives & Key Results. | https://www.youtube.com/watch?v=pbkI--GvEZY (accessed 07.07.24)

Obsession, compelling

"I am not as goal obsessed as I am process obsessed." *– Lady Gaga*

Winning managers make their ambitions a compelling obsession (like writing this book). They understand the need to be focused, to keep moving their obsession along, to every day make a movement towards the future goal, no matter how small.

The key to achievement is focus on the process, the journey, and the incremental steps to success. Marginal gains, measured by day, week, month, or even over years, provides evidence of *movement towards* (see **Emotional Drivers™**) and the feelings of achievement and satisfaction which come with that. Achievement, no matter how minor, provides belief, strengthens self-image, and spurs us on to further investments of energy.

The ambition must be compelling for this to happen, obsessively so. We create our own compelling obsessions when we make a firm decision, considered and non-negotiable, to achieve a stated goal. For some people writing the goal down, drawing a picture, or sharing an ambition with others, are means of leveraging the obsession. Then comes the application of effort, tireless, persistent, never-ending dedication to work towards your compelling outcome. It will require personal discipline, and an unswerving commitment sustained long after the initial rush of start-up excitement (see **Commitment mantra**).

Few people dedicate enough energy, over a sustained period, or are sufficiently resilient and adaptive to barriers and obstacles for major achievement to come their way. Some will say, *"I'd do anything to be able to do/achieve X."* No, they wouldn't. They talk a good game but don't put in the investment of self to make it happen. You can deliver remarkable results if you have a compelling obsession and act upon it, persistently, for a long time.

Lukewarm doesn't cut it. Neither does *trying* (see **Tentative is no good**), only unrelenting commitment and massive, sustained action achieves a compelling obsession.

Do you have a compelling obsession?

Further reading

Obsession Is A Positive Quality When It Comes To Improvement | Forbes, 2014 | Selk, J. | https://www.forbes.com/sites/jasonselk/2014/01/13/obsession-is-a-positive-quality-when-it-comes-to-improvement/?sh=79ba0f847181

What Makes Your Obsession Healthy or Unhealthy: Why some obsessions can turn into success | Psychology Today, July 2011 | Chamorro-Premuzic, T. | https://www.psychologytoday.com/us/blog/mr-personality/201107/what-makes-your-obsession-healthy-or-unhealthy

Occam/Ockham's razor

"Simplicity is the ultimate sophistication." *– Leonardo da Vinci*

I've worked with senior managers who make unnecessary complexity an art form. Maybe it's an urge to feel sophisticated, or to cover off all eventualities? Whatever the reason, when it comes to team management, simplicity is best. Employees have enough to do without having to navigate through a maze of algorithms.

William of Ockham (Surrey, England) was a Franciscan friar in the early 1300s. *Ockham's Razor* was his thinking process of *shaving off* unlikely explanations for unexplained phenomena and accepting the most obvious or simplest reason as most likely. His context, back then, was to explain *divine miracles*, as 'simply because it pleases God'.

Today, the principle of Ockham's Razor is still used in science as a reference point for thinking through theoretical models. Straightforward constructs are easier to test than more complex possibilities. The simplest explanation is the best.

Aristotle commented,

"Nature operates in the shortest way possible."

In organisational management, reflections of Ockham's Razor are found in the process improvement strategies of Total Quality Management, Kaizen, 5S and Value Stream Mapping, all favouring simplicity, and the removal of excess activity, considered *waste* (see **Lean management, Quality and TQM,** and **Quality circles and Kaizen**).

Simplification is a proven approach for efficiency of operations. It is a *pattern which connects* across organisational processes (see **Patterns which connect**). Simplicity in functional management is effective and easily understood by all those involved, directors, managers, and employees. For customers and service users too, convenience and simplicity are increasingly key factors in our decision making (see **Every Customer Wants®**).

No fuss, no frills; in value stream planning and in team management, simple is good. KIS(S) – Keep It Simple (no need for the Stupid).

Further reading

For a Better User Experience, Forget Alexa, Use Occam's Razor | CMSWire.com, 2018 | Miller, D. | https://www.cmswire.com/digital-experience/for-a-better-user-experience-forget-alexa-use-occams-razor/

Simplicity Is the Key to Success | Inc., September 2016 | Tredgold, G. | https://www.inc.com/gordon-tredgold/

simplicity-is-the-key-to-success-here-are-26-inspiring-quotes-to-help-you-on-tha.html

Occam's Razor: The simplest solution is always the best | Interaction Design Foundation, 2020 | Soegaard, M. | https://www.interaction-design.org/literature/article/occam-s-razor-the-simplest-solution-is-always-the-best

Options and choices

"For me, it is always important that I go through all the possible options for a decision." *– Angela Merkel*

Sometimes employees feel stuck, even trapped. Colleagues believe they have no choice. This is rarely true; there are options available in most situations. Outcomes from adopting a specific option may seem more, or less, appealing. Options exist.

Therapists understand many of the issues presented by patients are exaggerated through their impoverished recognition of choice. Part of a therapist's task, especially cognitive behaviour specialists, is encouraging patients to break free of restrictive thinking patterns and consider opportunities. Fresh perceptions of choice minimise feelings of anxiety and helps stimulate a resourceful state (see **Maps of the territory, Irrational thinking, Can't to Can Belief Busting®** and **I know you don't know**).

Wise managers cultivate a team habit of asking the question, *"What options do we have?"* This is a great starting point for addressing any challenging situation, or opportunity.

Lateral thought and innovation are helpful attributes. By urging colleagues to explore choice options, managers nurture solution-focused thinking within the work group. Radical *out-there* ideas are how innovation begins.

Thinking through possibilities, including the 'crazies', is a productive pattern for managers and team members to develop (see **Brainstorming, esrever, Decision making tools** and **Looking out of the window thinking**).

"What are the options here?" is a healthy management question.

Further reading

The Practice of Rational Emotive Behaviour Therapy | Free Association Books, 1999 | Ellis, A., Dryden, W.

Creative Problem Solving | Mind Tools | Editorial team, undated | https:// www.mindtools.com/a2j08rt/ creative-problem-solving

You Always Have a Choice | Personal Excellence | Chua, C. | https:// personalexcellence.co/blog/ you-always-have-a-choice/

Ownership

"Nothing is more powerful than individuals acting out of their own conscience." *– Vaclav Havel*

Quality performances evolve in a culture of personal responsibility. When employees own accountability for the quality of their work, compliance with standards increases, and non-conformances reduce.

There is an internal customer-supplier dynamic in every business (see **Customer, internal**). The supply chain includes materials or information. When your team receives 'supply' you want it to be fit for purpose, received on time, and delivered to specification. Your team expects a quality supply to subsequently do *their* job, to deliver added value on to your next-step customer, either internal or external.

In world class teams employees and managers take personal responsibility for their own quality. They deliver their part of the internal customer-supplier chain to customers, at specification, at first delivery, on time, on every occasion. In quality-speak, they *get it right, first time, on time, every time*. This is a fundamental premise of Total Quality Management (see **Quality and TQM**).

If you'd like your team to embrace principles of TQM, a briefing session or training event for colleagues makes sense, backed up by on-the-job coaching. Once the penny drops about quality principles of ownership, and personal quality, conversations with team members about performance become more informed and value adding. I have found employees (generalisation) buy-in to concepts of quality ownership once they understand TQM principles.

Training, coaching, team huddles, Keep In Touch meetings, and performance reviews all offer opportunity to emphasise principles of ownership and personal quality (see **Huddles**, **KIT meetings**, and **Appraisals and performance reviews**).

What strategies do you have in place, in your team, for establishing and maintaining a focus on individual ownership?

Further reading

The Toyota Way: 14 Management Principles from the World's Greatest Manufacturer | McGraw-Hill, 2004 | Liker, J.

14 Ways That Employees Can Take Ownership at Work | Indeed, March 2023 |

Birt, J. | https://www.indeed.com/career-advice/career-development/taking-ownership-at-work

Operations Management | Pearson, 2022 | Slack, N., Brandon-Jones, A., Burgess, N.

P

Past

"Your past does not equal your future." – *Tony Robbins*

Many of the managers I support are stuck in thinking patterns which loop back to past experiences, either good or bad. Bad seems to be the majority. Hurtful experiences are embedded in our minds as reminders for us to avoid repeating the same mistakes, and repeated pain. This is an evolutionary mechanism, it aids our survival, and the survival of our genes. It offers a useful notice to *be wary*.

The challenge comes when continuing focus on our historical reference points overpowers our present-day thinking, hampering opportunity, becoming a psychological straight jacket, pulling us back from exploring new ventures. It creates in us a mindset of low resourcefulness and inhibits our development ambitions.

For many managers I work with, the best thing about their past is it's over.

It is helpful to recognise your 'learns'. Make a pledge to yourself to draw knowledge from them and move on. Burton and Bodenhamer (2000) describe how we hold a mirror up to the past and choose to live in a previous world. The past refers to *what was*, not *what is* and certainly not *what will be*. What happened in the past does not dictate the future: unless you choose to live there.

I have made calamitous errors as a manager, absolute howlers! That was then, and this is now.

There is a reason why your car windscreen is bigger than the rear-view mirror. The past has gone. It may be useful to refer to from time to time and acknowledge what's behind you, but it is over. Look ahead. What's next?

I remind managers in our sessions; *how you got here is irrelevant, its where you chose to go which counts.*

Further reading

The Little Book of Resilience | Robinson, 2015 | Johnstone, M.

Hypnotic Language: Its Structure and Use | Crown House Publishing, 2000 | Burton, J., Bodenhamer, B.

Patterns which connect

"What pattern connects the crab to the lobster, and the orchid to the primrose and all four of them to me? And me to you? … The pattern which connects is a meta pattern. It is a pattern of patterns. It is that meta pattern which defines the vast generalisation that, indeed, it is patterns which connect." *– Gregory Bateson*

Humans are talented recognisers of pattern. We use (according to theories of patterning) *feature detectors* to compare new information with experiences already recorded in our long-term memories.

We compare incoming information against established knowledge we have stored as templates. We check for similarity and difference. This is helpful for our survival instincts. It includes information sequencing, logic flows or 'seriation', facial recognition, language development, and other life factors, including music.

Gregory Bateson was a polymath, an expert in different fields. He started his career in biology, then anthropology, and became a thinker and commentator on a range of disciplines including psychology, systems thinking and cybernetics, ecological integrity, and environmentalism.

From my book *Fast Coaching* (2016),

The most intriguing of all Bateson's ideas was his reference to what he called Patterns Which Connect. He highlighted how patterns in nature are repeated in diverse sets of animals, plants, and organisms. He identified patterns which connect in language, in communities and in communication. He proposed connectivity and patterns are everywhere!

Pattern recognition is useful in developing a career in management.

I joined the merchant navy at 16 and went to sea. I spent a few years as a deck officer cadet. There were occasional glamorous watches on the bridge in tropical whites. Mostly though, it was chipping off old paint, wire-brushing, and red-lead painting. Scrubbing out the inside of freshwater tanks was claustrophobic, and it seems crazy now to put a boy seaman in charge of the engine-room pumps, redirecting the ballast water on a bulk carrier, without any supervision – though it only went wrong once (see **Decision making, navy style**). It was hot and greasy down on the bottom plates of the engine room, not the romance of navigation work with charts, compasses, and radar screens I had hoped for.

The four to eight watches twice a day was tough, and six-on-six-off during dockside operations was a shift pattern to make or break a young lad. My longest watch was 49 hours in Suez, splicing and re-splicing hawsers with shipmates, as the wash from passing super tankers broke our shorelines. On the hour, every hour, over two days, another tanker would pass. We snatched moments of sleep before the next torn rope thwacked against the bulwarks and the hawser repairs started again. I have never been so tired as that day – and night, and day, and night.

During my first trip to sea, westbound across the Atlantic, I remember a full-on dressing down from a wily old seadog, a petty officer who (quite reasonably, looking back) took umbrage at my directive and bossy communication style. The learning I took from that incident, about respect for others, is still embedded in in my mind 47 years later.

Everyone thinks they're in control of their emotions until they sail deep-sea into an Arctic storm. In the North Atlantic, in mountainous waves, some way east of Newfoundland, I cried on deck in the bitter conditions. The seas were terrifying, my hand had stuck to the frozen bulwark, it wouldn't budge, and I didn't know what to do. I was seventeen.

These experiences were laying foundations for my future career and personal life. Although I didn't realise at the time, I was learning masses about personal discipline, persistence, resilience, team dynamics, communication styles, internal customer-supplier chains, about quality standards, consistency of delivery, the sustainability of excellence, and continuous professional development.

I was learning patterns for future life.

Patterns which connect are everywhere. Good team leaders are mindful of this in their daily management activities. Patterns of success in one environment may work equally well in another context.

For example,

- Senior management is about to introduce a programme of change. The manager observes that the pattern may have similarities to a change scenario they experienced in another organisation. What useful insights emerged from those earlier circumstances?
- A team member is not performing to her usual high standards. There is a pattern of behaviour the manager recognises from coaching under-performing employees in another industry. What happened on those previous occasions? What worked well? What worked less well (see **Good and less good**)?
- A process is proving problematic in a commercial business. Team members are creating workarounds to compensate for the ineffective procedure. Something similar happened in a public sector environment and a solution was found. Could a public sector solution work in a private sector context?

Of course, experience is valuable, but what if a manager is young in service? Management development resources can help. Learnings are available from:

- *Mentoring.* More experienced managers may have *seen this movie before.* The context may have been different, or the environment, and probably the organisation. A Mentor may suggest a solution *pattern* to consider (see **Mentoring**).
- *Reading and research.* The best team managers read; extensively. Over years, they compile a compendium of management and organisational behaviour knowledge, of *patterns*, which they can draw on when needed (see **Continuous Professional Development [CPD]** and **Reading**).

Becoming aware of a pattern requires a certain amount of objectivity, or dissociation. Managers can step back and ask (internal dialogue), *"What is going on here? What is the pattern? Have I seen or heard this pattern before? What happened on previous occasions?"*

Further reading

Mind and Nature: A Necessary Unity | Hampton Press, 2002 | Bateson, G.

Language Ability Linked to Pattern Recognition | Voice of America | Editorial team, May 2013 | https://www.voanews.com/a/language-ability-linked-to-pattern-recognition/1670776.html

Understanding Gregory Bateson: Mind, Beauty, and the Sacred Earth | State University of New York Press, 2008 | Charlton, N.G.

Performance management

"Without standards there can be no improvement." – *Taiichi Ohno*

Monitoring individual and team performance is a management function. Addressing underperformance is necessary when there is a gap between what is required and what is delivered.

Newly promoted managers and team leaders may feel uncertain, or uncomfortable, about challenging performance issues. Fortunately, there is a simple framework for managers to use when a team member is not delivering to requirement.

Standards of performance need to be explicit for all job roles within an organisation. If they *are* explicitly described, and have been trained out through the organisation, you have a reference point for discussion with the team member. If they are *not* explicitly described, or have not been trained out, there is more fundamental work to be done within your operation before meaningful performance discussions take place (see **NDK Performance Model®**).

With explicit standards of performance identified we can draw a simple graph for joint discussion with the employee,

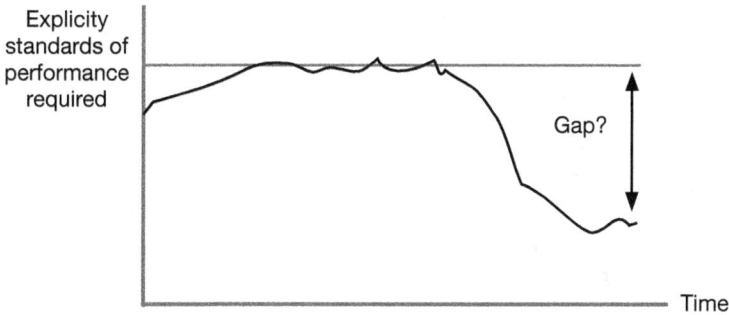

As with all communication, a manager's conversation with a team member about personal performance requires empathy and warmth. Remember, the discussion is about the performance, not the person's character.

Here are ten performance questions to explore,

1. Is there a gap between the explicitly described standards and the employee's performance?
2. If so, how big is the gap?
3. How long has there been a gap?
4. What is the reason for the gap? Allow plenty of time to explore.
5. Is it necessary to close the gap, fully, or partially?
6. Do factors merit a change to standards for this team member, perhaps temporarily?
7. What would have to happen to close the gap (see **Freedom questions**)?
8. Is the employee willing to take the action needed to close the gap?
9. Is there a requirement for the manager to act to help close the gap?
10. Will the action take place (see **Commitment mantra**)?

The above approach is effective when there is clarity on explicit standards. Stick to the facts, and the ten questions above, and you won't go far wrong.

Further reading

10 Performance Management Process Gaps: And how they negatively impact employee intentions. | Ken Blanchard Companies, Employee Work Passion, volume 7, 2014 | Zigarmi, D., Houson, D., Diehl,J., Witt, D.

Performance Management Playbook, The: 15 Must-Have Conversations To Motivate And Manage Your People | Pearson Business, 2021 | Bird, H

Persistence

"People's desire to have things, greatly exceeds their
willingness to do things." – *George Zalucki*

Some managers' desire to grow, to achieve goals, to be recognised and rewarded, or be promoted, generally exceeds their willingness to *invest long-term hard work*.

There is a reluctance to engage in continuous study, to read, or make sacrifices. There is resistance to operating in areas of discomfort or uncertainty, or to repeatedly step up from knockbacks (see **Resilience**).

Success comes from persistence, putting in the hard yards, grafting day after day to make a difference, investing in ambition, and overcoming barriers. As Ollie Ollerton, the celebrated special forces soldier and author states, *"Persistence beats resistance"*.

The history of achievement is full of stories about persistence. Henry Ford went bankrupt before he set up Ford Motor Company, Walt Disney was fired from his newspaper job because allegedly his cartoons weren't good enough, Bill Gates and Paul Allen's first tech inventions were failures, and Richard Branson struggled at school. J.K Rowling's first manuscripts were rejected by publishers. There are many similar stories.

A successful career in management requires dedication and the repetitive application of sound practice. Knowledge of *principles* gained through self-study, training, mentoring, coaching, or experiential learning is only valuable if the principles are applied, persistently over time, as sustained *behaviour.* Principles and behaviours are not the same thing. Remember,

Knowing what to do is not the same as doing what you know.

Persistence is key. When proven behaviours are applied repetitively, they become *habit-ual.* Habitual application of good practice will, over time, lead to managerial successes (see **Habit**).

I know it's tough sometimes, I have my own scars from operational management. In the face of difficulty and adversity though, know your routine use of professional management behaviours *will* pay dividends. Keep going!

As Churchill said,

"KBO! Keep buggering on!"

Further reading

Quitless: The Power of Persistence in Business and Life | Leaders Press, 2021 | Rutkowska, A. et al

How to Be an Overnight Success | Ebury Press, 2018 | Hatzistefanis, M.

Break Point | Blink Publishing, 2020 | Ollerton, M.

Turning the Flywheel: A Monograph to Accompany Good to Great | Random House Business, 2019 | Collins, J.

PESTLE

"Change before you have to." *– Jack Welch*

A PESTLE analysis considers the wider context of work, and the environment within which your team or organisation exists. An early version of PESTLE was PEST developed in the 1960s by Francis Joseph Aguilar of Harvard University. PESTLE raises questions about how external factors might impact on business decisions, and how they may affect your management considerations.

The name PESTLE means:

- Political (factors)
- Economic
- Social
- Technical
- Legal
- Environmental

Sometimes a variant of PESTLE it is presented as PESTEC, replacing *Legal* with *Cultural*. Other versions include PEST, STEP, STEEPLE, SLEPT, STEPE: you can seek out which is best for you by checking out these variants. Completing a contextual analysis may be a simple or complex process. It all depends how thorough you'd like to be.

Your PESTLE factors might include,

POLITICAL	ECONOMIC
Government policies	UK economic situation
Government term and change	Overseas economies and trends
Inter-country relationships/attitudes	Seasonality/weather issues
Terrorism	Market and trade cycles
Political trends	Exchange rates
Local council influences	Tax issues
SOCIAL	**TECHNOLOGICAL**
Demographic changes (age, gender, race, family size,)	Manufacturing advances
	Global communications
Lifestyle changes	Information technology
Population shifts	Transportation
Consumer attitudes and opinions	Quality assurance
Media views	Design capability
Crime and disorder	
LEGAL	**ENVIRONMENTAL**
Future legislation	Ecological
European/international legislation	Environmental issues
Regulatory bodies and processes	Environmental regulations
Environmental regulations	Customer 'green' values
Employment law	Supply chain shifts
Local legislation	Local issues

You may be thinking, for front line managers, team leaders and supervisors, aren't these PESTLE considerations outside the scope of the job role? Maybe. Or maybe gifted leaders forecast beyond the now and consider what may be coming. Certainly, if you have ambitions for managerial advancement, these are thinking habits to cultivate for the future.

What PESTLE factors are likely to affect your team leadership role? What might be coming? Are you ready?

Further reading

Chartered Institute of Personnel and Development | https://www.cipd.co.uk/knowledge/strategy/organisational-development/pestle-analysis-factsheet

PEST Analysis Ultimate Guide: Definition, Template, Examples | PESTLE Analysis, September 2020 | Frue, K. | https://pestleanalysis.com/pest-analysis/

Planning

"Logic will get you from A to B. Imagination will take you everywhere."
– Albert Einstein

Planning is a prime management function. It is the starting point for all action. Attempting to manage without considered planning is unprofessional and borderline reckless. Managers are employed to plan, it's a fundamental function of the role (see **About management – an overview**).

Planning requires *contemplative* thought, *logical* thought, and *creative* thought.

It benefits from diarised time. Plans may relate to immediate, medium, or longer-term business activity. The horizon distance is immaterial; the accountable manager has a professional responsibility to prepare. It requires planning.

Management planning might include thinking about,

- Why an activity is required. Clarity of purpose is vital.
- What is the goal, or desired outcome, specifically?
- What information is needed to be fully informed, before making the plan?
- What are the contextual factors to consider?
- What options are available?
- Which strategy should be employed?
- What will be the impact of implementing the strategy?
- How should the strategy be implemented?
- What resources will be required?
- Who should be involved in the strategy?
- What training or preparation will they need?
- When? What are the timelines involved?
- Which activities within the plan may run concurrent with others?
- Which activities need to be sequential? What is the critical path?
- How much float (contingency) time should be built into the plan?
- When and how will implementation be monitored, measured, reviewed, adapted?
- How will successful application be known?

Management planning requires *informed* thinking. It may benefit from more than one perspective. Team members' input may be helpful, depending on context. Robert Townsend's management mantra offers encouragement to engage employees in the planning process,

"Ask the people, they know where the wheels are squeaking."

Thinking is underrated as a management activity. Managers are employed to think and make judgements. Simply taking time out to reflect, before *doing,* is the professional way to operate (see **Looking out of the window thinking**).

Further reading

The Role of Planning as a Fundamental Management Function for Achieving Effectiveness in Business Organisations | University Goce Delcev, 2017 | Kareska, K

The Resource Management and Capacity Planning Handbook: A Guide to Maximizing the Value of Your Limited People Resources | McGraw Hill, 2014 | Manas, J.

Up the Organisation: How to Stop the Corporation from Stifling People and Strangling Profits | Jossey-Bass, 2007 | Townsend, R., Bennis, W.

Positivity

"Once you replace negative thoughts with positive ones, you'll start having positive results." – **Willie Nelson**

My pal Henry has a positive and radically optimistic outlook on life, even in the most challenging of contexts. You may already know the old joke, *"He went bald years ago. He's so optimistic he still takes a hairdryer on holiday";* Henry summed out magnificently.

Here's the challenge; a positive mental attitude on its own won't make much of a difference. It helps, of course. Positivity leverages action and oils the wheels of persistence. It keeps us going when progress is slow or troublesome. The key to achievement though, is to *Decide, Plan, Act,* and *Persist.*

Professional, successful managers,

1. *Decide* to implement their strategy (see **Decision making, navy style**).
2. *Plan* a strategy (see **Planning**).
3. *Act* decisively and with a compelling obsession (see **Obsession, compelling**).
4. *Persist* until the strategy is successfully implemented (see **Persistence**).

Training your mind to think in positive terms about the past, present, and future is a healthy management regime. Managers set examples of behaviour for team members to model and replicate (see **Past, Framing and reframing, Planning, Modelling excellence,** and **Culture**).

Would you like your team members to think and act in a positive, or negative fashion? Positive, of course. Then it is necessary for you, the team manager, to think and act in a positive manner. Support your positive mentality with the pragmatic approach of *Decide, Plan, Act* and *Persist* and you will have a robust operating model in place.

Further reading

The Power of Positive Thinking | Touchstone; Reprint Edition, 2003 | Peale, N.V.

Awaken The Giant Within: How to Take Immediate Control of Your Mental, Emotional, Physical and Financial Life | Simon & Schuster, 2001 | Robbins, A.

Pre-framing

"Life will bring you pain all by itself. Your responsibility is to create joy."
– Milton Erickson

Pre-framing is a method of instilling, in self or others, a positive thinking frame around a future event.

Framing and *Reframing* are helpful disciplines for shaping and reshaping the way we perceive the past, or our present circumstances. Encouraging employees to adopt these thought habits helps stimulate positive energy in team operations (see **Framing and reframing**).

A *pre-frame* relates to the future. It is what hypnotherapists call a *direct suggestion*, an assertive instructing message. A pre-frame instructs the listener to accept a suggestion about a future scenario. When employed as an influencer, towards positivity, it encourages a mindset of optimism. Examples could include,

- The new software will make life so much easier for us!
- We can make Q3 our most successful sales quarter so far!
- You're going to love the new product range for our customers!
- We'll have a much more comfortable workspace in the new office!
- The revised warehouse systems will improve fulfilment!

Pre-frames are often exhortations (hence the exclamation marks), delivered with energy and enthusiasm. They persuade and cajole listeners to embrace a suggestion and to be equally enthusiastic about the future state it refers to.

Inspirational team managers are also people *leaders*, so leadership behaviours are an important part of a manager's toolkit. Promoting positivity and can-do culture in the team is a pre-requisite for success.

How could you employ pre-framing with your team?

Further reading

Preframing: A Stoic Principle For Living a Less Stressful Life | Medium, May 2021 | Oppong, T. | https://thomas-oppong. medium.com/preframing-a-stoic-principle-for-living-a-less-stressful-life-5f3921f14224

Hypnotic Realities: The Induction od Clinical Hypnosis and Forms of Indirect Suggestion | Irvington, 1976 | Erickson, M.H., Rossi, E.l., Rossi, S.I.

Presentations

"All the great speakers were bad speakers at first."

– Ralph Waldo Emerson

My coaching sessions with managers frequently reveal the coachee's ambitions to improve their presentations skills. The ambitions are usually self-identified by the manager although on occasions a senior sponsor will ask for the topic to be included in a person's development plan (see **Continuous Professional Development [CPD]**, **CPD cascading**, and **Get Even Better Ats [GEBAs]**).

For some, the development activity is to brush up on a few techniques, or to remind themselves of forgotten good practice. For others, the needs are more basic, and there is fear in the manager's eyes as they discuss an upcoming presentation. Conference time seems to bring out the most intense neuroses.

I remember my own terror as a twenty-something year old college lecturer being allocated a weekly presentation to groups of women attending a *Women into Management* course. The groups invariably contained super-assertive, ambitious delegates, and the sessions were designed to inspire as much as educate. I knew I had to be *in state*, the right state of mind, brimming with enthusiasm and valuable insights. I was terrified!

I'd learnt about using karate kata, patterns of disciplined movement, to instil a resourceful mindset. I developed a dramatic (and ridiculous) *personal power move,* and a set of affirmation statements for facing challenging scenarios. None came more challenging than the *Women into Management* group.

Over time I toned down the mindset regime, gradually reducing the preparatory drama as the years went by. I still have an internal dialogue I use in preparation for major presentations, large seminars, and conference work; it's a simple, quietly (internal) spoken message to myself, a piece of self-talk to centre me in readiness. I say to myself,

"Be professional. Help these people with valuable insights.
Enjoy the day!"

In the early days, what I was missing mostly (I was missing a lot by the way), was structure.

The first format I found helpful was the *Tell 'em x 3* pattern. The model has a simple high-level outline,

1. *Tell 'em what you're going to tell 'em.* Introduce your presentation by explaining what it will contain and how the message content will help the audience.
2. *Tell 'em.* Present.
3. *Tell 'em what you've told 'em.* Summarise and reaffirm your presentation messages.

Tell 'em x 3 was a good starting point. I needed more structure though. I came to know and employ a framework I found particularly helpful, the

6 Ps. This format is useful when presenting to an audience of decision makers. Here's the structure,

6Ps

P1 – Preface.

Introductions, niceties, what the presentation will address, what the audience will learn, and decide upon, or do, resulting from the presentation. Play down self (no-one likes a show-off) and promote the learnings to be had from the session, *"My name is Nick and I'm here to offer some ideas. By the end of this presentation, you will be able to…".*

P2 – Position.

What is the current state? What is the status of a specific topic? What is the context of this status? What developments have created this current state? What is happening right now?

P3 – Problem (or Opportunity Problem).

What is the challenge or opportunity associated with the current Position? What are the limitations, dangers or threats, or opportunities, which the current state presents to the audience? Why should the audience consider options for change? What are the consequences of doing nothing?

P4 – Possibilities.

What are options for change, including the option of no change? Which possibilities are least or most radical? What are the potential impacts of each approach? What are the likely drivers and resistors to implementation (see **Forcefields**)? What is the required investment in resources, in energy and emotional hope? What is the return on investment and payback schedules for each possibility?

P5 – Proposal.

Which option is being proposed? Why is it the best choice? What would have to happen to make the proposal happen (see **Freedom questions**)? What are the next steps?

P6 – Postscript.

Thank you to the audience for listening, observing, considering. Availability (now, or subsequently) for questions. Contact details for follow up.

I still use the *6Ps* framework where appropriate. Once the sequence is installed in the presenter's mind it requires only subject knowledge and presentations techniques (see **Presentation behaviours**) to address an audience of decision makers with confidence.

Further reading

The Art of Persuasion Hasn't Changed in 2,000 Years | Harvard Business Review, 2018 | Gallo, C.

The Presentation Secrets of Steve Jobs: How to Be Insanely Great in Front of Any Audience | McGraw Hill, 2009 | Gallo, C.

Presentation behaviours

"Presenting the Oscars was the most nerve-racking job I have ever done in show business. It's very much a live show: they have comedy writers waiting in the wings, and as you come off between presentations, they hand you an appropriate gag to tell."

– Michael Caine

If only I could have fast tracked through my presentations learning experiences. I'd have saved a lot of time and silliness if I had found a mentor to guide me back in the early 1990s (see **Mentoring**). These days I mentor others, providing information and guidance to help managers develop presentations skills.

We address two categories,

1. Format (6 Ps, or alternative structure)
2. Behaviours (including internal dialogue/self-talk)

We've already explored a useful and proven presentations framework with the 6Ps (see **Presentations**). Presentation behaviours bring a format to life.

Talented presenters seem to have an aura about them; there's an elegance about their communication. They appear relaxed and charming, almost magical in their ability to captivate an audience. There is no magic though, only structure. They may not even be consciously aware of their structure. This is a common feature of experienced performers. Fortunately, when the structure is isolated, codified and learnt, it can be replicated by almost anyone. This is how modelling works (see **Modelling excellence**).

Talented presenters complement an effective format with mastery of the three prime elements of face-to-face group communication (see **Words, song, and dance**),

Language patterns used

Presentation audiences respond best to language with which they are familiar. Avoid unnecessarily complex patterns. Simple, straightforward language is easy for the audience to digest and comes across as genuine. Flowery, convoluted words and phrases are perceived as pompous and pretentious.

The *Power Pause* is a formidable tool in presentations. Nervous presenters are fearful of pauses. Fear comes from anxiety of an audience member asking a question, or challenging part of the presenter's proposition. Nervousness manifests itself in different ways.

One common pattern is to speak quickly, without breathing breaks (less likely to be interrupted), with the consequence of reduced oxygen intake and the physiological repercussions. Another is the unconscious habit of verbal tics such as *"ok?"*, *"right?"*, *"er…"*, *"you know"*, *"know what I mean?"*, *"does that make sense?"*. These verbal tics get in the way of the message.

Slow down and breathe! Use pauses, it gives time for message impact, for presenter thinking time, and for audience members to absorb the presentation content.

Tonality employed

Maintaining an upbeat and varied tonality keeps an audience interested (remember the pauses though). Offering a range of speech tones, volume, inflections, cadence, and emphasis makes for a vibrant and memorable presentation.

Nervous presenters tend towards monotone speech. There is a mammalian reason for this behaviour, based around the fight-flight-play dead pattern (see **Fight, flight, play dead**). Robert Anton Wilson (1983) was right, we are still domesticated primates. By minimising movement and noise, our primitive survival minds believe as presenter, and therefore prey, we are less likely to be noticed by predators, which professionally seems illogical as the point of our presentation is to be noticed.

Non-verbal, physiological expression
(facial, breathing, minor and major motor movements)

Animation and variety of physiological movement keep a presentation stimulating. Not too much though. There seems to be two polarity extremes when it comes to presenter movement:

Polarity A.

Play dead is an inhibitor in physiological presentation, as well as tonal. Minimisation of movement is an obvious *play dead* strategy. Hold on to the lectern at all costs! Avoid smiling or facial expression. Minimise breathing, keep it shallow. Do not move a muscle, stay still! The predator can't see the prey (Wilson again). Consequently, the presenter's message transfer is dull and uninspiring.

Polarity B.

Prancing around the stage or presentation area, constantly moving, waving arms, swinging legs, 'dancing around a handbag', or being a pen clicker. Audiences soon become irritated by the scampering about, and message impact is compromised.

Polished performers know the importance of finding a presentation middle ground, one which mixes animated communication with emphasis on a core message.

Aligning non-verbal communication with the verbal or written (think PowerPoint) messages is important.

The integrity of a message is enhanced when all three primary communication channels of words, tone, and physiology, are in tune with each other. An audience is more likely to be influenced by a presentation which says the right message, sounds like the right message, and looks and feels like the right message (see **VAK[OG] representational systems**).

Below is a summary of typical *Begin Tos* (see **Coaching, Continue & Begin Fast Coaching®**) emerging from my coaching sessions with managers on presentation style. The aggregated list includes presentation behaviours managers have decided to work on. These come from genuine coaching action plans,

- *Act As If* I'm a polished performer.
- Heighten my self-awareness of Words, Song and Dance.
- Maintain a strong posture, planted and powerful.
- Embrace my stature and be proud. Stand tall. Be planted.
- Continue to share eye contact love with all members of the audience.
- Advance to centre stage for core messages.
- Enhance my use of the *Power Pause* to embed information and allow the audience to digest before moving on to the next idea.
- Less coin jingling, touching my face, or gyrating around the dance floor handbag.
- No more 'doing the Charleston' with my flicking foot during presentations. Stay grounded.
- Become more spatially aware during presentations, my personal movement and proximity of others. No more entering another presenter's physical space.
- Tell 'em x 3.
- Use the 6 Ps of effective presentation proposals.
- Develop variety in the tonality of my 'song'.
- Include appropriate humour.
- 360 view and eye contact love for all audience members
- Be more aware of my tendency to be monotone in delivery and the value of varied facial expression, including eyebrow movement.

- Research and model TED talks and other professional presenters. Model what I see and hear.
- Incorporate movement away/movement towards into my presentations.
- Use features, benefits, feelings as a hook for influencing my audiences.
- Use a self-talk affirmation tool to help me get ready to present.

Remember, best practice in *Continue & Begin Fast Coaching*® is to work on only a few *Begin Tos* at a time, certainly no more than three, and preferably one or two key development areas. There will be an opportunity to focus on additional skills another time.

Further reading

How to Give a Killer Presentation | Richard Turere TED Talk | Harvard Business Review, 2013 https://hbr.org/2013/06/how-to-give-a-killer-presentation | Anderson, C.

Prometheus Rising | New Falcon Publications, 1983 | Wilson, R.A.

Presentations Goal Map®

"Always remember, your focus determines your reality." – *George Lucas*

The goal map on the next page (see **Goal Mapping® by Brian Mayne**) illustrates one manager's ambition, and his strategy, to develop presentation skills, specifically for a project plan he will be presenting to senior managers in a few weeks' time.

Notice the required development actions shown as branches on the left side of the goal map 'trunk', and, on the right side, the individuals who can make the actions happen. Also, observe the *Why?* questions at the top of the plan; levers for the goal mapper's commitment to develop this skill.

How could you use a Goal Map® to enhance your presentations skill set?

Further reading

Goal Mapping® | Watkins Publishing, 2020 | Mayne, B.

Self Mapping | Watkins Publishing, 2009 | Mayne, B.

Life Mapping | Vermilion, 2003 | Mayne, B., Mayne, S.

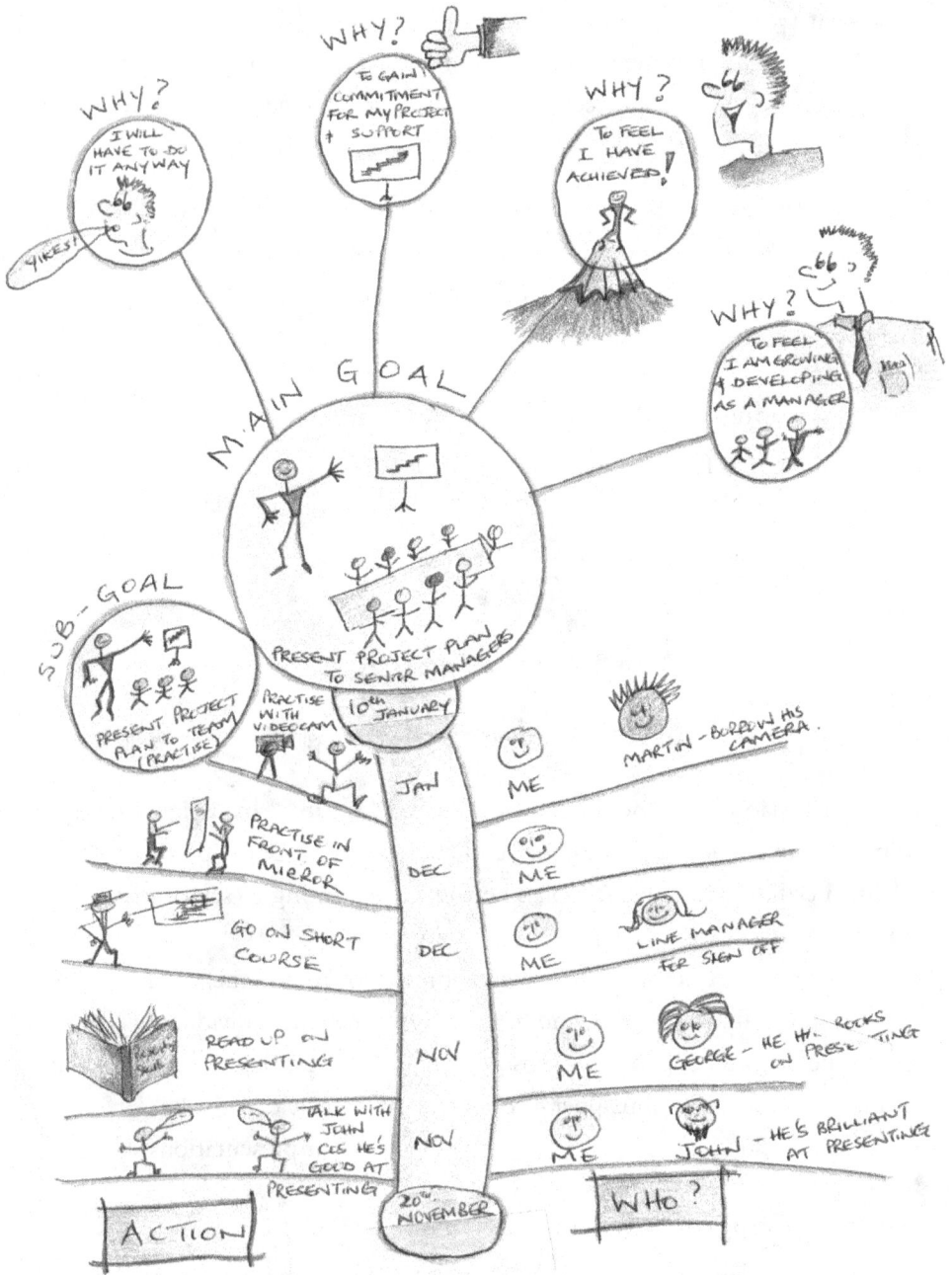

With acknowledgement to Brian Mayne!

Presuppositions

"Science, like art, religion, commerce, warfare, and even sleep,
is based on presuppositions." – *Gregory Bateson*

Presupposition is a noun. Its associated verb is *to presuppose.*

A presupposition is an idea assumed as a *truth.* It presents an implied assumption the presupposition sentence must be true for a subsequent related sentence to make sense. Presuppositions are powerful linguistic tools for influencing others. By asking questions which include a presupposition we can elicit value-adding responses to build on what has been presupposed.

In coaching a team member about work performance, we could ask the following questions, each of which includes a simple presupposition,

- *Which parts of your performance were you particularly pleased with?*
- *What would you like to begin to do differently?*
- *How do you think your improved performance will impact on the business?*

The questions presuppose something,

- *Which parts of your performance were you particularly pleased with?* Presupposes there are parts of the performance of which a team member is particularly pleased.
- *What would you like to begin to do differently?* Presupposes the coachee would like to begin to do something differently.
- *How do you think your improved performance will impact on the business?* Presupposes the coachee will improve his/her performance.

Presuppositions are sometimes incorporated into a statement-question structure, such as,

- *As the new machinery increases our production flow, how will you manage quality?* Presupposes the new machinery will increase production flow.
- *Once the document sharing system is available next month, and you're up to speed on it, we won't have to forward reports by email anymore.* Presupposes the document sharing system will be available next month and presupposes the employee will be up to speed on it.

- *When you've completed your professional qualification, how do you see your role changing?* Presupposes the team member will complete the professional qualification.

Notice these presuppositions refer to a future state. Elegant use of presuppositions by team managers smooths the way for employee performance improvement, or for the implementation of change (see **Change**).

Once you've re-read this section on presuppositions, and practised constructing them, how will you make use of presuppositions in managing your team?

Further reading

The Structure of Magic: A Book about Language and Therapy, Volume 1 | Bandler, R., Grinder, J. | Science and Behavior Books, 1975

Understanding Gregory Bateson: Mind, Beauty, and the Sacred Earth | State University of New York Press, 2008 | Charlton, N.G.

Pride, encouragement of

"Pleasure in the job puts perfection in the work." *– Aristotle*

I was a young executive, promoted to a new post of Personnel & Training Manager in a rapid growth leisure group. The business operated hotels, nightclubs, restaurants, bars, casinos, bingo halls, betting shops, and tourism attractions around the UK. As with many fast growth businesses, infrastructure lagged growth. My job, based at head office with national travel, was to design and implement human resource standards and processes for group businesses to adopt. It was a fabulous job.

A specific task was to establish a set of specimen job descriptions for use across operational businesses, for adaptation by local operational managers. I toured the country meeting with directors, managers, supervisors, and frontline employees. I asked questions about their jobs, the purpose of their employment, their main responsibilities, and the key tasks involved in performing their roles. Most interviews took around an hour to gather the information I needed to compile a first draft document.

A job description for cleaners was needed. Fortunately, there was a group hotel a few minutes from my home. Ideal! I arranged to meet with two employees and set off to meet them at their workplace. It would be a quick job.

Except it wasn't.

Sheila and Tina taught me a lesson about pride and personal motivation at work. Professional cleaning in hospitality venues is not as simple as I thought. What followed during the (two hours) interview was an instructional guide on how to manage cleaning services within a large hotel, to the highest standards of professionalism. I remember being struck by the importance of sequence; each cleaning task should fit within a larger logical flow of activity. Technicalities around mirror and floor cleaning became new knowledge for me.

What impacted most though, was the professional dignity, and dedication to quality, with which these two women conducted their roles. I was humbled.

The intense professional pride of Sheila and Tina was not driven by their hourly rate, or from the comforts of working in a plush hotel. It came from personal standards and, critically, the respect paid to them as professionals by the hotel's general manager Gavin. I met with Gavin to find out more. He explained how he encouraged each employee to create their own high standards, to feel confident and have pride in their work (see **Explicit Standards, Quality and TQM,** and **Ownership**).

Over thirty years later I still remember my learning from Gavin, Sheila, and Tina.

Further reading

Take Pride: How to Build Organisational Success Through People | Unbound, 2018 | Parry, S.

How to Foster Company Pride at Work in 2023 | teambuilding.com, July 2022 | He, G. | https://teambuilding.com/blog/company-pride

Procrastination, Hammer it!

"If it's your job to eat a frog, it's best to do it first thing in the morning.
And if it's your job to eat two frogs, it's best to eat the biggest one first."

– Mark Twain

Procrastination is the dithering, stalling or avoidance of *doing*. Procrastination is a resistor to action, a sapper of management energy, and a barrier to effectiveness.

There is so much to do! But then there's that thing you've been putting off. Team management is one long list of tasks waiting to be addressed. Even as you complete tasks, they are being backfilled with more. For each interesting activity on the management *to do* list, there are two dull, time-consuming activities which need to be dealt with. Eventually. Maybe after you've done some of these other things…

Perhaps it is complex and requires hard thinking? Are you apprehensive about tackling it? Or is it plain boring for you? Or has it been on the list so long you barely notice it anymore?

Some tasks seem overly challenging. We haven't yet found an obvious first step and we begin to worry about them. They lurk in our minds as 'I really ought to do something about that' and then do nothing. It stays in our mental inbox cluttering our thinking and causing frustration and tension.

Fretting about doing something is more tiring than getting on and resolving it. We feel better when we take the first step to actioning a task. If you want to remove a problem, *act* (see **Act**).

A contributor to procrastination is what time management students refer to as *flapsi hapsi;* the feeling of being unstructured, disorganised, and lacking prioritisation. There's a hazy overview of management direction, though it lacks clear planning or priorities. Tasks are numerous. *Flapsi hapsi* causes us to start a task, then move to another, and another, repeatedly, without completing any (see **Time is a budget item**).

A lack of structured analysis and application causes anxiety. If everything is urgent and everything *must* be done now, which task should be the first?

Complex time-consuming projects requiring deep thought, and the unpleasant ones being avoided, might stay on your *to do* list for a little while longer. And yet you know you'd feel better if the chore was dealt with, right?

Seneca, the Roman philosopher, knew this. He talked about the people who are always getting ready to start; but never do. We've all been there at some time. What's called for is a mental framing exercise, a way of thinking which removes personal inertia and stimulates activity.

You can escape from procrastination by using a structured approach, fuelled with massive determination. I refer to this as *Hammer It!* task management.

1. Remind yourself *"What am I here for?"* (see **What am I here for? What is my management purpose?**).
2. Create a list of outstanding management tasks. Use the Importance/Urgency grid (see **Time is a budget item**) to prioritise your list as,
    a) Important and Urgent – *do now.*
    b) Important but Not Urgent – *diary plan a block of dedicated time.*
    c) Not Important but Urgent – *deal with quickly now, or delegate if possible.*
    d) Not Important and Not Urgent – *eliminate or ignore.*
3. Adopt a mindset of determination and total conviction, and *Act As If* (see **Act as if**).
4. Focus on *one* task and eliminate all distractions. *Hammer it!* with sustained energy.
5. Celebrate your task completion!
6. Line up your next task and be ready to *Hammer it!*

Productive managers face up to their to do lists, decide to act, then *Hammer It!*

Further reading

Eat That Frog! Get More Of The Important Things Done Today | Hodder, 2013 | Tracy, Brian

How to Stop Procrastinating: Powerful Strategies to Overcome Laziness and Multiply Your Time | Independently published, 2020 | Walter, D.

Instantly Stop Procrastination: 4 Powerful Concepts That Will Help You Effectively Complete the Tasks You Keep Avoiding | Winner Media Publishing, 2022 | Drechsler, P.

Q

Quality and TQM

"Responsibility is the price of greatness." – *Winston Churchill*

Managers are responsible for the quality of their operations.

Total Quality Management (TQM) continues to be embraced by customer-centric organisations, due to its emphasis on customer focus and personal responsibility. TQM is closely associated with the Toyota corporation's quality management philosophies and principles.

Principles of TQM include,

- Quality can and must be managed.
- Everyone has a customer and is a supplier.
- Processes, not people are the problem.
- Every employee is responsible for quality.
- Problems must be prevented, not just fixed as they occur.

- Quality must be measured.
- Quality improvements must be continuous.
- The quality standard is defect free.
- Goals are based on requirements, not negotiated.
- Focus on life cycle costs, not front-end costs.
- Management must be involved and lead.
- Products or services are to be delivered to customers (external or internal) *right, first time, on time, every time,* and failure to do so is non-conformance.

And importantly, products and services must be *fit for purpose*.

All employees work with processes in one form or another. TQM states processes must be *managed and improved*. This includes,

- Defining the process.
- Measuring process performance (metrics).
- Reviewing process performance.
- Identifying process shortcomings.
- Analysing process problems.
- Making process changes.
- Measuring the effects of process changes.

Plan, Do, Check, Act

A feature of many continuous improvement activities (see **Lean management, Change, Quality Circles and Kaizen**) is Plan, Do, Check, Act. This sequence is sometimes described as *Plan, Do, Study, Act* or *Plan, Do, Check, Adjust,* or other minor variations.

PDCA emerged from the early days of the process improvement management at the Bell Telephone Laboratories in the 1920s. It is sometimes referred to as the Shewhart Cycle, after its originator Walter Shewhart. It was later developed further by quality guru W. Edwards Deming (he preferred *Study* rather than *Check*), and consequentially you may hear PDSA referred to as the Deming Wheel.

PDCA/PDSA is used in continuous improvement work through its repeated application, until a problem is solved, or process refined.

P	Plan	Plan an improvement. What processes are needed? Resources? Methodology?
D	Do	Implement the plan.
C/S	Check/ Study	Analyse data from results. Review implementation, its impact, effectiveness, efficiency.
A/A	Act/Adjust	Reflect on performance, adjust activities where necessary, repeat the PDC/A cycle.

You and your team members may wish to choose which PDCA/PDSA version works best for your team environment. How could you incorporate elements of TQM and PDSA into your team management role?

Further reading

Total Quality Management and Operational Excellence: Text with Cases | Routledge, 2021 | Oakland, J.S., Oakland, R.J., Turner, M.A.

Managing Quality: An Essential Guide and Resource Gateway | Wiley, 2016 | Dale, B.G., Bamford, D., van der Wiele, T.

The Simply Lean Pocket Guide – Making Great Organizations Better Through PLAN-DO-CHECK-ACT (PDCA) | MCS Media, 2008 | Tapping, D.

Quality Circles and Kaizen

"Without continual growth and progress, such words as improvement, achievement and success have no meaning". *– Benjamin Franklin*

Kaizen is part of a philosophy of constant improvement. Quality-focused organisations establish a cultural mindset referred to as a *Quest for Continuous Improvement*, or *QCI*. It becomes part of the fabric of an organisation's culture.

A Quality Circle, or Kaizen, meeting brings together colleagues in a voluntary capacity to explore quality issues within a workplace function. Meetings are usually brief, around an hour, and targeted on a specific topic. Quality circles are intended to identify improvements to workflow activities, operational processes, or design. The purpose is to enhance the quality of products or services offered to customers, both internal and external.

In my experience, the ideal size for a Kaizen quality circle is between eight to twelve members, some of whom may attend only occasionally to add value on specific elements of a quality issue.

A success factor is for ideas to be developed and promoted by team members, not driven by managers. It's quite common for a quality circle to be facilitated by an employee who is not in a management role.

Air Cover (see **Air Cover sponsorship**) for support is fine, whereas overt management influence is restrictive; it stymies free flow of discussions and lateral thinking. If you are thinking of a Kaizen quality circle approach in your organisation, it makes sense to train up a few non-management facilitators.

Kaizen works because meetings encourage small-scale suggestions with low resource requirements and are quick to implement. It engages employees in designing their own workplace and work practices. Suggestions come from employees who understand how each change will improve a process or system. Robert Townsend of Avis (2007) described how frontline team members know *where the wheels are squeaking.*

By creating numerous small incremental improvements, a Kaizen culture improves service quality.

The best Kaizen quality circles:

- Are voluntary.
- Encourage participants to address internal process or systems topics.
- Are regularly scheduled.
- Take place during usual work times.
- Are led by a trained facilitator.
- Analyse workflow or system problems.
- Make well-argued recommendations for change.

You can shape and format your Kaizen quality circles however you like. Here are well-proven approaches worth considering,

- Keep circle size manageable so everyone has opportunity to contribute. 8 to 12 participants is about right.
- Hold meetings away from the work area. People get distracted by the comings and goings of colleagues. No phones.

- The duration and frequency of quality circles can be agreed. It's important the scheduling offers a best fit for your organisation. New circles could, for example, meet for one hour, once per week. Once the activity is up and running participants decide on how frequently a circle should meet and for what duration. The nature and scope of the quality problem to be solved will influence this.
- Each quality circle meeting should have a clear agenda and objective.
- If helpful, a circle may wish to call on outside or expert help to add value to the kaizen process.

How could you integrate Kaizen quality circles into your QCI operations?

Further reading

One Team on All Levels: Stories from Toyota Members | CRC Press, 2012 | Turner, T.

Kaizen: The Japanese Method for Transforming Habits, One Small Step at a Time | Bluebird; Main Market edition, 2019 | Harvey, S.

Up the Organisation: How to Stop the Corporation from Stifling People and Strangling Profits | Jossey-Bass, 2007 | Townsend, R., Bennis, W.

Quality standards

"Well done is better than well said." *– Benjamin Franklin*

Quality standards are measures related to specific elements of operational quality.

Within the UK, the United Kingdom Accreditation Service (UKAS) is the national accreditation body, appointed by government, to assess agencies providing certification, testing, inspection, and/or calibration services.

Internationally recognised standards of quality include those prescribed by the International Organization for Standardization, including,

- ISO 9000/9001 quality management series accreditation. Standards relating to business processes mapped, made explicit and followed.
- ISO 14000/14001 series accreditation. Standards relating to environmental management processes mapped, made explicit and followed.
- ISO 19011. Standards relating to auditing processes mapped, made explicit and followed.

- ISO 31011. Standards relating to risk management mapped, made explicit and followed.
- ISO 26000. Standards relating to social responsibility, mapped, made explicit and followed.
- ISO 22000 series accreditation. Standards relating to food safety management processes mapped, made explicit and followed.
- ISO 27000 series accreditation. Standards relating to information security processes mapped, made explicit and followed.
- ISO 17065 accreditation. Standards relating to certification of technology enabled care services.
- ISO 45001 accreditation. Standards relating to occupational health and safety management.

UK specific quality standards,

- Customer Service Excellence Standard (previously Charter Mark). Standards relating to public sector customer care.
- Investors in People accreditation. Standards relating to human leadership, people management, their professional development and personal growth processes are mapped, made explicit and followed.

Industry specific quality standards,

- Sector accreditation, e.g., *Michelin Star* in hospitality.

Quality standards provide a threshold of requirements for an organization (or part of an organization) to meet, to achieve compliance, accreditation, or certification.

I encourage team managers to explore their industry sector quality standards. You may wish to consider which (if any) quality standards are, or could be, relevant to your workplace activities.

Further reading

United Kingdom Accreditation Service www.ukas.com

International Standardization Organisation www.iso.org

European Accreditation www.european-accreditation.org

Quality and 5S

"In the midst of chaos, there is also opportunity." – *Sun Tzu*

Involving team members in quality management activities makes good sense for both continuous improvement and employee engagement. A proven tool to help with this is *5S*, or *Workplace Organisation*; it's a core component within the Kaizen process.

5S is useful to improve workflow, reduce waste, and create a standardised approach to service delivery or production. Although best known in manufacturing businesses, it's popularity in service sector industries is increasing, as the benefits of 5S become more widely known as part of *Lean Services*.

The 5S philosophy suggests operations work best when the work environment is clean, tidy, and organised. There are messages in 5S disciplines about pride in the workplace and work role, efficiencies, safety, and the impressions offered to customers.

5S thinking considers all enterprises as potentially wasteful. Waste has many forms, in manufacturing and in service environments. 5S suggests waste is a *cost* to be eliminated, or at least reduced.

Waste is cost, absorbed into an organisation. Waste-cost has implications. Cost is passed on, as either,

- Inefficiency (see **Lean management**).
- A higher price to customers, to maintain profit margin, and the potential impact on competitiveness.
- Price maintenance, and consequential reduced profit margin.
- A combination of both.

Organisational waste may include,

- Waste from making more than needed – over production.
- Waste from waiting time in process flow.
- Waste from movement of materials.
- Waste from movement of parts or machinery.
- Waste from movement of people.
- Waste from inefficient processing.

- Waste from excessive inventory, stock, or raw materials.
- Waste from producing error waste, defective or damaged goods, non-conformance services, or incorrect information.
- Waste of a people time.
- Waste of energy.

Notice the similarity of the 5S emphasis on waste, with the approach promoted in Value Stream Mapping (see **Value Stream Mapping**).

The Japanese origin of 5S translates conveniently from words beginning with S (at least, aurally) in Japanese to English words also starting with S.

The 5S's are,

1. *Seiri/Sort – Clear out time.* Put aside all the equipment, machines, materials, and resources no longer needed, and *eliminate* them.
2. *Seiton/Straighten, Systemize – Categorise.* Arrange the remaining required items and clearly mark them. Make them easy to find, *a place for everything and everything in its place.*
3. *Seiso/Scrub, Shine – Clean and make ready.* Clean all equipment, machines, and the wider workspace ready for production activity, safe from contamination.
4. *Seiketsu/Standardise – Consistency.* Operate processes and behaviours in a consistent manner. Make workplace maintenance, cleaning and organising, a regular routine for all team members.
5. *Shitsuke/Sustain – Sustain-ability; the ability to sustain.* Keep the first 4 steps alive, every day, with every team member, and constantly seek to improve 5S processes.

Think about your workplace and the wastes described above. Where are the opportunities for you and your colleagues to embrace 5S into workplace operations?

Further reading/watching,

Total Quality Management and Operational Excellence: Text with Cases | Routledge, 2021 | Oakland, J.S., Oakland, R.J., Turner, M.A.

How do you train 5S | Bourton Group | Editorial team, February 2021 | https://www.bourton.co.uk/how-do-you-train-5s/

R

Rapport

"Prosperity is full of friends." – *Euripides*

Rapport. You won't get far without it.

A skill for managers is to elegantly build rapport with direct reports, peers, your boss, and your wider network. Rapport is about finding shared territory, being empathetic and building a relationship. Here's the good news… if you've got at least one friend, then you already know how to do it.

Obvious examples of rapport are a common bond, shared interests or beliefs, using the same phrases and tone of voice, even adopting the same posture (see **Clean language** and **Matching and mirroring**). Why? Because we like people who are like us. Think about it. When was the last time you said to yourself, *"Oh yes I like him, he disagrees with me on most things."*? The concept of *opposites attract* rarely holds water in business relationships.

Most of all, rapport is about being friendly. Team managers can do the same with colleagues. Even recently appointed managers already know how to be friendly and approachable – it's a social skill we learn from an early age.

To learn about developing rapport at a deeper level, read on…

Further reading

How to win Friends and Influence People in the Digital Age | Simon & Schuster, 2011 | Dale Carnegie

It's Not All About Me: The Top Ten

Techniques for Building Quick Rapport with Anyone | Robin K. Dreeke, 2011 | Dreeke, R.

Rapport, advanced skills

Qui se ressemble, s'assemble. *– French proverb*

Communication bonds between two or more people flourish through physiological, tonal and word content similarities (see **Clean language**, **Matching and mirroring** and **Words, song and dance**).

Therapists use advanced communication techniques for building trust and confidence. Beyond 'standard' communications skills are subtle methods for enhancing relationship dynamics.

Cross-Over Matching

You can match or mirror one physiological behaviour or tonality with something quite different, and with the same frequency. For example, you may see someone's foot tapping beneath a table, perhaps concentrating on a matter of importance to them. Or they might be heel-lifters, rhythmically raising and lowering their heel at a fast pace. There will be a cadence to this movement. It is simple to set up a similar frequency with finger movement above the table. This is elegant because:

- The subject does not know you have recognised the (e.g.) foot tapping beneath the table.
- The subject is not consciously aware of your finger movement above the table.
- The subject is not consciously aware of the relationship of the finger movement to the foot tapping, or heel lifting.

Cross-Over Matching of Breathing Patterns

Taken a step further, an elegant cross-over pacing activity is to match breathing patterns with minor motor movements. The process is not recognised by the subject, at a conscious level, although the unconscious mind is fully aware, and is likely to fall into empathetic trust.

You can match the frequency and intensity of another person's breathing pattern with some form of minor motor movement from yourself. Operated elegantly, this is a proven winner and a rapport building strategy to build rapid connection.

By raising and lowering a finger, hand, or other minor motor movement, in time with the breathing pattern of another, we build an unconscious recognition from the subject of being 'in sync' with them. Consciously there is no recognition of the technique being employed, whereas the two unconscious minds are chattering away to each other like old friends re-united.

Cross-Over Matching of Eye Blink Patterns

A more challenging technique is to cross-over match the subject's blink rates with minor motor movements. This requires the minor motor movement to take place immediately after the blink, so it is seen by the unconscious mind. Blink matching is tough to learn due to the high concentration levels needed to accurately observe the blink rate, and to avoid flicking a finger at random intervals.

Critical Success Factors

- Not everyone thinks the same way as you. The top rapport builders, the wizards, and magicians of communicating, rarely make this mistake. They know the way you and I see the world is different from their perception. It must be, we've all experienced different lives – how could we all be the same? The master communicators know to enter our world, using the skills we have described above (see **Maps of the territory** and **Get inside their world**).
- The congruence with which we use these skills. Make sure you match or mirror a person's (key) words, their tonality, and their physiology. Getting the physiology right whilst speaking in an incongruent tone will send a mixed message.

- Adopt any combination from your subject's communication,
    - tonality.
    - colloquialisms, phrases, jargon, speech patterns.
    - breathing patterns.
    - posture, shifts in weight.
    - hand gestures.
    - foot movements.
    - facial expressions, eyebrow movements.
    - muscle tensions.
    - head positions.

If this sounds hard work, you're right; it may be at first. New skills take time to develop. It's worth persevering. When you have rapport, you can influence.

Further reading

Ericksonian Approaches, A Comprehensive Manual | Crown House, 1999 | Battino, R., South, T.

How to Build Rapport: A Powerful Technique | Psychology Today, April 2015 | Civico, A. | https://www.psychologytoday.com/intl/blog/turning-point/201504/how-to-build-rapport-a-powerful-technique

Rarely, sometimes, always

"Who looks outside, dreams; who looks inside, awakes."
– Carl Gustav Jung

Rarely, sometimes, always, is a great way to calibrate performance against an explicit standard or ambition. Take any competence or required performance, reflect a while, and ask the question,

"Is this something (I-we-you) do Rarely, Sometimes, or Always?"

For example,

"Our customer experience protocols require us to ask prospective customers at least three questions to gain an understanding of their needs and wants. Is this something I-we-you do Rarely, Sometimes, or Always?"

I've used this approach during professional development work across sectors and professions. Because it's a generic approach it has universal application.

Rarely, Sometimes, Always response options are clearly limited (one of three). We can create more flexibility by adding a numerical Red Amber Green 'RAG' option to responses. For example, we may feel a *Sometimes* response is appropriate, although maybe more towards the *Rarely* end, say a 4, or perhaps nudging on the edge of *Always,* perhaps a 7?

Here's an example from leadership,

B. Team Leadership	Rarely 1 2 3	Sometimes 4 5 6 7	Always 8 9 10
1. Promotes innovation. Asks team members for ideas to help solve problems and improve performance.			

Recognising a numerical as well as colour scale position statement on the 1-10 RAG report allows a more precise evaluation. It offers scope for gradual personal improvement towards a competency goal. As a coaching resource *Rarely, Sometimes, Always* suggests insights for discussion.

You may a have a set of management or leadership competences in mind from which you could develop your own table for a RAG self-assessment.

How could you use *Rarely, Sometimes, Always,* with your team, and yourself?

Further reading

Chartered Institute of Personnel and Development | Leadership | https://www. cipd.co.uk/knowledge/strategy/leadership

8 Behaviours of the World's Best Managers | Gallup, 2019 | Pendell, R. | https://www. gallup.com/workplace/272681/habits-world-best-managers.aspx

Top 27 Self-Assessment Questions for Managers | PeopleGoal Inc, March 2021 | Kelly, L. | https://www.peoplegoal.com/blog/self-assessment

Reading

"Without training they lacked knowledge.
Without knowledge they lacked confidence.
Without confidence they lacked victory".

– Julius Caesar

Leaders are readers, or audiobook listeners, or video watchers. Experiential learning is fine; trial and error is a proven method of gaining knowledge and skill. It may be impactful, unfortunately, it is a slow way to grow.

Reading, or any other channel for knowledge acquisition, creates a mental repository of reference material for managers to dip into as circumstances require. The more reading, the more knowledge, the more reference points.

You can make time to learn.

For some managers learning through reading has, historically, been a challenging experience. Memories of enforced reading at school, or the horror of being made to read out loud to the class. No wonder there is remembered pain and a reluctance to read.

Many of the managers I work with, including high performers, have dyslexia in various grades of severity. Some use avoidance tactics to minimise their exposure to the written word. Others have developed coping strategies.

Information gathering and learning is still available for them, maybe just not in book format. Today we are blessed by audiobooks (you can listen to my book *Fast Coaching* on Audible), podcasts, webinars, online film, all of which offer a gateway to professional knowledge. Nowadays academic institutes and vocational education centres are more aware, and better equipped, to offer non-traditional learning methods.

The most helpful book I read as a young operational manager was *Management & Organisational Behaviour*, by Laurie Mullins. I still have a copy now and refer to it from time to time. Like this book, it has a reference framework, and is accessible by subject matter rather than a sequential text requiring a start-at-the-beginning-continue-to-the-end approach.

If reading about management or leadership is new for you, textbooks may seem burdensome. That's ok, there are excellent short books which offer great value, without the need to plough through hundreds of pages. Or books like this one, which have a dip-in-dip-out format, allowing you to search on the sections you find most interesting.

Read, read, read. Or listen to audiobooks, or podcasts. Or watch YouTube. Or find a mentor. The most successful leaders and managers absorb new learning through an obsessive thirst for new knowledge.

You don't know what you don't know.

Further reading

Management and Organisational Behaviour | Pearson, 2016 (11th Edition) | Mullins, L.

The New One Minute Manager | William Morrow, 2015 | Blanchard, K.H., Johnson, S.

Who Moved My Cheese: An Amazing Way to Deal with Change in Your Work and in Your Life | Vermilion, 1999 | Johnson, S.

Management Basics in Easy Steps | In Easy Steps Ltd, 2019 | Rossiter, T.

Receive, and transmit

"A wise man speaks because he has something to say;
a fool because he has to say something". *– Plato*

Managing as a *Transmitter* might be helpful, occasionally, in delivering ideas and instructions. Astute managers are wary of spending time in transmitter mode. Turning on your *Receiver* mode helps information flow even better (see **Hallucination**).

There is danger in becoming a habitual *Transmitter*. You know these people, the ones who talk and talk, consumed by their own experiences and opinions, seemingly oblivious to the audience's world and perspective. There is minimal opportunity for recipients to contribute as the stream of noise continues one-way in your direction.

The Latin root of the word communication is *communicare*, meaning to share. The only sharing for *Transmitters* is the downloading of their thoughts and proposals to the poor *Receivers*, on the receiving end of a didactic lecture. Notice the emphasis on downloading; there is little in the way of receptive uploading.

Chronic *Transmitters* are insensitive communicators, domineering, or uncaring about the views and opinions of *Receivers*. There's a reason for their being stuck on transmission (see **Emotional Drivers™**), it is an urge to move towards feeling good, perhaps the self-esteem from imparting knowledge, of feeling significant. Or maybe it's an urge to move away from pain, from being perceived as dull, boring, or even worse, lacking in significance.

The *feel-good*, or avoidance of *feel-bad*, is short lived. It requires constant reinforcement from repetitive transmission to reducing levels interest from *Receivers*. Eventually *Transmitters* are perceived as tiresome.

Worst of all, *Transmittters* miss out on the true richness of *communicare*, the *sharing* of thoughts, ideas, and knowledge. Feedback for them is limited to non-verbal messages and pre-verbal grunts from *Receivers*. Email and other digital communications are particularly troublesome. With *zero* biofeedback *Transmitters* have freedom to impart information as frequently, and in as much volume, as they choose.

Who suffers the most? Is it the *Transmitter* who doesn't benefit from feedback, or the *Receiver* who switches off? Both participants are stuck in a Lose-Lose pattern (see **Win-win**).

Further reading

Message Received: 7 Steps to Break Down Communication Barriers at Work | McGraw Hill, 2021 | Donohue, M.E.

Reasons You Don't Listen | PsychCentral, June 2021 | Cassata, C. | https://psychcentral.com/lib/reasons-you-dont-listen

Remote working, remote management

"When the best leader's work is done the people say,
'We did it ourselves'." – *Lao Tzu*

The Covid-19 pandemic changed employment behaviours, with remote working emerging as a format for keeping organisations moving. We found ourselves adapting to new ways of communicating, harnessing the power of electronic media. We learned to use digital platforms to see and hear each other.

For some, the concept of working from home (WFH) was already a familiar phenomenon. Organisations had flexible working practices in place long before Covid. The benefits afforded by lower bricks and mortar overheads, and the reduced time waste of travel, made sound business sense.

For others, the shift to a home-based working format proved problematic. Technical investment was a resisting force (see **Forcefields**), as was the learning required for employees to become competent users of digital communications. Domestic circumstances became a major factor in making WFH viable.

Cultural shift was an issue. The discomfort of 'meeting' remotely was apparent, as was the change in interpersonal dynamics. The motor movements and mini transmissions of face-to-face communication was affected. Breathing patterns, skin colour changes, shifts in posture, minor motor movements of eye dilation, hands, fingers, feet, nostrils – via digital communication all these message-giving channels become less obvious to the conscious and unconscious mind of co-communicators. We adapted (see **Adapt**).

Today, remote working, or some version of it, is commonplace. Hybrid working is a norm for many organisations, with team members working a mix of home and office, or other on-site operations. Team management becomes interesting when colleagues are working with a blended approach to 'attendance'.

Good management practices are now evident, and well-proven after such an intensive period of adjustment. What is clear in hybrid and remote working is the importance of trust, and the role of management in clearing the way to allow employees space, opportunity, and the resources, to get on and succeed on their own without micro-management.

Here is a summary of suggestions for remote team management, drawn from respected employment agencies and advisory groups. Also included are empirical research findings I've discovered from client organisations I am fortunate to work alongside.

- *Stay connected* – regular scheduled and ad hoc online check ins and KIT team meetings. Physical in-person meetings, whenever possible, are the new *full fat* version. The richness of physical meetings becomes more noticeable after extended periods of hybrid and remote arrangements (see **KIT meetings**).
- *Be clear on expectations* – clarity is good. Performance requirements, delivery schedules, quality definitions, explicit standards, all become more significant. Expectations are best described in unambiguous language (see **Explicit standards, NDK Performance Model®** and **Aims & objectives, clarity on**).
- *What is our purpose?* – keep team purpose highlighted, and use business plans, quarterly goals, campaign initiatives, and other ambitions visible and regularly updated with progress reports. Teams and team members work best when there is direction, purpose, and progression. There is no difference here to good management practice within static environment work groups.
- *Review performance individually and team performance collectively* – performance still requires management and measurement irrespective of workforce location.
- *Keep communication channels open* – active 360 communications are a feature of successful hybrid or remote working teams. Creating a safe

Open area of Johari is key to stimulating team communication. Healthy teams communicate politely, with frankness, and without fear (see **Johari, adapted for management**).

- *Words, Song, and Dance* – when we remove an element of human interaction, we automatically impoverish the quality of interpersonal communication. Think carefully about how you as team manager, and your colleagues as team members, use their comms skills in a digital setting. The words we use, the tone with which we use them and the way we use our bodies, and facial expressions, are all accentuated in remote delivery. Smiling is a good start (see **Words, song, and dance**).

- *Equity, diversity, inclusion* – changing expectations around working practices will create new dynamics in the way people feel. For some, shifts in working arrangements will be embraced. For others, with habits embedded over a long period of time, change will be an experience of seismic proportions. What seems easy for some may feel insurmountable for others. Your team members are individuals, with unique character-istics. Be empathetic (see **Empathy** and **Diversity, Equity, Inclusion (DEI), or Equity, Diversity, Inclusion [EDI]**).

- *Stay healthy* – the dangers of overwork are ever present in remote teams. Screen breaks, parameters around aggregated working hours, and encouragement to take physical exercise away from the remote worksta-tion, all help foster healthy working practices. Think about initiating a 'no late-night/no weekend working' policy, except of course, where it is helpful to a team member's personal or domestic circumstances to do so. Consultation here is the key.

- *Employee engagement research* – if your organisation doesn't already have one, think about introducing a team-based engagement survey, asking colleagues for their thoughts on what is working well as a remote or hybrid team, and what is working less well.

- *Newbies* – recruits to any organisation expect and benefit from close support during their early days. This doesn't change in a hybrid or remote context. *More* attention is generally the rule to go by. Readily accessible and friendly online faces and voices are reassuring for new joiners. Retention issues and churn are prominent during the early stages of employment. Remote physicality makes uncertainty and anxiety more likely. For a new starter, training, mentoring, and coaching are all imperatives to help bedding-in and feelings of comfort.

- *Collaboration* – when workers have opportunity to work with colleagues remotely on a common cause, feelings of team-ship and belonging increase. There's an implicit reminder in the group task of togetherness and team collective purpose. What could you do to engage your team members in a partnership work assignment?

- *Keeping the good stuff* – the motivational factors for colleagues in face-to-face work teams are still relevant in remote scenarios. Principles of motivational psychology remain valid. Helping team members feel good about their worth, celebrating their successes, recognizing achievement, providing meaningful, value adding responsibilities, and providing a forum for acknowledgement of performance; these factors can still be fulfilled in a remote or hybrid team. It may require some innovation; that's ok, new thinking brings freshness and excitement.

Remote and hybrid working is here to stay. As technological communication tools evolve, we will become more accustomed to how we manage ourselves and our colleagues. Skilful managers will continue to balance performance emphasis with the health and welfare of team members and the team collective.

Further reading

Managing and Supporting Remote Workers; Guidance for Line Managers | Chartered Institute of Personnel and Development, January 2021 | https://www.cipd.org/uk/knowledge/guides/remote-working-line-manager-guide/

Remote working causes communication gap between managers and employees | HR Magazine, March 2023 | Machell, M. | https://www.hrmagazine.co.uk/content/news/remote-working-causes-communication-gap-between-managers-and-employees

6 Trends Leaders Need to Navigate This Year | Gallup, January 2023 | Wigert, B., Pendell, R. | https://www.gallup.com/workplace/468173/workplace-findings-leaders-need-navigate-year.aspx

Resilience

"What is demanded from us all is something more than courage and endurance; we need a revival of spirit, a new unconquerable resolve."

– King George VI

Resilience is a choice. It is a decision, like the creature in nature whose house is destroyed by environmental circumstance, who starts again, ceaselessly moving forward. Our species, like others, is programmed to rebuild and survive, to perpetuate the genes.

Team management can be a rocky ride. Resilience is a worthwhile characteristic to develop. There are resources to organise and monitor, and all will be problematic at times. Inevitably, the most volatile resource is people. Communicating with team members, both individually and collectively, is a task sure to result in occasional disagreement, and maybe conflict. You will make management decisions which are unpopular, and you will make mistakes of judgement and of implementation.

You are a fallible human being who gets things wrong and learns. I've made colossal management errors. I'm glad I did though because it means I've learned how not to operate in the future. They were valuable experiences, even if painful at the time. It helped me become resilient, to absorb the learning and bounce back, just like sports team do after a poor result.

Imagine if you didn't bounce back? You'd be saying to yourself, *"Well I messed up, I'd better not try anything like that again"*, and before long you're treading water.

You are going to get plenty of knockbacks in your management career. Absorb the learning, take stock, reflect, and think, *"Ok, I've experienced something useful here. I will be a more rounded manager because of this."*

Be resilient; go again. And again.

Further reading

The Little Book of Resilience: How to Bounce Back from Adversity and Lead a Fulfilling Life | Robinson, 2015 | Johnstone, M.

Resilience in the Workplace: How to Be Resilient at Work | PositivePsychology.com, March 2023 | Craig, H. | https://positivepsychology.com/resilience-in-the-workplace/

Resistor busting

"It can be surmised that the extent to which social research is translated into social action depends on the degree to which those who carry out this action are made a part of the fact-finding on which the action is to be based." *– Kurt Lewin*

In *Forcefield Analysis* a push-pull dynamic of arrows is used to illustrate the balancing effect of *Driver* and *Resistor* forces in a stable equilibrium, or *homeostasis*. A forcefield describes the position statement of an organisation, a work group, or an individual (see **Forcefields**).

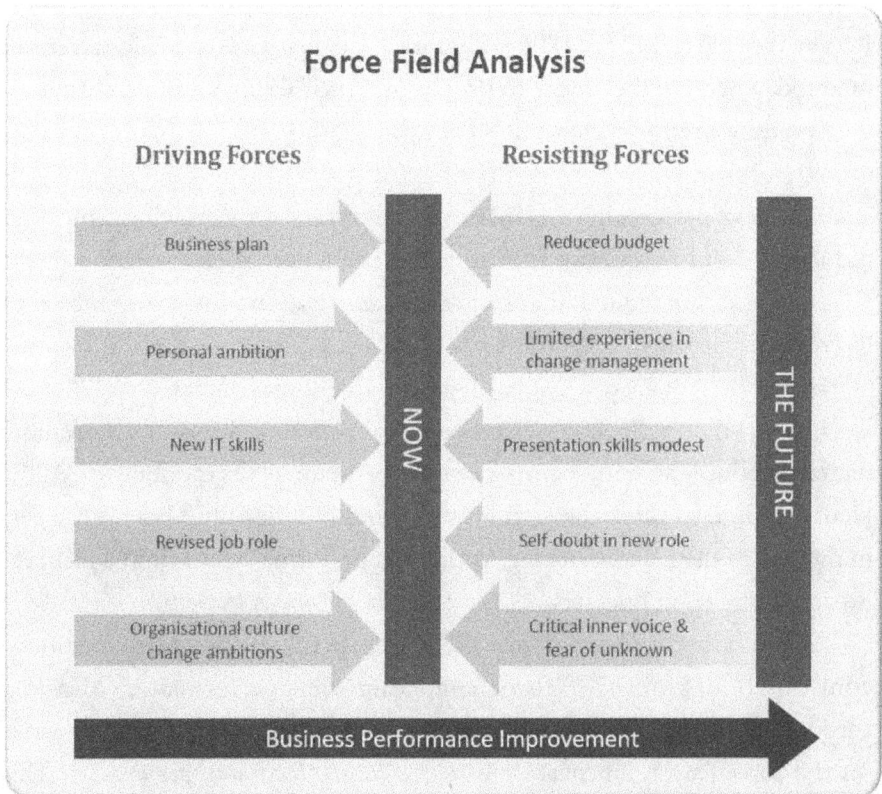

Force Field Analysis

Driving Forces	Resisting Forces
Business plan	Reduced budget
Personal ambition	Limited experience in change management
New IT skills	Presentation skills modest
Revised job role	Self-doubt in new role
Organisational culture change ambitions	Critical inner voice & fear of unknown

NOW — THE FUTURE

Business Performance Improvement

A position statement is a helpful starting point; it provides clarity of status. It doesn't change the status. To create change, to move towards the right, requires a stimulus.

So, what could be done to stimulate change and create a revised forcefield?

Should we increase the *driving forces?*

No.

If you studied science at school, you may remember Isaac Newton's Third law of Motion,

'For each force there's an equal and opposite force'.

In managing change the primary resistors are often people's attitudes and belief systems, including those of managers and team members. For each newly introduced forcefield driver there is someone who responds with *"Ah, but it won't work because…"* (see **Change** and **Behaviour breeds behaviour**).

As long ago as 1969 Paul Lawrence understood the nature of human resistance and described these factors eloquently in his Harvard Business Review Paper *How to Deal With Resistance to Change*. Lawrence's ideas remain valid today because they relate to people, and their feelings around change.

Should we remove the *resisting forces?*

Yes.

The best performing businesses concentrate on removing, diluting, reducing, or in some way lessening the influence of the *resisting forces*. Experience shows reduction of resistor influence allows the *driving forces* to leverage performance improvement.

Here's how managers can facilitate this in a team context,

List down on a flipchart, whiteboard – or a message board if it's a remote digital meeting – as many *resisting forces* as team members can think of. Allow plenty of time to think through logically, and emotionally, about what gets in the way of the team achieving world class performance – within whichever discipline the team operates.

At first, resistor suggestions will be 'out there', outside team members' control, about external factors hampering their performance. Mid-way through the process, with a marker pen, and without comment, I write on the top of each flipchart or board, *'What about you, personally?'* This usually changes thinking patterns, sometimes with a degree of discomfort, and highlights at least some *resisting forces* as being attitudinal, rather than externally 'caused'.

Once a rich list of *resisting forces* has been created, it's time to address them.

Ask the group to review their list and identify,

- which *resistors* are external forces outside their locus of control.
- which are directly within their sphere of influence.
- which could be indirectly influenced, perhaps by persuasion, lobbying, report writing, or other activity.

Mark the *resistors* on the flipchart as either **E** (external), **I** (internal, either directly, or indirectly) or **E/I** for those forces which may be a bit of both.

This is a critical moment because for some folk within the group, particularly the *CAVE people*, *R-Buts*, *MGs* and *20/20s* this may be the first time they have admitted to themselves they have personal control over some *resisting forces* (see **Behaviour breeds behaviour** and **Case Study: On Growing Managers [and our Business]**).

Acknowledgement of this may be uncomfortable for some. On the upside, it is often the turning point in shifting mindsets towards recognition of personal *response-ability*; the ability to respond.

Once the *resisting forces* are categorised, take next steps. We can do nothing about external forces. Fact. So, let's get on with life and deal with the things we *can* influence. Select one of the **I** resistors (any) and bust it.

We do this is through poetry.

Rudyard Kipling was clearly an organisational change specialist ahead of his time. His poem in the *Just So* story *The Elephant's Child* is instructive in how to bust forcefield resistors. Here is the introductory verse,

I keep six honest serving men
(They taught me all I knew)
Their names are What and Why and When
And How and Where and Who.

We begin with the *Why* question. *Why* is it important we address this resisting force? This is the leverage we need for action. There must be a perceived benefit from busting the resistor.

Second up is the *What* question. *What* (specifically) are we going to do about it? This is the call for action. The remaining questions are answered in any order.

So, the question set goes like this:

1. *Why* is it important we bust this *resistor*?
2. *What* (specifically) are we going to do to bust this *resistor*?

And then in any order…

- *How* (specifically) are we going to do it?
- *Who* (specifically) will be involved?
- *When* (specifically) will we do it?
- *Where* (specifically) will we do it?

The skill in facilitating answers to these questions is to be specific and precise. The perils of ambiguity are always present. Once the group have answered the questions with precision and specificity you will have the beginnings of a plan for eliminating, reducing, or diluting the *resisting force* – a plan for change.

Of course, the plan only is a list of words until put into action (see **Act**).

Bust more *resisting forces* and you'll be getting closer to your team ambitions for the *future* position statement.

Further reading

Planned Change: Why Kurt Lewin's Social Science is Still Best Practice for Business Results, Change Management, and Human Progress. | Routledge, 2021 | Crosby, G.

How to Deal With Resistance to Change | Harvard Business Review, January 1969 | Lawrence, P.R. | https://hbr.org/1969/01/how-to-deal-with-resistance-to-change

Review and reflection

"Children always want to look behind mirrors." *– Joseph Joubert*

In the section **About management – an overview** are headline ideas from some of the early thinkers and writers on management principles. If we aggregate these ideas, and find patterns which connect, we can propose an outline description for a management role,

1. *Plan* – set objectives and establish goals for employees.
2. *Organise* – allocate work to the right team members.
3. *Motivate* – communicate with the team and within the organisation.
4. *Control* – set targets and measure results.
5. *Develop people* – encourage learning and growth for team and self.
6. *Review – reflect on performance and adjust tactics.*
7. *Improve* – continuously improve processes.
8. *Re-plan* – restart functions 1- 8.

(6.) above is a critical component for management activity.

Too few team managers, in my experience, invest sufficient dedicated time to reflection,

- To be curious, to *look behind the mirror.*
- To think about how and why a circumstance evolved, and its subsequent progression.

The best managers I've worked with reflect. They consider a recent flow of events, from planning through to completion. What worked well? What worked less well (see **Good and less good**)?

- What happened? What stimulated the need for decision making and action?
- What did we decide to do about it?
- Why did we choose the strategy?
- Which parts of our actions proved helpful, or successful?
- What worked less well, or was less useful?
- What learnings have we gathered form this experience?
- What could be transferable *patterns which connect* to future scenarios?

The 4Fs model developed by Dr Roger Greenaway is a framework designed to aid the reflective process. Included in 4Fs is recognition of the emotional element in reflection – how we felt before, during and after the experience of the management event. The four Fs are,

- *Facts:* an objective account of what happened.
- *Feelings:* emotional reactions to the situation.
- *Findings:* learning to take away from the experience.
- *Future:* how can learning be used in future scenarios.

Review and reflection time offers *learning experiences* for all team managers. What do you do, or could you do, to review and reflect on your management decisions and actions?

Further reading

Experiential Learning: A Practical Guide for Training, Coaching and Education | Kogan page, 2018 | Beard, C., Wilson, J.P.

The four F's of active reviewing | The University of Edinburgh, November 2018, adapted from Roger Greenaway's 'The

Active Reviewing Cycle'. | https://www. ed.ac.uk/reflection/reflectors-toolkit/ reflecting-on-experience/four-f

The Notebooks of Joseph Joubert: A Selection | NYRB Classics, 2006 | Joubert, J.

Root cause analysis

"Knowledge of the fact differs from knowledge of the reason for the fact." *– Aristotle*

Root cause analysis is about finding the *Cause of the Cause* of a problem. Understanding the origins of a problem can give you a head start in resolving it and preventing a re-occurrence.

Here is a simple example:

The delivery van is showing a warning light.

Why? Because…
Coolant is low. There is no obvious water leak though…

Why? Because...
Water is leaking within the system.

Why? Because...
The exhaust gas recycling cooler is faulty.

Why? Because...
The van has not been maintained.

Why? Because...
No one has been given the task of managing the van maintenance programme.

Why? Because...
I haven't allocated the task to anyone.

Why? Because...
I didn't take time out to consider how to manage our equipment and resources this year. We don't have a preventative maintenance programme. I'd better sit down and think about this. I'll ask the team for their thoughts.

Why? as a repeat question gets to the originating cause of a problematic situation. Notice how in the example above the *Why?* question acts as a funnel, gradually creating clarity by searching for the genesis of a set of circumstances.

Root cause analysis encourages operational managers to investigate a problem using good questions to dig out what's going on. *Why?* is one good question to use. Others are: *What? How? Who? When? and Where?* These can all be employed to help investigate the origins of a problem (see **Resistor busting**).

Further reading

Root Cause Analysis Handbook: A Guide to Efficient and Effective Incident Management, 3rd Edition | Rothstein Associates, 2008 | ABS Consulting, Vanden Heuvel, L.N., Lorenzo, D.K., Hanson, W.E.

5 Whys: The Ultimate Root Cause Analysis Tool | Kanbanize | Editorial team, undated. | https://kanbanize.com/lean-management/improvement/5-whys-analysis-tool

S

Scrums and sprints

"First, have a definite clear practical goal, an objective. Second, have
the necessary means to achieve your ends; wisdom, money, materials
and methods. Third, adjust all your means to that end."

– Aristotle

Software development disciplines are a great reference source for team
managers. Patterns connect between project organisation and team organisation (see **Patterns which connect** and **Agile management**).

In technology and 'dev' project teams, colleagues meet up regularly to
discuss stage planning and performance, and subsequent progress meetings.
These sessions are known as *scrums*, an analogy from the sport of rugby.
Scrums review performance, determine new short-term goals, and plans for
implementation, before restarting the game.

Work activity following the *scrum* is known as a *sprint*. As the name suggests, a sprint is a short, fast paced work assignment covering a specific project element. At the end of each sprint phase the team reconvenes for another scrum, reviews progress, make changes where necessary, and prepare for the next sprint. Sprint phases are of whatever period works best for your team project. Maybe once a month could be appropriate? Fortnightly? Weekly? You and the team decide.

During sprints, project teams will have *daily stand ups*, super quick team meetings, physical or digital, of typically ten minutes, conducted whilst stood (remotely is fun). The purpose of the *daily stand up* is to update colleagues on progress for specific elements of the project, recent or emerging obstacles, and any immediate changes team members should be aware of. First thing each morning is a common time for daily stand ups, creating focus for the day, and energising team members.

Some organisations I work with refer to daily stand ups as *huddles*, or *remote huddles*. Whatever you call them, a super quick pre-work meeting sets team members in the right mindset ready to deliver outstanding performance, with the team's pre-agreed goals in mind.

Think about your work team. How could you use *scrums* and *sprints* in the management of your projects and daily workflow?

Further reading

Scrum Mastery: The Essential Guide to Scrum and Agile Project Management (Audiobook) | SD Publishing, 2020 | Caldwell, G.

Scrum sprints | Atlassian, undated. | Rehkopf, M. | https://www.atlassian.com/agile/scrum/sprints

Secondary and tertiary impact: The Law of Unintended Consequences

"Science is the knowledge of consequences, and dependence of one fact upon another." *– Thomas Hobbes*

Good chess players think a few moves ahead, and super talented players think many moves ahead. They consider the possible outcomes of playing strategies. Intelligent team managers do the same; they think through the implications of decision making, the likely effects on performance, on internal and external customers, on the team, and on individual colleagues. Decision making though, is just a thought process, nothing happens until action, or *non-action*, creates effect.

Non-action?

Yes, those times when a manager 'lets it go' and ignores non-conformance behaviour, or minor drops in performance standards, and *decides* to take no action.

Taking no action is an action. It allows standards to be ignored; it says to team members, *"Don't worry about it, it's not really important..."*. Either a work team has performance standards, or it doesn't. Non-action about under performance is a decision made by team members, and its manager, to ignore a standard. It's a slippery slope from there.

The *Law of Unintended Consequences* states actions and non-actions may have unplanned impact. Consequences of actions or non-actions come in different forms,

Primary consequences

The immediate impact of actions taken because of a team manager's decision. These impacts are usually anticipated and are intended outcomes of the action.

Secondary consequences

Any decision, followed by its action, has a primary impact, and secondary impact – sometimes unexpected. These secondary impacts may be classed as *unintended consequences*. For example, delivering improved customer experience (CX) will, over time, lead to customers expecting these higher standards of performance as the norm; known as *enhanced CX benchmarks*.

Tertiary consequences

There may also be a third or tertiary level of impact, again potentially unintended or unexpected; for example, learning and development activities for team members will require updates to address these higher CX expectations. There may be resource investment implications connected to this.

Winning managers think about decisions in bigger terms. They think not only of the immediate intended impact of a decision and its action; they consider chess moves beyond their initial planned move.

Think about decisions you make about,

- Work allocation.
- Staffing rotas.
- Working practices.
- Workplace environment.
- Remote or hybrid arrangements.
- Absence and attendance management.
- Organisation and reorganisation.
- Succession planning.
- Recruitment.
- Employee training.
- Appraisals format.
- Coaching schedules.
- Staff wellbeing.
- Designing and developing explicit standards of expected performance.
- The all-encompassing term, *change management.*

What might be the consequences, of your next management decision? How many chess moves will you think ahead?

Further reading

Beware of Unintended Consequences | Remote Leadership Institute | https://www.remoteleaderinstitute.com/ | Eikenberry, K.

To Be A Successful Business Leader, Think Like A Chess Player | Forbes, October 2022 |

Chevannes, S. | https://www.forbes.com/sites/forbesbusinesscouncil/2022/10/11/to-be-a-successful-business-leader-think-like-a-chess-player/?sh=158cbe863985

Secondary gain

"You cannot escape the responsibility of tomorrow by evading it today."

– Abraham Lincoln

Secondary gain describes a side benefit of a presenting behaviour pattern. It is well documented in medicine. In work contexts secondary gain is a phenomenon familiar to occupational therapists who see patterns which connect to employment scenarios (see **Patterns which connect**).

An employee who avoids certain tasks or functions, or over-invests in an activity, is doing so for a reason, either through conscious thought or unconsciously.

There is a planned beneficial return on their behaviour, either an avoidance of discomfort, or anticipated feelings of pleasure (see **Emotional Drivers**™). For example,

- A colleague who finds an excuse not to present at a team meeting – what is the side benefit of this excuse? Avoidance of anxiety? Fear of interrogation by peers? Fear of failure?
- An employee who uses workarounds to avoid using new technology. What is the secondary gain? Avoidance of discomfort in learning new skills? Moving outside current feelings of competence? Fear of feeling vulnerable?
- A colleague so 'busy' with urgent, but trivial, matters, they have no time for important considerations. How is this beneficial for them? Do they get to avoid difficult thinking, or uncomfortable future realities? Does 'busy-ness' offer significance for them (see **Significance**)?
- The team member who speaks at length, quickly, and without offering opportunities for co-communicators to comment. What is the planned pay-off for this behaviour? Preventing others from contradicting them? Avoiding searching questions and potential feelings of exposure? Wanting to dominate and force an opinion or argument?

Secondary gain strategies, whether consciously intended or unconsciously derived, are a game being played (see **Games people play**).

Being mindful of potential secondary gain in a team member's behaviour has advantages when scrutinising performance. All behaviour has a positive intent. What is the reason behind someone's behaviour? The *real* reason?

Secondary gain behaviours require empathy, and investigation.

Further reading

Handbook of Occupational Health and Wellness | Springer, 2012 | Gatchel, R. J., Shulz, I.Z.

What Keeps People from Solving their Problems Series: Secondary Gain | AliceBoyes. com, September 2010 | Boyes, A. | https://www.aliceboyes.com/secondary-gain/

Self-awareness

"Knowing yourself is the beginning of all wisdom." – *Aristotle*

Stage one in any good management development programme is an investigation of self.

I remember, as an over-confident 24-year-old leisure centre manager, embarking on my first professional qualification, a Certificate in Management Studies. The CPD programme meant attending a Further Education college one day per week, for one academic year, with lectures, assignment work, a residential long weekend, and a project dissertation, with a *viva voce* examination (oral questioning on the dissertation) at the conclusion of the programme.

I was energised and keen to gather knowledge about professional management. There was so much to learn and apply!

Imagine my disappointment then, when the first few weeks of the course centred on my existing management characteristics, my learning styles, and the underpinning patterns of my personality/ies. I was frustrated and annoyed. Where were the insights into management excellence? The techniques for motivating team members, and the technical know-how to manage professionally? I wanted to *get on with it.*

No, it was (in my immature mind) unnecessary navel gazing and nonsense psychobabble, akin to reading an agony aunt column, or astrology stars in the morning paper.

Then the penny dropped. I had been blissfully unaware of my gregarious communications style, its often-negative impact on others, and the opportunities I had to uncover new ways of interacting with people in my working world. I began to take a meta position about my interpersonal communications, adopting as best I could a *helicopter view* of objectivity, looking down on my behaviours.

How was I communicating? To whom? In what way? What variances and adaptive approaches was I employing, if any? How agile, or not, was I in different environments? I began to reflect on my personal effectiveness as a communicator. This was new, enlightening, a little embarrassing, and hugely beneficial (see **Continuous professional development [CPD]**, **Empathy**, **Emotional Intelligence (EQ)**, and **Johari, adapted for management**).

Nowadays I smile inwardly, and (I confess) sometimes outwardly, when working with young up-and-coming managers, brim full of energy, effervescent in communication, with absolute certainty… and limited self-awareness.

Awareness of self is the right starting point for professional development. Recognising your communication style, in all forms of words, song and dance helps develop elegance in your interactions (see **Language to help** and **Words, song, and dance**).

How can team managers develop self-awareness?

Colleagues

You could start by asking an honest colleague, a line manager, mentor, or trusted team member, to describe your management style, and any patterns of note. To minimise awkwardness, it helps to ask for two communications patterns they consider are positive attributes of yours, and one area you could develop to become even better (see **Coaching, Continue & Begin Fast Coaching®**).

Johari

Reviewing self against the Johari Window is a useful assessment activity. The top right quadrant in Johari is *Blind*, those behaviours and presenting styles of which we are unaware. As with the *Colleagues* approach above, asking for commentary on these is the most direct way to gain an objective view and a helpful assessment (see **Johari, adapted for management**).

Commercially available self-assessment inventories include,

Belbin

Meredith Belbin developed his approach to team role analysis and team collaboration in the 1960s. It remains a popular method for evaluating self or others against a team effectiveness framework. A self-perception questionnaire identifies a participant's *preferred* team roles. Belbin categorised team functions into (originally) eight categories, *Chairman (nowadays 'Co-ordinator'), Shaper, Plant, Monitor-Evaluator, Company Worker (now 'Implementer'), Resource Investigator, Team Worker,* and *Completer-Finisher.* Belbin subsequently added a ninth category of *Specialist.* In addition to self-perception testing, colleagues and team assessments offer additional insights for participants.

https://www.belbin.com

Big Five

The Big Five, sometimes known as the OCEAN or CANOE model, considers five personality characteristics, measured through reference to self-descriptive sentences, or in some test versions, single adjectives. The Big Five categories include *Openness, Conscientiousness, Extraversion, Agreeableness,* and *Neuroticism.*

Testing is usually conducted via self-report questionnaires. Supporters promote the idea of 'dimensions' rather than 'types', suggesting qualities all people possess in varying degrees.

Commercial agencies offer testing and assessment services.

Clifton Strengths®

Developed by Gallup®, this assessment considers four 'domains', of *executing, influencing, relationship building,* and *strategic thinking.* Domains have subsets of 34 strengths areas, or themes.

The assessment asks participants to consider a series of opposing statements and asked which statement they most closely relate to. A subsequent report presents five specific strengths which the process suggests have been scored most highly by the participant. Guidance is offered on how to make best use of the identified strengths.

https://www.gallup.com/cliftonstrengths/en/252137/home.aspx

DISC

DISC assessments are behavioural self-assessments originally created by psychologists William Moulton Marston in 1928. DISC is used in recruitment activities to predict job performance. The acronym DISC refers to four proposed characteristics of an individual, *Dominance, Inducement/Influence, Submission/Steadiness,* and *Compliance.* Participants may uncover one or more characteristics as significant for them.

Commercial agencies provide DISC assessments in a range of formats, some recognising the variance in behaviour in differing circumstances, e.g., the participants 'standard/default' behaviour patterns, and how the assessment suggests behaviour may shift emphasis at work, or during stressful periods.

Emotional Intelligence (EI/EQ)

The term *Emotional Intelligence* first appeared in a 1964 paper by Michael Beldoch. It became well known through Daniel Goleman's 1995 book *Emotional Intelligence, Why It Can Matter More Than IQ* (Bantam). In team management, emotional intelligence has become a topic of interest.

Developed awareness of our own and others' emotions helps improve interpersonal communication, by using *feeling* insights to steer our thinking and subsequent behaviours. Observers debate the 'correct' abbreviation for emotional intelligence. Some prefer EI, others EQ. Assessment tools exist, available through commercial agencies.

Enneagram

Enneagrams suggests, and explores, nine interconnected personality characteristics, or 'enneatypes',

Peacemaker, Reformer, Helper, Achiever, Individualist, Investigator, Loyalist, Enthusiast, and *Challenger.*

Personality measurement instruments, assessing a participant against the enneatypes, are offered by agencies, including the Riso-Hudson Type Indicator (RHETI®) and the Stanford Enneagram Discovery Inventory.

https://www.enneagraminstitute.com/

Insights Discovery

Insights Discovery is a framework used in recruitment circles, informed by a self-completion profiling tool of 100 questions. It seeks to identify the participants' observable behaviour patterns, known as *colour energies,* and described as *Cool Blue* (cautious, analytical), *Fiery Red* (competitive, demanding), *Earth Green* (caring, encouraging) and *Sunshine Yellow* (demonstrative, enthusiastic).

https://www.insights.com/products/

Myers Briggs

The Myers-Briggs Type Indicator dates to mid-20th Century. It is a self-completed personality inventory, describing competing characteristics, or 'dichotomies', e.g., *Introvert – Extrovert, Thinking – Feeling, Sensing – Intuition*, and *Judging – Perceiving*. Completed questionnaires produce a summary of 'personality type' in four letter formats, representing the first letter of each component of the dichotomies, e.g., INTJ, ISTP, ESFP, ENFJ.

www.myersbriggs.org

Strengthscope® inventory

Strengthscope®, as it sounds, explores the talents of a participant, creating a strengths profile from a combination of self-assessment and the contribution of others. Awareness of personal and professional strengths helps develop a positive self-image, creating empowering feelings of resourcefulness (see **Coaching, Continue & Begin Fast Coaching®**).

Strength attributes are clustered into four categories, Emotional, Relational, Thinking, and Execution, each with subsidiary components, measuring against a total of twenty-four strengths.

https://www.strengthscope.com/

360 degree feedback

Typical contributors to a 360 assessment are peers, line managers, and team employees, providing insights from within the employing organisation. External perspectives from customers and suppliers offer potential to further broaden an assessment.

To be effective, 360 assessments require honesty from assessors. For managers, comparing colleague perceptions against self-image may be unnerving, especially when receiving observations from direct reports. 360 programmes require considered thought regarding implementation, and the sensitivities involved in receiving observations from others.

Criteria for assessment should be carefully described to focus on specific areas of interest, for example, *leadership style under pressure, empathy, clarity of direction,* or *support for team members.*

Software programmes are available commercially to assist in 360 assessments.

Self SWOT

SWOT analyses are commonly associated with team or organisational activities. Self-assessment SWOTs are useful for managers. As a reminder, SWOT = *Strengths, Weaknesses* (*'Potential'* is better), *Opportunities*, and *Threats*.

Strengths and *Weaknesses-Potential* are usually related to internal resources, with *Opportunities* and *Threats* considered as external factors. Here is a simple grid of a self-assessment SWOT,

Self-Strengths	Self-Weaknesses/Potential
Technical skills.	Reluctance to change.
Industry experience.	Over work, long hours.
KPI management.	Fear of delegation.
Support for team members.	Micro-managing team members.
Opportunities	**Threats**
Develop presentation skills.	Organisational change.
Increase knowledge on marketing.	IT skills dated.
Network with senior colleagues.	Insufficient reading on topical management matters.

Video of Self

Reducing the *Blind* area of Johari is a fast track to personal development. There's no better way to do this than see and hear yourself on film. In terms of continuous improvement, I'm fortunate (questionable) to regularly see and hear my professional performance on video. Even after all these years I still find myself wincing at elements of my personal presentation. It's an opportunity to rapidly review what is working, and what could be enhanced.

How could you set up a video recording of elements of your team manager performance?

Further reading

Five proven Methods to Achieve True Self-Awareness | Chartered Management Institute, January 2021 | Makoff-Clark, A. | https://www.managers.org.uk/knowledge-and-insights/article/five-proven-methods-achieve-true-self-awareness/

Emotional Intelligence: Why It Can Matter More Than IQ | Bantam Books, 2005 | Goleman, D.P.

Best Personality Tests of 2024 | Forbes Health, 2024 | Laurence, E., Lloyd, M. | https://www.forbes.com/health/mind/best-personality-tests/

Self-talk, critical inner voice, empowering inner voice

"If you hear a voice within you say you cannot paint, then by all means paint, and that voice will be silenced." *– Vincent Willem van Gogh*

Self-talk or *inner dialogue* is the chatter we hear in our minds. How we manage our mental voice impacts on our performance and wellbeing. We can choose our internal musings to be constructive and empowering, or critical. Sometimes our self-criticism is harsh.*

Positive self-talk strengthens our confidence and inner belief. Constructive *rational* self-appraisal of our abilities and performances is a healthy resource-building activity. By contrast, *irrational* negative inner dialogue about self, interferes with our goal ambitions.

Finding a balance between celebration of successes and continuing personal development makes sense for everyone, including managers. Team managers are imperfect, fallible human beings. We can achieve our goals and still make mistakes. We will succeed sometimes, and then miss the mark.

We can train our minds to be measured and proportionate in how we talk to, and about, ourselves.

A *Critical Inner Voice (CIV)* is at work in everyone's mind from time to time, offering internal commentary about our capabilities, our performance, and the likelihood of future success. It can be useful when acting as a coun-

---

* Let's be honest, you've been beating yourself up for years about 'stuff', haven't you? Enough. You've had a good run of it, self-flagellating, and feeling bad about what you've done or not done or said or not said. It's time to give it a rest. There are more healthy outlooks available to you. Let's move on, ok?

terbalance to over-confidence. Sometimes though, the critical inner voice gets in the way of achievement. When this happens, it is time to act.

So, you might not have achieved the business outcome you wanted, the personal performance you'd hoped for at the meeting, or maybe the presentation you gave didn't go as well as you had wished. You can be disappointed; this is a *healthy*, negative emotion. You can also get over it quickly, bounce back, and use it as leverage to future change.

Hanging on to negative feelings and internal dialogue about self is *unhealthy* and will limit your ability to manage effectively, and more importantly, to be happy.

- How active is your CIV?
- How do you respond to the CIV when it talks?

Therapists will suggest the CIV is a part of our unconscious mind, protecting us from harm. Being critical is its way of reigning in our enthusiasm, by suggesting we don't embark on potentially dangerous adventures. It means well.

Strategies are available to manage your CIV in a healthy way.

- A proven approach is to recognise and acknowledge the CIV is in operation, *"I notice my CIV is suggesting I am not capable of XXXX. This is just a form of thinking. I can change my thinking."*
- Another tactic for managing your CIV is to thank it for its well-intended advice. You are grateful. You have considered the advice and you are going to proceed with your goal because you realise it's the healthy thing to do. *"Thank you CIV, I appreciate your concern. I won't be needing quite so much criticism from you on this activity, I have plans to succeed."*
- An imaginative procedure is to enter the control room of your mind and turn down the volume dial of the CIV until it clicks off. Then leave the room and turn the light off.
- Some managers tell me their most successful strategy to quell troubling self-criticism is to tell the CIV to *"Pipe down!"* (Or more robust language).
- You may have your own proven strategy for calming your critical inner voice?

- Or maybe you have cultivated a counterbalance *Empowering Inner Voice (EIC),* boosting your feelings of resourcefulness?
- Affirmations work well for some people, with self-talk mantras and repeated reminders of existing capability and inner resourcefulness.
- Affirmations may be couched in present tense, or future tense language, for example,

"I am a competent presenter", or

"I will be a competent presenter".

Research suggests a present tense approach is helpful for people with positive *high pot* self-esteem. By contrast, present tense affirmations are a tough ask for folk with *low pot* confidence. For these individuals, future tense affirmations are more palatable (see **Celebrating successes, Pot Fillers**)

Further reading

Conquer Your Critical Inner Voice | New Harbinger Productions, 2002 | Firestone, R., Firestone, L., Catlett, J.

Peoplemaking | Science and Behavior Books, 1972 | Satir, V.

Servant leadership

"The best way to find yourself is to lose yourself in the service of others."

– Mahatma Gandhi

In traditional leadership models the 'boss' determines direction, goal, and method of delivery, whilst team members perform as instructed, in compliance with the boss's instructions.

Servant leadership adopts a different approach, with greater freedom for team members to shape working methods. Goals are still established (in most cases) by the senior team, or individual leader. What differs in a servant leadership culture is *who* decides on *how* those goals are fulfilled.

In a continuum model servant leadership may be presented as the inverse of traditional leadership authority,

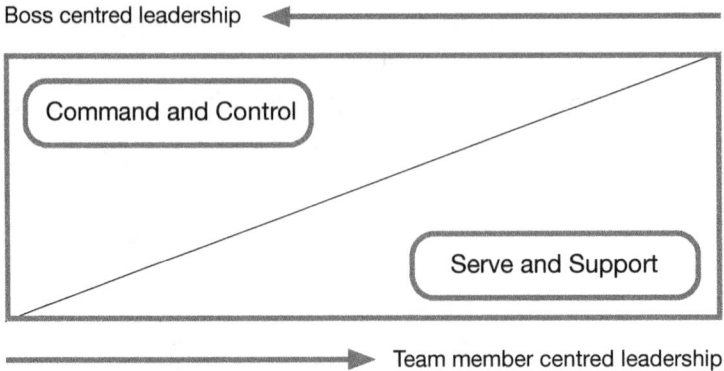

Boss centred leadership

Command and Control

Serve and Support

Team member centred leadership

A critical feature of servant leadership is the role the leader plays in enabling the activities of team members to achieve their ambitions, aligned to business goals. The leader's role becomes one of serving the needs of team members to help them fulfil their aspirations. The essence of servant leadership is to encourage personal growth in employees, to empower them, and to allow freedom for colleagues by handing over 'control' to the team.

Ken Blanchard, renowned business writer and author of *The One Minute Manager*, defines servant leadership as,

> "Servant leadership is all about making the goals clear and then rolling your sleeves up and doing whatever it takes to help people win. In that situation, they don't work for you; you work for them."

Servant leaders make employees the central point of attention in their new 'servant' role. Leaders focus on supporting colleagues, including the development of new skills, to help with goal achievement.

Servant leadership goes beyond the delivery of task. Wellbeing for employees, and their feelings of safety and security in the work environment, are high on the list of priorities (see **Johari, adapted for management**). Servant leaders recognise team members as fallible human beings, who will make errors of judgement in their freedom. This is part of the learning phase.

What benefits does research suggest?

Return on investment for organisations is the enhanced affinity employees feel towards their employer. Encouragement of personal growth has benefits for colleagues too, outside the working environment. Research findings hint at happier home lives as employees find employment more fulfilling. Self-image, self-worth, and self-esteem grow and transfers into life beyond work.

Traditional leadership styles are at odds with a libertarian approach. Understandably, managers may feel uneasy in a new cultural world. Where is the control? It rests with the team members, within the parameters of clearly articulated goals. Gulp! Isn't it a risk?

David Marquet was a US Navy submarine captain who, due to operational imperatives, adopted a servant leadership style on a vessel under his command. Marquet took the unusual step in a military environment of handing over leadership of key roles to his crew. In his TED Talk presentation *How Great Leaders Serve Others*, he describes how he inherited a crew trained for compliance. They complied even when his orders were clearly misguided. Marquet worked to develop a crew of specialist submariners trained for critical thinking, not compliance. He became a leader in service to his crew.

Servant leadership principles are unorthodox, even radical. Managers may feel uncomfortable. In some organisations a *giant leap* for managers from a command-and-control culture to act as servants of team members may be too much in one go.

What about *Servant Leadership Lite*? Are there stepping stones to servant leadership worth considering for your team management role?

Further reading

Servant Leadership [25th Anniversary Edition]: A Journey into the Nature of Legitimate Power and Greatness | Paulist Press, 2002 | Greenleaf, R.K.

Servant Leadership: Its Origin, Development, and Application in Organizations | Journal of Leadership & Organizational Studies, September 2002 | Sendjaya, S., Sarros, J. C.

How Great Leaders Serve Others | TEDx Talks, June 2012 | Marquet, D. | https://www.youtube.com/watch?v=DLRH5J_93LQ

The One Minute Manager | Penguin Putman, 1997 | Blanchard, K.H.

Significance

"Glory ought to be the consequence, not the motive of our actions."
– Pliny the Younger

Everyone has ego.

Most employees seek opportunities to be thought of as *significant*. Significance is related to self-image, self-worth, and self-esteem. Team members may be talented as specific parts of a job function, and are considered by colleagues, and maybe customers, to be exemplars of a particular performance trait. This pleases (most of) them. There are different types of significance,

Performance Significance

- Best at handling customer concerns.
- Highest customer satisfaction ratings.
- Top of the sales ladder.
- Highest attendance, lowest absenteeism rate.
- Best technical operative.
- Expert in (specific) software packages.
- High/highest productivity.
- High/highest quality performance, least non-conformances.
- Creative excellence and wizardry.
- Earliest in to work, latest to leave.
- Considered an Oracle within the organisation, knows everything.

Not everyone seeks significance in relation to their job role. Some colleagues will display self-worth in activities outside work.

Community Significance

- Sporting or physical prowess.
- Family focus.
- Cultural, or faith related commitments.
- Hobbies or recreational interests.
- Political affiliation.

Significance may present itself as behaviour unhelpful to the work group. Some team members will display characteristics in work which seem counter-productive, apparently negative, or disruptive in nature, as a means of achieving significance within their team. For example,

Group Influence significance

- Cares less about *win-win* dynamics. Is focused purely on *win*, often with short-term focus.
- Uses passive-aggressive behaviour to achieve wins.
- *"Management can't push me about."*
- Speaks, allegedly, for others – *"I represent everyone's views."*
- Uses universal quantifier language to assert authority of argument, *"Everyone knows…"*, *"No-one wants it…"* (see **Universal quantifiers**).
- Behaves in ways to make a point – *"See, I was right".*
- Will regularly challenge management decisions.
- Is cynical of management purpose.
- Is manipulative-aggressive.
- Uses passive-aggressive behaviour to delay or derail management plans.

To be clear, these behaviours are all routes to feelings of *significance* for the individual, whether consciously intended or not.

Recognition of the significance strategies employed by team members is helpful for thinking through how you plan to manage each character.

Further reading

Help your employees find purpose—or watch them leave. | McKinsey, April 2021 | Dhingra, N., Samo, A., Schaninger, B., Schrimper, M. | https://www.mckinsey.com/capabilities/people-and-organizational-performance/our-insights/help-your-employees-find-purpose-or-watch-them-leave

Employees Seek Personal Value and Purpose at Work. Be Prepared to Deliver | Gartner, March 2023 | Turner, J. | https://www.gartner.com/en/articles/employees-seek-personal-value-and-purpose-at-work-be-prepared-to-deliver

Sleep on it

"Never go to sleep without a request to your subconscious."
– Thomas Edison

Grandma was right; sleep on it.

Perhaps without even knowing, she was encouraging us to use our unconscious minds to think through options for dealing with *the troubling thing* that's been causing unrest (see **Unconscious mind, trusting the**).

How is it, having stopped thinking about *the troubling thing*, sometime later we find a solution, potential solutions, often after a good night's sleep. Our unconscious minds have a habit of making sense of our inner world whilst we rest.

Mother Nature uses sleep as a restorative period, allowing our mind and body to recuperate after the trials of the day. Sleep helps repair us physically, with overnight scheduled service maintenance, and mentally, with software upgrades fortifying our wellbeing. Deep sleep for physical rest, REM sleep for information processing.

During REM sleep, including through dreams, our minds are making sense of the world we have experienced. Sleep allows us time to file information in appropriate folders and clear the way for less cluttered thinking. No wonder we discover new possibilities in our minds when we wake, or later in the day.

With practice, we can rely on our sleeping state, harness the power of our dreamworld, our unconscious mind, or whatever name label you choose. It will process information on our behalf, as we enjoy a peaceful night of sleep, and subsequently provide us broader options to consider.

We can avoid the temptation to make rushed decisions. For significant issues, even though it may seem counter intuitive, learn to leave a problem alone. We can allow our sleeping mind to sort, file, and clear away the junk, and offer up possible solutions to dealing with *the troubling thing* (see **Zzzz – REM sleep**).

Sleep on it. The answer will come unexpectedly.

Further reading

The Magic of Sleep Thinking: How to Solve Problems, Reduce Stress, and Increase Creativity While You Sleep | Dover Publications, 2018 | Maisel, E.

Why We Sleep: The New Science of Sleep and Dreams | Penguin, 2018 | Walker, M.

Stoicism

"How ridiculous and how strange to be surprised at anything which happens in life." *– Marcus Aurelius*

I encourage clients and management students to explore stoic philosophy. At the heart of Stoicism is the principle; *It is what it is.* We can't control what has happened, nor can we always control present or future events, but we *can* control how we respond to circumstances, in thought and in behaviour.

Stoic philosophy emerged from the teachings of writers in Greek and Roman cultures. Seneca, Cato, Epictetus, and perhaps the most well-known character, the Roman emperor, Marcus Aurelius. Aurelius kept a daily journal, recording his thoughts through his remarkable life. His collected papers are still available today in *Meditations*.

A few stoic principles are noted here,

Epictetus,
The Enchiridion, Epictetus, c.135AD
- *"What disturbs men's minds is not events, but their judgements on events."*
- *"Some things are in our control and others not."*
- *"It is impossible for a man to learn what he thinks he already knows."*

Marcus Aurelius (Marcus Aurelius Antoninus)
Meditations, Marcus Aurelius, Roman Emperor, 161–180AD
- *"Today I escaped from anxiety. Or no, I discarded it because it was within me, in my own perceptions – not outside."*
- *"You're better off not giving the small things more time than they deserve."*
- *"Choose not to be harmed and you won't feel harmed. Don't feel harmed and you haven't been."*

Seneca (Lucius Annaeus Seneca the Younger)
Essays & Letters, Seneca, 4BC–65AD

- *"We suffer more often in imagination than in reality."*
- *"We learn not for school, but for life."*
- *"Being poor is not having too little, it is wanting more."*

In team management, stoic thinking helps us deal with the incidents and accidents which come our way, with calm consideration, and sometimes acceptance – *to be expected*. Emotional responses to events rarely help resolve management challenges. It is during difficult times stoicism becomes useful.

Supervisors and managers who learn stoic principles are, in my experience, better placed to deal effectively with challenges than those who exhibit stimulus-response emotive behaviours (see **Case Study: On Growing Managers [and our Business]**).

There is a health benefit for stoic thinkers too. Anxiety levels are generally lower for managers who adopt stoic approaches, than for those who allow external factors to influence their thinking, their resultant emotions, and the rash behaviours associated with impassioned decision making (see **Stress management, patterns of healthy thinking**).

Rudyard Kipling's advice works for team managers,

"If you can keep your head when all about you are losing theirs…"

Critics of stoicism point to the lack of emotion in stoic thinking and behaviour. Stoicism can be seen as dry and humourless, not filled with joy. It's true, there is an avoidance of emotive response in stoic behaviour, especially when faced with obstacles. This is the point though, to assess circumstances calmly, without undue negativity, excessive celebration, or fervent emotional reaction; this is the essence of stoicism in team management.

Is it necessary to be devoid of emotional experience at work? Of course not.

Another school of thinking in ancient times was the Greek philosophy of Epicureanism. Epicurus (341 – 270 BC) promoted a lifestyle of tranquillity and freedom from pain.

Epicureans are often unfairly labelled as hedonists, as single-minded seekers of physical pleasure. It is true, pleasure, including physical and *pleas-*

ures of the mind (happiness, absence of fear, feelings of contentment) are promoted in Epicureanism as ambitions for a fulfilling life.

As much as *movement towards pleasure* is an important element of Epicureanism, for Epicurus, a core ambition was the avoidance of pain and suffering, a *movement away from pain*. This was a life goal he wished for himself and others. Contentment, relaxation, and freedom from physical discomfort are at the heart of Epicurean philosophy (see **Emotional Drivers™**).

Whilst the Stoics may seek control over mind and emotion; Epicureans know a thing or two about living a comfortable and pleasurable life. For busy team managers, maybe there's room for a bit of both?

Further reading

Lessons in Stoicism: What Ancient Philosophers Teach Us about How to Live | Penguin, 2020 | Sellars, J.

The Obstacle is the Way | Profile Books, 2014 | Holiday, R.

Meditations | Penguin Classics, 2006 | Marcus Aurelius

Epicureanism: A Very Short Introduction | OUP Oxford, 2015 | Wilson, C.

If: A Father's Advice to His Son

The Complete Works of Rudyard Kipling | Kipling, J.R. | Happy Hour Books, 2023

Stress management, Mrs Erickson's mindfulness relaxation technique (5-4-3-2-1)

"Peace comes from within. Don't seek it without." – *Buddha*

Team management is exhilarating, challenging, and periodically stressful.

When the pressures of work impact on emotional wellbeing it helps to have a collection of stress-busting techniques at hand. Exercise may help, whether vigorous or gentle, or a creative hobby, reading, spectating at sports, cultural events, or other distraction activities.

During challenging times, I have found meditation and specifically mindfulness helpful as a means of shutting out the external pressures of life.

Mindfulness is a method for anchoring thoughts on what is happening right now in our personal experience, being aware of what is in our immediate world, without judgement. It encourages focus on the present and not on past events or worry about uncertainty or imagined future scenarios. It gives us a break from the anxious thinking patterns we often experience during times of strain, including work overload.

When our mind wanders off into worry (again) we can pull it back to a focus on the here and now, recognising what is happening in our immediate experience. It's a mental training regime which helps break the patterns of critical or anxious thoughts.

There are numerous approaches to achieving a mindful or meditative state. I discovered the Betty Erickson 5-4-3-2-1 approach many years ago, and found it worked well. I still use it today.

Betty Erickson was the wife of celebrated clinical hypnotherapist Milton Erickson. Mrs Erickson was a talented hypnotherapist herself. She developed her own method for achieving a state of relaxation, sometimes known as Mrs Erickson's 5-4-3-2-1 technique. Here is the approach,

- Sit or lie in a comfortable position. Allow your hands to relax, separately, by your side.
- Keep your head still and focus your eyes on a point ahead of you.
- Notice what you *see, hear,* and *feel.*
- Say to yourself gently (out loud, or as internal dialogue),

"I can see... [name any object in your field of vision, or peripheral vision]"

and repeat for 5 different objects, for example,

— "I can see a picture."
— "I can see a wall."
— "I can see a lamp."
— "I can see a book."
— "I can see a radiator."

- Then say to yourself,

  "I can hear... [name any sound you can hear]"

  and repeat for 5 different sounds, for example,
    - "I can hear the ticking of the clock."
    - "I can hear traffic outside."
    - "I can hear my breathing."
    - "I can hear a door creaking."
    - "I can hear the wind."

- Then say to yourself,

  "I can feel... [name any feeling or sensation you experience]"

  and repeat for 5 different sensations, for example,
    - "I can feel my feet on the floor."
    - "I can feel the cushion behind my head."
    - "I can feel the tongue in my mouth."
    - "I can feel my legs against the chair."
    - "I can feel my hand on my lap."

- Repeat the sequence, this time naming only 4 things you see, 4 things you hear, 4 things you feel. The images, sounds and sensations can be the same as last time, or different – it doesn't matter.
- At this point some people *close their eyes* and begin to *imagine* things they can see, hear, and feel, perhaps from a favourite place, or imaginary location?
- Repeat, naming 3 things you can see, 3 things you can hear, 3 things you can feel.
- Repeat, naming 2 things you can see, 2 things you can hear, 2 things you can feel.
- Repeat, naming 1 thing you can see, 1 thing you can hear, 1 thing you can feel.

By now, if you are not already in a meditative state, you will feel more relaxed, with much less 'chatter' in your mind.

5-4-3-2-1 is used for insomnia as well as general relaxation in stressful situations, e.g., during work breaks, before an interview, in preparation for an exam or before difficult meetings, or simply as a general de-stressor.

Go back to this whenever you'd like to re-access a mindful state of relaxation.

Further reading

Hypnotic Realities | Irvington Publishers, 1976 | Erickson, M.H., Rossi, E.L., Rossi, S.I.

The Little Book of Meditation: 10 minutes a day to more relaxation, energy and creativity | Gaia, 2019 | Collard, P.

Stress management, self-trance

"There is nothing really important… except the activity of your unconscious mind." *– Milton Erickson*

Hypnosis, or trance, is much misunderstood, and consequently an underused resource for managing personal stress.

Forget images of stage hypnotists encouraging chicken noises and raw onion eating, swinging pocket watches, or *look into my eyes* nonsense, trance state is a naturally occurring phenomenon we all experience, every day. Momentary periods of deep thought, looking out of a window, daydreaming, or meditating, or simply resting our eyes for a few moments; these are all forms of natural trance state, with no therapist or agent of change involved.

Hypnosis is simply a relaxed state of altered consciousness, allowing us to access our unconscious mind, and create healthy embedded thinking patterns. Our unconscious minds know far more than our conscious thinking can ever hope to achieve. Think of this as your mental hard drive, or Cloud files, compared to a desktop.

The unconscious mind eats a conscious mind for breakfast.*

---

* Apologies to Peter F. Drucker for hijacking his claim "Culture eats strategy for breakfast."

Our unconscious mind stores everything we've ever seen, heard, felt (external feel or internal emotion), everything we've smelled, tasted, or experienced, and stores it away in our mental files. Sometimes we forget to remember things useful for us, healthy resources we've misfiled or left hidden under other thoughts. Hypnosis can help re-access these.

By contrast, our conscious mind fills quickly, it overloads. George Miller, the cognitive psychologist, highlighted this in his research paper, *The Magical Number Seven, Plus or Minus Two: Some Limits on Our Capacity for Processing Information* in which he explored, amongst other topics, the limitations of short-term memory.

Our unconscious mind also manages our autonomic nervous system, the operations of our vital functions without us having to consciously think about them, for example, heart rate, breathing, eye blinking, digestion, instinct awareness, and other behind the scenes activities.

We don't have to consciously think, *"Hmmm, it must be time for another breath... here we go..."*. It does it for us.

The unconscious mind protects us, and this includes during hypnotic trance. It will never allow harm to come to us during a hypnotic experience.

By entering a relaxed state, unencumbered by the noises and distractions of daily life, we can access our unconscious mind and ask it for help, or provide instruction for resetting our unconscious thinking habits to healthy alternatives. It is this principle which underpins clinical hypnotherapy, a world apart from the entertainment activities of stage performers.

For example, I regularly ask my unconscious mind for help when troubled by a problematic situation. A proven method (for me) is to achieve a level of relaxation and quietness from mental chatter, a mild state of trance. I then firmly, and politely, ask my unconscious mind to consider the matter I'm finding challenging and to work on it in the background whilst I get on with my daily activities.

Programming my mind just before a gym session, or before a cycle ride, has developed into a successful personal strategy. It is, I suppose, a version of *sleep on it* (see **Sleep on it**).

An answer, or options, often pop into my mind sometime later. I'm careful to thank my unconscious mind for its efforts. Whether this is scientifically valid, or just a useful fiction doesn't matter. It works for me (see **Useful fiction**).

Clinical hypnotherapists are skilled in assisting patients (or *subjects*) to access a trance state. Trance induction, in its varied forms, is a precursor to making suggestions to the patient's unconscious mind, encouraging more healthy thinking or behaviour patterns. Proposals are made by the therapist as direct suggestions, indirect suggestions, or in the form of metaphor, determined by the clinician's skill in identifying a best fit approach for each patient.

How does this relate to a team leader feeling under stress?

Well, trance induction and healthy proposals to the unconscious mind can be self-managed. We already do this with our unconscious minds, although maybe not always in a self-induced trance state of self-hypnosis.

There is a simple 3 step framework to self-hypnosis.

1. *Trance induction.* There are various methods to achieve a relaxed state. You can read about them.

2. *Suggestions to your unconscious mind.* For example, healthier behaviours, instructions to reduce anxiety, installing beliefs of greater contentment and feelings of relaxed confidence, or ego strengthening messages to aid self-confidence.

3. *Awakening process.* Filled with positivity and empowering messages of self-esteem, personal wellbeing, and resourcefulness.

To understand more about how self-hypnosis can reduce stress and create healthy resourcefulness, explore the sources of learning available from reputable professional bodies.

There's no need to eat raw onions or make chicken noises.

Further reading

British Society of Clinical Hypnosis www.bsch.org.uk

London College of Clinical Hypnotherapy International https://lcchinternational.co.uk/

Handbook of Hypnotic Suggestions and Metaphors | Norton, 1990 | Hammond, D.C.

Hypnotic Realities: The Induction od Clinical Hypnosis and Forms of Indirect Suggestion | Irvington, 1976 | Erickson, M.H., Rossi, E.l., Rossi, S.I.

The Magical Number Seven, Plus or Minus Two | Miller, G. | The Psychological Review, 1956 | http://psychclassics.yorku.ca/Miller/ (accessed 24.07.23)

Stress management, patterns of healthy thinking

"If you're feeling sad, just do a roly-poly and all the sadness will fall out."
– Claire Drake-Knight

Fifty of my personal thinking habits are listed here, in no sequential order. I refer to these patterns from time to time. Everyone benefits from a healthy reminder. Maybe some could be helpful for you?

1. *Pain from the past.* The best thing about the past is… it's over.
2. *My timeline shows how far I've come and how much I have developed.* If I can do that, what else can I do?
3. *My mistakes and stupid behaviours help me learn.* I laugh with myself when I act clumsily or do something daft.
4. *I've beaten myself up about 'that thing' for a long time.* That's enough now. Learning has been banked. I will reference *that thing* only when helpful.
5. *Forward thinking.* How I got here is irrelevant, its where I choose to go which counts.
6. *I will listen and understand first.* I learn more from receiving than transmitting.
7. *I will own responsibility, not subcontract it out.* If it is to be, it is up to me.
8. *I will make things happen.* I'm driving the bus; I am not the passenger in my life.
9. *I will Act As If.* Its only pretend, and it works.
10. *I will accept inevitability.* It is… to be expected.
11. *There are no unresourceful people, only unresourceful thinking patterns.* I will think in a resource-seeking fashion.
12. *It is the behaviour, not the person.* They/I am a good person. The behaviour may stink though.
13. *Its ok if I screw up sometimes.* Fallibility is a human condition. It is normal.
14. *Self-talk of demand is unhealthy.* I will avoid inner dialogue of *must, should, have to, got to, ought to, need to*, and will listen for signs in others. I can find compassionate language.

15. *Big problems, take a first step.* Taking a first step to addressing an issue helps me feel better. I'm doing something positive.

16. *I will focus on what I want, not what I don't want.* Energy flows where focus goes.*

17. *I don't know the answer yet. I'll ask my unconscious mind to mull it over.* My unconscious mind has immense power beyond conscious thought. I trust it to protect me.

18. *State management helps.* I know I can *get in state* appropriate to circumstances.

19. *Feel the caution.* When I feel unease about a scenario, there is a reason to tread carefully.

20. *Confusion is helpful.* It's good to be confused, it's when we learn best.

21. *Dissociation helps objectivity.* I will stay above the event, observe with objectivity, to aid my understanding.

22. *Emotion. I can choose to let go of a feeling.* I chose it, so I can discard it.

23. *Stoicism #1. What disturbs my mind is not events, but my thoughts about them.* I can frame or reframe to healthy thoughts.

24. *Stoicism #2. Some things are within my control and others not.* I will control what I can control.

25. *Stoicism #3. I suffer more often in imagination than in reality.* Imagination is not real.

26. *Grief, sadness, regret, and guilt are always with me.* I can acknowledge them and live with compassion for myself. These feelings are useful (occasionally); they help me reflect and learn.

27. *Before I formed a belief, I decided to believe it.* I can change my decision, and my belief.

28. *Commitment is doing the thing I said I would do, long after the mood I said it in has left me.*† I will sustain my commitment; it is the mark of a disciplined mind.

29. *I know when I'm tired or anxious I am more susceptible to irrational thinking.* I will be aware of the impact of tiredness and anxiety on my thought patterns.

---

* Acknowledgement to Tony Robbins
† Acknowledgement to George Zalucki

30. *I will use my 'nightmare management' strategy.* If a situation is causing me difficulties, I will face it, challenge it, and deal with it.

31. *I will recognise when I am feeling a strong emotion and acknowledge it to myself.* e.g., I notice I am feeling; defensive, competitive, frustrated, anxious, tense, elated...

32. *I don't have to like it.* I can accept some circumstances are outside my control. I can bear it.

33. *Discomfort provides learning.* I will learn by experiencing discomfort.

34. *New beliefs take time to become habit.* It can take time for new patterns to bed in.

35. *Procrastination is unhelpful.* I will act.

36. *I own my goals.* I will set goals, identify actions, set timelines, resource them, and act.

37. *I can model.* No matter how talented someone is, I can model, codify, and replicate at least some of their excellence.

38. *Everyone is carrying something, even (especially?) uber confident people.* They just hide it well. If I can help them, I will.

39. *I will live in congruence with my own propaganda.* Congruence aids authenticity and integrity.

40. *Adults are just children who have grown tall.* * I will be kind to their inner child.

41. *So long as we have our imagination, we can really distress ourselves.* Or we can use our imagination to feel good.

42. *I can reframe my nervousness as excitement.* It releases the same hormones.

43. *My resourceful inner voice is telling me I can, my critical inner voice sometimes tells me I can't.* I can listen to my empowering inner voice, turn up the volume, turn up the resourcefulness, and *Act As If.* I can turn down (or switch off) the volume of my critical inner voice.

44. *I can use the control room of my mind to manage my thinking and my emotions.* I can choose how I feel.

45. *When I feel worry about future possibilities, I remember Michel de Montaigne's message, "My life has been filled with the most terrible of misfortunes, most of which didn't happen."*

---

* Acknowledgement to Dr. Richard Bandler

46. *When anxious about a situation, I remember the advice from my friend Dr Danny Zamir, "Anxious thoughts are just thoughts."* I know how to change my thoughts.*

47. *My ethics, morals, and personal values are more important than fee earning.* Integrity beats money.

48. *Professionalism.* I will share my knowledge and skills, be supportive to others, and enjoy the assignment.

49. *Be Kind.* My team members, peer colleagues, customers, and suppliers, have their professional and personal challenges which trouble or excite them. We are people with hopes, anxieties, and inner dialogues, some helping, some hindering. I will be mindful of the individuality of the people I interact with and be kind.

50. *Work Life Balance.* Our children, and grandchildren, take priority over any work assignment.

Further reading

The Practice of Rational Emotive Behaviour Therapy | Free Association Books, 1998 | Dryden, W. and Ellis, A.

Stop Feeding Your Worry: Understand and Overcome Anxious Thinking Habits | The Glendon Association, 2023 | Zamir, D. | https://www.glendon.org/shop/stop-feeding-your-worry-understand-and-overcome-anxious-thinking-habits/

Structure of Well-Done-Ness®

"There is no magic in magic, it's all in the details." – *Walt Disney*

In my book *Fast Coaching* I propose ill-defined praise as a scourge of modern management. The urge to be nice, to offer vague *well-done* plaudits without definition or rationale behind the praise, has negligible long-term benefit (see **Chocolate Praise®**).

Only when a team member understands *precisely* what they did well, and the component parts of their excellence, will they understand how to replicate outstanding performance.

---

* Acknowledgement to Dr. Daniel Zamir

Team members, and team performance, benefit when excellence is understood as a construct, a sequence of behaviours and actions contributing to the whole. Employees flourish when they recognise *why* what they have done has been successful. Replication is dependent on understanding process. *Continue & Begin Fast Coaching®* helps this (see **Coaching, Continue & Begin Fast Coaching®**).

Excellence has a framework. There is no magic, only structure.

Further reading

Boomerang! Coach Your Team to Be the Best | Dandelion Digital, 2007 | Drake-Knight, N.

Fast Coaching. The Complete Guide to New Code Continue & Begin® | Dandelion Digital, 2016 | Drake-Knight, N. |

Audible https://www.audible.co.uk/pd/ Fast-Coaching-Audiobook/B07TTKD13T

The Motivation Agency | https:// themotivationagency-online.com/course/ begin

Supervision sessions

"All learning has an emotional base." *– Plato*

Supervision sessions are well established in social work teams and in health and care sector environments. Colleagues benefit from regular opportunities to share their experiences of work with a supervision practitioner, who may or may not be their line manager. Sessions consider how work events are being processed by the employee and the impact it is having on them personally.

During 'supervision' the employee reflects on their current caseload and identifies any health or wellbeing factors associated with work pressures. The activity offers employees opportunity to offload emotional hurdles and share feelings they have been experiencing. For a brief period of respite, the supervisor 'holds' the team member's anxiety.

Supervision is emotionally supportive, whilst challenging beliefs and behaviours (see **Beliefs, you can choose or change** and **Beliefs, limited**).

Supervision might discuss ongoing work projects, personal reflections, and learning. It offers a space to review recent work events and the impact on the supervisee's emotional wellbeing. Sessions might include advice and guidance from the supervisor. It could be an opportunity for coaching around a specific topic or as a launch pad for further training (see **Coaching** and **Continuous Professional Development [CPD]**). Supervision is intended as a supportive activity.

A long service mental health nurse, Mike, shared with me his experiences of supervision sessions. He described what works for the supervisee, and what doesn't,

> "For a nurse practitioner working in the front line of patient care, the purpose of supervision should be for the practitioner to review their practice, share any significant emotional impact of specific cases, and to develop their skills.
>
> Although it should be planned as a regular activity, supervision should also be available on-demand for the practitioner, if they are experiencing particularly traumatic cases.
>
> The supervisor should be on a peer group level with the practitioner. Supervision should not involve management or performance monitoring – I feel that detracts from the effectiveness of a supportive supervision process, potentially making it a negative experience."

There are parallels in supervision with human leadership (see **Human leadership**) principles of authenticity, empathy, and adaptability.

The individuality of employee experience is a core value of human leadership. A useful illustration for individuality is to think of 100 employees working on a common assignment as having 100 different perspectives.

Supervision sessions respect the unique nature of each employee's experience of work. It offers freedom to explore the team member's feelings as well as professional performance.

For a supervision session to work effectively the supervisee needs to feel safe with the supervisor, to let their guard down, make themselves vulnerable, and reflect critically on their own performance, or the situation they find themselves in (see **Johari, adapted for management** and **Human leadership**).

How could you incorporate supervision sessions into your management activities?

Further reading

Supervision | Social Work England | https://www.socialworkengland.org.uk/cpd/supervision/

BASW: UK Supervision Policy | British Association of Social Workers, May 2011 | https://www.basw.co.uk/resources/basw-uk-supervision-policy

Effective supervision in social work and social care | SCIE Research Briefing 43 | Social Care Institute for Excellence, 2012 | Carpenter, J., Webb, C., Bostock, L., Coomber, C.

Surface structure, deep structure, specificity

"The structure of language determines not only thought, but reality itself."
– Noam Chomsky

Linguists understand the different pools of vocabulary available to us and how we select words from these pools to communicate meaning. We're not very good at it.

Researchers tell us most reasonably educated adults have an active vocabulary (words used) and a passive vocabulary (words understood and rarely used) of between 20,000 and 40,000 words.

When we consider how to describe a thought, a feeling, or an experience, we have access to this impressive library. We have a large collection of words known as our *deep structure*, or D-structure, relating to our meaning. These are the relevant words at our disposal. Sourced from these words are those we select and subsequently speak, that is, our *surface structure* (S-structure) language, or *utterance* used to convey our meaning.*

My book *Fast Coaching* includes a transcript from a seminar I ran for operational managers who were learning to use *Continue & Begin Fast Coaching*® with their teams. Below is an extract from the transcript, featuring a conversation between myself and a seminar delegate Michelle. We were exploring the nature of S-structure and D-structure language, and the brief utterances people make when describing personal experience.

The conversation highlighted the extent to which experience is described during conversation, and the limited language used, despite available vocabulary. The net effect is deletion, generalisation, and potential ambiguity (see **Deletion, Distortion, Generalisations** and **English is rubbish™**).

NDK: Ok, who's had a long drive here today?

Michelle: I have.

NDK: Tell us about your journey…

Michelle: It was ok. Got stuck on the ring road though.

NDK writes on flipchart… It was ok. Got stuck on the ring road though.

NDK: What time did you leave home Michelle?

Michelle: 6.45

NDK: Did you come by car?

Michelle: Yes.

---

* There is debate amongst linguists as to the nature of D-structure and S-structure language. Some linguists evolved their propositions over time, creating disagreement between language specialists. Peak argument occurred through the 1960s and 70s, during what became known as the *Linguistics Wars*, as academics argued over their respective understandings of these terms. For our purposes we can assume the explanation offered in this book is a useful fiction (see Useful fiction), which adequately describes how we limit the use of our vocabularies to describe experience, creating potential for misunderstanding.

NDK Did you drive or were you a passenger?

Michelle: I drove.

NDK: Were you alone in the car?

Michelle: Yes.

NDK: Where was your car parked?

Michelle: On my drive.

NDK: Facing your home or facing away from your home?

Michelle: Facing my home.

NDK: What sort of car is it?

Michelle: It's a VW Golf

NDK Ok, colour?

Michelle: Red

NDK: 4 door or 2 door?

Michelle: 4 door.

NDK: Is your driveway level or on a slope?

Michelle: Bit of a slope actually, up towards the garage door.

NDK: You've got a garage door! You never mentioned that!

Michelle: You didn't ask!

(Laughter)

NDK: Ok, well I suppose you reversed out of your drive...

Michelle: Yes.

NDK: Onto a side road? A main road? A cul-de-sac?

Michelle: It's quite a busy road.

NDK: Much traffic about this morning?

Michelle: Kind of. There's road works and temporary traffic lights.

NDK: Ok. Was there music playing in your car?

Michelle: Yes.

NDK: Radio?

Michelle: Off my phone.

NDK: Ok. What was the music?

Michelle: All sorts, I had it on shuffle.

NDK: Ok, thanks Michelle. And ladies and gentlemen, we haven't even started the journey yet... What was the question I asked Michelle? Who remembers?

Audience member: "Tell us about your journey."

NDK: Correct. And what was Michelle's response to that question? It's written here!

Audience member: "It was ok. Got stuck on the ring road though."

NDK: Correct. Michelle's response was what's called a surface structure utterance. It's the initial response. It was an overview of what she thought was relevant information.

When we, or others, communicate meaning we do so by selecting language from our D-structure and S-structure depositories.

In team management, accuracy of communication helps drive performance. Inquisitive managers consider whether the utterance of a team member is providing an accurate representation of meaning. What has the team member deleted? Distorted? Generalised? For precision of understanding, it's helpful to consider what is meant, specifically?

Remember, *English is rubbish*™.

Further reading

Boomerang! Coach Your Team to Be the Best | Dandelion Digital, 2007 | Drake-Knight, N.

Fast Coaching. The Complete Guide to New Code Continue & Begin® | Dandelion Digital, 2016 | Drake-Knight, N. |

Audible https://www.audible.co.uk/pd/ Fast-Coaching-Audiobook/B07TTKD13T

The Motivation Agency | https:// themotivationagency-online.com/course/ begin

T

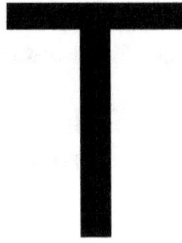

Team evolution

"Coming together is the beginning. Keeping together is progress.
Working together is success." – *Henry Ford*

Teams evolve over time, including work teams. People leave, others join, and the dynamics of relationships, communication, and performance shift with the evolution. All the while, team members are growing in experience and capability, and maybe in their expectations and ambitions of work?

Managing the shifting shape of a team requires consideration and objective thinking. What is happening here in this team? How is it transforming? If I look and listen, what do I see and hear? What do I feel?

Professional managers think ahead, certainly when thinking about recruitment and integration of new players into the team (see **Induction, preboarding, onboarding, reboarding**).

Bruce Tuckman had interesting ideas about team evolution and the stages of 'life' a team goes through as it matures, shifts shape, and matures again. Tuckman suggested four stages,

- *Forming* – the group begins its work together. Emotions are evident as enthusiasm, hope, and uncertainties reveal themselves, and as team members get to know each other and prepare for the work ahead. Relationships are high on the agenda; members of the new team are polite and respectful of others' ideas and skills; at least at first.
- *Storming* – a few glitches appear in the relationships dynamic. Team members question ideas, become tetchy and irritated by colleagues.

Tensions rise as disagreements emerge in project planning and delivery. Team unity becomes fractious, and members form cliques at odds with other parts of work group.

- *Norming* – the team begins to normalise as members acknowledge and accept the idiosyncrasies of colleagues, applauding their attributes and embracing diversity of ideas. The work group integrates and builds momentum and starts to deliver against objectives.

- *Performing* – the team has matured into its role and purpose. It is productive, delivering towards the goals for which it was originally established. Team members communicate effectively with internal and external customers (see **Customers, internal**).

Tuckman and Mary Ann Jensen later added a fifth stage of team evolution they labelled as,

- *Adjourning* – the team's work is done, completely or in part, and the group begins to disband. Group member focus wavers as thoughts turn to the next project or role change.

Project-dedicated work groups is not typical of all organisations. More common is established teams, or departments, with long term programmes of work, shifting organically as business imperatives dictate, and as team members come and go.

For this reason, I highlight the concept of *Mourning*, the stage of team evolution leading up to, and immediately after, a team member leaves the group. Relationships built up over time dissolve as established colleagues move on. There may be genuine hurt and emotional turmoil for those 'left behind'. New starters discover a work group still processing the loss of their teammate, and sometimes genuine friend.

In sad circumstances where a colleague has died, the mourning can have painful and deep emotional impact on individuals and the group. Just as in life outside of work, grieving is an important healing process which takes time. Emotions can run high and inconsistent, even odd, behaviours are common.

Managers who recognise the stages of team evolution are well placed to deal with changing dynamics (see **Case Study: On Growing Managers [and our Business]**).

Anticipating each stage of evolution is mature management. Evolutionary phases can be forecast and prepared for by manager and team members. As each emerges, colleagues may conclude, *"Ah, yes, this is to be expected."*

Further reading

The One Minute Manager Builds High Performing Teams | Fontana 1993 | Blanchard, K., Carew, D., Carew, E. P.

Will it Make the Boat Go Faster? | Matador, 2011 | Hunt-Davis, B., Beveridge, H.

The Jersey. The All Blacks: The Secrets Behind the World's Most Successful Team | Pan, 2022 | Bills, P.

Developmental Sequence in Small Groups | Tuckman, B.W. | Psychological Bulletin, 1965

Stages in Small-Group Developmental Revisited | Tuckman, B.W., and Jensen, M.A.C. | Group Facilitation: A Research and Applications Journal – Number 10, 2010

Teeth, show them (if necessary)

"To know what people really think, pay regard to what they do, rather than what they say." *– René Descartes*

If managers fail to address inconsistencies in performance, creeping non-compliance, and non-conformances, expect overall team performance to deteriorate. It's tougher to get back on the track, than it is to stay on it.

Performance standards exist to maintain quality of production or service. Class-leading organisations explicitly describe expected performance standards and provide training and coaching to help employees implement and sustain their delivery (see **NDK Performance Model®**).

Weak managers avoid confrontation and allow dips in standards to go unchallenged. When performance drops below explicitly described expectations, strong managers act (see **Performance management**). There are times when strength of character is tested, when a manager will require the personal confidence and mental grit to challenge a team member, or a collective group, and address underperformance.

Some find this difficult. Recently promoted managers working with former peers may feel uncomfortable with the change in relationship dynamics and a role requirement which requires standards monitoring and occasional remedial action. This is to be expected (see **Stress management, patterns of healthy thinking**).

Adopting an appropriate communication style is important. Assertion skills are helpful in these circumstances, and avoidance of aggressive language, tone, or body language (see **Words, song, and dance**). You can make your point in a friendly yet firm manner, focusing on standards, not personalities.

The winning mindset is to think about the standards and not the relationship, especially where friendships are involved (see **Friends, managing them at work**). Stick to a conversation about standards and the relationship dynamics subside. This is not a battle, it's a collective endeavour to achieve workplace goals and ambitions. It's the job of a team manager to help colleagues maintain standards of operations, behaviour, and values.

Be prepared to *show teeth* when necessary.

Further reading

Armstrong on Reinventing Performance Management: Building a Culture of Continuous Improvement | Kogan Page, 2019 | Armstrong, M.

Showing Teeth | Essential Communications, December 2015 | Henschel, T.

Developmental Sequence in Small Groups | Tuckman, B.W. | Psychological Bulletin, 1965

Stages in Small-Group Developmental Revisited | Tuckman, B.W., and Jensen, M.A.C. | Group Facilitation: A Research and Applications Journal – Number 10, 2010

Tentative is no good

"If you have an important point to make, don't try to be subtle or clever. Use a pile driver. Hit the point once. Then come back and hit it again. Then hit it a third time – a tremendous whack."

– Winston Churchill

Tentative thinking, uncertainty, timid and hesitant behaviours, impoverish a team manager's effectiveness. Team members become frustrated. Performance suffers. Respect for the team leader diminishes.

Proficient managers consider, calculate, and evaluate options – then decide on action and drive it home. Uncle Eric was right (see **Decision making, navy style**),

"An officer always makes a decision; good or bad, as long as he makes one. Got it nipper?"

"Yes Eric".

Sport offers helpful reference points. My sport as a younger man was rugby. I played a very poor standard, for a very long time. 39 years of being bashed about every Saturday afternoon imprinted some useful learning about human behaviour.

One such learning point was the power of certainty as a leader. I was a forward, one of the 'fat lads', the *piano shifters* rather than the gifted *piano players* in the backs.

Each pack of eight forwards has a *Pack Leader*, a focal point for the players to follow. It helps if the pack leader communicates with impact, has charisma, certainty, and the ability to stir emotions. As in nature, pack members follow a convincing leader. A pack leader exudes confidence and clarity of purpose. The plan is set, a leader makes it happen.

Rugby clubs around the world train players in leadership, communication, and resolve. There is no place for tentative behaviour. I am sure the same principle applies to many other sports.

The way we think, and the way we give ourselves instructions, is a critical factor in achieving success in any endeavour. Our minds respond to firm instructions. When we provide clear and unequivocal requirements to our unconscious mind, it works on our behalf and does what is asked (see **Unconscious mind, trusting the**).

How is it when we set our alarms for an especially early start, we somehow wake up a minute or two before the alarm rings? How can it be? It's because, for once, we gave such firm instructions our mind did what was asked and took care of us. That's the job of our unconscious mind, to protect us from danger. It requires firm unambiguous instruction though, nothing fluffy, tentative, confused, or uncertain.

Tentative is no good.

When we hear people say, *"I'm going to try to stop smoking, lose weight, stop drinking, go to the gym, go running regularly, stop eating chocolate..."*, well, good luck, because it's not going to happen.

"I'll give it a go…"

"Hopefully…"

"I'll do what I can…"

"I'll see how I feel…"

"I might be able to…"

"I'll try and…"

Hopeless. Whatever it is, it won't happen. *Try* doesn't work. *Do* is more determined.

In *Fast Coaching* I promote commitment, resolution, and persistence to make things happen. The words we use with ourselves, and others, offers insight into determination level,

We know from therapeutic practises our minds respond to firm assertive instructions… like the presupposition stuff we explored in *"What else…?"* and *"Anything else…?"* We respond more immediately to firmness than we do to weak tentative requests.

This applies equally to internal dialogue… or self-talk. Imagine a drill sergeant… you know…a Sergeant Major kind of character… imagine him… it's usually a him… imagine him coming out onto the parade square and he says… *(NDK has quiet, hesitant voice, legs crossed, avoiding eye contact, looking down at hands, picking at fingernails)…*

"Er, I wondered if … er… I don't know… er… I wondered if maybe…
you know… er… if you might like to… er… do a bit of marching…
er… what do you think?"

No! Of course he doesn't! He comes onto the parade group and shouts *(NDK adopts pose of drill sergeant, leaning forward, chin extended, scowling, imaginary pace stick under his arm…*

"Right you 'orrible lot… I'm your mother now!…atten…shun!"

And all the squaddies jump to attention and do exactly as they're told. That's your unconscious mind for you. Give it firm instructions and it does what it's told... you don't have to shout at it... be firm... be tentative though, and you've got a lazy teenager on your hands... *"Yeah, whatever..."*

Tentative is no good.

Further reading

Boomerang! Coach Your Team to Be the Best | Dandelion Digital, 2007 | Drake-Knight, N.

Audible https://www.audible.co.uk/pd/ Fast-Coaching-Audiobook/B07TTKD13T

Fast Coaching. The Complete Guide to New Code Continue & Begin® | Dandelion Digital, 2016 | Drake-Knight, N. |

The Motivation Agency | https:// themotivationagency-online.com/course/ begin

Thank You

"Gratitude is not only the greatest of virtues, but the parent of all the others." *– Marcus Tullius Cicero*

Thank you is one of the most powerful people stimulants. The psychologist Fred Herzberg included the importance of *recognition for achievement* as a motivational force, up there with *job satisfaction* and *purposeful, meaningful work.*

Researchers have solid evidence to back up Herzberg's work; *Glassdoor for Employers* (2013) found 81% of employees reported being motivated to work harder when shown appreciation for their work by their line manager.

The Journal of Positive Psychology (2019) highlighted enhanced social connection from offering genuine, authentic gratitude and reduced feelings of stress. Praising another's qualities was especially influential in developing feelings of warmth and affiliation to the person offering gratitude. People feel good when we thank them.

Managers who offer genuine, authentic *thank yous* to their teams are providing the recognition Herzberg referred to and confirming to employees the value and significance of their contribution.

A *thank you* is best aligned to something specific rather than a generic note of gratitude. What exactly has the team member done which merits recognition? There are dangers of a *Chocolate Thank You*, a message to employees of general thanks, creating a short-term lift in spirits, without identification of what specifically the employee has done to merit the applause.

I refer to *Chocolate Thank Yous* in the same way as we do in *Continue & Begin Fast Coaching®* when we describe *Chocolate Praise™*, that is, the generic *"Well done"* statement providing a short-term sugar rush, with an inevitable downer once the sugar rush has subsided, and the substance for applause is uncertain (see **Coaching, Continue & Begin Fast Coaching®**).

Highlighting why an employee's or team's contribution is valuable to a wider goal is equally important. Contextual understanding provides significance for the employee's efforts.

In *Continue & Begin®* we talk about the *Structure of Well-Done-Ness®*. When a colleague understands the specific patterns of their success, the building blocks of their excellence, they can replicate it in future. *Thank you*, therefore, has more value than simply ego-strengthening. When used judiciously, and with the *Structure of Well-Done-Ness®* in mind, it serves as a reminder and embedder of behavioural excellence (see **Structure of Well-Done-Ness®**).

A genuine, authentic *thank you* is an influential motivational force. For maximum impact, ensure your message of thanks is conveyed by congruent communication, with words, tone, and body language all expressing a common meaning of gratitude (see **Words, song, and dance**) and related to a specific action of merit.

Further reading

The Secret to Productivity and Positivity: Show Your Appreciation | Forbes.com 2019 | Abbajay, M. | https://www.forbes.com/sites/maryabbajay/2019/02/28/the-secret-to-productivity-and-positivity-show-your-appreciation/?sh=54628dcd26c4

The Ripple Effects of a Thank You | Greater Good Magazine, December 2019 | Suttie, J. | https://greatergood.berkeley.edu/article/item/the_ripple_effects_of_a_thank_you

Employers To Retain Half Of Their Employees Longer If Bosses Showed More Appreciation; Glassdoor Survey | Glassdoor | Editorial team, November 2013 | https://www.glassdoor.com/employers/blog/employers-to-retain-half-of-their-employees-longer-if-bosses-showed-more-appreciation-glassdoor-survey/

Gratitude enhances the beneficial effects of social support on psychological well-being | The Journal of Positive Psychology, November 2019 | Deichert, N.T., Fekete, E.M., Craven, M.

Time is a budget item

"You may delay, but time will not, and lost time is never found again."
– Benjamin Franklin

Time is a management resource, as are people, machinery and equipment, workspace, finance, and information.

The difference with time resource is its fleeting nature, it is here and then not, never to reappear or be re-used. Once managers consider *time* as a temporary supply to their business operations, it becomes more obvious how this raw material requires planning and allocation. As with the middle aisle of some supermarket chains, *once it's gone, it's gone.*

For many years my friend Richard was a hotelier. During my early management career, I learnt a prized lesson from him about the value of prudent management of time. It still resonates for me now,

"Nick, you can't sell yesterday's bedroom."

Let's think about the tasks of a manager and the limits of time available in which to complete them. Management tasks come in two forms,

1. Positive Active Tasks

Positive Active tasks are developmental, they evolve from considered thinking about how to improve performance or quality (see **Looking out of the window thinking**).

Developmental activities are usually about future ambition, searching for improvements in working methods. They are *important.* Forward thinking allows managers to allocate chunks of ringfenced diary time to these positive active tasks. Examples might include,

- Appraisals and performance reviews.
- Team building sessions.
- Product or service development discussions.
- Process improvements.
- Training, coaching, and mentoring.

2. Reactive-Response Tasks

Reactive-Response tasks are different. These are the requests and obligations received by managers every day, requiring resource and process time. They may be couched in language of *urgency*. They are often notable for revealing someone else's urgency, and not necessarily yours. Reactive tasks are rarely self-motivated or developmental. They are the junk landing on your desk every day.

Time efficient managers diarise contingency for the inevitability of inbound reactive tasks. In project management this is known as *float*. Float time is the spare capacity built into a project plan to accommodate unexpected bumps in the road. Team leaders are, in effect, project managers, constantly adjusting their team's project plan to accommodate external requests.

Importance and urgency

Importance and urgency are not the same thing. How many times have you been asked to react to a request because it is important, only to discover it isn't important at all, it just has a short timeline for delivery? This isn't *importance*, it is *urgency*.

- *Important* activities require dedicated thinking time. Important topics relate to your team's purpose, and their ability to achieve goals, now and in the future. They are to do with core principles, and strategies, not tactics. Important tasks can be planned and diarised ahead with significant chunks of allocated time, e.g., a developmental initiative (see **What am I here for? What is my management purpose?**).
- *Important* activities with a short, or immediate deadline (*important* and *urgent*) require dedicated management time, now, e.g., a health and safety issue, or key customer concern.
- *Urgent activities, with modest importance*, require prompt action, though with minimal time invested, e.g., responding to a short deadline information request. Delegate if possible.
- *Urgent request activities with negligible importance* may benefit from being delegated or bounced back to the requester. Not everything can fit into your own or your team's working time. As a mentor once advised me,

"You can only get a pint in a pint pot. Choose what you put in your pot."

You may have seen the importance and urgency framework, sometimes known as the Eisenhower 4 Box Grid, named after General Dwight D. Eisenhower, 34th President of the United States. His model is widely used as a prioritisation and decision-making aid. Here is an adapted version for team managers,

Important and Urgent	Important, but Not Urgent
This issue requires prompt management attention and action now.	This needs management attention, and dedicated future diary time, for consideration and action.
Do	*Decide*
Not Important, but Urgent	**Not Important, Not Urgent**
This requires immediate management attention. It is not important, so, if possible, delegate to others or briefly deal with it personally.	This is not worthy of your management attention currently.
Delegate	*Delegate, bounce back, delete, or ignore*

Flapsi hapsi

Flapsi hapsi is a phrase known in time management circles, made popular by the training company *Time Manager* in the 1980s. We've all been there in our management roles; there is so much to do! Tasks are everywhere, lists, part completed jobs, our minds are muddled, and we feel overloaded.

We start an activity and get distracted by another task, and then there's that other task to do as well. We move from one project to another without dedicated energy to completing one, before moving onto the next.

Dedicated, single focus is the key to task completion. From time to time, I find myself aware of my own *flapsi hapsi* and decide to concentrate on one selected task (see **Self-awareness**).

Discretionary time and Time Eaters

Day to day team management is busy! There's so much to consider and limited opportunity to take time out to *think*. Not transitory thinking, in-the-moment mental processing, but the deep thought, proactive thinking about purpose, goals, strategy, business planning and implementation. Thinking about development, about improvements to service proposition and delivery. About resource allocation and people growth. About medium and long-term evolution. The type of thinking which needs dedicated time. It requires planning into a manager's diary.

It is during *discretionary time*, that is, time not constrained by necessity, where managers have the psychological freedom to *ponder* (see **Looking out the window thinking**).

Discretionary time is the space for managers, free from reactionary tasks; those stimulus-response activities brought by team members, by line managers, by colleagues across the organisation, or from customers, either external or internal (see **Customers, internal**). Other tasks are demanded by systemic internal processes.* For most, discretionary time is a rare commodity.

Here then is the challenge for managers; discretionary time is under attack from multiple forces. In Ken Blanchard, William Oncken Jr, and Hal Burrows' book *The One Minute Manager Meets the Monkey*, the authors describe how discretionary time is diminished by boss-imposed time, system-imposed time and 'monkeys', those difficulties brought by direct reports as unsolved problems (see **Monkeys, management of**).

Blanchard, Oncken, and Burrows missed a crucial component in their modelling. External forces, including market and societal factors, place a root-cause demand on managers' discretionary time.

For example, in multi-site retail operations, and in the wider service sector, talent acquisition, recruitment, development and retention, are prime factors in delivering quality service to customers. In today's markets, availability of appropriate staffing, supply chain reliability, and changes to customer expectations, are challenging and time consuming. Think about the dynamics of this,

- Labour shortages, staff turnover rates and associated induction training implications.
- Inflationary wage expectations.
- Wage jumping (moving from one employer to another for minor pay increases).
- Active 'poaching' of staff by competitors.

---

* Educated managers know how *Lean* interventions eradicate non-value adding procedures (see **Lean management**).

- Career acceptance of short-term employment periods, before 'next move'.
- Labour market's evolving demand for meaningful work life balance (see **Work Life Balance**).
- *Gen Z* perceptions of 'work' and their expectations of employers.
- Consumer requirements of service delivery, including quality, convenience, and speed.
- Product and materials availability in volatile supply chains.

Managers are already juggling focus and dedicated time to keep on top of these and other market variables before internal demands add to the burden.

Discretionary time is fighting for survival on (at least) four fronts,

1. Boss imposed *Time Eaters.*
2. System imposed *Time Eaters.*
3. Market imposed *Time Eaters.*
4. *Monkeycare Time Eaters.*

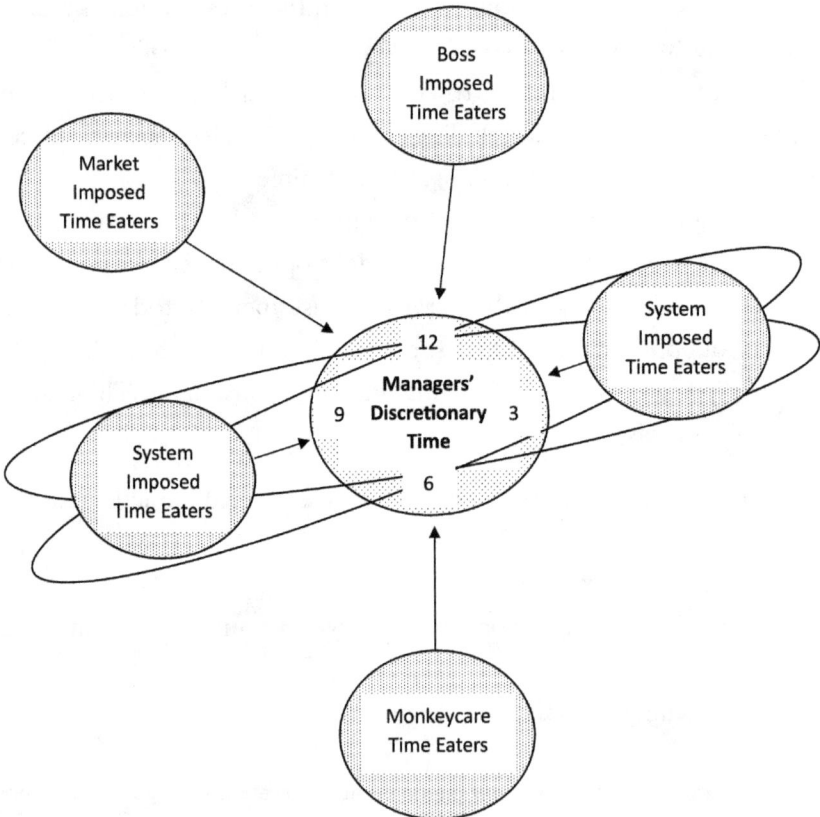

An optimistic manager might attempt to influence boss-imposed and system-imposed *Time Eaters* through lobbying, via business case presentation, or other persuasive means. There may be possibilities. Good luck with market-imposed *Time Eaters* though, that's a tough ask. The market doesn't care about your quest for discretionary time.

One area where managers *can* minimise impact on discretionary time is *Monkeycare Time Eaters.*

By adopting the principles proposed by Blanchard and others in various versions of *The One Minute Manager*, and by growing the capabilities and self-sufficiency of team members, it is possible to reduce the time-eating impact of team members bringing problems they hope the manager will take ownership of, and resolve.

Too many managers I meet are zookeepers, specialising in primate care. Monkeys are running wild, creating manager overload, *flapsi-hapsi* ineffectiveness, and team member frustration. Professional managers don't accept upwardly delegated monkeys. The monkey stays with the team member.

Reduce *Monkeycare Time Eaters*, increase discretionary time, plan, do, and review.

Elephant eating

You can't eat an elephant in one go; or any other large mammal, come to that. Efficient time managers know the value of carving your elephant (your management accountabilities) into smaller parts, to become more manageable.

If your elephant is *Team Supervisor role*, then the smaller parts (elephant steaks?) might include the team supervisor's *Key Result Areas* (KRAs), for example,

- Productivity.
- Quality and compliance.
- Budget; revenue, expenditure, or both.
- Team recruitment and retention.
- Employee engagement and satisfaction.
- Health, safety, and welfare.

KRA elephant steaks are best carved into smaller tender morsels to chew, swallow and digest. Some tender morsels might be delegated to colleagues, as part of your management of team time.

Visible success

To Do lists are helpful. Be wary though of becoming overwhelmed by the never-ending additions to your workload. It can help personal motivation to recognise what has already been completed.

A tip I learned as a young manager is to keep the finished tasks visibly marked as completed, at least for a while, struck through, as a reminder of how much you've achieved, and how productive you have been already.

Managers benefit from empowered thinking just as much as team members. When we feel good about ourselves, about our productivity and management successes, we become energised and resourceful, ready to take on new challenges and those projects still on our task list (see **Coaching, Continue & Begin Fast Coaching®**).

Plan in the big things, fit in the little things

Analogies are helpful (or irritating). Think about a road trip, a family holiday or similar. The car is about to be filled with luggage, bags, clothes, accessories, and all the paraphernalia of family life. What do you pack first? If you load up all the little things, the big things won't fit in. Plan the big things first, fit in the little things second.

My younger grandchildren love playing with toy animals. There are two storage jars in our playroom packed full of elephants, tigers, giraffes, cows, crabs, sheep, dolphins, and every other animal you can think of. The children have learned, through trial and error, and an occasional gentle steer from Papa, to put the big animals in first, and then the little ones will fit around them.

You're ahead of me, I suspect. Your diary has a finite amount of space. *You can only get a pint in a pint pot. Choose what to put in your pot.* Get the big things planned in first and the little things will fit around them.

What are the big things? The positive-active tasks, planning and strategy thinking, dedicated time for your people, the developmental activities, the *important*, not the *urgent*.

What are the little things? What are the reactive-response tasks, daily chores, the *urgent* but not *important* activities, the routine jobs, some of which you can delegate to team members. How about building in float time for the inevitable *"Can you just..."* requests?

Net Time

A simple diary optimisation technique is to adopt *net time* principles. Net time represents the period from the start of one or more activities, through to completion. Wherever practical more than one activity can run at the same time, each in parallel to others.

At home you can load the dishwasher whilst the kettle is on, and pop bread in the toaster. The overall time from start to finish of these parallel activities is *net time*.

Project managers are familiar with running concurrent events simultaneously rather than sequentially. Running in parallel means the overall time required and allocated for a project can be minimised. Where some activities are necessarily sequential, the overall time required to complete events in series is known as the *critical path*. Any extension or delay to activities on the critical path results in an increase in *net time*, and a delay for the overall project.

Which management activities could you run in parallel to reduce *net time*?

Time Boxing

Blocking off, or 'boxing' chunks of time is a useful tactic for dedicated focus on specific management functions. It works especially well for *important* (not *urgent*) developmental activities. It's also an effective method for minimising distractions during the working day.

Skilled *Time Boxers* are disciplined in avoiding temptation to be side tracked by inbound calls, emails, or messages. They ring fence set times during the day, say 3pm to 5pm each afternoon, or Monday afternoons and Friday mornings, for managing communications.

Time Boxers manage time in a structured manner beyond the world of work. Managing our busy timetable includes home, family commitments, and social contexts. Health and wellbeing, holidays and breaks away from work, are important considerations. Time boxing can help us isolate and dedicate time portions to these parts of our life.

The challenge, always, is the personal commitment to protect these pledges from other pressures.

Pomodoro method

Francesco Cirillo developed this method in the 1980s as an aid to productivity. Pomodoro is the Italian word for tomato, and the design of Cirillo's kitchen timer he used for this time management technique.

In *pomodoro*, work is carved into short chunks, with 25 minutes of dedicated activity on one task, followed by a 5 to 10 minutes break. After 4 consecutive *pomodoros*, a longer break is taken, typically 20 to 30 minutes. A kitchen timer, or perhaps today a phone alarm, is used to set the 25 minutes pomodoro working period. Traditionalist *pomodoro* users believe the winding of an analogue timer adds to the theatre of time management and focuses attention on workflow. Hmmm, maybe.

Choose Your Time Management Tools

Evidently, there are numerous time management concepts, some more theoretical than pragmatic. Real life applicability is the yardstick for measuring value. An approach I find helpful as an *applied* time management idea is the CLEAR® model developed by my friend and colleague Steve O'Neill at www.sondevelopment.com

CLEAR®: Catch | Locate | Execute | Adapt | Review

Step	Aim	Action
Catch	Grab each idea–thought-problem as it happens.	Paste. To a pre-defined inbox (book, in-tray, or digital device). Action. Immediately, if it takes less time than writing them down.
Locate	Move what you've caught to a best place.	Rubbish. Dump them. Reference items. Move to a storage space. Actions. Use a positive verb. Place in a task manager or calendar.
Execute	Select 3 items for your impactful day.	Calendar. Block out time for impactful work. Tasks. Prioritise using an impact-effort matrix.
Adapt	3 times each day. Check in with yourself.	On track. Is it all working? Divergence. What's changed? Agile. Do I need to adapt?
Review	Daily. Weekly.	Daily. What worked, what didn't, what shall I change tomorrow? Weekly. Pull out impact actions and plan for next week.

The stoic philosopher Seneca (see **Stoicism**) was right when he said,

"It is not that life is short, but that we waste a lot of it."

Time is a budget item, a management resource to be used with care. There is a limited amount of this precious material and high calibre managers use it wisely.

Which of the above ideas would work for you in allocating your time budget?

Further reading

Indistractrable: How to Control Your Attention and Choose Your Life | Bloomsbury Publishing, 2020 | Eyal, N.

The One Minute Manager® Meets the Monkey | Thorsons, 2011 | Blanchard, K., Oncken Jr, W., Burrows, H.

How to Use Time Blocking to Manage Your Day | Very Well Mind, December 2020 | Gordon, S. | https://www.verywellmind.com/how-to-use-time-blocking-to-manage-your-day-4797509

The Pomodoro Technique: The-Life-Changing-Time-Management System | Virgin Books, 2018 | Cirillo, F.

CLEAR® | sondevelopment, 2023 | O'Neill, S. | www.sondevelopment.com/clear

Timeline empowerment

"The kingdom of heaven is within you, and whosoever shall know himself shall find it." – *Ancient Egyptian proverb*

Timelines are mental constructs used to explore past, present, and future life positions. The purpose of timeline exploration (NDK style) is to strengthen ego and identify healthy ambitions for the future.

Timelines represent a flow of time from as far back in your personal history, and as far forward into your future, as you would like to consider.

As with many metaphors and useful fictions (see **Useful fiction**), timelines are not real, they are made up imaginary concepts which offer a thinking framework. Timeline users acknowledge their lifetime achievements to date, feel good about them, and then consider their ambitions, along a visualised path from past to future.

Note the language, *achievements,* and *ambitions.* Timelines are best used with a positive mindset, employing healthy language to celebrate personal development and empower aspirations.

Here's one method for developing and using your personal timeline,

- Take a comfortable seat away from outside distractions.
- Place your hands palm down on your thighs.
- Allow your mind to rest and self-chatter to subside.
- Breathe easily.
- If you'd like to, close your eyes.

Now, think about which direction your historical life stories come from, along a pathway, a road, a track, a 'neural pathway', or some other form. Does it come from directly behind you? From beneath or above you? From the left, or right? And in which direction does your future timeline travel?

Looking back along your timeline (only pleasant memories), seek out the significant positive events, the helpful steppingstones on your journey, to where you are now. Each steppingstone is another stage in your personal and professional development.

Look how far you have come!

Confidence and resourcefulness come from acknowledging what you have already achieved.

Now, having recognised your progress to date, look ahead along your timeline. In which direction does it travel? How far ahead would you like to explore? Use only positive empowering thoughts of what you would like to achieve, and by when. What ambitions do you have? Dreams?

There's something good waiting for you there; what is it? What would you like it to be?

My timeline comes from behind me, drifting up from a misty background. I see it in my mind as a long train track, the type I played with as a child. At key points back along my timeline are circumstances which were significant growth events for me, some career related, some personal. They appear as markers in the ground at each development stage.

Ahead of me is my timeline future. It goes forward from my mind and, for some reason, veers up and to the right and in a slow curve. Along my future timeline are ambitions I have for what remains of my life, some are date marked, and including visual imagery, or sounds. Others are less precisely described. All are based around positive feelings.

I use my timeline to remind myself of my achievements, and the skills I have gathered so far in life. I feel empowered and resourceful and use these feelings to address new challenges with optimism and feelings of possibility and opportunity.

I introduce timelines to managers where there is a lack of self-recognition of progress to date. Almost every time, having conducted a brief retro review of their timeline, managers will (usually reluctantly) acknowledge their successes and professional development so far. More times than not it ignites an inner resourcefulness for their hopes and dreams – mapped out on their future timeline of course!

How could you use a timeline to celebrate your own growth to date, and empower your ambitions?

Further reading

Time Line Therapy and the Basis of Personality | Crown House, 2017 | James, T., Woodsmall, W.

Timelines: A simple exercise? | Counselling Directory | Editorial team, June 2019 | https://www.counselling-directory.org.uk/memberarticles/timeline-a-simple-exercise

Time off

> "If you are quiet enough, you will hear the flow of the universe. You will feel its rhythm." *– Buddha*

Working hard is a mindset familiar to managers.

Deadlines, performance indicators, standards management, staffing and resource management, all require a work ethic. It can go too far though. There is only so much work a manager can absorb before negative indicators emerge.

Performance deteriorates as work sessions extend, we become tired, make errors and ill-considered decisions. Maybe we act impulsively. Tiredness results in reduced efficiency and a loss of perspective. The impact of overwork on personal wellbeing and relationships is well documented.

Time away to rest and recharge mind and body is vital. Incidentally, the etymology of 'vital' originates from Latin, meaning 'belonging to life'. How appropriate!

Extensive global research by the World Health Organisation (WHO) and International Labour Organisation (ILO) revealed the damaging impact of excessive working hours, trending upwards from data points in 2000, 2010, and 2016. In extreme cases overwork leads to acute and chronic illness, heart disease, stroke, and potentially death. The research found consistently working 55 hours or more each week presents a 35% increased risk of stroke, and 17% more likelihood of dying from heart disease, compared to workers engaged for 35 to 40 hours per week.

In the UK, the Health & Safety Executive reported over 900,000 people experiencing work-related stress, depression, or anxiety during 2021/22.

Strategies for managing your stress levels will help, of course (see **Stress management, Mrs Erickson's mindfulness relaxation technique (5-4-3-2-1), Stress management, self-trance,** and **Stress management, patterns of healthy thinking**).

Better though, is to have a complete break from work, away from the ingredients of your working life, experiencing life beyond the goldfish bowl you work within.

It's difficult, I know. I've been there. Sometimes a break away will help restore perspective about what is important in your life. I work with many managers who have microscopic focus on their job role. A healthy activity I encourage is to consider what exists beyond the immediacy of their job role? Their team? Department? The employing organisation? The industry? The sector? Work?

Looking up from the intensity of deliverables brings a healthier recognition of where work exists within your wider life. Taking time off helps achieve objectivity and perspective, if only for a (healthy) while.

Take a break. Relax on a holiday. Go away for a few days, long enough to wash away thoughts of work. Take mid-day breaks away from the work environment. Take your lunch break. You think you can't find the time for a walk? Take the time.

Grandma was right (again); the ironing will still be there in the morning.

Further reading

Working Too Hard Makes Leading More Difficult | Harvard Business Review, December 2014 | Friedman, R. | https://hbr.org/2014/12/working-too-hard-makes-leading-more-difficult

Long working hours increasing deaths from heart disease and stroke: WHO, ILO | Environment International, September 2021 | https://www.who.int/news/item/17-05-2021-long-working-hours-increasing-deaths-from-heart-disease-and-stroke-who-ilo

Burn-out an "occupational phenomenon": International Classification of Diseases | World Health Organisation | Departmental news, May 2019 | https://www.who.int/news/item/28-05-2019-burn-out-an-occupational-phenomenon-international-classification-of-diseases

Work-related stress, anxiety, or depression statistics in Great Britain, 2022 | Health & Safety Executive, November 2022 | https://www.hse.gov.uk/

Tissue paper prisons

"Man often becomes what he believes himself to be. If I keep on saying to myself that I cannot do a certain thing, it is possible that I may end by really becoming incapable of doing it. On the contrary, if I have the belief that I can do it, I shall surely acquire the capacity to do it even if I may not have it at the beginning." *–Mahatma Gandhi*

Long term stability as a manager might feel nice and secure, except it doesn't help us grow and develop. If we don't continually evolve our management skills and competences, we become stale and inflexible. In today's fast changing world of work this is a high-risk strategy.

Living, working, and thinking within a homeostatic comfort zone is at best unfulfilling, and potentially career threatening. Managers today have an opportunity to learn and grow, rapidly. Leading edge expertise is available at the touch of a button. Dynamic operators are constantly on the lookout for new knowledge, fresh insights, and a competitive edge.

So why do people stay within their comfort zones? George Zalucki talked about self-created mental straw prisons, restraining an individual within limiting boundaries. Straw is a tough natural material. I label these restricted thinking patterns as *tissue paper* prisons.

Can we break free from our *tissue paper prison*? Of course. We can step through the tissue paper any time we like and explore expansive, enriching territory. Yet people choose not to. Why? Because they have a secondary gain from living and thinking within the *tissue paper prison* (see **Secondary Gain**).

The secondary gain will be associated, commonly, with not having to place oneself in a position of vulnerability, or to feel uncertain, to experience low confidence about a potential professional 'failure', or of personal embarrassment. By staying in the *tissue paper prison* these threats are minimised. Sophisticated, self-manipulating lies will be constructed to justify staying inside. Self-denial about the benefits of personal and professional growth will inhibit change.

The resulting limitation of this mindset is the missed opportunities, the experiences of growth and achievement and thrill from taking a managed risk and stepping beyond the tissue paper. Sadness comes from a comfort zone becoming a prison for the future.

Some managers wish to stretch and grow. Some want to stay in the *tissue paper prison*. Some would like to step through the tissue paper but don't know how. For these managers, see **Can't to Can Belief Busting®** and check it out on YouTube.

Further reading

Boomerang! Coach Your Team to Be the Best | Dandelion Digital, 2007 | Drake-Knight, N. |

Fast Coaching. The Complete Guide to New Code Continue & Begin® | Dandelion Digital, 2016 | Drake-Knight, N. | Audible https://www.audible.co.uk/pd/ Fast-Coaching-Audiobook/B07TTKD13T

The Motivation Agency | https:// themotivationagency-online.com/course/ begin

Can't to Can Belief Busting | Continue and Begin Ltd | Drake-Knight, N. | https:// www.youtube.com/watch?v=yeb3nc7w2_8

To be expected

"Life is largely a matter of expectation." *– Homer*

In cricketing terms, life and work have a habit of throwing us inswingers, outswingers, and the occasional nasty bouncer. We can stress about these or, in the spirit of stoicism (see **Stoicism**), accept unwelcome events as bumps along the road for us to experience.

A thought response I've found helpful over the years is the framing of outcomes as an *inevitability* of circumstances, that whatever difficulties arise; these are *to be expected*.

It seems the retrospective acceptance of an outcome as inevitable is a healthy, strain-reducing, mental construct which reduces anxiety and creates equilibrium; it simply acknowledges the development as a reality. When we accept an outcome we avoid the discomforting early stages of shock, denial, anger, and depression, described so elegantly in the much-adapted grief experience model developed by psychiatrist Elisabeth Kubler-Ross.

An evolving adaptation of Kubler-Ross's work became widely recognised in organisational development circles as the *change curve*, using parts of the original death and grief management model as inspiration to represent the path employees travel along as they experience profound change to their working lives.

An (NDK) version of the *change curve* is shown as,

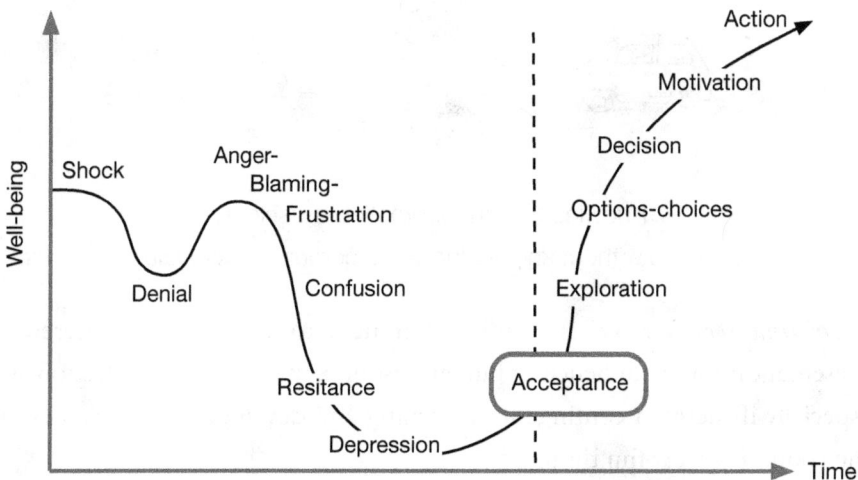

To be expected

By adopting a thinking pattern of *to be expected*, we fast forward through the first stages of the change curve and begin our journey of adaptation at *Acceptance.*

We *act as if* (see **Act As If**) the circumstances were *To be expected*, and therefore make the early stages of the change curve redundant. There is less relevance to feelings of shock, denial, anger, and frustration, if the outcome was *To be expected.*

Whether the outcome really *was* expected is secondary to the benefits of thinking it so. This simple mental construct is a *useful fiction* (see **Useful fiction**).

Think back over recent years, with the benefit of emotional distance, and consider a work-based circumstance where you could usefully have employed the mindset, *"Hmmm, yes, to be expected."*

Further reading

On Death & Dying: What the Dying Have to Teach Doctors, Nurses, Clergy & Their Own Families | Macmillan, 1969 | Kubler-Ross, E.

Putting theory into practice: Kübler-Ross Change Curve | Warwick Business School, November 2021 | Potter, A. | https://www.wbs.ac.uk/news/putting-theory-into-practice-kuebler-ross-change-curve/

Training doesn't work

"Knowledge without practice is useless.
Practice without knowledge is dangerous." *– Confucius*

"Training doesn't work" is a radical comment to include in a conference presentation for an audience of human resource management professionals, especially if there's a contingent of learning and development colleagues in the room. Its great fun though.

Listen to the sharp intakes of breath!

Large audiences are best for impact, although it works equally well in smaller meetings. Why? Because it is a deliberately provocative statement, contrary to many established beliefs we have about the value of professional development. L&D pros and their human resource colleagues squirm in their seats, look worryingly at each other, and feel anxious.

> "Who is this provocateur? How dare he say such harmful things about some of the core beliefs I have about learning and growth? Who invited him?"

I go on to say,

> "Training is a complete waste of time, energy, resource, and worst of all, hope. It is wet mud thrown against a wall; most of it slides off immediately. It leaves a little bit of sediment and forms a muddy puddle on the floor. Hopeless. We're all kidding ourselves that training works, particularly soft skill training. Employees leave your training rooms, and you can see the learning falling off them as they walk out the door. By the time they're home they've forgotten most of it. When they get to work the next day, a colleague will ask 'How was the training' and they'll say 'Lunch was good', or worse, 'Lunch was awful'. Training doesn't work."

Audible gasps in the room! There's a sense of anxiety and suppressed anger as the audience feels threatened by this assault on their professionalism.

Then the release...

> "Unless... ('What? You mean there's hope?') ... unless two things happen. 1. New knowledge from the training is turned into behaviour by the learners. 2. The new behaviours are sustained, long after the excitement of the training event itself... every day, every week, every month, every quarter, every year, in every circumstance, every time. Then? Then the training programme has been valuable. It is providing a return on investment. This only happens though, if those two things occur, turning new knowledge into new behaviour, and sustaining

those new behaviours. And this is where local on-the-job coaching,
by team leaders, creates stickability."

The relief and joy on the faces of L&D and HR members in the audience is palpable. I know I shouldn't really laugh, but I do.

So no, training doesn't work, unless the two follow-up pieces are in place,

1. New knowledge is implemented, as new behaviour.
2. New behaviour is sustained, through local coaching, by team leaders who have been trained how to coach!

Further reading

Boomerang! Coach Your Team to Be the Best | Dandelion Digital, 2007 | Drake-Knight, N.

Audible https://www.audible.co.uk/pd/ Fast-Coaching-Audiobook/B07TTKD13T

Fast Coaching. The Complete Guide to New Code Continue & Begin® | Dandelion Digital, 2016 | Drake-Knight, N. |

The Motivation Agency | https:// themotivationagency-online.com/course/ begin

U

Unconscious mind, trusting the

"You don't even have to listen to my voice…
because your unconscious will hear it.

Your unconscious can try anything it wishes… but your
conscious mind isn't going to do anything of importance."

– Milton Erickson

The unconscious mind is a wonderful resource, much undervalued and underutilised in the world of work. Clinical hypnotherapists know the power of the unconscious mind and make use of its influence in helping patients change their lives or the better.

The unconscious mind, therapists say, operates independently of the conscious mind and has one primary function; to protect us. Behind the scenes it will look after our breathing, our heartbeat, eye blinks, eye dilation, sneezing and coughing, sweating, or shivering, awareness of smell, taste, sight, sound and touch, and a whole range of instinctive physiological responses to our environment, including fight, flight and play dead reactions. Our (unconscious) autonomic nervous system controls many of these behaviours.

Clinicians believe the unconscious mind can be harnessed to help us navigate life in a healthy and productive manner. Patients are induced into a trance state by the therapist and offered suggestions, which may subsequently stimulate healthier thinking or emotional responses when 'awake'.

Hypnotic subjects are encouraged to trust their unconscious mind and allow it to work on problems whilst the patient goes about his or her daily life. Milton Erickson, the innovative clinical hypnotherapist said,

> "And it is very important for a person to know their unconscious is smarter than they are. There is a greater wealth of stored material in the unconscious. We know the unconscious can do things, and it's important to assure your patient that it can." – *Hypnotic Realities, 1976*

I regularly ask my unconscious mind to work on matters problematic to me, and to report back once progress has been made. Over the years this has been a successful strategy for uncovering fresh thinking (see **Stress management, self-trance**).

Move a problem or issue to your unconscious mind and allow it to work in the background and you will discover to your delight new, perhaps unexpected answers.

I use a rowing machine in my gym at the bottom of the garden. A strategy which works is to plug in a problematic issue into my unconscious mind, give it a firm and friendly instruction to *"Work on it while I row"*, and wait for the answers to come. Often a new idea will come whilst rowing, sometimes later in the day, or maybe the next day.

Rarely does my unconscious mind let me down. I make a point of thanking it for its kindness and help.

Of course, this may be a hogwash idea. Except in my experience, it works. Or perhaps it is a useful fiction (see **Useful fiction**).

Further reading

Hypnotic Realities: The Induction of Clinical Hypnosis and Forms of Indirect Suggestion | Irvington Publishers, 1976 | Erickson, M.H., Rossi, E.L., Rossi, S.I.

Handbook of Hypnotic Suggestions and Metaphors | Norton, 1990 | Hammond, D.C.

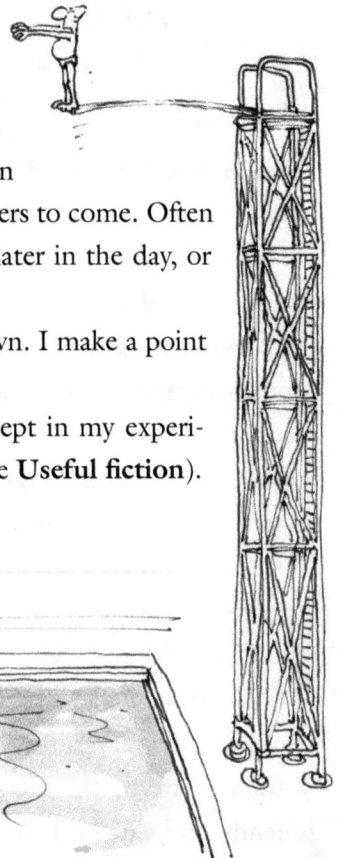

Universal quantifiers

"Always remember that you are absolutely unique.
Just like everyone else" – *Margaret Mead*

Linguists refer to language patterns of totality as *universal quantifiers*. These include extremity words and phrases such as, *never, always, no-one, nobody, nothing, everything, totally, completely, full, empty, ever, everyone, everybody, every time, any, all, none, hopeless, useless, best, worst*, and others.
For example,

- "She never shows up on time."
- "You always say that."
- "It happens every time."
- "Everyone knows that."
- "This is completely hopeless, it never works."

   and

- "You never empty the dishwasher!"

Universal quantifier statements, therefore, have a 100% or 0% polarity. These patterns are a form of generalisation.

People use universal quantifiers when feeling anxious. Anxiety leads to emotive responses in communication. When a team member is experiencing stress or frustration, anger, or fear, it is common (in my experience) to notice the frequency he/she uses polarity language. This provides insight.

Listen out for universal quantifiers in language patterns. Explore what is going on in the other person's mind. A handy way to do this is to repeat the language pattern back, politely and with empathy, and ask what *specifically* they mean,

"Oh no! So, when you say, 'It's hopeless' and 'it never works', in what circumstances has it not worked? When specifically, has it not worked?"

"Well, it didn't work just now, and Tina couldn't get it to work yesterday either when she took over from me. It works if the battery is completely charged but otherwise its rubbish."

And now we have additional information to explore, an opportunity to find a root cause and a solution (see **Generalisation** and **Root cause analysis**).

Further reading

The Structure of Magic: A Book about Language and Therapy, Volume 1 | R. Bandler, J. Grinder | Science and Behavior Books, 1975

Coaching out Universal Quantifiers (Absolute Language) | Continue and Begin Ltd | Drake-Knight, N. | https://ndk-group.com/coaching-universal-quantifiers-absolute-language/

Useful fiction

"An idea whose theoretical untruth or incorrectness... is not... practically valueless and useless; for such an idea, in spite of its theoretical nullity, may have great practical importance."

– Hans Vaihinger

Hans Vaihinger developed his concept of a *Useful Fiction* to illustrate how ideas which may, or may not be true, can be valuable to us. Some models of the world are not necessarily proven, and yet they help us make sense of what is going on around us and how we can deal with situations.

- Is it true counting to ten is scientifically proven to help us stay calm when feelings of anger begin to surface? Maybe. Or maybe it should be count to five, or twenty, or fifty? Or maybe there's no proof at all counting helps.
- Is it true, when instructed to do so, our unconscious mind will work on a problem, perhaps overnight, and subsequently provide us with the answer we seek? Possibly.
- Is it helpful, during a workplace presentation, to pretend to be confident, even though you may feel nervous?
- Is it useful, when learning a new task or skill, to believe you will achieve expertise in time?
- Can it be helpful to visualise some future time and place where you have overcome a limiting belief or restricted thinking pattern?
- Would it be helpful, in changed workplace circumstances or conditions, to think your existing skillsets may be transferable to the new environment?

- Are personality inventories valid? Are the various self-assessment questionnaires scientifically accurate and proven? Or do we belief the results as presented?

- Other than for safety reasons, it necessary to wear specific clothing at work? Uniforms? Suits? Ties? Skirts? Shoe styles? Norms of personal grooming? Dress like the boss? Or does cultural compliance help create harmony within the workplace?

- Might it be helpful to consider all human behaviours are driven by an urge to move towards feelings of comfort, or to move away from feelings of pain? Or both?

- Does reading, listening to audiobooks or podcasts, or watching personal development film clips help us to perform better at work? Or is better to learn by experience?

Are the above scenarios true? Or useful fictions?

The most valuable useful fiction I've encountered, and have used since early adulthood, is the principle of *Act As If*. If we *Act As If* we are competent at a given task, then we will, over time, become competent (see **Act As If**).

This book is a *Useful Fiction*. It offers ideas and techniques available to us all. Whether they are true, or not, you decide.

Further reading

The Philosophy of As If: A System of the Theoretical, Practical and Religious Fictions of Mankind | English translation from CreateSpace Independent Publishing Platform, 2015 | Vaihinger, H., 1922

Useful Fictions: Why Beliefs Matter | Psychology Today, March 2017 | Gautam, S. | https://www.psychologytoday.com/us/blog/the-fundamental-four/201703/useful-fictions-why-beliefs-matter

V

VAK(OG) representational systems

"Love is, of all the passions, the strongest, for it attacks
simultaneously the head, the heart and the senses." – *Lao Tzu*

You may be familiar with *Visual, Auditory* and *Kinaesthetic* communication styles. This idea proposes we process information, at specific times, through a preferred 'sense' channel, either visual, auditory (hearing), kinaesthetic (feeling), olfactory (smell), or gustatory (taste) to best understand the communication message or experience. This framework is known as VAKOG, commonly referred to as simply VAK.

This is one of the best-known propositions from Neuro Linguistic Programming, or *NLP*, co-created by Richard Bandler, John Grinder and Frank Pucelik in the 1970s. NLP was concerned with the nature of communication between people and with oneself.

One proposition from NLP is that words selected during conversation offer hints at how information is being processed by a communicator *at a moment in time.*

NLP suggests, when we describe our thinking, even in casual conversation, we are quite literal in meaning. Colleagues who say things like *"I see what you mean"* are most often processing information *at a precise moment in time* in a visual mode. They have organised their internal representations into images; they are making pictures from the words they hear. *"It doesn't sound right to me"* (auditory) and *"It's going along smoothly"* (kinaesthetic) are further examples.

It seems preference for a representational channel, during conversation, is temporary and fleeting. An individual is using a specific channel at a specific moment, in specific circumstances. These are transitory channels which may change suddenly. Please do not fall into the trap of labelling a person as a *visual learner,* or having an *auditory preference,* a *kinaesthetic thinker* or similar.

British schools have made enormous errors of judgement in applying a misinterpreted version of VAK in misguided attempts to help students. A child is not a 'kinaesthetic learner' any more than she is an auditory or visual or olfactory or gustatory learner. Representational preferences are temporarily adjusted to fit an environment, nothing more.

Students may have a tendency to use one representational system more than others, during a particular period of development. Does that mean this channel should majored on, minimising access to new ways of processing information? School children are learning how to learn. Education establishments which label a child as visual, kinaesthetic, or auditory processes are creating an impoverished learning environment.

Rant over.

Nonetheless, we can be conscious of a person's clue words *at a specific time, in a specific environment,* and identify their most highly valued or dominant communication style *in a specific circumstance.* The words and phrases people use are clues to their processing. These are known as *predicates.*

With practise, you can match your language patterns to predicates used by another and build commonality of communication. We like people like us, who use the same words as us (see **Clean Language**, **Rapport**, and

Rapport, advanced skills). Persistence is required to master this skill, so why not start today? Identify the representation system, at a given moment, of the next person you meet.

Here are some phrases you can interpret on your own.

- Looks about right.
- Feels about right.
- Sounds about right.
- I'm uncomfortable about this.
- The way I see it...
- There's a lot of noise around this.
- Get an eyeful of this.
- In a manner of speaking...
- Is it going smoothly?
- What does it say to you?
- Can you get to grips with this?
- I don't follow you.
- I see what you're saying.
- He's a pain in the neck.
- It's rather short sighted of him.
- Can we get this project landed on time?
- I don't see how it could.
- We need to take a view on this.
- Give me an account of it.
- It's how it appears to me.
- There's a hidden message here.

How about this though, a childhood friend of mine (still) has a habit of referring to how a situation *tastes* to him, or how it *smells*. What representational systems is he using in these moments? How could you respond in a similar style?

Further reading

The Structure of Magic 2: A Book about Communication and Change | Science & Behavior Books, 1976 | Grinder, J., Bandler, R.

Peoplemaking | Science and Behavior Books, 1972 | Satir, V.

Value Stream Mapping

"All we are doing is looking at the timeline, from the moment the customer gives us an order to the point when we collect the cash. And we are reducing the timeline by reducing the non-value adding wastes".

– Taiichi Ohno

Value Stream Mapping (VSM) is a Lean technique evolved from production management. It is now used extensively in service delivery organisations, in both private and public sectors. VSM is used to analyse and redesign the flow of materials and information required to bring a service to a consumer. It is applicable in most value chains.

Value Stream Mapping describes visually how a work process flows and is constructed using symbols in a process diagram.

The process of Value Stream Mapping begins by describing the *Current State* of processes within an organisation. VSM activities map the current state and then analyse where opportunities exist to remove waste, retain value, and create an improved *Future State*.

Mapping works best when a cross section of managers and team members engage in the *Current State* and *Future State* mapping process

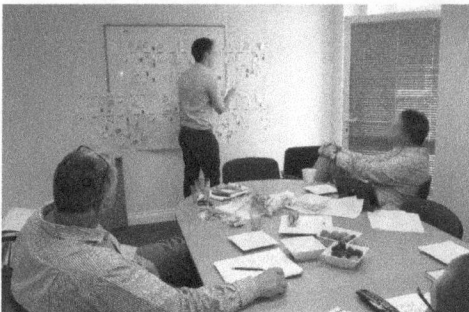

Images from
VSM exercises

Typical Application of Value Stream Mapping

- Identify the target service, or specific element of service delivery.
- Draw a *Current State* value stream map, which shows the current steps, delays, and information flows required to deliver the target service. VSM uses symbols to represent different activity types and key moments in the supply chain.
- Assess the *Current State* value stream map and seek opportunities to create 'flow' in momentum and reduced time lag, by eliminating waste, including 'time waste'.
- Draw a *Future State* value stream map.
- Work toward the future state condition.

Value Stream Mapping Symbols

There are variations on symbols mapping. There are no laws or rules on how to present them. The symbols described here are an adapted version of 'standard' VSM. It makes sense for organisations to consider how best to visually describe critical stages in their Value Streams. For example,

 Outside organisation

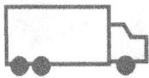 Transport

 Inventory

 Push

Communication

Additional symbols are created to represent other typical VSM concepts. You can design your own imagery, there are no VSM branding police.

- Activity undertaken & time taken to complete the activity.
- Customers & suppliers including internal market.
- Management control.
- First in first out.
- Niggles.
- Inventory, or stock.
- Cloud idea.
- Danger or risk.
- Information needed.

Images from
VSM exercises

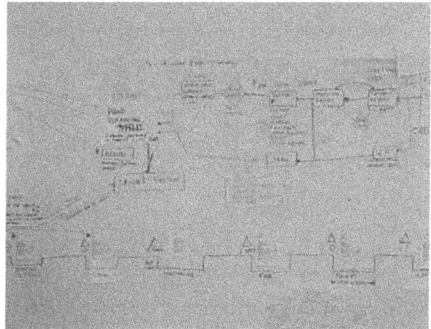

Creating a *Future State* map is not enough. Unless action is taken to implement new practices, *Future State* is a dream about how things *could* be. The secret to VSM is to be specific in determining the actions to be taken, who will take them, when they will be completed and how the review process will be managed.

Further reading

The Toyota Way: 14 Management Principles from the World's Greatest Manufacturer | McGraw-Hill, 2004 | Liker, J.

Value Stream Mapping: The Definitive Guide | Kanbanize | Editorial team, undated | https://kanbanize.com/lean-management/value-waste/value-stream-mapping

Visual management

"We can easily forgive a child who is afraid of the dark.
The real tragedy of life is when men are afraid of the light." – Plato

Visual management is the display of information in signage, visual data boards, floor area markings, shadow boards, and any form of workplace information easily understood through imagery. Visual stimuli are generally quicker to absorb cognitively than the written word. Visual management is used extensively in organisations which adopt Lean processes (see **Lean management**).

Visual controls help with safety compliance, and process conformance. It provides latest updates on workflow status for teams and the wider organisation. Visual controls help with employee engagement too, by offering regular reporting on performance, often in real time, in relation to known KPIs or OKRs (see **Objectives, management [MBOs and OKRs]**). People know how they're doing.

Visualisation is a great way to illustrate how a task or process should be completed, especially for workers who find written instructions a barrier to understanding.

Examples of visual management include,

- Safe walkways.
- Danger areas.
- Highlighted floor areas, positioned at information boards, for stand-up meetings and huddles (see **Huddles**).
- Shadow boards for tools.
- Task processes.
- Live performance data on productivity or quality.
- Daily, weekly, monthly, quarterly, year-to-date performance data.
- Red, amber, green (RAG) dial boards showing performance of specific workflows.
- Project status boards, including Gantt charts and critical paths (see **Planning**).
- Kanban boards and cards (see **Kanban**).

- 5S reminder boards, highlighting commitments to 5S protocols (see **Quality and 5S**)
- SQDCP huddle boards used for continuous improvement stand up discussions. These relate to *Safety, Quality, Delivery, Customers, People.* Typically, whiteboards are used to log a concern from the team, then recorded, action is decided, and responsibility allocated, with a timeline.
- 'Andon' lights are employed in some manufacturing organisations. These are visual information alarm systems which team members light up (pull cords or button press) when a major quality or safety issue is identified. Andon lights are the manufacturing equivalent of *pull the cord to stop the train.*
- Value Stream Mapping is a great example of visual management in action. A value stream map describes current state operations in each area of an organisation, with visual symbols depicting processes and activities in the operational flow. Future state maps depict how a revised approach will reduce activity and create a leaner operation, reducing waste and reducing cost (see **Value stream mapping**).

Below are examples of visual management. Notice how the images send a message of in-the-moment adaptation, handwritten and bang up to date. They present visual management as a meaningful activity, kept alive by contributors, both management and team members,

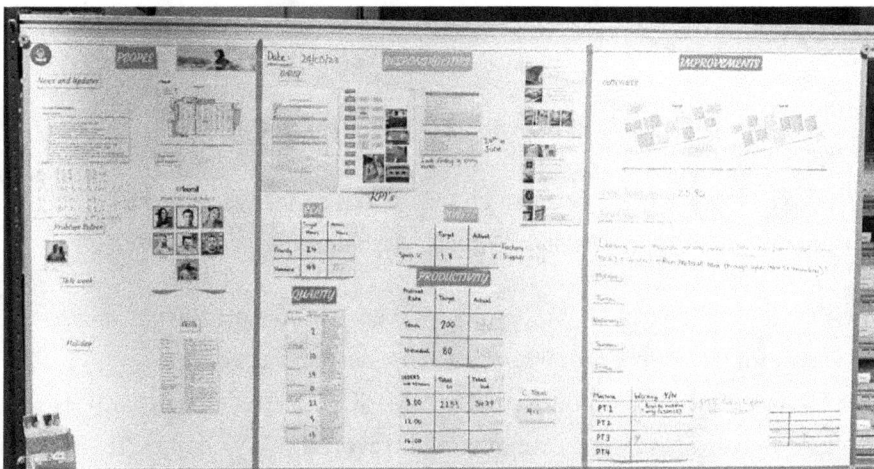

Visual management doesn't have to be a complex activity. Any form of visual representation of business information is useful to team managers and team members. Technological visuals can be helpful, of course. Call centre operators, for example, are outstanding at providing digital live information to team members. I prefer handwritten visual management, it has a more visceral, 'alive', feel to it.

Gareth Ellis, Head of Manufacturing at Teemill Tech Ltd www.teemill.com provides pragmatic guidance on the use of visual management,

> "The best visual management systems present raw information. Information is provided by, and managed by, the team. It's their information, not mine. They own it and understand what it means for them and the business."

Think about your own area of management responsibilities,

1. Which information, if visualised, would help you and colleagues better understand how activities are progressing?
2. What form of visual management would highlight where your team's processes and quality could be further improved?

Further reading

Visual Controls: Applying Visual Management to the Factory | Productivity Press, 2018 | Ortiz, C. A, Park, M.

One Team on All Levels: Stories from Toyota Members | CRC Press, 2012 | Turner, T.

VUCA management

"Doubt is not a pleasant condition, but certainty is absurd."
– Voltaire (François-Marie Arouet)

VUCA, a term coined by academics Warren Bennis and Burt Nanus, is an acronym for *Volatility, Uncertainty, Complexity* and *Ambiguity*.

VUCA describes a contextual world of constant change and evolution; sometimes, as in the case of Covid, revolutionary change. It suggests value in awareness, anticipation, and readiness. VUCA has some parallels with PESTLE analysis, which is the study of external influence including political, economic, social, technological, legal, and environmental factors (see **PESTLE**).

The Covid-19 pandemic taught us to expect the unexpected, and be prepared to think and act, swiftly.

Some organisations and the managers within them were quick to adapt to radically changing conditions, adopting agile thinking (see **Agile team management**) and creative solutions.

In early 2020, as Covid emerged as a threat, senior leaders in one brand I was privileged to support, set about creating a temporary operating model, to keep key workers and emergency service vehicles moving throughout the pandemic.

Their new operating model was agile, it changed frequently, often overnight, to address evolving factors in the fight against Covid. It was a constantly updating system, pivoting and shape shifting to keep up with changing medical realities and new government instructions. Protocols were drawn up and implemented, and almost as soon as these were established, new requirements caused a rethink on how best to adapt.

VUCA management was in abundance.

From Day One of Covid-19 there was a *can-do* mindset throughout the business, a determination to keep emergency vehicles moving. As the landscape around living with Covid evolved, so did strategies and tactics to maintain their service. There was no *try*, only *do* (see **Tentative language**) and the agile approach continued, as each new challenge appeared.

A mindset of agility became their norm, encapsulated by a mantra whenever faced by harsh conditions,

"Ah, yes, to be expected" (see **To be expected**).

Some enterprises, and the leaders and team members within them, have a special way of thinking and acting in adversity. Ryan Holiday's magnificent book *The Obstacle is the Way* offers insights into the benefits of stoic thinking habits during times of difficulty (see **Stoicism**).

Team managers, the ones who stand out as exemplars, are aware of VUCA, they are aware of PESTLE, and they understand the value of a preparedness to be agile, and an expectation of obstacles.

How prepared are you and your colleagues to operate in a world of VUCA?

Further reading

What VUCA really means for you | Harvard Business Review, January-February 2014 | Bennett, N., Lemoine, G.J. | https://hbr.org/2014/01/what-vuca-really-means-for-you

The Obstacle is the Way | Profile Books, 2014 | Holiday, R.

W

What am I here for?
What is my management purpose?

"Be kind, for everyone you meet is fighting a battle." – Socrates

I facilitated a management development programme for department heads (HODs) of a Further Education College. Over a series of half day events, we explored a range of management and leadership topics, and tied back each exploration to the job functions of each participating manager.

A standard approach.

It was interesting to work with subject area specialists who had found themselves promoted into management positions. Although they were bright people, it soon became apparent there was scope for them to learn about management good practice.

The best management development programmes involve a preparatory fact-finding phase, which usually takes a consultative approach, in advance of learning design and subsequent delivery. It proved helpful on this assignment. Discussions with the College's senior management team and my one-to-one discussions with each delegate, were revealing. We discovered even basic supervisory skills and knowledge was missing from the HODs.

The programme began with a typical round of self-assessment and self-evaluation activities, considering a range of behavioural models and self-perception inventories (see **Self-awareness**), plus a standard learning styles inventory to uncover how each manager processed information and absorbed learning. Nothing new in this approach. We were almost ready to start delving into the subject matter, compiled from the consultation process referred to above.

Before we began on 'content', I asked the group a direct and blunt question,

> "Why are you employed as a Head of Department? What is the
> purpose of your managerial post? What are you here (at the
> College) for? You are an expensive resource, there must be a
> purpose to your position?"

It was deliberately provocative, delivered with a smile of course, and it stopped these professional academics in their tracks. There was thought, and a few mumbled suggestions, vague, ambiguous and brim full of generalisations (see **Generalisations** and **Fuzzy language**).

I presented each manager with a 'sticky' badge, approximately 10 cm in diameter, with the question *What Am I Here For?* in large font. I offered the managers a challenge; to stick the badge to their suit, shirt, blouse, or whatever they were wearing, *upside down,* so they would see the question each time they looked down at their desk, or laptop, or sat in meetings. The challenge required delegates to wear the badge in full view of colleagues and students for one whole working day, before we met up for our next session together.

There was questioning from managers, and bags of uncertainty – ideal conditions for learning.

It wasn't a new idea; I'd seen it used in other organisations I'd been associated with. This was different though, because customers would see the badges, potentially hundreds, maybe thousands, of students; and of course, the managers' colleagues and departmental team members. One brave Head of Department accepted the challenge, and soon others followed in agreeing to the task.

Off they went, out into the enormous community of people moving around a busy college campus. Students and staff adopted awkward poses as they met each manager, sort of twisting at the hip and neck, head at an angle, trying to read upside down. It was funny!

The following week we met up. Each of the Heads said they had worn the badge around the College for one full day during the previous week.

What followed was fabulous. One by one, each manager explained how the 'badge' activity had caused them to think and feel *differently* about their role at work. Words we heard included,

- Vulnerable.
- Naked.
- Exposed.
- Uncertain.
- Explorative.
- Open minded.
- Curious.
- Enthusiastic.
- Committed.
- Dedicated.
- Clear.
- Purposeful.
- Focused.
- Responsible.
- Student centred.
- Supportive.
- Developmental.
- Questioning.
- Aligned (with College Values).

Quite a range!

Managers expressed agreement around high level themes of,

- Supporting the College *Mission*.
- Striving to deliver the College's *Vision*.
- Behaving and communicating in line with College *Values*.

I didn't believe that tripe.

Then, after a while, the good stuff came...

The managers headed up department teams of between 10 to 40 colleagues. Gradually, we built a list of *"What am I here for?"* statements.

Here's a summary,

- Encourage the team to…
- Influence others, to help the team to…
- Find resources for the team to…
- Mentor the team to…
- Train the team to…
- Coach the team to…
- Review with the team…
- Celebrate with the team…
- Provide air cover to the team… (see **Air Cover**).
- To develop as a manager by asking team members for commentary on my presenting style.

A week later, after learning of the Johari Window, there was a willingness to improve self-awareness of their *Blind* quadrant behaviours (see **Johari, adapted for management**),

Wow! What a series of sessions, and what a result in exploring *"What Am I Here For?"* The activity caused managers to think deeply about their roles as Heads of Department, managing teams of academics, and support staff.

How about you? Will you consider the same question,

"What Am I Here For?"

Will you wear the badge for a day?

Further reading

The New One Minute Manager | William Morrow, 2015 | Blanchard, K., Johnson, S.

What is Management? Objectives, Functions, and Characteristics | Knowledge Hut,

July 2023 | Hati, S. | https://www.knowledgehut.com/blog/others/what-is-management#frequently-asked-questions

Why? Purpose and meaning

Dear Mr Bin Man,

I am five years old.
I am very worried
about lots of rubbish.

Will there be enough
room left for me in the
world when I am a
grandad?

Where does all the
rubbish from my
dustbin go?

– Martin Drake-Knight, age 5 (1991)

Class-leading work groups have a collective ambition to stimulate team attention. We know from psychology that people work most effectively with a goal-oriented purpose. Alfred Adler (1956) and others referred to this as *teleological thinking*. Goals are helpful in focussing effort.

Even more powerful is to have a *compelling obsession* and inner motivation of purpose. When we understand and 'get' the reason we want to do something, our endeavours have meaning.

Brands with purpose provide a vehicle for employees to make a difference and achieve special outcomes. President John F. Kennedy toured NASA in 1962 and chatted to a janitor carrying a broom. When asked about his role at NASA the janitor replied,

"I'm helping to put a man on the moon."

In more earthly contexts, a collective underpinning *Why* leverages inner drive for employees.

Fred Herzberg (1964, 2008), the industrial psychologist, is known for his two-factor theory of motivation. Beyond his identification of *hygiene factors* as potential dissatisfiers at work, he proposed *true motivators* as responsibility, achievement, recognition for achievement, advancement, and valuable meaningful work. Value and meaning become more tangible when they are expressed in terms of clear purpose.

My sons are founders of Teemill Tech www.teemill.com a business with strong purpose and meaning for their 100+ employees, encapsulated in the company's headline mission, *Helping Brands End Waste.*

Teemill is the world's biggest dedicated circular economy e-commerce and supply chain platform. It works with more than 10,000 clothing brands providing an open-access circular design and supply chain platform.

In the traditional linear economy, products are designed from the start to be used, then thrown away. Worst still, over production by corporate clothing manufacturers ensures stockpiled garments are landfilled, even though they've never been worn. At Teemill every product purchase is manufactured at the point of order, in real time. Products are designed from the start to come back and be remade into new clothing using the fibre materials from worn-out garments. Zero waste. This is the *circular economy.*

Helping Brands End Waste is the *Why* driving performance at Teemill. It permeates throughout the business across all teams and is the reasoning behind employee passion.

What is the *Why* in your team? The *Purpose and meaning*? If you can't immediately present an answer in a simple statement, it is worth thinking through. This is a critical employee motivating factor.

Included in *Further reading* below, are links to businesses that my four adult children are involved with. Each one has meaning, ethical purpose, and a strong *Why*. As a result, my children and their colleagues are rightly proud to be part of them.

Further reading

Start With Why, How Great Leaders Inspire Everyone to Take Action | Penguin, 2009 | Sinek, S.

The Motivation-Hygiene Concept and Problems of Manpower | Personnel Administration, January 1964 | Herzberg, F.

One More Time: How Do You Motivate Employees? | Harvard Business Review Press, 2008 | Herzberg, F.

The Individual Psychology of Alfred Adler | Basic Books, 1956 | Adler, A.

TEDx talk, 2022 | *Dear Mr. Bin Man* | https://youtu.be/heIXdS7Gs7c | Drake-Knight, M.

Rapanui Clothing | https://rapanuiclothing.com/

Teemill Tech | https://teemill.com/

Roake Studio | https://roake.studio/

American Battery Technology Company | https://americanbatterytechnology.com/

Win-Win

"The greatest virtues are those which
are most useful to other persons". *– Aristotle*

We know from assertion theory selfish 'wins' can be achieved through manipulative, aggressive and self-serving tactics. Note the word *tactic* – an action or strategy carefully planned to achieve a specific end. Tactics are often focused on short term horizons, designed to create an immediate advantage or benefit (see **Assertion and assertiveness**).

Professional team managers look beyond the immediacy of *now* and think in bigger terms; their thoughts and actions are *strategic*. Farsighted team discussions have the goal of achieving a Win-Win outcome of mutual benefit. This is the ambition of professional negotiating strategies, or at least those managed with integrity in mind.

As far back as the early 1900s Mary Parker Follett (see **Management, about – an overview**) understood the management benefits of striving for win-win outcomes.

Transactional analysis and assertion principles describe four positions of the win-lose dynamic,

I win	I win
You win	You lose
You win	You lose
I lose	I lose

I Win-You Lose (aggression), *You Win-I Lose* (submissive), and *You Lose-I Lose* (mutual disaster), are all detrimental to long term workplace relationships. Team managers who favour *Win-Win* as their management philosophy, in my experience, create tighter knit work groups, with well-balanced task-team-individual dynamics.

Habitually use *Win-Win* as your baseline approach to team and individual communications and you'll build trust, respect, and commitment from your colleagues.

Next time you're communicating with your team or an individual team member, ask yourself, is my ambition a *Win-Win?*

Further reading

How to Win Friends and Influence People | Vermillion, 2006 | Carnegie, D.

The Management Theory of Mary Parker Follett | Business.com | February 2023 | Peak, S. | https://www.business.com/articles/management-theory-of-mary-parker-follett/

Words, song, and dance

"All communication must lead to change." – Aristotle

The purpose of our communication with team members may vary; perhaps to inform, or to seek information, to reassure, or challenge, or to influence thinking and behaviour. We communicate with colleagues, and they with us, through three primary channels,

Words

The language choices we make; meaning the words themselves, the phrases we use and their appropriateness in a workplace environment, or for a specific context.

Song

The tone with which we converse with colleagues; our talking volume, the speed or cadence of our speech, the inflections and variety in our voice, the emphasis we place on key words, and the upward or downward ending to our sentences. Message meaning is conveyed in *how* we sound as much as *what* we say.

Dance

The non-verbal body language signals we adopt, including posture, major limb and minor motor habits, our head positioning, facial expression, whether smiling, frowning or blank 'mask', our eye contact, blink rates, eyebrow movements, mouth shape, our breathing patterns and skin colouration. It's helpful to remember the positive impact of *Smile Power!* Everyone understands a genuine smile, in every language.

Impact

Congruence, or sameness of meaning, from all three channels of expression is important in conveying a genuine message. Research tells us, if there is a difference in message between any of the *Words, Song* and *Dance* routine – an incongruence – then the *Words* become less believable to a co-communicator than the *Song* and the *Dance*.

Words, Song and *Dance* elements vary in significance depending on channel, for example, when communicating by phone, by email, face-to-face in person, via a digital platform, or if working with a face covering.

Some of our communication patterns are unconscious to us – we operate without realising how our presenting style impacts on others. This is why, for customer facing professionals, call recordings and video mystery shopping are valuable personal development resources; it helps us acknowledge our patterns and understand the likely impact, good or less good, of our interaction with others (see **Case Study: On Growing Managers [and our Business]**).

A great way to develop communication skills, without the need for digital recording, is to ask colleagues for commentary on what they see, hear, and feel when they observe and listen to your communication patterns and style. What do they like? What could you do differently, or even better? Ask them!

Mehrabian miss-quotes

Beware the much miss-quoted 7% words, 38% tone, 55% physiology ratio promoted by those with only a surface knowledge of Alfred Mehrabian's work on communication channels. These numbers relate to a specific context in Mehrabian's work, referring to incongruence, published in his book *Silent Messages* (1970).

Like many research findings, Mehrabian's proposals have been hijacked and used in generic terms as an easy explanation, supposedly leveraged by academic research. My guidance is, if you're going to quote research findings, make sure you check the research source.

Think about your WS&D channel mix and how you currently communicate with team members and other colleagues. What's working well? How could you operate even more effectively?

Channel	What do I do well? What could I do even better? In which circumstances?
Words	Good - Less good -
Song	Good - Less good -
Dance	Good - Less good -

Further reading

Silent Messages | Wadsworth, 1971 | Mehrabian, A.

The Definitive Book of Body Language: How to read others' attitudes by their gestures | Orion, 2017 | Pease, A., Pease, B.

Work life balance

"The whole life of a man is but a point in time; let us enjoy it." *– Plutarch*

Work is an important part of people's lives. In stressful environments the pressures of a job role may overflow into life beyond the workplace, causing challenges for home and family. Creating boundaries for work and home makes sense, although in today's world of hybrid flexible working, the lines can seem blurred.

Team managers have a responsibility to team members, and to themselves, to create a working environment where employees can switch off physically and mentally from the rigours of work.

In recent years, work life balance (WLB) has become a broader phenomenon, encompassing aspects of life beyond the employment-family dynamic. Personal wellbeing in all its forms is now recognised as significant parts of the WLB equation.

The Covid-19 pandemic did much to reshape employees' and employers' thinking about how work fits into a society more conscious of fundamental life factors. Industries notorious for long hours, and high pressure/high rewards cultures, have found a workforce less willing to give so much of their souls to the employing organisation. The *hustle factor* is being questioned more, as employees think in bigger terms about what is important to them.

A radical decrease in staffing in the 50+ age labour force sector is an example. It's not just the older workforce though. Parents who became accustomed to spending time with children and families during lockdown, and subsequently in the new world of hybrid working, are considering how they wish to manage their professional and personal lives. The Gen Z labour force segment have made their expectations of work clear to employers.

Markets dictate, and as employers seek out the best talent for their operations, so they are adjusting working practices to attract a labour market now more discerning about which employer they commit to, and the shape of their working lives.

For team leaders, in busy operational environments, taking time to think through your own work life balance is important. You're busy though, right? Thinking about work life balance would be easier if you had more time.

How about if you had an easy access reference tool, quick to review and monitor?

One handy way to keep an eye on your work life balance is to build, and occasionally refer to, a *Wheel of Life*. A compelling *Wheel of Life* includes criteria important to *you*, rather than a universal model found online. Decide on what elements of life are import at to you and design a wheel appropriate for *your* needs, not what someone else thinks should be included.

If you have the tech skills to design something electronically, great. If you think it's a bit of a faff to get the laptop out, design your *Wheel of Life* by hand, it works just as well.

Here's an example,

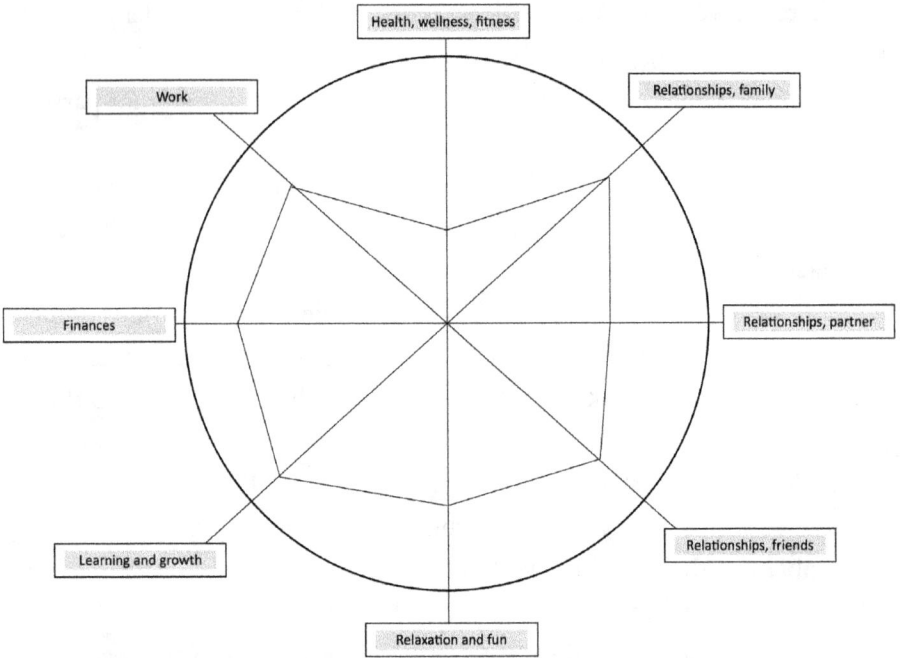

Hand drawn works just as well,

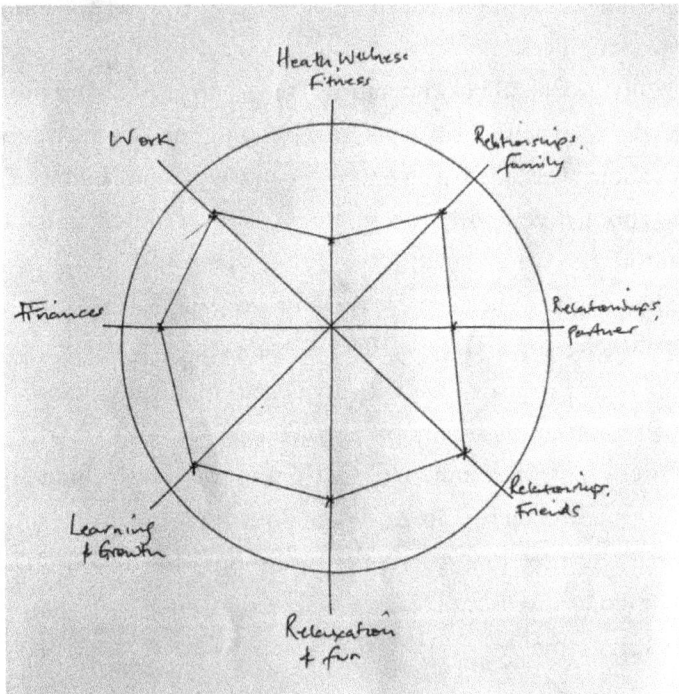

The *Wheel of Life* illustrates criteria important to the designer and heightens awareness of the status of each criterion in the person's life. The designer of the wheel illustrated above might reflect on the obvious message the imagery offers; there's a concern here about health, wellness, and fitness.

How would you design a *Wheel of Life* for you? What will be your criteria? How will you score? What will you do with your raised awareness, to improve your work life balance?

You may wish to share the *Wheel of Life* idea with your team members. Each colleague will have their own criteria to plot on the wheel; imperatives significant to them.

Further reading

Hustle culture: Is this the end of rise-and-grind? | BBC Worklife, April 2023 | Carnegie, M. | https://www.bbc.com/worklife/article/20230417-hustle-culture-is-this-the-end-of-rise-and-grind

Work-life balance | Mental Health Foundation | https://www.mentalhealth.org.uk/explore-mental-health/a-z-topics/work-life-balance

If Your Co-Workers Are 'Quiet Quitting,' Here's What That Means | Wall Street Journal, August 2022 | Ellis, L., Yang, A. | https://www.wsj.com/articles/if-your-gen-z-co-workers-are-quiet-quitting-heres-what-that-means-11660260608

Work Life Balance | Sharp Podcast series, episode STP070 | SON Development, 2023 | O'Neill, S. | www.sondevelopment.com/podcast

Retention On The Rise: What's Driving The Trend For Satisfaction And Staying | Forbes, August 2023 | Brower, T | https://www-forbes-com.cdn.ampproject.org/c/s/www.forbes.com/sites/tracybrower/2023/08/06/retention-on-the-rise-whats-driving-the-trend-for-satisfaction-and-staying/amp/

World's worst question

"The worst of all deceptions is self-deception." – *Plato*

A debilitating language pattern I hear managers ask team members is, *"Why can't you do it?"*

This is the *World's Worst Question*.

When a team member is asked, *"Why can't you X?"* the individual searches the files of their mind to find the document folder headed, *"Why I Can't X."* Once found, it's simply a case of opening the folder and presenting all the

good reasons for *"Why I Can't X."* It's an effective strategy for confirming you can't do something.

When we ask someone, *"Why can't you?"*, there is a presupposition (see **Presuppositions**) implicit in the question: *"We both know you can't do it."* This is not conducive to stimulating ambition about possibility. George Zalucki states (*Mind and Emotions* audio tape), in a slight paraphrase,

> The Thinker thinks and the Prover proves.
>
> If the Thinker thinks "I can't", the Prover proves it right.

Ask someone why they can't do something, and you reinforce their belief they can't, even when with a little resourceful thinking and behavioural changes, they may be able to. Ask *"Why can't you?"* and you immediately impoverish the resourcefulness of team members.

Off they go to search through their mental files of *"Why I can't X?"* and up pops a reason or two to helpfully illustrate why they can't, and confirmation they were right all along. So, you see, they really can't do that thing, ok?

> "Why can't you get here on time?"
>
> "I can't because…"

> "Why can't you follow the correct procedure?"
>
> "I can't because…"

"Why can't you network more?"
"I can't because…"

"Why can't you contribute to team meetings?"
"I can't because…"

"Why can't you hit your KPIs?"
"I can't because…"

"Why can't you complete the report on time?"
"I can't because…"

"Why can't you sell more warranties?
"I can't because…"

"Why can't you come to team socials?"
"I can't because…"

These examples of the *World's Worst Question* all lead to responses of justification, reasons why it is not possible for the individual to do the thing they say they cannot do. They search for and present evidence to support their proposition of *"I can't do that thing…"*

So, what can a team manager do in *"I can't…"* situations to change a team member's mindset and drive performance? Fortunately, an empowering coaching method exists to break through restrictive thinking patterns. It is a solutions focused language pattern included within *Continue & Begin Fast Coaching®*, known as *Can't to Can Belief Busting®* (see **Can't to Can Belief Busting®** and **Freedom Questions**).

Further reading

Boomerang! Coach Your Team to Be the Best | Dandelion Digital, 2007 | Drake-Knight, N.

Fast Coaching. The Complete Guide to New Code Continue & Begin® | Dandelion Digital, 2016 | Drake-Knight, N. | Audible https://www.audible.co.uk/pd/Fast-Coaching-Audiobook/B07TTKD13T

The Motivation Agency | https://themotivationagency-online.com/course/begin

Can't to Can Belief Busting | Continue and Begin Ltd | Drake-Knight, N. | https://www.youtube.com/watch?v=yeb3nc7w2_8

Worry

"There is only one way to happiness and that is to cease worrying about things which are beyond the power of our will."

— Epictetus

Its normal and healthy to be concerned about challenging workplace matters.

Worry is our way of stimulating us to act on something of importance. It gets us primed, thinking through options and potential strategies. Psychologists refer to *foresight* as being helpful, it's a healthy mental activity embedded within us through evolution. It is a survival mechanism. Thinking ahead about possible threats to our safety is a human condition to support our livelihood.

It can go too far.

If worry is repetitive, ingrained, and excessive, it becomes a debilitating habit. When it impacts on our work performance, and more importantly on health, it's time to think about how to manage your anxiety. We can manage some worry habits ourselves. Self-help is a good starting point for moderate levels of anxiety.

This insight has helped me over the years; it comes from Michel de Montaigne, the 16th Century French philosopher:

"He who fears he shall suffer, already suffers what he fears. My life has been full of terrible misfortunes most of which never happened."

Most worry comes to nothing at all. Anxious thoughts are just thoughts.* You can change your thoughts (see **Stress management, patterns of healthy thinking**).

In chronic or severely acute cases health practitioners offer services which may be useful. Generalised Anxiety Disorder, or 'G.A.D.', is a condition therapists address. Cognitive behaviour therapy (CBT), mindfulness, meditation, hypnotherapy, rational emotive behaviour therapy (REBT), and other 'talking' support are effective for some people.

---

* With thanks to my friend Dr Daniel Zamir and the team at The Glendon Association https://www.glendon.org/ for insights on this management topic.

For many of us, worry is a self-generated habitual pattern. If we can influence a situation, then great, let's get on with taking preventative or remedial action. If we can't change a circumstance, we are in a state where Stoics (see **Stoicism**) will say,

"It is what it is, it will be what it will be."

Those wise old Stoics from ancient times were wrestling with worry, just as we do now. Stoic principles include, from Epictetus,

"It is not events which disturb men's minds, but their thinking about the events".

"Some things are within my control and others not".

From Marcus Aurelius,

"Today I escaped from anxiety. Or no, I discarded it because it was within me, in my own perceptions – not outside."

From Seneca

"I suffer more often in imagination than in reality".

In many cases of worry, the events haven't even happened yet, so just as de Montagne counselled us centuries ago, that's our imagination taking over.

How do you manage worry? Which ideas in this book would help you?

Further reading

9 Scientifically Backed Ways to Stop Worrying | The Huffington Post, 2013 | Chan, A. | https://www.huffingtonpost.co.uk/entry/stop-worrying-anxiety-cycle_n_4002914

Stop Feeding Your Worry: Understand and Overcome Anxious Thinking Habits | The Glendon Association, 2023 | Zamir, D. | https://www.glendon.org/shop/stop-feeding-your-worry-understand-and-overcome-anxious-thinking-habits/

Would you follow you?

"My own definition of leadership is this: The capacity and the
will to rally men and women to a common purpose
and the character which inspires confidence."

– Bernard Law Montgomery, 1st Viscount Montgomery of Alamein.

Would you follow you? Although this is a leadership question, remember, effective managers incorporate leadership traits to get the management job done.

Think about the great managers you've known (if you have known one?). What was it you admired? What behaviours, processes, or communication styles made a positive difference for you? What inspired you? What caused you to think,

"I feel motivated to follow my manager's ideas and plans. I'm
enthusiastically onboard with the direction we're going in".

What can you do to create the right conditions for your team members to enthusiastically follow you? Research into the attributes of motivational managers reveals common patterns of success.

Listed below is a sample of competences to stimulate your thinking. Which are strengths you excel in? Which could you develop to become an even better *Follow Me* manager?

This *40-Follow-Me Competences* self-assessment table is presented in *Rarely, Sometimes, Always,* format. Be as honest as you can, avoid being overly generous to yourself, or too harsh. None of us are perfect and remember this is a stimulus to aid self-awareness, nothing more. Maybe think about asking a colleague or two to help you with the assessment process?

Continue and Begin Ltd, 40-Follow-Me Competences

A. Achievement Focus	Rarely 1 2 3	Sometimes 4 5 6 7	Always 8 9 10
1. Inspires and motivates team members towards team direction and goals.			
2. Aligns team and individual task with purpose. Does everyone understand why we are doing this? Where we are going?			
3. Creates explicitly described standards of performance for team and team members.			
4. Gives clear direction, and goal specificity.			
5. Makes decisions and communicates them.			
6. Demonstrates enthusiasm for team goals.			
7. Assesses team performance against goals, celebrates successes, and improvement opportunities, and communicates to the team.			
8. Celebrates 'good', as well as 'excellent', performance.			
9. Translates opportunities into actions beneficial for the team.			
10. Regularly returns team focus to stated goal ambitions.			

B. Team Leadership	Rarely 1 2 3	Sometimes 4 5 6 7	Always 8 9 10
1. Promotes innovation. Asks team members for ideas to help solve problems and improve performance.			
2. Delegates authority to match responsibility, holds team members accountable for agreed commitments.			
3. Involves team members in decisions and team plans.			
4. Promotes productivity by being clear about output expectations.			
5. Creates a 'safe space' culture to encourage openness and frankness.			
6. Has regular keep-in-touch talks with each team member, face-to-face, or remotely.			
7. Supports team members to manage their work life balance.			
8. Applies appropriate level of pressure within the team, to leverage performance.			
9. Recognises early-stage conflict within the team and takes pre-emptive action.			
10. Reorganises team where necessary.			

C. Talent Development	Rarely 1 2 3	Sometimes 4 5 6 7	Always 8 9 10
1. Considers succession planning within the team.			
2. Promotes job enrichment and variety, to reduce staff turnover.			
3. Creates opportunities for team members to grow and develop professionally.			
4. Encourages team members to take the lead and drive results locally.			
5. Allocates work activities to suit each team member's skillset and personal motivators.			
6. Promotes sharing of expertise to support team and individual learning.			
7. Enables team member potential to take over new responsibilities, recognizing the Latent Potential in team members.			
8. Sets a personal example of continuing professional development.			
9. Celebrates team's continuing contribution to business goals.			
10. Presents business cases to budget holders, to secure CPD investment in team members.			

D. Influence Prowess	Rarely			Sometimes				Always		
	1	2	3	4	5	6	7	8	9	10
1. Leads, as well as manages.										
2. Self-presents with gravitas, stimulating respect and trust from others.										
3. Communicates effectively and comfortably with senior management.										
4. Communicates with confidence and charm, verbally, physiologically, and in writing.										
5. Has professional and elegant formal presentation skills. Has positive 'impact'.										
6. Is competent in Transactional Analysis and effective assertion techniques.										
7. Anticipates reactions and maintains momentum for team goals.										
8. Own 'receiver' skill and habit is as well-developed and refined as 'transmitter' skill and habit.										
9. Is aware of impact, and congruence or incongruence, of own 'Words, Song and Dance'.										
10. Makes decisions and implements.										

How did you do? Would you follow you?

Further reading

8 Behaviours of the World's Best Managers | Gallup, November 2019 | Pendell, R. | https://www.gallup.com/workplace/272681/habits-world-best-managers.aspx

Leadership Brand: Would you follow you? (Part 1) | Medium, December 2020 | Pestelos, I. | https://medium.com/move-the-average-up/leadership-brand-would-you-follow-you-part-1-d616a18084e

X

X Factor management and leadership

His encore is always the best bit!

"It isn't positions which lend distinction,
but men who enhance positions." – *Agesilaus*

Some managers seem to have an intangible presence about them, a special kind of competence we find compelling. Maybe it's their communication style, or their ability to calmly deal with challenging situations, their analytical skills, or how they bring the best out of people. They have an aura about them which inspires confidence from team members and peers.

Do they have a special kind of magic? A wizardry? Of course not. There is no magic, only structure (see **Structure of Well-Done-Ness®**).

X Factor management and leadership has a structure, there's a construct going on, a combination of behaviours creating a sense of management excellence. Some exemplars of effective team management are fully aware of the component parts to their wizardry, and how they use them.

Others, maybe the majority, are partially aware of their behaviours and why they employ their concoction of tactics in getting the best from their teams. Some aspects of their behaviours are unknown to them, they may be *unconsciously competent*. Modelling could help raise their awareness of how they excel (see **Modelling excellence**) and create *conscious competence*. Their methods can be codified and taught to others, perhaps to junior managers within an organisation.

A question for readers to consider may be,

"How can I learn and exhibit X Factor management and leadership?"

The answer is contained to some extent in this book. The structure of X Factor is a combination of component parts, like building blocks, constructed in different forms to suit each circumstance. It can be learnt.

There is no magic, only structure.

The more your read, the more you'll know. The more you know, the more you can implement. The more you implement, the more feedback loop learning you'll benefit from. The more feedback loop learning you experience the more you can hone your skills and adapt to each new situation (see **Agile management**).

The starting point is learning. Reading. Watching. Listening. Modelling. Applying new knowledge and absorbing from the feedback loop. It can take time to build X Factor levels of competence, but it *can* be developed.

You've already started the process by digesting knowledge from this book and beginning your journey to becoming an X Factor team manager.

Leaders are readers.

Further reading

20 Leadership Qualities that Make a Great Leader (With Tips) | uk.indeed.com, 2022 | Wike, E.

Leading | Hodder and Stoughton, 2015 | Ferguson, A., Moritz, M.

What Makes a "Great" Manager? | Dare 2 Dream Ltd, July 2023 | Gardiner, J. | https://johngardiner.substack.com/p/what-makes-a-great-manager

Y

Yes Sets, building confidence in others

"When you first went to kindergarten… this matter of learning letters
and numbers seemed to be a big insurmountable task. To recognise
the letter A, to tell a Q from an O was very, very difficult… But you
learned to form a mental image of some kind."

– Milton Erickson

Dmitri (Dmitry Nikolaevich) Udnadze was a Georgian psychologist who explored how repetitive mental habits create embedded patterns of thinking.

Udnadze is famous for his experiment presenting a pair of spheres of marginally different size to his research students. He asked each student to identify which was the smaller sphere and which the larger. The tests were repeated numerous times until the subjects were presented with spheres of equal size. Participants continued to think in comparative terms and again identified one sphere as being larger, one smaller. Udnadze suggested there exists a tendency to continue along a line of repetitive thinking, as habit forming.

A *Yes Set* capitalises on this form of repetitive thinking. Therapists use *Yes Sets* to build trust and suggestibility, aiding therapeutic interventions.

Yes Sets are used in sales organisations to encourage a potential customer to maintain a momentum of 'yes' statements leading up to, and including, the closing question of *"And so, would you like to place the order now?"*.

In organisational people development *Yes Sets* are valuable in strengthening self-esteem, self-worth, and self-image.

For example, *Yes Sets* in an adapted form are used in *Continue & Begin Fast Coaching®*, where the coachee is encouraged to identify a series of recent successes to encourage feelings of resourcefulness; the *Continue To* behaviours. A *Yes Set* is used to build a momentum of positive self-assessment thinking.

In one-to-one and team dynamics a *Yes Set* is a healthy way to stimulate positive thought patterns. I've used *Yes Sets* successfully in team performance scenarios. Here's a (very) simple illustration,

"OK, so let's think back over January. What good things did we achieve this month? What's gone well? Great! What else? Excellent! Let's think through some more achievements.... Yes, that's another success. Congrats on that one... What else? Amazing! Feel good about what we've done? Yes? Quite right too! Which successes could we continue to do well through February? And what new ambitions should we consider?"

How could you use *Yes Sets* in your team manager role?

Further reading,

International Bureau of Education | *PROSPECTS: The Quarterly Review of Comparative Education* (Paris, UNESCO: International Bureau of Education) vol. 24, no.3/4, 1994, p. 687-701 UNESCO: International Bureau of Education, 2002.

The Psychology of Set | Uznadze. D.N. | Translated by Basil Haigh. | New York: Plenum Publishing Corporation, 1966. | Published online by Cambridge University Press, January 2018.

Z

Zzzzz – REM sleep

"Even a soul submerged in sleep is hard at work;
and helps make something of the world." – *Heraclitus*

Get plenty of sleep, it is nutritious for mind and body.

A good 'solid 8' of sleep each night would be wonderful, wouldn't it? Not everyone can manage that, for physical or environmental reasons. According to sleep expert Matthew Walker (2018) any sleep is good, even a nap. Sleep can reduce anxiety, lower blood pressure, and help with learning retention.

A full night of sleep includes a series of different types of sleep, repeated several times during a full night of slumber. First up is introductory light sleep, followed by deeper sleep and then a return to 'almost awake' rapid eye movement sleep, or dream sleep, before cascading back down into the deep sleep phase again. Each cycle of deep sleep, to REM sleep, and back to deep sleep, is typically of around 90 minutes duration, and is repeated a few times each night.

According to sleep psychologists, REM (rapid eye movement) sleep is especially good for us. REM sleep was first identified by scientists when sleeping babies were observed to have periods when their eyes moved rapidly side to side during slumbers.

Research has since revealed REM sleep to be close to the waking state, when eye movements, breathing patterns, and heart rates are close to those during normal daytime functioning. Brain functioning is particularly active during REM phases of sleep. This is markedly different to the deep non-REM periods when deep sleep features slower breathing, reduced heart rate, and partial muscle tone relaxation, sometimes known as Slow Wave Sleep (SWS).

REM periods occur typically 4 to 6 times during a full night's sleep, the first of which may begin around 90 minutes after falling asleep and is then repeat every 90 to 120 minutes. REM periods become gradually longer, and more frequent, as a full night of sleep progresses.

Here's an approximation of a typical night of sleep with REM and SWS described,

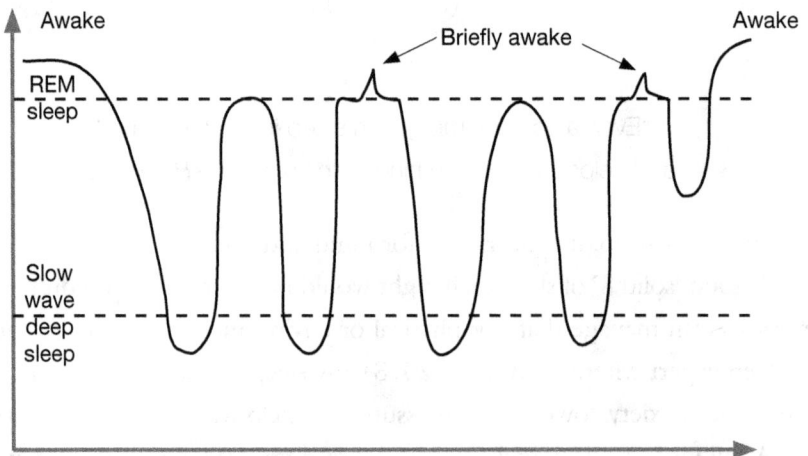

There is still debate about the genetic purpose of REM sleep. There appears a consensus amongst researchers of a processing benefit, of REM helping us make sense of the world, and playing a role in memory consolidation. It seems valuable then, for us to get our daily dose of rejuvenating sleep, including as many REM periods as we need.

Broken sleep, or simply insufficient long periods asleep, will impact on our ability to process the world and our experiences within it. We've all had times, perhaps extended periods, where we have not had enough sleep. We feel jaded, irritable, forgetful, maybe confused during these times – because we haven't had sufficient REM processing time.

So, even if the benefits of REM sleep may be a useful fiction (see **Useful fiction**), if it encourages us to avoid burning the candle at both ends – not always possible in our busy family and work lives – getting a regular decent night of sleep seems beneficial to our wellbeing and performance.

Alcohol, and especially a heavy drinking session, is an inhibitor to healthy sleep, and is known to impact of REM phases. This is why I tease training delegates to be careful about alcohol consumption post-event.

No surprise, caffeine also has a detrimental effect on sleep quality; it blocks our sleep machinery from acting efficiently. Its best to avoid caffeine content well before bedtime because it lingers in our body system for many hours. Caffeine has a half-life (is half as strong) of around 5 hours, so a caffeinated coffee at 12 noon still has 50% presence in our body system at 5pm, and 25% at 10pm. That's something to think about.

Strategies for improving the chances of a good restorative night of sleep, recommended by experts, include,

- Be habitual, go to bed at the same time each night if possible.
- Limit caffeine, alcohol, nicotine, other drugs.
- Exercise, well before bedtime though.
- Write down your worries, empty your mind of them.
- Avoid laptop, tv, or phone screens, immediately before bedtime.
- Darken your environment an hour before bedtime, prepare your mind for impending sleep.
- Keep your sleep area dark (think dark cave).
- Keep your sleep area cool to allow to reduce body temperature (think cool cave).

- If you wake up and can't get back to sleep after 30 minutes, perhaps thinking about something on your mind, get up for a short while, break the spell of rumination and then go back to bed, re-programmed for sleep.

At the conclusion of training seminars and conference events I encourage delegates, if they wish to absorb and apply their learning experience, to adopt the above principles. It seems a shame to retain an impoverished version of the learning due to insufficient quality sleep.

As you read parts of this book, you'll need deep and REM sleep to make sense of your new knowledge, so tomorrow you're ready for another day of exceptionally productive team management.

Further reading

Why We Sleep: The New Science of Sleep and Dreams | Penguin, 2018 | Walker, M.

Sleep is Your Superpower | TED Talk, 2019 | Matt Walker | https://youtu.be/5MuIMqhT8DM

NHS Every Mind Matters | https://www.nhs.uk/every-mind-matters/mental-health-issues/sleep/

Reflections

"The ignorant man affirms
The scientist doubts
The wise man reflects".

– Aristotle

I hope you've enjoyed this book of management ideas.

Take a while to enjoy looking out of the window, feet up and your phone on silent. Skim read the book again. Maybe notice some ideas you missed the first time. Or choose a random letter from the alphabet and discover where it takes you?

Now, let your imagination begin to wonder... you may be curious to know *how* changes will begin, and how *soon* you'll notice a difference in your behaviours. In the days and weeks ahead, you will be surprised and delighted to discover *new patterns* in your management style.

Enjoy your journey.

NDK
Andros, 2024

And to follow...

"I do not insist this is a full adventure,
but it is the beginning of one,
for this is the way adventures begin."
– Miguel de Cervantes Saavedra

As a *pattern which connects*, it doesn't get more tenuous than referencing a 400-year-old literary classic. Miguel de Cervantes wrote his masterpiece *The Ingenious Hidalgo Don Quixote of La Mancha* in two parts. Part 1 was published in 1605, covering Quixote's first two adventures as a Knight Errant.

Cervantes offered a concluding tease from the book's narrator,

> "These were the verses that were legible; since the others were worm-eaten, they were handed to an academician for him to decipher. It is reported that he has done so, after long vigils and much toil, and that he intends to publish them, as we await Don Quixote's third sally."

Part 2 of Don Quixote and his squire Sancho Panza's adventures wasn't published until 1615, ten years after Part 1. So, in the spirit of Cervantes, a note here to suggest… an update to *Alphabet Management* may take a while.

In the meantime, you can direct your own learning. Where will you go next, to expand your knowledge?

Further reading

The Ingenious Hidalgo Don Quixote of La Mancha |
Penguin Classics, 2003 | Cervantes, M., Rutherford, J. (translator).

Acknowledgements

My thanks to,

Katy Loffman and Lesley Pollinger at Paper Lion Ltd for their encouragement and wisdom, through Covid and beyond, to persevere and make *Alphabet Management* happen.

Jonathan Baker at Seagull Design for his patience and expertise in preparing this book in such a professional format.

Dame Irene Lucas-Hays, DBE, DL for her kind Foreword.

Simon Hiorns, for his generous contribution *On Growing Managers*, and the pleasure of working together over so many years to develop a successful organisation.

Rupert Besley for his fun illustrations.

Chantal Orlik, Ian Luxford, and the team at The Motivation Agency for incisive perspectives.

My good friend Brian Mayne, for creating and sharing his *Goal Mapping*® method, and our too infrequent chats over coffee.

Mike Notman at Bourton Group for his tutorship and steerage.

Rebecca Braund and Mike Janvrin for insights into the health and social care sector and patterns of relevance for commercial managers.

Mike King for reminders on performance strategies within elite teams.

Steve O'Neill for introducing me to his *CLEAR*® model of personal and professional effectiveness.

Gareth Ellis, Byron Coleman, and Sergio Kulikovsky, at Teemill Tech for their manufacturing advice and photography expertise.

My friends at The Glendon Association for their long-standing warmth and support.

Frank Farrelly, who taught me over lunch the importance of communicating with *"…an open heart, a twinkle in the eye, and a smile around your lips"*. And to keep motorcycling until at least 75 years old.

Gregory Bateson, whom I never met, and yet feel such gratitude towards, for introducing the most valuable personal development resource of all, that of *patterns which connect*.

To other writers and teachers from whom I have learnt and continue to learn from.

To the characters and personalities included in this book, thank you for contributing to my learning and growth.

And finally, a thank you to the thousands of managers I have worked alongside, or supported in the development of their management careers, over so many years. I have learnt far more from you, than you from me.

NDK

Andros, 2024

Case Study

On Growing Managers [and our Business]

Simon Hiorns, President, Protyre Motorsport

I was fortunate to be given the opportunity to develop a retail business from a base of 16 tyre fitting garages with 200 team members. Over 15 years we grew largely by acquisition, to 184 autocentres with 1648 colleagues, offering a full range of tyre, mechanical and EV services.

Here is a brief overview of our journey.

I joined Micheldever Tyres in June 2007 as Retail Director. A year earlier the business was bought by Graphite Capital. At that time the retail arm of Micheldever Tyres (Protyre) was run with the support of local entrepreneurs across the 16 locations, all of whom left within 12 months. We had a highly respected local business with no leadership.

My role was to develop a retail business of 100+ centres.

Stage 1 – Create a clear vision and guidelines to work within and communicate this to the team.

We used the NDK Performance Model® as our framework,

CONTINUE&BEGIN LTD

To be clear, we were at the base level with no consistent policies, operating procedures or even health and safety guidelines. We worked with the very knowledgeable operators we had, to agree and set our *Explicit Standards.*

Our focus at this time was creating clarity and consistency around the way in which we presented our business, did our jobs, and interacted with both internal and external customers. Once everyone was bought into our *Explicit Standards,* we wrote them down.

We could then start to set goals for the business. At the senior management level this covered a three-year time span (what was the direction of travel), at operational level this became at set of monthly KPI's and an annual plan (sales, costs, profit contribution) with SMART objectives. Operationally delivering the short-term plan was vital to our long-term goals, bearing in mind we were working in a Private Equity environment.

We wrote down our values as *Care, Honesty, Expertise and Trust.* At this stage they were simply words

We held our first conference in the lounge area of The Hampshire Golf Club near Andover. The 16 Centre Managers attended.

Stage 2 – Develop our leadership structure and our leaders to support a growing business.

This was the tough bit. Writing down *Explicit Standards* and your vision and goals is the easy bit. Most companies are good at it (and put it up on the wall).

If we wanted to move off the base layer of the *NDK Performance Model®* and deliver *Consistency* and *Sustainability* we needed to develop and attract a group of leaders to deliver it. We knew what type of leaders we wanted: a positive mindset, prolific communicators, people-orientated individuals, who were results focused. We were looking for authentic, empathetic, and adaptable leaders.

One thing we were certain about was that what we had written down, would need to be adapted.

To offer some context: the industry at that stage had many so-called 'leaders' who actually *managed* a set of short-term goals and KPIs. Many were asked to support up to 20 centre managers. They were the score keepers, the police, auditors, compliance officers, or as I would describe them 'clipboard warriors.'

We wanted to develop a different business and leadership model. In our model our senior leaders would be supporting 12 centres and would be expected to develop their teams as well as developing their businesses.

Our senior team all came from the garage sector and most from the workshop itself; technically very good but with little or no management or leadership training and low confidence in their academic ability or their ability to learn.

I have had the pleasure of watching academically nervous individuals grow into confident leaders with an appetite for learning and personal development. Many have gone beyond internal support we provided to take on external qualifications including level 5 apprenticeships in Operational Leadership (equivalent to a degree!).

Nick Drake-Knight has supported our business at organisational level and at individual level since 2010. Nick understood our framework and developed a programme to support our journey. We meet as a group once a year and twice a year every member of the senior management team has a personal 1:1. Each time we met with Nick we had a clear purpose and our group meetings set the agenda for the year ahead.

My role as leader was to set the tone for our business, a positive attitude with belief and optimism, a can-do attitude, fast paced and supportive. Throughout our journey we communicated prolifically our goals, our successes, and our challenges. It was important our *words, songs and dance* matched our ambition. In time the senior team language changed from 'why are we?' going through this change programme, introducing a new system, and new ways of working to 'how can we help deliver?' the new way.

NDK helped us understand where were and where we were going. From *forming* through *storming*, to *norming*, and ultimately *performing*, via *Can't to Can* attitudes, *resistor busting*, *the obstacle is the way* (and many more) he helped, as we looked to develop and grow. At operational level the *Continue and Begin*® coaching philosophy enabled us to deliver fast positive coaching to our customer facing teams, that they bought into.

This is when we started to achieve *Consistency* and *Sustainability*.

Protyre is now a national business with industry leading customer service and employee engagement. In March 2023 we had a 5-Star Trust Pilot rating from close to 100,000 reviews and a Gallup 12 score of 75.4*

Following extensive consumer, customer and colleague research conducted by an external marketing agency our values were confirmed as **Caring, Honesty and Expertise**. The research company stated they very rarely come across a business where their values were delivered so well at operational level.

Our most recent conference was held at the NEC with over 200 delegates as we launched our new brand image.

Simon Hiorns
President of Protyre Motorsport

---

* 75.4 is based on results from research calculated from employee engagement responses to 12 questions, modelled on the Gallup Q12® approach.

Appendix 1

Continue & Begin Fast Coaching®: its application in call centre operations

Q&A Podcast transcript from www.callcentrehelper.com

Charlie Mitchell: You have a technique for contact centre coaching called Continue & Begin Fast Coaching. What does this involve?

Nick Drake-Knight: So, you're right, Charlie. Continue & Begin Fast Coaching's been around for a while. It's used extensively in contact centre operations. It's used by class-leading brands every day across the world these days, and for some years now we've been working with global brands helping them to sustain their preferred processes, their performance standards, and behaviours. And we do that through fast coaching. So, the success of Continue & Begin Fast Coaching lies really in its positivity, and the speed of its application. It drives up performance and crucially it does it quickly. The emphasis, the essence rather, of Continue & Begin is an emphasis on celebration. And we celebrate the call centre team member's successes first, and then we build on that confidence, and we do that … crucially, we do that before we start thinking about development plans, and personal improvement.

A core skill of an effective Continue & Begin coach is to make careful use of language during the coaching processes, which initially stimulates that success celebration. And what we do is we use specific language patterns which are helpful in the coaching process. We also identify and isolate during training programmes some key phrases and patterns that are less helpful in the coaching context.

Charlie Mitchell: I think the key bit there is to celebrate advisor successes, and do you think this is something that sometimes contact centres don't do enough because they feel like, oh, we have to give them some sort of reward, not just a simple thank you, which might even suffice?

Nick Drake-Knight: Well, it's more about the emphasis on improvement, Charlie. I've been doing this a very long time and experienced lots of different development programmes. It seems to me that too many organizations are quick to get onto the development and the improvement ladder as a first step. Now what we know from heaps of research is that when people are being coached, certainly in the early phases, maybe the first time that they've been coached, they're feeling pretty vulnerable, pretty fragile. And I guess what we do in Continue & Begin is we start by strengthening that confidence, that ego, so that they're strong enough, they feel good enough, they feel powerful enough, resourceful enough to be able to take on additional development opportunities. But to start with that initially, how can we improve, it seems to me that that's not a very helpful way of operating.

So, you're right, the essence of it, the emphasis initially, is let's celebrate successes, let's feel good about the things that you're already doing well in your role in a contact centre. And now when your ego's strong, you're feeling powerful, you're feeling resourceful, now we can start talking about how we might want to do just one or two things a little bit differently, and perhaps even better. But let's not start with that, let's start by helping people feel good.

Charlie Mitchell: Interesting. So, do you think the starting approach of making people feel good is one of the reasons why Continue & Begin is different?

Nick Drake-Knight: Well, there's a number of reasons why it's different, but that's one of the primary ones. It's because it makes people feel good. So essentially there are four things that make Continue & Begin different. The first is that it's fast. So, it's a far quicker coaching approach than most established methodologies. Many coaching methods, they require anything from sort of 20 minutes to over an hour to create a meaningful change plan for an individual coachee in a call centre. Now with Continue & Begin we can get substantial impact in less than two minutesf and a really comprehensive change strategy within five or six minutes, depending obviously on the call centre environment and the complexity of the coachee's ambitions. There's the first thing, it's really fast.

The second, as I alluded to just now, it makes people feel good. So, call centre employees are much more likely to take on fresh challenges and new goals when they're in the state of confidence and personal feel-good. And the starting point for a successful Continue & Begin Fast Coaching session is to focus on the coachee's recent successes and a celebration of performance, when that's measured, of course, against some kind of previously agreed standards, or rules, or ambitions. What we do, Charlie, is emphasize existing competence and capability, so the coachee's stimulated through this process to recognize their self-worth and their self-image. And we enhance the ego and personal competence. So, if you contrast that, a person who's got some sort of impoverished self-perception, they're much less likely to feel confident and capable or willing to take on further stretch. That's the second reason, the feel-good.

Third is that it's content-free. So, there's no industry- or environment-specific jargon or set of references. Continue & Begin's used in a diverse range of circumstances, way beyond call centres and contact centres. Because it's so flexible, there are very few, if any, scenarios where a contact centre coachee can't be helped to further his or her competencies. So, the core framework remains the same, whatever the environment, but it's content-free; we can put anything through this method.

And finally, I guess what makes a difference is the language patterns are carefully crafted. So, we talk about how the questions are specific and we use words like specificity to elicit responses that aid the coachee in achieving her ambitions, so that these patterns come from transformational grammar or other linguistic sciences, and they stimulate personal growth.

So those are the four things that make it different. It's fast, it makes people feel good, it's content-free, we can use it with anything, and the language patterns are very carefully constructed. It's those four things together that makes Continue & Begin different.

We'll help brands to map out and design their preferred behaviour patterns for call centre staff. We do that at the front end of the programme, especially around customer service and sales patterns, and of course, whatever processes and guided conversations that form part of the call centre operations. So, we talk about making sure the expectations around employee performance are presented as what we call explicitly described standards that everyone can understand. So, there's no ambiguity. And once these have been trained out in the call centre to the team members, once they've been trained out, then we can start coaching people around those standards.

Most of the world-class operators that we've worked with over the years use what I call the NDK Performance Model. So, if you can imagine a triangle with four levels, so at the bottom, level one, we've got explicit standards. These explicitly describe a set of performance standards that spell out exactly what is expected of employees. The approach applies irrespective of the discipline or the industry sector. People need to know what's expected of them if they're going to work to a given standard, so let's make them explicit, there's the starting point.

And then the second part is about achieving consistency. I go around the world and I meet with call centre leaders and they tell me they get frustrated about inconsistency, that they've got some pockets of excellence, parts of the organization, parts of the operation where performance and individual standards delivery is exemplary, and they'll say that that's good. But it's far from comprehensive. In fact, most of them say, Charlie, that the majority of their people are sort of doing okay. And then they sadly tell me they have a few pits of despair, where folk, no matter what support they've got, just don't seem to be able to deliver to the high standards of those pockets of excellence.

But here's the thing, we can create the consistency temporarily through effective training. Temporarily. Consistency is of limited value if it's only temporary, because what we know is, performance excellence is going to be delivered day in, day out, long after the latest training initiative has been launched. And I'm going to say this, in some organizations, and surprisingly some really impressive organizations, training is like throwing mud against the wall. Most of the mud slides off the wall immediately and leaves a puddle of brown water, a little bit of sediment on the wall, but most of it slides off. And when people leave the training room, you can see the learning falling off them as they walk out the door. And I've got to say, sometimes they get back to work and the line manager will ask them, *"What was training like?"* And they'll say, *"Well, lunch was good."*

So training's great, and it achieves consistency, but it only does it temporarily, that's the reality of it, but don't let anybody from L&D hear that story. Unless, and this is where we get with coaching, Charlie, unless we can sustain that new knowledge. We can do two things, if we can do these two things then suddenly the training becomes monstrously successful, just uber successful. Here's the first thing, first thing is the training has to turn knowledge into skill, into behaviours. If we can do that as a starting point, the second thing is having created that changed behaviour, can we sustain it, can we keep it going? Can that call centre agent, that operator, can that team member deliver the new behaviours, the new skills that they've learned every day, every week, every month, every quarter, every year with every call? Because if they can do that, if they can sustain that new knowledge, that new learning, suddenly the training is exceptionally valuable.

And the way that we do that is through coaching, but it has to be local coaching, and it has to be local team leaders who keep the momentum up and the training alive. Otherwise, it's a coach who flies in every week or two weeks to do some kind of momentum work. Much better if it's the local team leader who's doing that on a daily basis. So that's level three, if you like, to sustainability. So, we've got level one, the explicit standards. Level two, the consistency achieved through training. Level three is the sustainability through coaching. And level four, the tiny little bit right at the top of the triangle, I call it QCI. Certainly, your listeners from a quality background will be familiar with it from Total Quality Management days, QCI, the Quest for Continuous Improvement. And that's about saying that what's good today is not good enough for tod so what can we do to improve our service proposition to even higher levels? And what we do in that scenario is we get the people involved in the discussion.

So, there we are, that's in my view the answer to your question, as it fits with call centre standards. It's about creating those explicit standards, it's about creating consistency of delivery, it's about sustaining them, and it's about continually looking to see how it could be improved. Does that answer your question?

Charlie Mitchell: It does, indeed, and I think it was very interesting, those four levels, because these four levels can go beyond the Continue & Begin and just for any coaching programme that anybody puts into place. But just focusing again on Continue & Begin, how is that kind of structured within the contact centre?

Nick Drake-Knight: Well, I guess the clue's in the title, Charlie, Continue & Begin. So let's start with the *continue to*. What we do is, we identify a set of productive positive behaviours that are exhibited by the coachee and that relate to a given set of known standards, those explicit standards on level one. And then we can help the team member celebrate her existing or evolving excellence. And by doing that we can build an ego strong enough for her to take on further personal development ambitions in the form of guess what? The *begin to* commitment. It's essential that the *continue to*s are self-identified by the coachee, so it's a self-assessment process, self-evaluative, and the evaluation on the self-assessment is against those explicit standards.

So once again, it's critical that the organization maps out what's expected so that the individual team member can then self-assess against those standards to see how they're getting on. Rather than, and this is a real bee in my bonnet, rather than being told by the coach. There's a massive difference between coaching and providing feedback. I'm really not into that. Self-awareness is the beginning of this. When people are self-aware, they're much more likely to move forward. Being told, and told, and told, and told is a really inefficient way of helping people grow. So, this is a ... if you like, it's a key differential, and it's at the core of Continue & Begin Fast Coaching.

It's imperative the coachee is empowered by self-reflection, and our goal as Continue & Begin practitioners is to arouse, if you like, a strong psychological sense of resourcefulness and confidence before she embarks on her plans for improvement. So that's the first of the structure, the *continue to*.

You'll recognize the second part clearly as the *begin to*s, and these are developmental. In many coaching methodologies, this is in my view wrongly the starting point. In Continue & Begin we don't even consider improvement, or self-development, or remedial work until a set of continued successes have been loudly hailed and celebrated to strengthen the individual self-perceptions up. Once we've got a coachee confident, then we can activate the *begin to* phase with a small set of targeted specific ambitions. Not too many. The number of the *begin to*s identified is deliberately kept to a modest number, so a maximum of three ambitions for change, and in many cases I prefer just one or two key ones.

So the rationale, I guess, Charlie, for this, is sort of based on the short-term memory capacity, and the ability of people to consciously consider new ideas during performance. Sometimes we hear about people being asked to do loads of things differently; they can't compute it in their short-term memory, on the desktop, if you like, of their mind. Therapists understand this. They call it performance anxiety. It's exacerbated by overload. And there's also research by a fellow called George Miller who investigated that. So, in Continue & Begin, we ask the coachee to focus on just a few new ways of operating. And then in the personal development plan, we ask them to concentrate just a little bit, but it makes sense for those ambitions, if they are only going to have a few of them, to be significant and value-adding, not trivial. If you're only going to have a few, let's make sure they're really juicy ones.

So that's the way we go about the structure. The *continue to* is to celebrate, and then the *begin to* is for the developmental piece.

Charlie Mitchell: Excellent. And I think there's one bit there that I really want to pick up on, and that's the maintaining sustainability in training, because I'm sure you've witnessed training classes where maybe two weeks later advisors have only remembered 10% of what was taught during that class. How can we do a better job in sustaining training in the long run?

Nick Drake-Knight: Well, you're absolutely right, and in terms of the call centre colleagues that's true. But think about it from an organizational point of view as well. Think about it, if you're a senior player in an organization and you put together some significant investment in developing the training programme, and getting people to operate in new ways, fabulous new pieces of equipment are being used, but it's not sustained. And as you say, a week, two weeks, a couple of months, maybe a year after, people have resorted to their old ways, or the impact is not what it was intended to be. And the senior player in the organization, the sponsor, the investor quite reasonably says, "Well, hang on a minute, didn't we do something on this earlier in the year? We put a significant amount of energy into this, and it's not having the impact." Well, no, because the training is not sustained, the new behaviours are not sustained. The coaching piece isn't in place, or the coaching piece is so tortuous and so unpopular that people do everything to avoid it.

It's crucial that we get this bit right. Training's great at creating consistency, but it's of limited value if it's temporary. What we're going to do is to create a coaching philosophy, and a skill set that allows local managers to keep the plates spinning long after the training event has passed. Sustainability through local coaching, local managers, keeps that momentum up and the training alive. So as long as the coaching experience is helpful, as long as it's not too onerous, and dare I say, as long as it's enjoyable, people can start to enjoy celebrating the things that they're doing well, feeling good about their successes, and being hopeful and anticipatory about the things that they might be able to do in the future that will make their performance even better than it already is. When you can do that, then the training can be sustained in the long run.

Charlie Mitchell: I guess having a clear coaching philosophy, as you say, though, goes halfway to answering my next question, actually. But I did want to ask, what advice do you have for changing employee mindsets and getting them excited about coaching?

Nick Drake-Knight: Well, yeah, you're right, some way through that, but let's just think about this. I mentioned it earlier; too often Charlie, coaching is camouflaged in name because it's really feedback, and feedback isn't coaching. And too many folk have been through that painful experience of being told, often with best intention, that there are things they're doing well, and things that they should, need to, have to, got to, ought to improve on. Feedback is didactic, it's an imposition of will, it's forceful. It should not be about that. We've got to change that perception, because coaching becomes popular, people enjoy it, they get a buzz out of it, they're saying,

"Hey, why haven't I had a coaching session recently?" They start to operate in this really dynamic, forward-thinking developmental way when it's experienced as a positive, value-adding, ego-strengthening activity. Because when people feel good, when they leave the coaching conversation feeling better than when they started, that's when organizational culture begins to change.

We know people grow best, they develop best, when they want to. Not when they're forced to. When the focus starts with a celebration of success, we change the thinking paradigm. When we focus on what's wrong in our lives, we shut out positivity and opportunity. When we start by focusing on what's not being done properly, we shut down that enthusiasm. Transfer this reality to the world of coaching and we create this kind of stunted thinking and limited possibilities. In fact, there's some recent research in the last few years analysing brain image patterns, and it highlights how important it is to think productively about potential outcomes rather than current limitations. And this is the essence of Continue & Begin Fast Coaching. And you can read the research at Harvard Business Review. There's a number of pieces there, but essentially it illuminates, and it emphasizes that thinking in a positive developmental sense is far more productive in terms of changed behaviour than identifying what's not being done so well.

Charlie Mitchell: There's a number of interesting points there that you mentioned, and one of them was that a lot of the existing coaching models aren't even coaching models at all, but they're ways of giving feedback. So, I'm thinking two stars and a wish, or there's a model itself called the GROW model, and that's not actually helping people learn, that's just a way of giving people feedback through real-time coaching. I thought that was a very interesting point before I move on to another thing that I've heard you speak about, and that is something called the *"But Monster"* in a previous presentation. Do you just want to let our listeners know what you mean by this?

Nick Drake-Knight: Yeah, sure, and just before we do that, I don't want to diss other coaching models because, generally speaking, they all have a place, it's just that I believe that they're not always as productive as they could be. I think they're too lengthy. I think they're convoluted. And I don't think they have the same rapid impact, and I don't think they make people feel as good as Continue & Begin, but let's not diss them.

So yeah, the But Monster. Yeah, this is fun, listen to this language pattern, okay? Call centre, right? *"Well, you did pretty well on that call, some of the things you did were … they were helpful."* Now, Charlie, what word is coming next? What is it I'm about to say?

Charlie Mitchell: "But …"

Nick Drake-Knight: Yeah, see you know, we know intuitively, we understand the next word's going to be *but.* Let's run it again. *"You did pretty well on that call. Some of the things you did were … well, they were helpful."* You just know the next word's going to be *but,* don't you? So, but here's the interesting bit, how did you know? How did you know? Well, here's the thing. You know because of the tonality of my voice, you know because … well, if you could see me, you'd know because of the physiology that I illustrate with my facial expression, and my breathing patterns, and everything else. And you've heard and experienced these types of communicating many times in the past, Charlie, haven't you?

Charlie Mitchell: Too many.

Nick Drake-Knight: You know that the next word that's coming out is going to be a *but.* Now, what's coming after the *but?* Well, you know, you understand, intuitively you know the next thing that's going to be coming out is some form of criticism, some form of request for change, some sort of negative vibe. And you're getting ready for it. So just try it again. *"You did pretty well on that call, some of the things you did were … well, they were helpful."* You know a *but's* coming, Charlie, don't you?

Charlie Mitchell: Yeah.

Nick Drake-Knight: But you know that after the *but* there's going to be some request for change, it's what I call the But Monster and it's coming to bite you on the buttock.

So, the But Monster, what it does, it stops people from feeling good, and it gets them ready for some impending pain. Which is absolutely *not* what we want to do for Continue & Begin Fast Coaching. So, remember, we want people to feel good. And if you start to use the word *but*, all of those natural downward inflections in the voice, all of the physiology and the tonality gives the game away before you even say the word *but*, and then inevitably is that request for change.

So, my guidance to you, and I think in the piece that I wrote for you so many years ago, remove the But Monster from your coaching vocabulary, change the way that you help people to change. And if you want them to operate in a different way, use a different way of communicating. I remember in the first piece I wrote for you all those years ago about the But Monster, there were people writing in and saying, *"Well it's okay saying don't use the But Monster, but what can we use?"* Well, there's a great way of operating; instead of using the But Monster, we use the word *and*. And we keep the tonality up, we keep the facial expressions and everything else about the body language really positive. So here it goes, back in the call centre coaching session, *"Hey, Charlie, some of the things on that call this morning were fantastic. You've done some great stuff. And what would be really great as we progress is if you could also make the change."*

Now, you're hearing this, there's still a request for change, and instead of the But Monster, there's an and. You may not even have heard it, it was slick, right? It was quick. So, there's a difference between the But Monster and *and*. *And* you can use a similar approach if you like. *And* instead of using *and* we simply break the sentence into two with a full stop and a deep breath and a swallow in the middle of the two ideas, the current idea, the current performance, and the future idea, the future performance. Here it goes, *"Hey, Charlie, some of the things on that call this morning were fantastic. You've done some really great stuff."* Full stop, deep breath, swallow. *"And what'd be really great as we progress is if you could also ... "* You get the idea?

Charlie Mitchell: Yeah.

Nick Drake-Knight: We have the first idea, and we just simply stop, *"You've done some great stuff."* Full stop, deep breath, swallow. *"What would be really* *great as we progress is if you could also ...*" So, the *and*, and the full stop. With the increased upward tonality, the positive physiology, everything around that, we simply avoid the But Monster. It's a technique used extensively, by the way, in therapeutic contexts. Because some therapists know that *but* can jolt a patient out of feelings of comfort and relaxation. In fact, what it does, it creates anxiety. That's why they avoid the But Monster. And we don't want our Continue & Begin Fast Coaching team members feeling anxious, because anxiety is an inhibitor to learning.

Charlie Mitchell: Excellent stuff, and I think that's not only a piece of advice for contact centre coaches, but maybe that's something that can be taught to advisors as well to make sure they don't pass any feelings of anxiety on to customers, so I think it's all around a brilliant tip. And just picking up on that emotional aspect of these feelings of anxiety and things, that we hear a lot about how we should behave as advisors in terms of creating an emotional connection with customers. What advice do you have for advisors, for coaches wanting to teach advisors, for creating emotional connections with customers?

Nick Drake-Knight: Well, firstly, you're absolutely right, the But Monster and the avoidance of it is transferable to the world of communication with customers. And a lot of my work around customer service and sales work, we focus in on language patterns and the impact it has on people at an emotional level. So you're absolutely right, the two think together. So in my book *Meerkat Selling* and also my most recent book, *Fast Coaching*, I talk about something called the Emotional Driver. And what we have here is the reason for all human behaviour. That sounds pretty profound, and it's true. Everything we do is driven by an urge for feeling, and it's a truism, that all human behaviour has a positive intent. Let's just say that people do things for a reason.

So behaviour is driven by an underlying emotional need. Every single thing that we do, no matter how trivial, is driven by an emotional need, what I call the Emotional Driver. And it encourages us to make either a movement towards emotional pleasure, emotional comfort, emotional feel-good, or the other underlying emotional need is a move away from existing physical or psychological discomfort or pain. And importantly, also not only existing pain and discomfort, but also anticipated pain or discomfort. So we're driven by an urge either to have some nice feelings or to avoid having nasty feelings. Behaviours are driven by our emotions.

Incidentally, in terms of buying behaviour, you think about every single thing that you've ever bought, every single thing, no matter how trivial, it's driven by an urge either to have some pleasure or comfort, some feel-good, or it's driven by an urge to avoid feeling bad. In the sales world, in the customer service world, this is profound in its impact. A lot of my work is around that. So hey, you know better than me, I guess, but experienced call centre colleagues know all about emotional customers, right? So there are these two types, moving away, including the fear of potential future pain, moving toward feelings of relaxation, feelings of comfort, feelings of contentment.

Now, this is really important, one of those drivers, one of them, will be the initiating force or the dominant force. Sometimes it's both, but one is the initiating or the dominant force in customers' minds, in their hearts, when they're seeking some form of resolution. Either the reason for the call, for making the call to the call centre, or for accepting an outbound call. But here's the question, Charlie, here's the question. Which driver is it, which Emotional Driver is it that's causing the customer either to accept the call or to make the call? Is it moving away from pain, or is it an urge to move towards pleasure? So a key skill for call centre professionals is to uncover, as best they can, the Emotional Drivers of the customer. What is the feeling that she wants to move away from? Or what is the feeling that she wants to move towards? These are critical questions to consider.

But what we can do, is we can gain clues from the customer by listening carefully, and there's no better medium for listening carefully than a call centre. Listening carefully to the words that they use, and the evidence that he or she offers. So in my books, and I think also in some of the Call Centre Helper articles I've written for you guys over the years, I talk about using clean language to build a rapid rapport, and how a good set of questions, including something called The Permission Question, is incredibly power-ful. The Permission Question, how these approaches can help in uncovering the primary, initiating, or most dominant Emotional Driver of the customer.

So it all comes down, really, Charlie, to rapport and to questioning.

Charlie Mitchell: Excellent, and just for some of our listeners who may be unaware, what does The Permission Question involve?

Nick Drake-Knight: The Permission Question is precisely what it says. So, what we do is we very simply ask the customer, whether it's a customer service environment, or a sales environment, or any other scenario, we ask the question, "Charlie, just so I can help you, would it be okay if I ask you a few questions?" That's The Permission Question, and it's rare, very rare that the response is, "No, I do not wish you to ask me any questions." Normally, of course, the answer is, "Yeah, sure, fire away."

Charlie Mitchell: Yeah, excellent, and I imagine that question is actually, as you say, very insightful in terms of which Emotional Driver the customer has for making the call. But just one final topic that I want to focus on today is a very in topic within the context of industry at the moment. And that's gamification. Have you had any experience with using gamification for contact centre coaching?

Nick Drake-Knight: I love gamification.

Charlie Mitchell: Oh, wow.

Nick Drake-Knight: I love anything that brightens up the day, eh? I've got to say my favourite's Bingo, I'm sure lots of people use it, but it's still my favourite. One of my clients in Chicago, it's a global brand, they're involved in adventure clothing, a well-known brand. But one of the country managers in Chicago started using Bingo within her coaching team. And what she was doing, she was checking off some of the key Continue & Begin phrases and language patterns that were being used by her coaching colleagues, and four corners, and a line, and a full house and all that sort of stuff. It's a lot of fun. A lot of ... all around the world, my global clients, they use games to stimulate the use of sales and customer service language patterns, and it's a lot of fun. It's really crazy to see Bingo sheets or any other game, it's crazy to see them in so many languages too. I was in Oslo recently with country managers all over the world, and I've never played Bingo in Hungarian before. And yes, I know Oslo's in Norway.

Charlie Mitchell: I was about to pull you up on that, but, yeah. You got there. Excellent stuff, and there's also gamification software, which I'm sure our sponsor, Genesys, can help you with.

Nick Drake-Knight: Oh, great.

Charlie Mitchell: See what I did there, Nick?

Nick Drake-Knight: Yeah, I'll take a look at that.

Charlie Mitchell: Excellent, excellent. And just as a final kind of caveat for our listeners, where can they find out a bit more about the coaching techniques that you've discussed today, and maybe where can they even get in contact with you after listening to this podcast?

Nick Drake-Knight: Oh sure. continueandbegin.com. They can get onto the website there. Have a play around on YouTube, there's … I don't know how many films on there. Or drop me an email, Nick@NDK-Group.com. Or just put my name into the internet and I'm sure stuff will come up. I'm on LinkedIn as well if guys want to have a chat via that medium.

Hey, but finally, good luck to everybody in their coaching ambitions, because this is so important. We go back to that triangle, explicit standards are great. Consistency is great, but it's temporary. Sustainability is what it's all about. And we've got to continuously improve if we're to stay ahead of the game. So I wish everybody great good fortune in their coaching activities. If anybody wants to have a chat, get in touch, I'm happy to talk.

Appendix 2

Rob, Mart, and George are my sons. Rosie is my daughter, their sister. At the time of this (real) event they were teenagers. They're all adults in their thirties now, and have their own children. The facts presented in the passage are correct. The ten statements, however, are ambiguous. In relation to all statements the reality is.... *Information Not Given*.

Bibliography

A

A Conscious Rethink | *10 Good Reasons Not To Label People (Or Yourself)* | Editorial team, June 2023 | https://www.aconsciousrethink.com/13771/stop-labeling-people/ (accessed 25.07.23)

Abbajay, M. | *Mentoring Matters: Three Essential Elements of Success* | Forbes, 2019

Abbajay, M. | *The Secret to Productivity and Positivity: Show Your Appreciation* | Forbes, 2019 | https://www.forbes.com/sites/maryabbajay/2019/01/20/mentoring-matters-three-essential-element-of-success/?sh=65fb64eb45a9 (accessed 25.07.23)

Abrams, M | *47 Terms That Describe Sexual Attraction, Behavior, and Orientation* | Healthline, February 2023 | https://www.healthline.com/health/different-types-of-sexuality (accessed 24.07.23)

ABS Consulting, Vanden Heuvel, L.N., Lorenzo, D.K., Hanson, W.E. | *Root Cause Analysis Handbook: A Guide to Efficient and Effective Incident Management, 3rd Edition* | Rothstein Associates, 2008

Adair, J. | *How to Grow Leaders: The seven key principles of effective leadership development* | Kogan page, 2007

Adler, A. | *The Individual Psychology of Alfred Adler* | Basic Books, 1956

Adler, A., Brett, C. | *Understanding Life. An Introduction to the Psychology of Alfred Adler.* | One World Publication, 2009

Allen, J. | *As a Man Thinketh* | CreateSpace Independent Publishing Platform, 2006

Allen, S. | *How Thinking About the Future Makes Life More Meaningful* | Mindful.org, May 2019 | https://www.mindful.org/how-thinking-about-the-future-makes-life-more-meaningful/ (accessed 24.07.23)

Anderson, C. | *How to Give a Killer Presentation*, Richard Turere TED Talk | Harvard Business Review, 2013 https://hbr.org/2013/06/how-to-give-a-killer-presentation (accessed 26.07.23)

Anderson, D.M., Stritch, J.M. | *Goal Clarity, Task Significance, and Performance: Evidence from a Laboratory Experiment* | Derrick M. Anderson, Justin M. Stritch, Arizona State University | Journal of Public Administration and Theory Advance Access, 2015

Andreas, S. | *Virginia Satir: the Patterns of Her Magic* | Real People Press, 1991

Armstrong, M. | *Armstrong on Reinventing Performance Management: Building a Culture of Continuous Improvement* | Kogan Page, 2019

Atlassian | *OKRs: the ultimate guide to objectives and key results*

Atria, A | *Good Managers Don't Grow On Trees* | The Motivation Agency, August

2023 | https://themotivationagency.co.uk/good-managers-dont-grow-on-trees/ (accessed 08.08.23)

Agile, 2019 | Sparks, R. | https://www.atlassian.com/agile/agile-at-scale/okr (accessed 24.07.23)

Atlassian | *What is Kanban?* | Agile Coach, 2019 | https://www.youtube.com/watch?v=iVaFVa7HYj4&t=15s (accessed 24.07.23)

Atria, A. | *Equality, equity, and inclusivity... What do they mean?* | The Motivation Agency, April 2023 | https://themotivationagency.co.uk/equality-and-inclusivity-is-changing-what-does-that-mean-for-organizations/ (accessed 24.07.23)

B

Baddeley, A.D. | *The Magical Number Seven: Still Magic After All These Years?* | Psychological Review, 101, 1994

Balogun, J., Hope Bailey, V., Gustafsson, S. | *Exploring Strategic Change* | Pearson, 2015

Bandler, R., Grinder, J. | *Patterns of the Hypnotic Techniques of Milton H. Erickson,* | *M.D. Volume 1.* | Meta Publications, 1975

Bandler, R., Grinder, J. | *The Structure of Magic: A Book about Language and Therapy, Volume 1* | Science and Behavior Books, 1975

Bateson, G. | *Mind and Nature, A Necessary Unity* | Hampton Press, 2002

Bateson, G. | *Steps to an Ecology of Mind* | University of Chicago Press, 1972

Battino, R., South, T. | *Ericksonian Approaches: A Comprehensive Manual* | Crown House Publishing, 1999

BBC | *Hustle culture: Is this the end of rise-and-grind?* | BBC Worklife, April 2023 | Carnegie, M. | https://www.bbc.com/worklife/article/20230417-hustle-culture-is-this-the-end-of-rise-and-grind (accessed 26.07.23)

Beard, C., Wilson, J.P. | *Experiential Learning: A Practical Guide for Training, Coaching and Education* | Kogan page, 2018

Beck, A.T. | *Cognitive Therapy and the Emotional Disorders* | Penguin, 1979

Behme, F., Becker, S. | *The New Knowledge Management: Mining the collective intelligence* | Deloitte Insights, January 2021 | https://www2.deloitte.com/us/en/insights/focus/technology-and-the-future-of-work/organizational-knowledge-management.html (accessed 26.07.23)

Bell, E.T. | *Numerology* | Williams & Wilkins, 1933

Bennett, N., Lemoine, G.J. | *What VUCA really means for you* | Harvard Business Review, January-February 2014 | https://hbr.org/2014/01/what-vuca-really-means-for-you (accessed 25.07.23)

Berne, E. | *Games People Play: The Psychology of Human Relationships* | Penguin, 1968

Berne, E. | *What Do You Say After You Say Hello: Gain control of your conversations and relationships* | Corgi, 2018

Bills, P. | *The Jersey. The All Blacks: The Secrets Behind the World's Most Successful Team* | Pan, 2022

Bird, H | *Performance Management Playbook, The: 15 Must-Have Conversations To Motivate And Manage Your People* | Pearson Business, 2021

Birt, J. | 14 Ways That Employees Can Take Ownership at Work | Indeed, March 2023 | https://www.indeed.com/career-advice/career-development/taking-ownership-at-work (accessed 26.07.23)

Blake, R.; Mouton, J. | *The Managerial Grid: The Key to Leadership Excellence* | Houston: Gulf Publishing Co., 1964

Blakemore, E. | *Race and ethnicity, explained* | National Geographic, February 2019 | https://www.nationalgeographic.co.uk/history/2019/02/race-and-ethnicity-explained (accessed 24.07.23)

Blanchard, K.H. | *Situational Leadership* | www.blanchard.com (accessed 07.07.24)

Blanchard, K.H. | *The One Minute Manager* | Penguin Putman, 1997

Blanchard, K.H, Carew, D., Carew, E. P. | *The One Minute Manager Builds High Performing Teams* | Fontana 1993

Blanchard, K.H., Johnson, S. | *The New One Minute Manager* | William Morrow, 2015

Blanchard, K.H., Oncken Jr, W., Burrows, H. | *The One Minute Manager® Meets the Monkey* | Thorsons, 2011

Bostic St. Clair, C., Grinder, J. | *Whispering in the Wind* | J & C Enterprises, 2001

Bourton Group | *Applying Lean in an Office Environment* | Editorial team, September 2022 | https://www.bourton.co.uk/applying-lean-in-an-office-environment/ (accessed 25.07.23)

Bourton Group | *How do you train 5S* | Editorial team, February 2021 | https://www.bourton.co.uk/how-do-you-train-5s/ (accessed 25.07.23)

Bower, S.A., Bower, G. H. | *Asserting Yourself – Update Edition: A Practical Guide for Positive Change* | De Capo Press, 2004

Boyes, A. | *What Keeps People from Solving their Problems Series: Secondary Gain* | AliceBoyes.com, September 2010 | https://www.aliceboyes.com/secondary-gain/ (accessed 25.07.23)

Brower, T | *Retention On The Rise: What's Driving The Trend For Satisfaction And Staying* | Forbes, August 2023 | https://www-forbes-com.cdn.ampproject.org/c/s/www.forbes.com/sites/tracybrower/2023/08/06/retention-on-the-rise-whats-driving-the-trend-for-satisfaction-and-staying/amp/ (accessed 07.09.23)

Brown, B. | *Dare to Lead: Brave Work. Tough Conversations. Whole Hearts* | Vermilion, 2018

Brown, K. | *Accountability Vs. Responsibility: Is There a Difference?* | Science of People, December 2022 | https://www.scienceofpeople.com/accountability-vs-responsibility/ (accessed 26.07.23)

Brownlee, D. | *Forget Traditional Brainstorming— Instead, Try This Technique To Spur New Levels Of Team Creativity* | Forbes, July 2021 | https://www.forbes.com/sites/danabrownlee/2021/07/28/forget-traditional-brainstorming-instead-try-this-technique-to-spur-new-levels-of-team-creativity/?sh=2468ca174d13 (accessed 24.07.23)

Bryant, A. | *How to Run a More Effective Meeting* | New York Times Business, 2023 | https://www.nytimes.com/guides/business/how-to-run-an-effective-meeting (accessed 25.07.23)

Burton, J., Bodenhamer, B. | *Hypnotic Language: Its Structure and Use* | Crown House Publishing, 2000

C

Caldwell, G. | *Scrum Mastery: The Essential Guide to Scrum and Agile Project Management* (Audiobook) | SD Publishing, 2020

Call Centre Helper | *Call Centre Etiquette: 15 Things You Should Never Say to a Customer* | Editorial team, February 2018 | https://www.callcentrehelper.com/11-things-a-call-centre-agent-should-never-say-but-many-do-68516.htm (accessed 26.07.23)

Capelli, P., Tavis, A. | *The Performance Management Revolution* | Harvard Business Review, 2016 | https://hbr.org/2016/10/the-performance-management-revolution (accessed 24.07.23)

Carnegie, D. | *How to Win Friends and Influence People* | Vermilion, 2006

Carnegie, D. | *How to win Friends and Influence People in the Digital Age* | Simon & Schuster, 2011

Carnegie, M. | *Cricket legend Ebony Rainford-Brent: "Anyone can suffer from imposter syndrome – it's part of who we are".* | The Independent, July 2023 | https://www.independent.co.uk/life-style/galaxy-the-ripple-effect/imposter-syndrome-anxiety-mental-health-work-wellness-b2369161.html (accessed 24.07.23)

Carpenter, J., Webb, C., Bostock, L., Coomber, C. | *Effective supervision in social work and social care* | SCIE Research Briefing 43 | Social Care Institute for Excellence, 2012

Carter, D. | *The Art of Winning. Ten lessons in Leadership, Purpose, and Potential* | Penguin, 2023

Cassata, C. | *Reasons You Don't Listen* | PsychCentral, June 2021 | https://psychcentral.com/lib/reasons-you-dont-listen (accessed 25.07.23)

Cast, C. | *6 Ways to Take Control of Your Career Development If Your Company Doesn't Care About It* | Harvard Business Review, 2018 | https://hbr.org/2018/01/6-ways-to-take-control-of-your-career-development-if-your-company-doesnt-care-about-it (accessed 24.07.23)

Cervantes, M., Rutherford, J. (translator) | *The Ingenious Hidalgo Don Quixote of La Mancha* | Penguin Classics, 2003

Chamorro-Premuzic, T. | *What Makes Your Obsession Healthy or Unhealthy: Why some obsessions can turn into success.* | Psychology Today, July 2011 | https://www.psychologytoday.com/us/blog/mr-personality/201107/what-makes-your-obsession-healthy-or-unhealthy (accessed 25.07.23)

Chan, A. | *9 Scientifically Backed Ways to Stop Worrying* | The Huffington Post, 2013 | https://www.huffingtonpost.co.uk/entry/stop-worrying-anxiety-cycle_n_4002914 (accessed 25.07.23)

Charlton, N.G. | *Understanding Gregory Bateson: Mind, Beauty, and the Sacred Earth* | State University of New York Press, 2008

Chartered Management Institute | www.managers.org.uk (accessed 26.07.23)

Chartered Management Institute | *CMI Professional Standard* | https://www.managers.org.uk/education-and-learning/professional-standards/professional-standard/ (accesses 25.07.23)

Chartered Management Institute | *Continuing Professional Development: Ensuring you have the skills to face a challenge* | https://www.managers.org.uk/education-and-learning/continuing-professional-development/ (accessed 26.07.23)

Chartered Institute of Personnel and Development (CIPD) | *Equality, diversity, and inclusion (EDI) in the workplace*

CIPD Factsheet, November 2022 | https://www.cipd.org/uk/knowledge/factsheets/diversity-factsheet/ (accessed 24.07.23)

Chartered Institute of Personnel and Development (CIPD) | Knowledge Hub | https://www.cipd.org/en/knowledge/ (accessed 24.07.23)

Chartered Institute of Personnel and Development (CIPD) | *Induction: A look at the induction process, and the purpose of induction for employer and employee.* | December 2022

Chartered Institute of Personnel and Development (CIPD) | *Leadership* | https://www.cipd.co.uk/knowledge/strategy/leadership (accessed 26.07.23)

Chartered Institute of Personnel and Development (CIPD) | *Managing and Supporting Remote Workers; Guidance for Line Managers* | January 2021 | https://www.cipd.org/uk/knowledge/guides/remote-working-line-manager-guide/ (accessed 25.07.23)

Chartered Institute of Personnel and Development (CIPD) | PESTLE Analysis |

https://www.cipd.co.uk/knowledge/ strategy/organisational-development/pestle-analysis-factsheet (accessed 26.07.23)

Chevannes, S. | *To Be A Successful Business Leader, Think Like A Chess Player* | Forbes, October 2022 | https://www.forbes.com/ sites/forbesbusinesscouncil/2022/10/11/ to-be-a-successful-business-leader-think-like-a-chess-player/?sh=158cbe863985 (accessed 25.07.23)

Chua, C. | *You Always Have a Choice* | Personal Excellence, | https:// personalexcellence.co/blog/you-always-have-a-choice/ (accessed 25.07.23)

Cialdini, R. B. | *Influence: The Psychology of Persuasion* | HarperBus, 2021

Civico, A. | *How to Build Rapport: A Powerful Technique* | Psychology Today, April 2015 | https://www.psychologytoday. com/intl/blog/turning-point/201504/ how-to-build-rapport-a-powerful-technique (accessed 25.07.23)

Clean Learning (Walker and Way Ltd) | *What is Clean Language?* | https://cleanlearning. co.uk/about/faq/what-is-clean-language (accessed 26.07.23)

Clear, J. | *Atomic Habits* | Random House Business, 2018

Cirillo, F. | *The Pomodoro Technique: The-Life-Changing-Time-Management System* | Virgin Books, 2018

Collard, P. | *The Little Book of Meditation: 10 minutes a day to more relaxation, energy and creativity* | Gaia, 2019

Collins, J. | *Good To Great: Why Some Companies Make the Leap... and Others Don't* | Random House, 2001

Collins, J. | *Turning the Flywheel: A Monograph to Accompany Good to Great* | Random House Business, 2019

Conradie, Y. | Having Hope: Motivator, Comfort, or a Curse? | MindTools, April 2022 | https://www.mindtools.com/blog/ having-hope-motivator-comfort-curse-mttalk/ (accessed 24.07.23)

Continue and Begin Ltd | https:// ndk-group.com/conference-presentations-8/ (accessed 24.07.23)

Counselling Directory | *Timelines: A simple exercise?* | Editorial team, June 2019 | https://www.counselling-directory.org.uk/ memberarticles/timeline-a-simple-exercise (accessed 26.07.23)

Covey, S.R. | *7 Habits of Highly Effective People* | Free Press, 1989

Craig, H. | *Resilience in the Workplace: How to Be Resilient at Work* | PositivePsychology. com, March 2023 | https:// positivepsychology.com/resilience-in-the-workplace/ (accessed 25.07.23)

Crosby, G. | *Planned Change: Why Kurt Lewin's Social Science is Still Best Practice for Business Results, Change Management, and Human Progress.* | Routledge, 2021

D

Dale, B.G., Bamford, D., van der Wiele, T. | *Managing Quality: An Essential Guide and Resource Gateway* | Wiley, 2016

Darwin, C. | *On the Origin of Species* | Wordsworth Editions (1998)

Day, G.S., Schoemaker, P.J.H. | *See Sooner, Act Faster: How Vigilant Leaders Thrive in an Era of Digital Turbulence* | The MIT Press, 2019

Deichert, N.T., Fekete, E.M., Craven, M. | *Gratitude enhances the beneficial effects of social support on psychological well-being* | The Journal of Positive Psychology, November 2019

Dilts, R.B., Gilligan, S., Meza, A. | *Generative Coaching Volume 1: The Journey of Creative and Sustainable Change* | International Assoc. for Generative Change, 2021

Dixon, M., Freeman, K., Toman, N. | *Stop Trying to Delight Your Customers* | Harvard Business Review, August 2010 | https://hbr. org/2010/07/stop-trying-to-delight-your-customers (accessed 26.07.23)

Doerr, J. | *Measure What Matters. OKRs – the Simple Idea That Drives 10x Growth* | Penguin Random House, 2018

Doerr, J. | John Doerr. OKRs. Objectives & Key Results. | https://www.youtube.com/watch?v=pbkI--GvEZY (accessed 07.07.24)

Donohue, M.E. | *Message Received: 7 Steps to Break Down Communication Barriers at Work* | McGraw Hill, 2021

Doran, G.T. | *There's a SMART Way to Write Management's Goals and Objectives.* | Journal of Management Review, 70, 35-36. 2018 | https://www.scribd.com/document/458234239/There-s-a-S-M-A-R-T-way-to-write-management-s-goals-and-objectives-George-T-Doran-Management-Review-1981-pdf# accessed 27.07.23)

Drake-Knight, M. | TEDx talk, 2022. | *Dear Mr. Bin Man* https://youtu.be/heIXdS7Gs7c (accessed 26.07.23)

Drake-Knight, N. | *Boomerang! Coach Your Team to Be the Best* | Dandelion Digital, 2007

Drake-Knight, N. | YouTube channel https://www.youtube.com/channel/UCbiVddbHqtlhXLGEE24iDOA

Drake-Knight, N. | *Can't to Can Belief Busting®* | Continue and Begin Ltd | https://www.youtube.com/watch?v=yeb3nc7w2_8 (accessed 26.07.23)

Drake-Knight, N. | Coaching out Universal Quantifiers (Absolute Language) | Continue and Begin Ltd, 2016 | https://ndk-group.com/coaching-universal-quantifiers-absolute-language/ (accessed 26.07.23)

Drake-Knight, N. | *Fast Coaching. The Complete Guide to New Code Continue & Begin®* | Dandelion Digital, 2016 | Audible https://www.audible.co.uk/pd/ | Fast-Coaching-Audiobook/B07TTKD13T (accessed 24.07.23)

Drake-Knight, N. | *Every Customer Wants®* | Continue and Begin Ltd | www.continueandbegin.com (accessed 26.07.23)

Drake-Knight, N. | *Meaning Deletion in Coaching Communication* | Continue and Begin Ltd, 2016 | https://ndk-group.com/language-deletion-generalisation-in-coaching-communication/ (accessed 26.07.23)

Drake-Knight, N. | *Meerkat Selling®* | Dandelion Digital, 2008

Drake-Knight, N. | *Motivation through a Kick in the Ass* | Call Centre Helper, May 2009 | https://www.callcentrehelper.com/motivation-through-a-kick-in-the-ass-3448.htm (accessed 24.07.23)

Drake-Knight, N. | *NDK Performance Model®*, 2016 | https://www.youtube.com/watch?v=n4sPW5N7w9E (accessed 24.07.23)

Drake-Knight, N. | *New Code Continue & Begin® – Analogue Marking* | Continue and Begin Ltd, 2016 | https://ndk-group.com/new-code-continue-begin-analogue-marking/ (accessed 26.07.23)

Drake-Knight, N. | Nick Drake-Knight YouTube channel | https://www.youtube.com/channel/UCbiVddbHqtlhXLGEE24iDOA (accessed 27.07.23)

Drechsler, P. | *Instantly Stop Procrastination: 4 Powerful Concepts That Will Help You Effectively Complete the Tasks You Keep Avoiding* | Winner Media Publishing, 2022

Dreeke, R. | *It's Not All About Me: The Top Ten Techniques for Building Quick Rapport with Anyone* | Robin K. Dreeke, 2011

Drucker, P.F. | *Essential Drucker: The Best of Sixty Years of Peter Drucker's Essential Writings on Management* | Harper Business, 2008

Dryden, W. and Ellis, A. | *The Practice of Rational Emotive Behaviour Therapy* | Free Association Books, 1998

Duckworth, A. | *Grit: Why passion and resilience are the secrets to success* | Vermilion, 2017

Duhigg, C. | *The Power of Habit. Why we do what we do and how to change* | Random House, 2013 | *Measure Twice, Cut Once!* | Psychology Today, February 2012

Dwyer, D.J. | https://www.psychologytoday.com/us/blog/got-a-minute/201202/measure-twice-cut-once (accessed 25.07.23)

E

Edmonstone, J. | *Action Learning in Health, Social and Community Care* | *Principles, Practices and Resources* | CRC Press, 2017

Edmonstone, J. | *Learning and development in action learning: the energy investment model* | Industrial and Commercial Training Vol. 35, February 2003

Eggert, M.A. | *Assertiveness Pocketbook* | Management Pocketbooks, 2011

Eggington, B. | *The Use of Adjectives and Adverbs in Journalism* | Media Helping Media (undated) | https://mediahelpingmedia.org/basics/the-use-of-adjectives-and-adverbs-in-journalism/ (accessed 26.07.23)

Eikenberry, K. | *Beware of Unintended Consequences* | Remote Leadership Institute | https://www.remoteleaderinstitute.com/ (accessed 26.07.23)

Ellis, A., Dryden, W | *The Practice of Rational Emotive Behavior Therapy* | Free Association Books, 1999

Ellis, A. | *Rational Emotive Behavior Therapy: It Works for Me – It Can Work for You* | Prometheus, 2010

Ellis, L., Yang, A. | *If Your Co-Workers Are 'Quiet Quitting,' Here's What That Means* | Wall Street Journal, August 2022 | https://www.wsj.com/articles/if-your-gen-z-co-workers-are-quiet-quitting-heres-what-that-means-11660260608 (accessed 26.07.23)

Environment International | *Long working hours increasing deaths from heart disease and stroke: WHO, ILO* | September 2021 | https://www.who.int/news/item/17-05-2021-long-working-hours-increasing-deaths-from-heart-disease-and-stroke-who-ilo (accessed 25.07.23)

Epictetus | *The Enchiridion*, c125 AD

Erickson, M.H., Rossi, E.l., Rossi, S.I. | *Hypnotic Realities: The Induction od Clinical Hypnosis and Forms of Indirect Suggestion* | Irvington, 1976

Ernst, F.J. | *The OK Corral: Grid for What's Happening* | http://ernstokcorral.com/OK_Corral.html (accessed 26.07.23)

Exploring Your Mind | *Showing Interest in Others Can Change Your Life!* | Exploring Your Mind, November 2020 | https://exploringyourmind.com/showing-interest-in-others-can-change-your-life/ (accessed 26.07.2023)

Eyal, N. | *Indistractable: How to Control Your Attention and Choose Your Life* | Bloomsbury Publishing, 2020

F

Farrelly, F., Brandsma, J. | *Provocative Therapy* | Meta Publications, 1974

Ferguson, A., Moritz, M. | *Leading* | Hodder and Stoughton, 2015

Ferrazzi, K. | *Keith Ferrazzi on How the Pandemic Taught Organizations to Be "Crisis Agile"* | Harvard Business Review, March 2022 | https://hbr.org/2022/03/keith-ferrazzi-on-how-the-pandemic-taught-organizations-to-be-crisis-agile (accessed 24.07.23)

Firestone, L. | *4 Reasons to Take Ownership of Your Feelings* | Psychology Today, July 2021 | https://www.psychologytoday.com/us/blog/compassion-matters/202107/4-reasons-take-ownership-your-feelings (accessed 24.07.23)

Firestone, R., Firestone, L., Catlett, J. | *Conquer Your Critical Inner Voice* | New Harbinger Productions, 2002

Flaxington, B.D. | *Understanding Other People: The Five Secrets to Human Behavior* | ATA Press, 2009

Forbes.com Coaches Council | *11 Ways To Stay Up On The Latest Industry Developments* | https://www.forbes.com/sites/forbescoachescouncil/2021/02/18/11-ways-to-stay-up-on-the-latest-industry-developments/?sh=e3f0d7b70fbc (accessed 26.07.23)

Friedman, R. | *Working Too Hard Makes Leading More Difficult* | Harvard Business Review, December 2014 | https://hbr.org/2014/12/working-too-hard-makes-leading-more-difficult (accessed 25.07.23)

Frue, K. | *PEST Analysis Ultimate Guide: Definition, Template, Examples* | PESTLE Analysis, September 2020 | https://pestleanalysis.com/pest-analysis/ (accessed 25.07.23)

G

Gallo, C. | *The Art of Persuasion Hasn't Changed in 2,000 Years* | Harvard Business Review, 2018

Gallo, C. | *The Presentation Secrets of Steve Jobs: How to Be Insanely Great in Front of Any Audience* | McGraw Hill, 2009

Gallup's Employee Engagement Survey: Ask the Right Questions with the Q12® Survey | Gallup | https://www.gallup.com/workplace/356063/gallup-q12-employee-engagement-survey.aspx (accessed 26.07.23)

Gardiner, J. | *What Makes a "Great" Manager?* | Dare 2 Dream Ltd, July 2023 | https://johngardiner.substack.com/p/what-makes-a-great-manager (accessed 26.07.23)

Gartner HR Research Identifies Human Leadership as the Next Evolution of Leadership | Gartner Newsroom, June 2022 | https://www.gartner.com/en/newsroom/press-releases/06-23-22-gartner-hr-research-identifies-human-leadership-as-the-next-evolution-of-leadership (accessed 26.07.23)

Gatchel, R. J., Shulz, I.Z. | *Handbook of Occupational Health and Wellness* | Springer, 2012

Gautam, S. | *Useful Fictions: Why Beliefs Matter* | Psychology Today, March 2017 | https://www.psychologytoday.com/us/blog/the-fundamental-four/201703/useful-fictions-why-beliefs-matter (accessed 25.07.23)

Gladwell, M. | *Blink: The Power of Thinking Without Thinking* | Penguin, 2006

Glaser, J.E., Glaser, R.D. | *The Neurochemistry of Positive Conversations* | Harvard Business Review, 2014 | https://hbr.org/2014/06/the-neurochemistry-of-positive-conversations (accessed 24.07.23)

Glassdoor for Employers | *3 Quick Wins for Establishing a Culture of Employee Engagement* | Editorial team, May 2021 | https://www.glassdoor.co.uk/employers/blog/3-quick-wins-for-establishing-a-culture-of-employee-engagement/ (accessed 26.07.23)

Glassdoor for Employers | *Employers To Retain Half Of Their Employees Longer If Bosses Showed More Appreciation; Glassdoor Survey* | Editorial team, November 2013 | https://www.glassdoor.com/employers/blog/employers-to-retain-half-of-their-employees-longer-if-bosses-showed-more-appreciation-glassdoor-survey/ (accessed 02.08.23)

Goleman, D.P. | *Emotional Intelligence: Why It Can Matter More Than IQ* | Bantam, 2005

Goleman, D.P. | *Leadership that gets results* | Harvard Business Review, 2000 | https://hbr.org/2000/03/leadership-that-gets-results (accessed 25.07.23)

Goman, C.K. | *6 Assumptions You Shouldn't Make – and 1 You Always Should* | Forbes, 2017 https://www.forbes.com/sites/carolkinseygoman/2017/01/15/6-assumptions-you-shouldnt-make-and-1-you-always-should/?sh=7e23a83676f0 (accessed 24.07.23)

Gordon, D. | *Therapeutic Metaphors: Helping Others Through the Looking Glass* | Independently published, 2017

Gordon, S. | Very Well Mind, December 2020 | *How to Use Time Blocking to Manage Your Day* | https://www.verywellmind.com/how-to-use-time-blocking-to-manage-your-day-4797509 (accessed 25.07.23)

Greenaway, R. | *The four F's of active reviewing* | The University of Edinburgh, November 2018, adapted from Roger Greenaway's 'The Active Reviewing Cycle'. | https://www.ed.ac.uk/reflection/reflectors-toolkit/reflecting-on-experience/four-f (accessed 25.07.23)

Greenleaf, R.K. | *Servant Leadership [25th Anniversary Edition]: A Journey into the Nature of Legitimate Power and Greatness* | Paulist Press, 2002

Griffiths, C. | *The Creative Thinking Handbook: Your Step-by-Step Guide to Problem Solving in Business* | Kogan Page, 2019

Grinder, J., Bandler, R. | *The Structure of Magic 2, A Book About Communication and Change* | Science and Behavior Books, 1976

Grove, A. | *What is an OKR? Andy Grove, OKR inventor, explains.* | https://www.youtube.com/watch?v=1ht_1VAF6ik (accessed 07.07.24)

Guttman, J. | *Are You Guilty of Making Too Many Assumptions?* | Psychology Today, September 2019 | https://www.psychologytoday.com/us/blog/sustainable-life-satisfaction/201909/are-you-guilty-of-making-too-many-assumptions (accessed 26.07.23)

H

Hagen, M., Bernard, A., Grube, E. | *Do It All Wrong! Using Reverse-Brainstorming to Generate Ideas, Improve Discussions, and Move Students to Action* | Sage Journals, 2016

Hammond, D.C. | *Handbook of Hypnotic Suggestions and Metaphors* | Norton, 1990

Harvey, S. | *Kaizen: The Japanese Method for Transforming Habits, One Small Step at a Time* | Bluebird; Main Market edition, 2019

Hati, S. | *What is Management? Objectives, Functions, and Characteristics* | Knowledge Hut, July 2023 | https://www.knowledgehut.com/blog/others/what-is-management#frequently-asked-questions (accessed 25.07.23)

Hatzistefanis, M. | *How to Be an Overnight Success* | Ebury Press, 2018

Hazlehurst, J. | *How to Lead When the World's Gone Crazy* | Management Today, 2019 | https://www.managementtoday.co.uk/lead-when-worlds-gone-crazy/long-reads/article/1523413 (accessed 24.07.23)

He, G. | *How to Foster Company Pride at Work in 2023* | teambuilding.com, July 2022 | https://teambuilding.com/blog/company-pride (accessed 25.07.23)

Health and Safety Executive, 2013 | *Managing for health and safety (HSG65)* | https://www.hse.gov.uk/pubns/books/HSG65.htm (accessed 26.07.23)

Health & Safety Executive, November 2022 | *Work-related stress, anxiety, or depression statistics in Great Britain, 2022* | https://www.hse.gov.uk/statistics/ (accessed 26.07.23)

Henley, D. | *Three Ways Great Leaders Show They Care About Their Team* | Forbes.com, July 2018 | https://www.forbes.com/sites/dedehenley/2018/07/20/three-ways-great-leaders-show-they-care-about-their-team/?sh=e7badd846e5c (accessed 26.07.23)

Henschel, T. | *Showing Teeth* | Essential Communications, December 2015 | https://essentialcomm.com/podcast/showing-teeth/ (accessed 25.07.23)

Hersey, P. | *The Situational Leader* | Prentice Hall & IBD, 1986

Herzberg, F. | *The Motivation-Hygiene Concept and Problems of Manpower* | Personnel Administration, January 1964

Herzberg, F. | *One More Time: How Do You Motivate Employees?* | Harvard Business Review Press, 2008 | https://hbr.org/2003/01/one-more-time-how-do-you-motivate-employees (accessed 24.07.23)

Hirano, H. | *JIT Implementation Manual – The Complete Guide to Just-In-Time Manufacturing* | Taylor and Francis, 2009

Hoffer, E. | *The True Believer, Thoughts on the Nature of Mass Movements* | Harper Brothers, 1951

Holiday, R. | *The Obstacle is the Way* | Profile Books, 2014

Horn, H., Sloan, N., Benjamin, B. | *Build a Customer-First Culture* | The Wall Street Journal, 2017 | https://deloitte.wsj.com/articles/build-a-customer-first-culture-1512968535?tesla=y&tesla=y (accessed 24.07.23)

Horn, R. | *The Business Skills Handbook* | Kogan Page, 2009

HRM Online | *A guide to reboarding an employee* | June 2021 | https://www.hrmonline.com.au/change-management/a-guide-to-reboarding-an-employee/ (accessed 26.07.23)

Hunt-Davis, B., Beveridge, H. | *Will it Make the Boat Go Faster?* | Matador, 2011

Hypnotherapy education and accreditation authorities | British Society of Clinical Hypnosis www.bsch.org.uk (accessed 26.07.23) | London College of Clinical Hypnotherapy International https://lcchinternational.co.uk/ (accessed 26.07.23)

I

Indeed | *6 Team Huddle Ideas for the Workplace (With Tips)* | Editorial team, March 2023 | https://www.indeed.com/career-advice/career-development/team-huddle- (accessed 24.07.23)

Indeed | *Top Email Etiquette Examples for Professional Communication* | Editorial team, July 2022 | https://www.indeed.com/career-advice/career-development/email-etiquette-examples (accessed 24.07.23)

Indeed | *What are the advantages and disadvantages of job enrichment?* | Editorial team, March 2023 | https://uk.indeed.com/career-advice/career-development/advantages-and-disadvantages-of-job-enrichment (accessed 26.07.23)

Institute of Risk Management, 2018 | *Horizon Scanning: A Practitioner's Guide* | https://www.theirm.org/news/horizon-scanning-a-practitioners-guide-revealed-at-irm-leaders/ (accessed 26.07.23)

International Bureau of Education | *PROSPECTS: The Quarterly Review of Comparative Education* (Paris, UNESCO: International Bureau of Education) vol. 24, no.3/4, 1994, p. 687-701 UNESCO: International Bureau of Education, 2002.

J

Jackson, B. | *I Think I'll Go to Sea* | You Write On Publishing, 2010

James, T., Woodsmall, W. | *Time Line Therapy and the Basis of Personality* | Crown House, 2017

Janzer, C. | *How to Manage Managers* | Society for Human Resource Management, July 2021 | https://www.shrm.org/resourcesandtools/hr-topics/people-managers/pages/managing-managers.aspx (accessed 26.07.23)

Jayaraman, R. | *8 Reasons Why Experiential Learning Is the Future of Learning* | eLearning Industry, 2014 | https://elearningindustry.com/8-reasons-experiential-learning-future-learning (accessed 24.07.23)

Johnson, J. A. | *Are 'I' Statements Better Than 'You' Statements?* | Psychology Today, November 2012 | https://www.psychologytoday.com/ca/blog/

cui-bono/201211/are-i-statements-better-you-statements (accessed 24.07.23)

Johnson, L. | *Frank Pucelik – His view on NLP's beginnings* | NLP Academy, 2010 | https://www.nlpacademy.co.uk/articles/view/frank_pucelik_-_his_view_on_nlps_beginnings/ (accessed 26.07.2023)

Johnson, S. | *Who Moved My Cheese: An Amazing Way to Deal with Change in Your Work and in Your Life* | Vermilion, 1999

Johnstone, M. | *The Little Book of Resilience: How to Bounce Back from Adversity and Lead a Fulfilling Life* | Robinson, 2015

Jones, C. | *Radical Clarity for Business: How to Empower People for Better Results at Work* | Clarity Press, 2020

Jordan, P.J. | *Dealing with organisational change: Can emotional intelligence enhance organisational learning?* | International Journal of Organisational Behaviour, 2004

Joseph, S. | *Authentic: How to be yourself and why it matters* | Piatkus, 2016

Joubert, J. | *The Notebooks of Joseph Joubert: A Selection* | NYRB Classics, 2006

K

Kahneman, D. | *Thinking, Fast and Slow* | Penguin, 2012

Kanbanize | *5 Whys: The Ultimate Root Cause Analysis Tool* | Editorial team, undated. | https://kanbanize.com/lean-management/improvement/5-whys-analysis-tool (accessed 25.07.23)

Kanbanize | *Value Stream Mapping: The Definitive Guide* | Editorial team, undated. | https://kanbanize.com/lean-management/value-waste/value-stream-mapping (accessed 25.07.23)

Kareska, K. | *The Role of Planning as a Fundamental Management Function for Achieving Effectiveness in Business Organisations* | University Goce Delcev, 2017

Kelly, L. | Top 27 Self-Assessment Questions for Managers | PeopleGoal Inc, March 2021 | https://www.peoplegoal.com/blog/self-assessment (accessed 25.07.23)

Kennedy, J.T., Jain-Link, P. | *Sponsors Need to Stop Acting Like Mentors* | Harvard Business Review, February 2019 | https://hbr.org/2019/02/sponsors-need-to-stop-acting-like-mentors (accessed 24.07.23)

Kipling, J.R. | *Just So Stories: Original Illustrated Edition.* | Independently Published, 2022

Kipling, J.R. | *If: A Father's Advice to His Son* | *The Complete Works of Rudyard Kipling* | Happy Hour Books, 2023

Kogan, M. | *Descartes Square: A Popular Decision Making Technique* | Westminster Business Consultants, April 2017 | https://wbcuk.wordpress.com/2017/04/07/descartes-square-a-popular-decision-making-technique/ (accessed 24.07.23)

Korzybski, A. | *Science and Sanity: An Introduction to Non-Aristotelian Systems and General Semantics (1933)* | Forest Hills; Institute of General Semantics, 1995

Kotter, J.P. | *Leading Change* | Harvard Business Review Press, 2012

Krech, G. | The Art of Taking Action: Lessons from Japanese Psychology | To Do Institute, 2014

Kubler-Ross, E. | *On Death & Dying: What the Dying Have to Teach Doctors, Nurses, Clergy & Their Own Families* | Macmillan, 1969

L

Laker, B., Pereira, V., Malik, A., Soga, L. | Dear Manager, *You're Holding Too Many Meetings* | Harvard Business Review, March 2022 | https://hbr.org/2022/03/dear-manager-youre-holding-too-many-meetings (accessed 26.07.23)

Lancefield, D. | *5 Strategies to Empower Employees to Make Decisions* | Harvard

Business Review, March 2020 | https://hbr. org/2023/03/5-strategies-to-empower-employees-to-make-decisions (accessed 24.07.23)

Laurence, E., Lloyd, M. | *Best Personality Tests of 2024* | Forbes Health, 2024 | https:// www.forbes.com/health/mind/best-personality-tests/ (accessed 25.06.24)

Lawrence, P.R. | *How to Deal With Resistance to Change* | Harvard Business Review, January 1969 | https://hbr.org/1969/01/how-to-deal-with-resistance-to-change (accessed 25.07.23)

Lean Competency Services Ltd | *Lean Competency System* | Cardiff University | https://www.leancompetency.org/lean-company-visits-uk/ (accessed 26.07.2023)

Lencioni, P. | *Make Your Values Mean Something* | Harvard Business Review, 2002 | https://hbr.org/2002/07/make-your-values-mean-something (accessed 23.07.23)

Lewin, K. | *Field theory in social science* | Harper, 1951

Liker, J. | *The Toyota Way: 14 Management Principles from the World's Greatest Manufacturer* | McGraw-Hill, 2004

Lloyd, S. | *Managers Must Delegate Effectively to Develop Employees* | Society of Human Resource Management, 2012 | https:// www.shrm.org/ResourcesAndTools/ hr-topics/organizational-and-employee-development/Pages/DelegateEffectively. aspx (accessed 24.07.23)

Lombardo, E. | *5 Ways to Reframe Failure* | Success, November 2014 | https://www. success.com/5-ways-to-reframe-failure/ (accessed 24.07.23)

Lombardo, M., Eichinger, R | *The Career Architect Development Planner* | Korn Ferry, 1996

Luft, J., Ingham, H. | *The Johari window, a graphic model of interpersonal awareness* | University of California, Los Angeles, 1955

M

Machell, M. | *Remote working causes communication gap between managers and employees* | HR Magazine, March 2023 | https://www. hrmagazine.co.uk/content/news/ remote-working-causes-communication-gap-between-managers-and-employees (accessed 26.07.23)

Maisel, E. | *The Magic of Sleep Thinking: How to Solve Problems, Reduce Stress, and Increase Creativity While You Sleep* | Dover Publications, 2018

Makoff-Clark, A. | *Five proven Methods to Achieve True Self-Awareness* | Chartered Management Institute, January 2021 | https://www.managers.org.uk/ knowledge-and-insights/article/five-proven-methods-achieve-true-self-awareness/ (26.07.23)

Manas, J. | *The Resource Management and Capacity Planning Handbook: A Guide to Maximizing the Value of Your Limited People Resources* | McGraw Hill, 2014

Marciano, P.L. | *Carrots and Sticks Don't Work: Build a Culture of Employee Engagement with the Principles of RESPECT* | McGraw-Hill, 2010

Marcus Aurelius | *Meditations* | Penguin Random House, 2006

Marquet, D. | *How Great Leaders Serve Others* | TEDx Talks, June 2012 | https://www.youtube.com/ watch?v=DLRH5J_93LQ (accessed 26.07.23)

Machell, M. | *Remote working causes communication gap between managers and employees* | HR Magazine, March 2023 | https://www.hrmagazine.co. uk/content/news/remote-working-causes-communication-gap-between-managers-and-employees (accessed 25.07.25)

MacLeod, D., Clarke, N. | *Engaging for Success* | Department for Business, Innovation, and Skills, 2009

Maslow, A., and Hudson, T.W. | *The Theory of Human Motivation* | Historical Recordings, 2020

Matta, C. | *Are Emotions a Choice?* | MentalHealth.net May, 2013 | https://www.mentalhelp.net/blogs/are-emotions-a-choice/ (accessed 26.07.23)

Mayne, B. | *Goal Mapping®* | Watkins Publishing, 2020

Mayne, B. | *Self Mapping* | Watkins Publishing, 2009

Mayne, B., Mayne, S. | *Life Mapping* | Vermilion, 2003

McGowan, H., Shipley, C. | *The Adaptation Advantage* | Wiley, 2020

McGregor, D. | *The Human Side of Enterprise (annotated)* | McGraw – Hill, 2006

Mehrabian, A. | *Silent Messages* | Wadsworth, 1971

Megginson, D., Whitaker, V. | *Continuing Professional Development* | Kogan Page 2007

Mesaglio, M. | How to Lead Better Remote Meetings | Gartner, May 2020 | https://www.gartner.com/smarterwithgartner/how-to-lead-better-remote-meetings (accessed 26.07.23)

Metathinking.org | https://metathinking.org/ (accessed 25.07.23)

Miller, D. | *For a Better User Experience, Forget Alexa, Use Occam's Razor* | CMSWire.com, 2018 | https://www.cmswire.com/digital-experience/for-a-better-user-experience-forget-alexa-use-occams-razor/ (accessed 25.07.23)

Miller, G | *The Magical Number Seven, Plus or Minus Two* | The Psychological Review, 1956 | http://psychclassics.yorku.ca/Miller/ (accessed 24.07.23)

Mind Tools | *Creative Problem Solving* | Editorial team, undated | https://www.mindtools.com/a2j08rt/creative-problem-solving (accessed 25.07.23)

Minow, M | *Equality vs Equity* | American Journal of Law and Equality, 2021

Mental Health Foundation | *Work-life balance* | https://www.mentalhealth.org.uk/explore-mental-health/a-z-topics/work-life-balance (accessed 26.07.23)

Mollor, C. | *The Rise of the Agile Leader: Can You Make the Shift?* | Prominence Publishing, 2020

Morgan, G. | *Images of Organization* | SAGE Publications, 2006

Morin, A. | *How Cognitive Reframing Works* | Very Well Mind, May 2023 | https://www.verywellmind.com/reframing-defined-2610419 (accessed 24.07.23)

Morin, A. | *Study Reveals a Conversation Trick That Motivates People To Change Their Behavior* | Forbes, January 2016 | Morin, A.

Morris, L. | *What is a RACI matrix?* | Project Management.com, October 2022 | https://project-management.com/understanding-responsibility-assignment-matrix-raci-matrix/ (accessed 26.07.23)

Mullins, L., Rees, G. | *Management and Organisational Behaviour* | Pearson, 2023 (13th Edition)

Murphy, K. | *You're Not Listening: What You're Missing and Why It Matters* | Vintage, 2021

Murphy, M. | *Leadership Styles: How To Discover And Leverage Yours* | Leadership IQ press, 2019

N

Nash, K. | *Positively Purple; Build an Inclusive World Where People with Disabilities Can Flourish* | Kogan Page, 2022

Nelson, S. | *The Business of Friendship: Making the Most of Our Relationships Where We Spend Most of Our Time* | HarperCollins Leadership; Illustrated edition, 2020

Newberg, A., Waldman, M. | *Words Can Change Your Brain: 12 Conversation*

Strategies to Build Trust, Resolve Conflict, and Increase Intimacy | Avery, 2012

NHS England Blog, March 2019 | *Can Huddles Really Help?* | Shanmugalingam, S. | https://www.england.nhs.uk/blog/can-huddles-really-help/ (accessed 24.07.23)

Nichols, M.P., Straus, M.B. | *The Lost Art of Listening*

Nicholson, N. | *How to Motivate Your Problem People* | Harvard Business Review, January 2023 | https://hbr.org/2003/01/how-to-motivate-your-problem-people (accessed 24.07.23)

NOBL Academy | *How 8 Organizational Metaphors Impact Leadership* | Editorial team, August 2019 | https://academy.nobl.io/gareth-morgan-organizational-metaphors/ (accessed 25.07.23)

Nordquist, R. | *A Receiver's Role in Clear, Effective Communication Is an Important One: Protect Yourself Better Knowing What Goes Wrong in Conversations* | ThoughtCo, July 2019 | https://www.thoughtco.com/receiver-communication-1691899 (accessed 26.07.23)

Nordquist, R. | Definition and Examples of Vagueness in Language | ThoughtCo, September 2018 | https://www.thoughtco.com/vagueness-language-1692483 (accessed 24.07.23)

Australia, 2015 | https://www.dca.org.au/research/project/building-inclusion-evidence-based-model-inclusive-leadership (accessed 24.07.23)

Ollerton, M. | *Break Point* | Blink Publishing, 2020

Oncken, W., Wass. D.L. | *Management Time: Who's Got the Monkey?* | Harvard Business Review, December 1999 | https://hbr.org/1999/11/management-time-whos-got-the-monkey (accessed 25.07.23)

O'Neill, S. | *CLEAR®* | sondevelopment, 2023 | www.sondevelopment.com/clear (accessed 14.08.23)

O'Neill, S. | *Work Life Balance* | Sharp Podcast series, work life balance stp070 | sondevelopment, 2023 | www.sondevelopment.com/podcast (accessed 14.08.23)

Onsight Insights | https://onsiteinsights.org/ (accessed 02.07.2023)

Oppong, T. | *Preframing: A Stoic Principle For Living a Less Stressful Life* | Medium, May 2021 | https://thomas-oppong.medium.com/preframing-a-stoic-principle-for-living-a-less-stressful-life-5f3921f14224 (accessed 26.07.23)

Ortiz, C. A, Park, M. | *Visual Controls: Applying Visual Management to the Factory* | Productivity Press, 2018

O

Oakland, J.S., Oakland, R.J., Turner, M.A. | *Total Quality Management and Operational Excellence: Text with Cases* | Routledge, 2021

O'Bryan, A. | *How to Practice Active Listening: 16 Examples & Techniques* | PositivePsychology.com, April 2023 | https://positivepsychology.com/active-listening-techniques/ (accessed 24.07.23)

O'Leary, J., Russell, G. and Tilly, J. | *Building Inclusion: An Evidence-Based Model of Inclusive Leadership* | Diversity Council

P

Parry, S. | *Take Pride: How to Build Organisational Success Through People* | Unbound, 2018

Peale, N.V. | *The Power of Positive Thinking* | Touchstone; Reprint Edition, 2003

Pease, A., Pease, B. | *The Definitive Book of Body Language: How to read others' attitudes by their gestures* | Orion, 2017

Pendell, R. | *8 Behaviors of the World's Best Managers* | https://www.gallup.com/workplace/272681/habits-world-best-managers.aspx (accessed 26.07.23) | Gallup, November 2019

Perls, F.S. | *In and Out the Garbage Pail* | Real People Press, 1969

Pestelos, I. | *Leadership Brand: Would you follow you? (Part 1)* | Medium, December 2020 | https://medium.com/move-the-average-up/leadership-brand-would-you-follow-you-part-1-d616a18084e (accessed 25.07.23)

Pirs, S. | *Human Leadership: What It Looks Like, And Why We Need It In The 21st Century* | Forbes, November 2018 | https://www.forbes.com/sites/sesilpir/2018/11/28/human-leadership-what-it-looks-like-and-why-we-need-it-in-the-21st-century/?sh=f990f2a29143 (accessed 24.07.23)

Porath, C., Boissy, A. | *Practice Empathy as a Team* | Harvard Business Review, February 2023 | https://hbr.org/2023/02/practice-empathy-as-a-team (accessed 24.07.23)

Potter, A. | *Putting theory into practice: Kübler-Ross Change Curve* | Warwick Business School, November 2021 | https://www.wbs.ac.uk/news/putting-theory-into-practice-kuebler-ross-change-curve/ (accessed 25.07.23)

Practical Psychology | *Fight or Flight (The Adrenal Response)*

Practical Psychology, March 2023 | https://practicalpie.com/fight-or-flight/ (accessed 24.07.23)

Profit.co | *10 Great Retail Store Operations OKR Examples* | https://www.profit.co/blog/okr-examples/10-great-retail-store-operations-okr-examples/ (accessed 26.07.23)

Prosci ADKAR® model | https://www.prosci.com/ (accessed 12.02.24)

Q

Quality accreditation bodies | United Kingdom Accreditation Service www.

ukas.com (accessed 26.07.23) | European Accreditation www.european-accreditation.org (accessed 26.07.23) | International Standardization Organisation www.iso.org (accessed 26.07.23)

R

Ratcliffe, R. | *What's the difference between leadership and management?* | The Guardian, July 2013 | https://www.theguardian.com/careers/difference-between-leadership-management (accessed 24.07.23)

Rehkopf, M. | *Scrum sprints* | Atlassian, undated. | https://www.atlassian.com/agile/scrum/sprints (accessed 25.07.23)

Reiss, H., Neporent, L. | *The Empathy Effect: 7 Neuroscience Based Keys for Transforming The Way We Live, Love, Work, and Connect Across Differences.* | Sounds True Inc, 2018

Robbins, A. | *Unlimited Power* | Simon & Schuster, 1986

Robbins, A. | *Awaken The Giant Within: How to Take Immediate Control of Your Mental, Emotional, Physical and Financial Life* | Simon & Schuster, 2001

Robinson, L., Smith, M. | *Dealing with Uncertainty* | HelpGuide.org

Robinson, L., Smith, M. | https://www.helpguide.org/articles/anxiety/dealing-with-uncertainty.htm (accessed 26.07.23)

Rock, D., Grant, H. | *Why Diverse Teams Are Smarter* | Harvard Business Review, November 2016 | https://hbr.org/2016/11/why-diverse-teams-are-smarter (accessed 24.07.23)

Rogelberg, S.G. | *Make the Most of Your One-on-One Meetings* | Harvard Business Review, November 2022 | https://hbr.org/2022/11/make-the-most-of-your-one-on-one-meetings (accessed 26.07.23)

Rogers, C. | *A Way of Being* | Houghton Mifflin, 1980

Ross, L. | *How To Stop the Halo and Horns Effect in Hiring and Reduce Unconscious Bias* | Vervoe, May 2022 | https://vervoe. com/halo-and-horns-effect-in-hiring/ (accessed 26.07.23)

Rossiter, T. | *Management Basics in Easy Steps* | In Easy Steps Ltd, 2019

Ruhl, C. | *Cognitive Bias: How We Are Wired To Misjudge* | Simple Psychology, July 2023 | https://www.simplypsychology.org/ cognitive-bias.html (accessed 24.07.23)

Rutkowska, A. et al | *Quitless: The Power of Persistence in Business and Life* | Leaders Press, 2021

Ryan, L. | *Management Vs. Leadership: Five Ways They Are Different* | Forbes, 2016 | https://www.forbes. com/sites/lizryan/2016/03/27/ management-vs-leadership-five-ways-they-are-different/?sh=5c9d9f8c69ee (accessed

S

Sands, L | *One-to-one meetings: a complete guide* | Breathe, May 2023 | https:// www.breathehr.com/en-gb/blog/topic/ employee-engagement/one-to-one-meetings-a-complete-guide (accessed 24.07.23)

Satir, V. | *Peoplemaking* | Science and Behavior Books, 1972

Selk, J. | *Obsession Is A Positive Quality When It Comes To Improvement* | Forbes, 2014 | https://www.forbes. com/sites/jasonselk/2014/01/13/ obsession-is-a-positive-quality-when-it-comes-to-improvement/?sh=79ba0f847181 (accessed 25.07.23)

Sellars, J. | Lessons in Stoicism: What Ancient Philosophers Teach Us about How to Live | Penguin, 2020

Sendjaya, S., Sarros, J. C. | *Servant Leadership: Its Origin, Development, and Application in Organizations* | Journal of Leadership & Organizational Studies, September 2002

Seneca | *Moral Letters,* c65 AD

Shannon, N, Frischherz, B. | *Metathinking: The Art and Practice of Transformational Thinking* | Springer, 2020

Shapiro, B., Doyle, S. | *Make the Sales Task Clear* | Harvard Business Review, November 1983 | https://hbr.org/1983/11/make-the-sales-task-clear (accessed 24.07.23)

Shellenbarger, S. | *Use Mirroring to Connect with Others* | Wall Street Journal, 2016 | https://www.wsj.com/ articles/use-mirroring-to-connect-with-others-1474394329 (accessed 25.07.23)

Sherman, J.E. | *Everything You Can Do, You Can Do Meta* | *A psychological key to smarter life navigation that you've never heard of* | Psychology Today, 2020

Shope Griffin, N. | *Personalize Your Management Development* | Harvard Business Review, 2003 | https://hbr.org/2003/03/ personalize-your-management-development (accessed 24.07.23)

Simkus, J. | *Sex vs Gender: What's The Difference And Why Does It Matter?*

Simply Psychology, June 202 | https:// www.simplypsychology.org/sex-gender.html (accessed 24.07.23)

Sinek, S. | *Start With Why, How Great Leaders Inspire Everyone to Take Action* | Penguin, 2009

Skusa, M. | *The ultimate project completion checklist* | Filestage, March 2023 | https:// filestage.io/blog/project-completion/ (accessed 25.07.23)

Slack, N., Brandon-Jones, A., Burgess, N. | *Operations Management* | Pearson, 2022

Social Work England | *Supervision* | https:// www.socialworkengland.org.uk/cpd/ supervision/ (accessed 26.07.23)

Society for Human Resource Management | *Human Capital Benchmarking Reports* | https://www.shrm.org/ ResourcesAndTools/business-solutions/

Documents/Human-Capital-Report-All-Industries-All-FTEs.pdf (accessed 26.07.23)

Soegaard, M. | *Occam's Razor: The simplest solution is always the best* | Interaction Design Foundation, 2020 | https://www.interaction-design.org/literature/article/occam-s-razor-the-simplest-solution-is-always-the-best (accessed 25.07.23)

Souders, B. | *The Science of Improving Motivation at Work* | PositivePsychology.com 2020 | https://positivepsychology.com/improving-motivation-at-work/ (accessed 25.07.23)

Souders, B. | *20 Most Popular Theories of Motivation in Psychology* | PositivePsychology.com 2019 | https://positivepsychology.com/motivation-theories-psychology/ (accessed 07.07.24)

Starr, J. | *Mentoring Manual, The: Your Step-by-step Guide to Being a Better Mentor* | Pearson Business, 2021

Storm, A. | *The Complete Guide to Business Networking [+8 Key Tips You Should Leverage]* | Hubspot, February 2023 | https://blog.hubspot.com/sales/what-is-business-networking (accessed 25.07.23)

Sullivan, W., Rees, J. | *Clean Language: Revealing Metaphors and Opening Minds* | Crown House Publishing, 2008

Suttie, J. | *The Ripple Effects of a Thank You* | Greater Good Magazine, December 2019 | https://greatergood.berkeley.edu/article/item/the_ripple_effects_of_a_thank_you (accessed 25.07.23)

T

Tahir, U. | *Lewin's Force Field Analysis (Change Management)* | Change Management Insight, November 2019 | https://changemanagementinsight.com/lewins-force-field-analysis-change-management/ (accessed 24.07.23)

Tannenbaum, R., Schmidt, W.H. | *How to Choose a Leadership Pattern* | Harvard Business Review Press, 2009

Tapping, D. | *The Simply Lean Pocket Guide – Making Great Organizations Better Through PLAN-DO-CHECK-ACT (PDCA)* | MCS Media, 2008

The Motivation Agency | https://www.themotivationagency-online.com/course/everycustomerwants (accessed 26.07.23)

The Motivation Agency | https://themotivationagency-online.com/course/begin (accessed 26.07.23)

The Motivation Agency | https://themotivationagency-online.com/course/meerkat (accessed 26.07.23)

Thomas, P. | *Why You Get What You Focus On* | Self Help for Life | https://selfhelpforlife.com/why-you-get-what-you-focus-on/ (accessed 24.07.23)

Tolle, E. | *A New Earth: Awakening to Your Life's Purpose* | Penguin, 2006

Tollman, P., Bixner, R., Keenan, P., Powell, K. | *Cascading Change* | Boston Consulting Group, 2009 | https://www.bcg.com/publications/2009/change-management-engagement-culture-cascading-change (accessed 24.07.23)

Torres, M | *5 Things You Must Do When You Get Promoted Over A Friend* | HuffPost, February 2022 | https://www.huffingtonpost.co.uk/entry/friend-job-promotion-tips_l_5cbdf2bee4b0f7a84a732e0b (accessed 24.07.23)

Townsend, R., Bennis, W. | *Up the Organisation: How to Stop the Corporation from Stifling People and Strangling Profits* | Jossey-Bass, 2007

Tracy, Brian | *Eat That Frog! Get More Of The Important Things Done Today* | Hodder, 2013

Trades Union Congress | *Equality* | TUC Workplace Manual, November 2021 | https://www.tuc.org.uk/resource/equality (accessed 26.07.23)

Trades Union Congress | *Health & Safety – Reps Guide* | TUC Workplace Manual, April

2021 | https://www.tuc.org.uk/resource/
health-and-safety-reps-guide (accessed
26.07.23)

Tredgold, G. | *Simplicity Is the Key to
Success* | Inc., September 2016 | https://
www.inc.com/gordon-tredgold/
simplicity-is-the-key-to-success-here-are-26-
inspiring-quotes-to-help-you-on-tha.html
(accessed 25.07.23)

Tuckman, B.W. | *Developmental Sequence in
Small Groups* | Psychological Bulletin, 1965

Tuckman, B.W., and Jensen, M.A.C. | *Stages
in Small-Group Developmental Revisited*
| Group Facilitation: A Research and
Applications Journal – Number 10, 2010

Turner, J. | *The 3 Qualities You Need To Be
A Really Effective Leader* | Gartner, October
2022 | https://www.gartner.com/en/
articles/the-3-qualities-you-need-to-be-a-
really-effective-leader (accessed 09.07.23)

Turner, T. | *One Team on All Levels: Stories
from Toyota Members* | CRC Press, 2012

U

Uznadze, D.N. | *The Psychology of Set* |
Translated by Basil Haigh. | New York:
Plenum Publishing Corporation, 1966 |
Published online by Cambridge University
Press, January 2018

V

Vaihinger, H. | *The Philosophy of As If: A
System of the Theoretical, Practical and
Religious Fictions of Mankind* | English
translation from CreateSpace Independent
Publishing Platform, 2015

Van Slyke, C. | *Risks and Benefits of
Generalizations* | Life Well and Flourish |
https://www.livewellandflourish.com/
blog/risks-and-benefits-of-generalizations/
(accessed 09.07.23)

Vervago, 2020 | *Precision Questioning* https:
//www.vervago.com/skill-sharpeners/
precision-questioning/ (accessed 24.07.23)

Vervago, 2020 | *Slippery terms: do you and I
mean the same thing?* | https://www.vervago.
com/slippery-terms-do-you-and-i-mean-
the-same-thing/ (accessed 24.07.23)

Villines, Z. | *What are the different types of
memory?* | Medical News Today, November
2020 | https://www.medicalnewstoday.
com/articles/types-of-memory (accessed
24.07.23)

Vista Projects | *3 Useful Ways to Eliminate
Redundancy from Written Reports* | Editorial
team, September 2016 | https://www.
vistaprojects.com/eliminate-redundancy-
written-reports/ (accessed 24.07.23)

Voice of America | *Language Ability
Linked to Pattern Recognition* | Editorial
team, May 2013 | https://www.voanews.
com/a/language-ability-linked-to-pattern-
recognition/1670776.html (accessed
25.07.23)

W

Walker, M. | *Why We Sleep: The New Science
of Sleep and Dreams* | Penguin, 2018

Walter, D. | *How to Stop Procrastinating:
Powerful Strategies to Overcome Laziness
and Multiply Your Time* | Independently
published, 2020

Walter, L. | *Highly delighted, bitterly
disappointed, ridiculously cheap: adverbs
for emphasis.* | Cambridge Dictionary
Blog, 2014 | https://dictionaryblog.
cambridge.org/2014/10/22/
highly-delighted-bitterly-disappointed-
ridiculously-cheap-adverbs-for-emphasis/
(accessed 24.07.23)

Welch, J. with Welch, S. | *Winning* | Harper
Collins, 2005 |

Why? Purpose and meaning brands, |
Rapanui Clothing https://rapanuiclothing.
com/ (accessed 02.08.23) | Teemill
Tech – https://teemill.com/ (accessed
02.08.23) | Roake Studio https://roake.

studio/ (accessed 02.08.23) | American Battery Technology Company https://americanbatterytechnology.com/ (accessed 02.08.23)

Wigert, B., Pendell, R. | 6 Trends Leaders Need to Navigate This Year | Gallup, January 2023 | https://www.gallup.com/workplace/468173/workplace-findings-leaders-need-navigate-year.aspx (accessed 25.07.23)

Wike, E. | uk.indeed.com | *20 Leadership Qualities that Make a Great Leader (With Tips),* 2022

Wilson, C. | *Epicureanism: A Very Short Introduction* | OUP Oxford, 2015

Wilson, P. | *Little Book of Calm at Work* | Penguin, 1999

Wilson, R.A. | *Prometheus Rising* | New Falcon Publications, 1983

Wiseman, E. | *Vogue editor Edward Enninful: 'Impostor syndrome is what drives me.'* | The Observer, 4th September 2022 | https://www.theguardian.com/fashion/2022/sep/04/vogue-editor-edward-enninful-impostor-syndrome-is-what-drives-me (accessed 24.07.23)

Wiseman, R. | *The As If Principle. The Radically New Approach to Changing Your Life* | Simon & Schuster, 2014

Woodward, C., Potanin, F. | *Winning!* | Hodder & Stoughton, 2004

Woolston, C. | *Why Appraisals Are Pointless for Most People* | BBC Work, May 2019 | https://www.bbc.com/worklife/article/20190501-why-appraisals-are-pointless-for-most-people (accessed 26.07.23)

World Health Organisation | *Burn-out an "occupational phenomenon": International Classification of Diseases* | Departmental news, May 2019 | https://www.who.int/news/item/28-05-2019-burn-out-an-occupational-phenomenon-international-classification-of-diseases (accessed 25.07.23)

Young, K. | *What you focus on is what becomes powerful – why your thoughts and feelings matter* | Hey SIGMUND, 2016 | https://www.heysigmund.com/why-what-you-focus-on-is-what-becomes-powerful-why-your-thoughts-and-feelings-matter/ (accessed 24.07.23)

Zalucki, G. | *The Mind and Emotions Set* | www.georgezalucki.com (accessed 26.07.23)

Zamir, D. | *Stop Feeding Your Worry: Understand and Overcome Anxious Thinking Habits* | The Glendon Association, 2023 | https://www.glendon.org/shop/stop-feeding-your-worry-understand-and-overcome-anxious-thinking-habits/ (accessed 25.07.23)

Zenger, J., Folkman, J. | *The Extraordinary Leader: Turning Good Managers Into Great Leaders* | McGraw-Hill, 2009

Zenger, J., Folkman, J., Sherwin, R.H., Steel, B. | *How to Be Exceptional: Drive Leadership Success by Magnifying Your Strengths* | McGraw Hill, 2012

Zhuo, J. | *The Making of a Manager: What to Do When Everyone Looks to You* | Portfolio, 2019

Zigarmi, D., Houson, D., Diehl, J., Witt, D. | *10 Performance Management Process Gaps: And how they negatively impact employee intentions.* | Ken Blanchard Companies, Employee Work Passion, volume 7, 2014